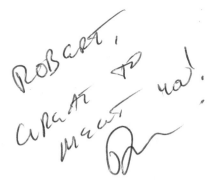

The Compliance Book

A leader's guide to understanding what the regulations and guidelines *really say* about information governance, information systems governance, and information technology governance.

Copyright stuff

Table of Contents

Foreword and Acknowledgements

A word about field editors

Ever wonder how we know so much? Field Editors! They keep us accurate, up-to-date, and honest. What do field editors get out of being able to contribute? *All* of the materials we work on together for *free*, an opportunity to collaborate with very smart people, and tons of deep discounts on everything we do.

Go ahead and read all about it at http://www.thecompliancebook.com/FE

We hope you sign up and here is some information about stuff that gets a 50% discount or more!

Systems Continuity Plan Pro

Disaster or auditor be ready for both! We worked with Palo Alto Softwware to bring you an application to conduct audits following our best practices, your audit guidelines, or with templates from well-known organization such as ISACA. Read all about it at http://www.paloalto.com/scpp

The Compliance Series

In addition to the main book, there are many parts to The Compliance Series. We have a slew of print and e-books available on topics ranging from Systems Continuity to How To Hire A Security Assessment Vendor. Just keep a look out at Amazon for our latest releases.

UCP Knowledgebase and Conferences

The Unified Compliance Project hosted by the IT Compliance Institute is based directly on The Compliance Series. Network Frontiers partners with ITCi on many conferences and the soon-to-be-released Control Objective Knowledgebase. Go ahead and take a look at
http://www.itcinstitute.com/ucp

790 days of research...

Over the last two years, we read through hundreds of regulations and standards, representing hundreds of thousands of pages of really, really tedious and redundant material. Now, true to Network Frontiers tradition of making complex concepts tangible, we present to you an approach to regulatory compliance.

We've determined the method you can use to reduce the number of "control objectives" you have to maintain by at least half (if you are being held to more than one standard or regulation), and even more than that if you are being held to three or more regulations and standards.

And we've discovered some of the biggest reasons that many of us feel the auditing process is "a bit out of whack," along with a way to guide the process back toward reality.

If you read no other section of this book, read this one.

Should you be reading this?

You should read this if you are the one **paying for auditors** who are running amuck in your offices charging you money to audit ridiculous bits of IT trivia. This will show you how to bring them back in line.

You should be reading this if you are the **IS staff** who *knows* that there is a great deal of redundancy and weirdness in the auditing methodologies you have to put up with. This will show you how to bring being audited into synch with testing *real* policies and procedures that *really* show how information systems support the business properly.

You should be reading this if you are an **information systems auditor** who is a real pro and who wants to make a difference for your organization (if you are internal) or your client (if you are external). It'll provide you with a tool to raise your practice above the bricker-brack caused by folks mired in technicalities who aren't focusing on protecting business processes.

You should be reading this because you care about your leadership role in information governance – whether on the business side, the IS side, or the auditor side.

This is *not* a Sarbanes-Oxley, HIPAA, or Gramm-Leach-Bliley only work. There are plenty of those out there.

This is all about information governance in *your* world, the world of business, which has become a regulatory world. Some forget that in the Information Systems arena there are both information technology *and* information management. This is *not* about information technology per se – it is about information management. Because management implies organization, power, and politics. It is about making decisions that affect both the leaders and the followers. It is about proper control, and hence, regulatory compliance.

If you are in the position to affect the proper control of information within an organization, then *yes,* you should be reading this.

> One ship drives east and another drives west
> With the selfsame winds that blow.
> 'Tis the set of the sails
> And not the gales
> Which tells us the way to go[1].

Regulatory compliance is just another strong wind of change blowing through the corporate world. If you want to set the direction, we'll help you get there.

---

[1] Ella Wheeler Wilcox.

Our promise to you

The Compliance Book makes three promises:

1. We'll help you align regulatory compliance within the *reality* that you face day to day.

2. We'll help you aggregate the large volume of overlapping regulatory control objectives into a manageable set of criteria.

3. We know that everyone comes to these projects with their own goals and ideas, and *that* is what will continue to make this a rich experience for everyone involved. E-mail us and we'll make your voice heard in the work we do future forward[2].

Everyone has a viewpoint and a direction in mind. We don't promise to have all the answers – there is no certainty in our method, only a consensus that we can draw toward, *together*. Let's take a look at a few of them and see if we can't find a common course to take.

Dorian J. Cougias, Lead Author
Dcougias@netfrontiers.com

Marcelo Halpern, Lead Legal Analyst & Co-Author
Marcelo.Halpern@lw.com

Erikka Innes, Lead Research Analyst
einnes@netfrontiers.com

---

2   Information on becoming a field editor is listed at
http://www.compliancebook.com/FE

The regulators, such as the Sarbanes-Oxley crew, saw the need for compliance because someone was caught with their spreadsheet in the cookie jar. The same idea applies to a lot of the privacy regulations that we are facing (and will probably face more of); regulators feel the need to step in and set some boundaries for compliance that they feel we have either missed or have ignored.

The auditors then get the wonderful job of enforcement by, as Paul Strassmann would say, "guessing the menu by examining the leftovers."

And we wonder why some auditors think it's a pretty crappy job.

Most business people we talk to seem to see regulatory compliance as a fleecing by the government and the auditors. More and more CFOs believe that profit has been taken from their organization and their shareholders because it was diverted to the audit industry.

Can't say we blame them.

The IS staff basically looks at regulatory compliance as the next hoop to jump through, or as some put it "the new way management wants us to kill ourselves." One client said "if the standards I have stacked on my desk don't fall over and kill me, the budgetary and compliance reports will."

The Main Thing here is that we *aren't* taking a stance "fer or agin" regulatory compliance. Our stance is this; if you have to go through compliance, you might as well make it as painless as possible, and as complete as possible so that you don't have to re-double your efforts at a later date. This book is a guide to efficient and effective compliance (thus, the name).

Special Thanks

We'd like to begin this section with a grateful thank you to Paul Strassmann, upon whose work our thinking is founded[3]. And to our field editor team for their direct input to this section (in the order that we added the information to the material):

Michelle Garvey, John Sage, Wyatt Banks, Mike Ivanov, Charles Hibnick, Alan Hallauer, Steve Helwig, Donald Ford, Michele Hope, John Wollner, Vinny DiSpigno, David Salav, Maureen Beekman, Vickiy Zaman, Bryan Adams, JP Calderon Del Vecchio, and Cass Brewer.

A word about field editors…

Field Editors, to Network Frontiers, are our lifeline to reality. Even though we consult nationally and internationally on the topics we write about, we know that we aren't going to learn everything there is to learn about our subjects. Therefore, we turn to you, our readers, for advice and input. The term Field Editor was coined by one of our book readers named Moon Mullins back in the early nineties as a way of saying to us "hey, us folk in the field should be giving you input that those fancy editors at your publisher can't contribute." And he was right. Over the years, our field editors have made our books move from bland to semi-brilliant. From our viewpoint, to a truly global viewpoint. Information on becoming a field editor is listed at:

http://www.compliancebook.com/FE

We hope to hear from you soon.

---

[3] The three main pieces of material that we draw from that Paul has written are as follows: Paul Strassmann (1995). <u>The Politics of Information Management: Policy Guidelines</u>. New Canaan, Ct., The Information Economics Press; Paul Strassmann and John Klossner (1995). <u>Irreverent Dictionary of Information Politics</u>. New Canaan, Ct., Information Economics Press; Paul Strassmann (2004). The Governance of Information Management, The Information Economics Press.

What are the regulators really saying?

Somebody voided the warranty. Actually, a lot of somebodies voided the warranty. Any organization that lost the confidentiality of their information, compromised the integrity of their information, or lost the availability of their information therefore causing loss to their clients, suppliers, or shareholders voided the warranty. And as an organizational leader, the responsibility for any voided warranty is on *your shoulders* whether you were the one who committed the act or you are merely the leader of those who committed the act. In other words, this warranty thing is relevant to you because it exposes *you* to risk, and has introduced *you* to the world of regulatory compliance for information management.

What's this *warranty* that has been voided? The warranty we are talking about is the one that comes with the IT equipment that runs your organization, and is inherent in the information that you are using the systems to create and store.

 Information products and technology are no different than anything else we purchase as packaged, finished, or customized goods. We've come to believe that *all* products and services should have an implicit warranty. New and used houses, boats, anything with a large price tag has a warranty these days. Within the computer and electronic information world, this "warranty" holds certain promises of assurance. It is this warranty of confidentiality (🔐), integrity (📋), availability (💡), and accountability (📠) that guarantees assurance. However, a combination of threats and vulnerabilities can "void" this warranty.

- Disclosure can void confidentiality.
- Modification or corruption compromises integrity.
- Interruption or loss compromises availability.
- Neglect or staff ignorance compromises accountability.

To regulators, the concepts of integrity, availability and confidentiality are related, with each term implicating distinct legal and organizational considerations. *Integrity* (together with its close cousin, *accountability*) is targeted at preserving and authenticating the accuracy of data. *Confidentiality* is focused on how regulated information is used and disclosed by those with *authorized* access. Integrity answers the question of how to guaranty the accuracy and truthfulness of data, while confidentiality is focused on accountability and privacy of data when handled by known people and processes. *Availability* is a necessary, but by no means sufficient, component of both integrity and confidentiality by focusing on protecting both data and systems from loss or interruption of service.

More than a few organizations have caused this warranty to be voided either through direct actions or through neglect. And it is specific warranty-voiding actions and neglect that have brought forth the ire of the regulators which are too numerous to mention here.

Most regulations are reactionary adjudications

As we'll discuss in more detail, while virtually all of the major regulations address all of the concepts found in the warranty, they balance the factors differently. Some regulations approach the issue from the confidentiality angle, and are promoted as confidentiality rules, but soon discover the need to include availability and integrity rules in order to make confidentiality work. Similarly, other regulations start from the premise that integrity is the most important issue and discover that you can't have integrity without confidentiality, availability, and accountability. Part of the confusion engendered by this alphabet soup of regulatory acronyms comes from the fact the interrelationships of these concepts are not always well drawn out because of the focus on what is perceived to be the "more important" issues addressed by that particular regulatory scheme.

As an illustration of these ideas, walk through just a few of the significant pieces of legislation with us and see how the lens of the regulator affects the implementation of integrity, confidentiality, availability, and accountability rules.

If you really want to read the next couple of pages, you'll maintain your over-achiever status. But if time is of the essence, here are the Cliff Notes:

- Sarbanes Oxley focuses on integrity through better account-ability.

- Gramm-Leach-Bliley focuses on both privacy and accuracy (through integrity and accountability).

- California 1386 focuses on confidentiality and accountability.

- HIPAA regulators, being health-care based, had panophobia and regulated everything short of your pancreas.

At this point, you can either read more about each regulator's viewpoint, or you can skip this part and get directly to the point in the next section, the "regulators' message to our organizations: don't void the warranty."

Sarbanes-Oxley Act (SOX) — Integrity through Accountability

The Sarbanes-Oxley Act[4] (SOX) was passed in 2002 largely in response to the corporate scandals of Enron, Arthur Andersen and others that caused, in the minds of legislators if not in the public, a crisis of confidence in the public equity markets. Most public companies were required to comply with the more significant portions of the legislation by June 15, 2004; smaller U.S. businesses and foreign companies are required to comply by April 2006, although certain requirements are in effect already.

SOX approaches its job from the perspective of data integrity and, more specifically, through the tool of accountability. Because the primary objective of the act is to assure the integrity of the organization's financial statements, the CEO and CFO are required to certify the accuracy of reported financial statements as well as the disclosure controls and procedures by which those statements were developed. The act also addresses specific aspects of security and controls of accounting and auditing processes through the accountability lens by providing strict guidelines for publicly traded companies with respect to corporate governance and oversight of accounting and audit practices as well as retention, control and reporting of financial information. In this case, the security classification of certain stored information (*e.g.*, financial results) changes from company-confidential to public-use with the release of the financial statement, but it

---

4   (2002). The Sarbanes Oxley Act of 2002.

must undergo that transformation at a very specific time – if the information is released too soon or too late, the SEC may come knocking on your door.

Integrity is also maintained through requirements relating to retention of documentation that backs up the financial statements – a response to the alleged shredding of files in connection with Enron's collapse. Auditing firms, for example, have to keep *every* document that influences a report about a client, including e-mail, instant messaging, or even sticky notes with facts and figures – for at least seven years.

Section 404 of SOX mandates that a public company's annual report also contain an internal control report that states the responsibility of the organization's management in establishing and maintaining an adequate internal control structure as well as the procedures used for financial reporting. The control report must also contain an assessment, at the end of the company's most recent fiscal year, of the effectiveness of the internal control structure and procedures for financial reporting. The *auditor* (an independent third party CPA firm) must also attest to, and report on, the assessment made by management of the company.

In doing this, SOX therefore sets forth very strong requirements that organizations implement an internal control framework, of which general computer integrity and accountability controls play a key role.

Gramm-Leach-Bliley Act (GLB) – Privacy and Accuracy

The Financial Modernization Act of 1999, also known as the "Gramm-Leach-Bliley Act"[5] (GLB), includes provisions to protect consumers' personal financial information held by financial institutions. Of course data confidentiality is necessarily a major component of GLB compliance.

GLB limits the instances in which financial institutions may disclose non-public personal information about consumers to non-affiliated third parties. GLB also requires financial institutions to disclose certain privacy policies and procedures with respect to the organization's information sharing with third parties.

It is important to realize that "financial institutions" is very broadly defined by GLB and includes not only banks, securities firms, and insurance companies, but also companies providing many other types of financial products and services to consumers. Among these services are lending, brokering or

---

[5]   (1999). The Gramm-Leach Bliley Act (GLBA). 15 USC:**6801 and 6805(b)**.

servicing any type of consumer loan, transferring or safeguarding money, preparing individual tax returns, providing financial advice or credit counseling, providing residential real estate settlement services, collecting consumer debts and an array of other activities.[6]

There are three principal parts to GLB privacy requirements: the Financial Privacy Rule, Safeguards Rule and pretexting provisions. For information governance purposes, we are interested only in the Safeguards Rule, however this rule is again in support of the privacy rules. GLB gives authority to eight federal agencies and the states to administer and enforce the Financial Privacy Rule and the Safeguards Rule. The Department of the Treasury, the Federal Reserve System and the FDIC published the "Interagency Guidelines Establishing Standards for Safeguarding Customer Information" in support of this act[7]. Each agency later republished these guidelines in an appendix to their independent regulations with slight modifications for each. The Office of the Comptroller of the Currency (OCC) has also published bulletins supporting the Safeguards rule that provide guidance to banks on how to prevent, detect, and respond to intrusions into their computer systems and the information contained therein.

California SB 1386 – Confidentiality through Accountability

Concerns over the increased incidence of identity theft led the State of California in 2003 to pass the California Database Protection Act, better known by its numerical designation of Senate Bill 1386[8] (SB 1386). SB 1386 requires businesses to disclose to California residents any breach in the security of their computerized data if that breach may have resulted in the disclosure of personal information to unauthorized users. While this law applies to any person or business in California as well as government agencies, it also applies to any organization that holds a Californian's personal information in its database(s) – therefore the reach of SB 1386 is worldwide.

SB 1386 was prompted by a much publicized computer intrusion into a California state government system that stored payroll information on 265,000 state workers. Confidential data accessed included employee names and addresses, social security numbers, and bank information. The state did not become aware of the breach for some weeks and did not report the in-

---

6   (1999). Privacy Initiatives, Federal Trade Commission.

7   Links for this, and all other pertinent regulations can be found at the end of this section.

8   California Civil Code Section 1798.82.

trusion to the affected employees until well after it was discovered – too late to prevent harm.

The law requires any agency that *owns or licenses* computerized data that includes *personal information* to *disclose any breach of system security* that led to a resident's unencrypted personal information – or is reasonably believed to have led to being – acquired by an unauthorized person. In addition, the California Office of Privacy Protection has published recommended practices to comply with this law. The recommended practices are divided into three parts; privacy and prevention, preparation for notification, and notification.

Interestingly, SB 1386 does not mandate any particular security measures. Instead it aims to create incentives for firms to take data privacy seriously by creating potentially serious business and public relations consequences for any breach of security. In other words, it uses accountability as a tool to improve privacy and security.

Health Insurance Portability and Accountability Act (HIPAA) – Confidentiality, Integrity, Availability, and Accountability

The Health Insurance Portability and Accountability Act of 1996[9] (HIPAA) covers a wide range of topics. Of particular interest to information management professionals is Title II of HIPAA, known as the "Administrative Simplification" provisions which cover the privacy and integrity of healthcare information. (The irony of referring to thousands of pages of complex regulations and commentary as "Administrative Simplification" has not been lost on commentators.)

The HIPAA privacy and security regulations arose from concerns that an individual's health information could be misused in ways detrimental to the data subject. For example, employers could discriminate against potential employees based on medical conditions – *e.g.*, a history of cancer – that could increase the employer's insurance premiums. Certain medical conditions associated with particular protected classes – *e.g.*, AIDS is more prevalent (or at least is perceived to be more prevalent) among homosexuals – may be used to overtly or covertly discriminate against protected classes.

The HIPAA regulations of interest to us here are the Privacy regulations and the Security regulations. The Standards for Privacy of Individually

---

[9]   (1996). Health Insurance Portability and Accountability Act of 1996. Title II.

Identifiable Health Information[10] (Privacy Rule) issued under HIPAA restrict the use and disclosure of protected health information (PHI),[11] by entities that meet the Privacy Rule's definition of a covered entity.[12] As a general rule, a covered entity is not permitted to disclose PHI without consent of the patient unless the Privacy Rule specifically requires or permits such disclosure. Without getting into too much detail, the Privacy Rule permits a covered entity to disclose PHI only for treatment of the patient, payment for services, and certain operations of the covered entity providing the services and for little else. The primary purpose of the Privacy Rule is to protect the confidential information of the patient and ensure that it is used only in connection with the healthcare of the patient. It also empowers the patient to have access to his/her own information and to find out who else has had access to it.

The Security Standards for the Protection of Electronic Protected Health Information (Security Rule)[13] sets forth standards for safeguarding the integrity, availability, and confidentiality of PHI when stored in electronic form. It should be noted that much of the HIPAA guidance for security (physical and technical safeguards) has its origins from guidance published by the National Institute of Standards and Technology (NIST). Healthcare organizations must now assess risks and develop, document, implement, and maintain appropriate security measures to keep risk at an acceptable level. These security requirements will include a combination of administrative and technical measures covering software, hardware, policies and procedures[14].

The Security Rule breaks security down into four main categories: administrative (§ 164.308), physical (§ 164.310), technical (§ 164.312), and

---

[10]   67 Federal Register 53182 (August 14, 2002) (revising the Privacy Rule previously finalized in 2000).

[11]   45 C.F.R. § 164.501 (defining PHI as individually identifiable health information that is transmitted electronically, maintained in electronic media or transmitted or maintained in any other form or media).

[12]   45 C.F.R. § 160.103 (defining covered entity as: 1) a health plan; 2) a health care clearinghouse; or 3) a health care provider who transmits any health information in electronic form in connection with any of eleven specified transactions).

[13]   The Security Rule is primarily set forth in 45 C.F.R. § 160.300 *et. seq.* but relies heavily on cross references to the Privacy Rule and other portions of the HIPAA regulations for definitions and context.

[14]   The Prifacy and Security Committee (2001). Security and Privacy: An Introduction to HIPAA. NEMA.

organizational (§ 164.314). For each set of rules, the regulations designate certain implementation standards as being "required" and others as "addressable". Required implementations must be met as written in the regulations – period. With respect to addressable implementations, however, the covered entity is required to make a judgment as to whether the standard is "reasonable and appropriate" (within certain guidelines) to safeguard its environment. If the standard is found to be reasonable and appropriate, the covered entity must implement the standard as stated. However, if the covered entity determines that the standard is not reasonable and appropriate, the covered entity must (a) document why the implementation is not reasonable and appropriate and how the intent of the standard can still be met, and (b) implement an alternative and equivalent solution that addresses the standard.

The regulators' message to our organizations: don't void the warranty

The point we are making with this sampling of regulations is this – you can't void the warranty, the pledge of assurance that your information management practices will ensure confidentiality, integrity, availability, and accountability. You owe it to your customers, employees and your shareholders to uphold the warranty. But too many folks have already voided that warranty. Therefore, we are now in process of *imposed* warranty repair. The direction you as a leader need to provide your staff is one that will guarantee assurance of your information systems' working order.

Whether your organization is big or small, in the service business or construction – it runs on computer systems working in concert with each other. In order to assure the compliance and warranty of those systems you have to balance confidentiality, integrity, availability, and accountability in a way that each supports the other as shown in the following diagram.

Ensuring the warranty of "in working order"

Integrity has to support confidentiality, and visa versa. Your IT staff can insist on a strong password system for accessing your computers (good integrity), but if your users are writing their passwords on a post-it note stuck to the bottoms of their keyboards (or their monitors), you've lost confidentiality and therefore integrity.

Confidentiality and integrity have to support availability. If the passwords are easy to guess for your system (loss of confidentiality), or your system is easily compromised (loss of integrity), someone with malicious intent could easily deny the service of your systems, power, or even facilities. And that's a bad thing.

Finally, confidentiality and integrity must support accountability. A combination hotel and convention center we were at failed to have confidentiality and integrity support accountability. They put a plaque on the outside of their IT data center – they lost confidentiality. And the door bolt was taped over to ensure it stayed open. All of the security cameras were turned to the wall so that they faced a taped up piece of paper with a smiley face (☺) that said "your security has been breached." So they lost integrity. Wouldn't you have wanted to know that your security was down? We told the hotel manager, who ignored us. With leadership's reaction like that, do you wonder why information security was so poor?

The tone has to be set at the top

The message that the regulators *really* want us all to hear is this: we have to get our collective acts together and *not* void the warranty of assurance, the promise that we will maintain our information systems through proper information governance. Business leaders are being held accountable for the compliance and governance of information management.

In relation to regulatory compliance, the law makers and standards creators are asking our organizations to mirror our policies to be private equivalents of public laws and international standards. They are asking us to define acceptable conduct by individuals, and acceptable uses of information and information technologies. They are asking us to define our guidelines, not just in our written procedures, but also in the way we *conduct* information management. Furthermore, they are asking that we define them in a way that the members of the executive committee or the board can comprehend and legitimize them.

No matter what your explicit, written policies are, it is your implicit policies, your day-to-day actions, that count. In one way or another, those actions are legitimized by the leadership of the organization.

Our organizations are being audited for control objectives...

So the situation is that somebody voided the warranty and the regulators want it stopped. And the way that the regulators are going to ensure that we don't void this warranty in the future is to send in a bunch of auditors to inspect our organizations for control objectives. As the following diagram shows, the first problem that auditors encounter is this; if all they have to look at is the back end view of an organization's information governance stance – the control objectives – they have to *interpret* the leadership directives and governance stance of the organization. And that's not a good thing.

Seems compliant to me...

In order for auditors to really be able to do their job, they need to understand the direction and character of the organization that guided the information governance decisions and whether or not to mitigate or accept the apparent risks. That means that we need to understand two critical factors; the definitions of what we mean by *organization* and how the *control objectives* were chosen or bypassed in the first place. So let's start there.

The scope of your organization affects the control objectives

Your organization, your institute, association, business, or group – is defined by the coming together of people to do whatever it is you do. What makes a hospital a hospital? Not the building, but what happens there; the people and activities that take place every day. It is this scope of who is working together and who (and what systems) are handling the information processing that should be the determining factor for the materiality of the control objectives you employ in order to assure confidentiality, integrity, availability, and accountability. We're going to hold off on defining materiality for a bit so that we can first clear up what we mean by "scope" and how that should affect regulatory compliance and the framework for your control objectives.

The direction, character, and boundaries of your organization

All organizations have a few things in common that determine the *organization* of the organization – the human element and group dynamic involved in the leadership of the organization[15]. However it actually takes place, the process is pretty simple. Here's an oversimplified view that will do just fine for our discussion here. The leader(s) have a vision of direction that they want the organization to follow. A business plan for organizational activities lays out this vision in an orderly fashion. Once things get going, some form of risk management, monitoring, and measurement are put into place to ensure that organizational activities are heading in the right direction.

A simplified model of business leadership

This defines the *direction* and *character* of the organization, but not the boundaries. Your organization's boundaries aren't defined at all by that which exists inside your office's walls. Yes, your organization's boundaries are defined by *who* you work with and *how* you work with them. So when

---

15   We don't have the time, inclination, or space to argue this to its logical conclusion here. So you can either take our word for it, or you can read any (or all) of the following books that make the same point: Ichak Adizes (1988). <u>Corporate Lifecycles: How and Why corporations grow and die and what to do about it</u>. Englewood Cliffs, NJ, Prentice Hall; Lawrence M. Miller (1989). <u>Barbarians to Bureaucrats: Corporate Life Cycle Strategies, Lessons from the rise and fall of civilizations</u>. New York, NY, Fawcett Columbine; William Bridges (1992). <u>The Character of Organizations: Using Jungian Type in Organizational Development</u>. Palo Alto, CA, Davies-Black Publishing; Warren Bennis (1993). <u>Beyond Bureaucracy: essays on the development and evolution of human organization</u>. San Francisco, CA, Jossey-Bass Publishers; Michael Hammer and James Champy (1993). <u>Reengineering the Corporation: a manifesto for business revolution</u>. New York, NY, Harper Business.

the regulators and auditors are examining the way you work in order to determine the appropriate control objectives, they *should* be taking into account *how* you work and *who* you work with.

As an example, let's look at the boundaries that would be set by the **home office** of a national restaurant chain's organizational activities. To start, there are the people and processes within the home office per se. Within each outlying restaurant the business of making and selling food happens, with reports going back to the home office. Those involved in the reporting are now added to the group being audited. The organizational directive of a "just in time" supply chain directly hooks in the vendors that provide supplies to the restaurants. Which adds that process and those involved to the audit. E-commerce creates a virtual restaurant with hooks back out to each physical restaurant for delivery of goods sold – adding that process and those staff to the audit. In the end, what you have is an organization defined by connectivity (as defined by business needs).

The boundaries or your organization are determined by *who works together*. The scope of your compliance environment is therefore determined by the *processes, systems,* and *technologies* that support your business efforts. The diagram that follows shows the *people* element of an organization as played out against the backdrop of the *technological system* that supports it.

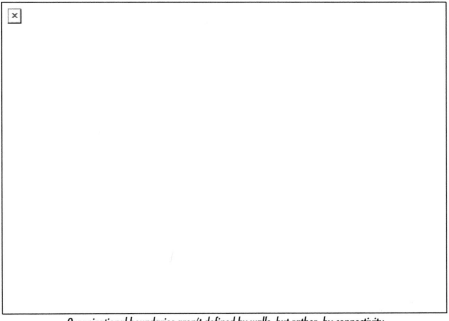

Organizational boundaries aren't defined by walls, but rather, by connectivity

Your organizational activities that are material to regulatory compliance are defined by how your workforce uses your computer systems to communicate with each other and carry out their day to day tasks.

From organizational activities to material control objectives

The information systems auditor's focus isn't the workforce using the technology. The information systems auditor's view is that of *activities* as played out against the backdrop of the technological system that supports it as shown in the diagram below. The point from the auditor's view is that your organizational activities can be evidenced in your computer activities.

Activities that play out on the backdrop of the technological systems

Using our example as a case in point, if your financial statements say that you sold 42 burgers on Tuesday at 2:00 pm, then the auditor can check everything from the back office ledger systems at corporate down to the records of the counter-top Point of Sale systems in the restaurants to ensure that all *activities, inputs,* and *outputs* align and say the same thing. But should they also check the firewall logs to ensure that a hacker hasn't changed the information? What about the backup logs to ensure that the information is being protected? Many times it isn't just the financial statements that the auditors want to look at to determine the scope of the organization's information management and information technology activities. They see evidence of, and therefore seem want to audit all sorts of IT management activities;

- 1. systems being designed, developed, and acquired,
- 2. new users being assigned systems to work on, and information to process,
- 3. day-to-day operational management activities, and recovery activities in the case where problems exist,
- records that are being created and manipulated for various and sundry reasons, and
- physical and technical safeguards being put into place to keep "the bad guys" out.

But how many of these activities are material to auditing the ledger system we are using as our example? In order for your organization and your auditors to come to terms on scoping the computer activities that have to fall within compliance, the auditors and your staff have to know where those activities *fit* within your organizational structure and the business process being audited. Going back to the example of the restaurant organization, here might be some typical questions coming from the auditor just for the food supply ordering process alone. Which ones would *you* deem important for the audit and which would *you* deem inconsequential when auditing the food supply ordering process?

- What were the controls you used to design or acquire the equipment you employ for the food supply ordering process?
- What controls do you use to define who has access to information and systems *usage* within the organization?
- What are your operational management controls for day-to-day maintenance of the system, and what controls do you have in place for continuity in case something breaks?
- What controls do you use in order to maintain the records that the system creates?
- What are your privacy controls for those records that you maintain?
- What are your controls for technical and physical security of those systems?

What the auditors are saying seems to be "I see the organization on the one hand, and these activities on the other hand, and I'm trying to interpret how the two go together." If you want to have a successful audit, and want to establish a solid regulatory compliance framework, then you'll need to **document** which processes, systems, and technologies are materially important and which are inconsequential for *your* organization according to the way that *you* do business.

Organizational decision making on one hand and organizational activities on the other

Who should be deciding the materiality of controls within your organization? Are these control questions about *procedures* at the information services team level, or are they questions about *policy* at the organizational leadership level? Or should they be handled within the organization as questions about *governance*, tying policy directly to procedures? We think the latter. Because this is where the big disconnect seems to be happening. Compliance of your information processes and systems is *an act of management*, not an act of technology.

Regulatory compliance is about policy, coordination, management, and if you are a reader of Paul Strassmann as we are, of politics[16] – or put more politely – governance. Which brings us to the very first point we are going to need to agree about – the nature of policy and governance in *your* organization.

Policy and governance – the explicit needs to be implicit

Your guiding principles and your course of action is what should define your information management organization as well as your information assurance framework.

There is a reason that the auditors need look beyond what our policy books and procedures have to say. That's because our organizational policies are defined both by our actions and our inactions, by our explicit and implicit policies, and by the tone set at the top. Too many businesses today will have an explicit policy state that all information system change management has to be reviewed for risks and business impact. And then the IT staff will up-

---

16   A wonderful piece that demonstrates this thinking is the following; Paul Strassmann (2004). The Governance of Information Management, The Information Economics Press.

grade servers and storage systems in their data centers without regard to risk assessment, business impact, or continuity service level agreements they are abrogating by not increasing the battery supplies needed due to new power consumption – because the *business* staff is urging speed and cost reductions. In this case the implicit policy (get it done *now* when management presses hard) is totally at odds with the explicit policy of analysis before action (i.e., conduct your risk analysis before making major changes). Which is the *real* policy? We the authors, and most auditors we know, would agree that it isn't what the organization writes in a policy, it is how they take action or inaction that sets the real policy. And your policies are a direct implication of your compliance stance.

Creating the explicit policies and control objectives

Your organizational policies should be a plan of action for tackling compliance governance issues, a written contract between your executive leaders, management, and end users that none should break. They should be made public (within the organization), expected to be followed, and have enough teeth in them to *ensure* they are followed.

And even the regulators have acknowledged time and again that there is no "one size fits all" policy for compliance. The policies your organization will create should be specific to your organization's needs and appetite for risk.

What is your team writing when they are writing information management policies? They aren't writing a strategic plan, a technology plan, or individual procedures for turning this wrench or attaching that card[17]. Policies for information governance are explicit business process *principles* and clearly explained as *attainable goals* written with enough clarity for implementation to occur[18].

*It is our **business process goal** to ensure complete legitimacy of end-user access in our information systems. Therefore, it is our **information services policy** that our HR systems, hiring, and termination procedures are directly tied to our organizational access directories so that as a full or part time staff member is hired, they are added to the organizational access directories. And as they are terminated, their privileges are immediately revoked from the organizational access directories.*

---

17   All too often, what we find when we look at policies in our client's policy books are just these – either procedures, proclamations of nothingness, or strategy guides. None of those are appropriate for compliance governance.

18   Implementation for the policies will be documented in your organizational procedures.

The success of any policy rests on two things: its clarity and the cooperation of all involved and affected by the policy. Does the staff understand the policy? If they don't you aren't even at ground zero. And if they do understand the policy, how will the policy affect the staff's roles and responsibilities? Its one thing for a policy to be understandable, something different for it to be attainable. And something *completely* different for it to be supported in your day-to-day activities (hence the problem between explicit and implicit policies).

And *that* is what the auditors should be checking for. They should be asking questions that follow along these lines:

- Has the scope and materiality of the information processes, systems, and IT assets been properly defined?

- Are the policies and procedures founded on the bedrock of solid information governance principles?

- What *are* those principles, and how are they brought to bear on the decisions which create the policies and procedures?

- Do the policies and procedures fall in line with (and directly support) the business plans of the organization?

- Do the policies and procedures fit the organization's risk profile and acceptance to exposure?

- Are the policies and procedures properly monitored, with the need for updates reported and acted upon in a timely and effective manner?

- Do the established controls fit the organizational activity model as designed by the leadership of the organization?

Can you answer those questions? **Are those the questions that the auditors are asking?** If you can't answer those questions, then you've lost the auditing game before you've begun it. Help for answering these questions is the basis of this book.

And if you are wondering, many organizational leaders can't answer those questions, leaving many auditors to bring in *their own* interpretations of both the questions and the answers. If the auditors are asking something other than what we've presented here, then they are introducing rules into the game that shouldn't be there. And *that* is what is driving many business people crazy about the audit process.

Is this a fleecing by the auditors?

If the goal is to balance confidentiality, integrity, availability and accountability, why do many of us feel as if we are being fleeced, or taken for a ride by our auditors? Is the government just trying to bolster the auditor's balance sheets in return for campaign contributions?

A typical business leader's view of regulatory compliance and auditors

To many business leaders, compliance seems just a tad bit ridiculous, many of the issues seem silly, and to some, the costs outrageous. We, the authors, feel the same way. We've heard stories of Sarbanes-Oxley auditors looking under the data centers floors (for what, a hidden accountant or a second set of books?). Other stories have auditors checking the heat-tempering of glass windows to ensure that data doesn't escape. These kinds of stories leave many CFOs to believe that compliance doesn't do a darned thing to enhance organizational systems or protect shareholders[19].

Q: How does being "dinged" on the *format* of audit forms affect the material well being of a financial system and an organization?

A: It doesn't, unless you count the fact that shareholders don't receive as much return because the organization had to pay for the auditor's time.

---

19 Amy Feldman (2005). Surviving Sarbanes-Oxley. <u>Inc. Magazine</u>. Inc. Magazine. **September:** 132-138.

Is this really a fleecing by the auditors? In some instances, it just might be. But in many instances, it is just compliance initiatives gone awry. In many instances, the new rules are too vague or their implementations by CPAs and other auditors are a bit over the top. The top of the list in most conversations we have with our clients and others we speak to is that the external review and auditing process is a costly mess[20]. One of our field editors, Wyatt Banks, had this to say about the auditors and the audit process:

"One thing that I hear pretty much from all my customers is that audits are a crap shoot. You pretty much never know what you are going to get. SOX audits are the worst, the interpretation of the regulation is subjective to what the auditor thinks. Often they get someone that is right out of college and has no idea about real work operations experience. But occasionally they get a seasoned auditor that really knows the business and what IT is trying to provide to the business. Also you get the scenario where the auditors are too focused on finding violations. They will not stop until they find something. Even the most ridiculous unimportant items can be the basis of the entire write up."[21]

If you want to feel another's pain, here are a few selected stories from our field editors about the auditing process gone awry. If you want to skip this part (it's pretty wild), then head down to the next section entitled "What was the point *supposed* to be?" to pick up the discussion again.

Field editor stories about auditors gone awry

All of the stories here were submitted by our esteemed field editor group and are assumed true. We asked them if they had any auditor stories to tell us, especially ones where the auditors were either over the top (pendulum swung one way) or extremely vague (pendulum swung the other way). We promised each and every one that we'd use the Chatham House Rule for their stories (that we will use the information received, but neither the identity nor the affiliation of the writer(s), nor that of any other participant). The only exceptions are where the field editor asked us to quote them.

---

20 A study by Nasdaq shows that public companies with less than $100 million in revenue were spending, on average, 1.3% of that revenue in compliance efforts.

21 Private e-mail communication between Wyatt and Dorian, 9/19/2005.

We'll start with a few real winners about external auditors. We've divided these into a couple of categories; too much, not enough, too vague, and "just goofey."

The too much category

A picture is worth a thousand words (and makes a big document)

"This fits into needing to actively monitor with alerts when software is installed outside of change control. Even if the organization has controls in place the auditor wanted to see screen captures of all auditing steps (this makes for a large document). The auditor wanted to know if any file in the *winnt* or *windows* directory was attempted to be deleted (successful or failure). All of these are weird requests and difficult to provide."

We'll see you next month for the next thousand servers

"Imagine selecting a random sample of servers from a list of several hundred or thousand servers, and asking to see how quickly and completely they could be restored, or proven that they were properly backed up…

In the case of the insurance company, the storage management team was faced with SOX-related audits every 30 days, from both internal and external auditors. To help it stay on top of these audits, the team produced its own SOX checklist that tracked and tested the effectiveness of eight backup/restore processes. These included how they secure and authorize access to backup tools and physical backup media, the steps they follow to perform automated backups, how they performed restore requests via the company's in-house incident management system, and the specific process followed for backing up new or changed data. The team also documented the process it followed to identify and resolve incomplete or failed backup jobs, and the quarterly backup audits it performed to ensure all servers were being backed up regularly.[22]"

The not enough category

Looks like a duck, so I guess it's a duck

"I just spoke with one of our field teams today that recently had a large customer who was undergoing a SOX audit by [auditor name withheld] and the auditor simply asked if they had a firewall and that would suffice for his/her security auditing purposes. Pretty scary."

---

[22]   Michele Hope (2005). Compliance: Process takes center stage, INfoStor.

Too much *and* too vague

Separate your duties, but we don't care what you do

"Our auditors were overly concerned with our database administrators using the *sys admin* accounts. So they forced us to create an individual's account (as opposed to an admin account) per each database administrator. Which is not a bad thing in and of itself. But what they failed to recognized is that if you have no way to audit their access to individual records and files (because they didn't set any audit triggers) this control is useless because you can not validate the control actions of the individuals using those accounts. The auditors wanted a separation of accounts, but didn't care what the database administrators did with those accounts because they didn't ask for any specific control triggers that would report on the database administrator's access to critical areas with the systems. They were clearly more worried about form over function.

In order to make SOX more useful, auditors need to identify all the key areas of these databases and make companies set audit triggers to only audit those items identified. I have not run into anyone that turns on Oracle auditing of *everything* just for fun. Most organizations leave it off because of the performance implications."

The too vague category

My format, or yours?

"My organization is being audited globally, both by internal and external auditors. In virtually all of the audits I have been through, there is an underlying issue of the auditors asking for information (during the pre-audit data gathering stage of the process), and not specifying the format that the information should be provided. We of course provide it in the format that we use internally. When the auditors arrive, they advise us that the format is inadequate and specify their own format, which forces us to throw more resources at supporting the audit than we planned.

During the active audit, they are asking for more information, based on the leads of their investigation. This is natural, but again, they do not specify the format until we provide the 'wrong' one, with more time wasted resubmitting the data in the format they want."

If we count the errors on each page, maybe we can make the problem seem bigger

"How about getting written up 5 times for the *same issue* in one audit? The issue, training documentation for employees, was cited as 'critical' in the audit for 5 different departments of the company. Although they hit us for other issues, this alone was enough to make us fail. To make matters even more distressing, our quality processes are defined for the development organization only, but we were hit on HR, IT, and other groups which we have absolutely no control over. So, management blames the development group for failing the audit even though the areas that were cited are not ours!"

Knock knock – Waddaya want? – can't tell you, I'm the auditor

"None of the auditors have provided either a game plan or a process prior to showing up at our door. We understand that they cannot provide a list of what they will look at, but some idea of the resources required (and when) would be more efficient for them and us. This lack of effective planning information essentially locks up the site team for the duration."

You did great, but you failed because we didn't **like** you

"Our new parent company requires that all the companies that they have purchased and their original parent company be audited both in Information Technology (IT) and Finance.

As part of an IT department we were subject to an annual IT audit. The parent company sent in 5 auditors with different backgrounds. They performed their auditing over a week's time. At the final exit interview with our top management, they told us how we did and what our rating was. The final report went to an audit board consisting of the board of directors and executive management of the parent company. There were 4 possible ratings with a rating of 1 being best and 4 the worst. Our rating was **3**.

When we asked how they derived this rating level for our company, they were vague and did not want to tell us. Eventually they told us **it was derived by a vote of the auditors that performed the audit.** Our question was how they could rate us in this manner and not on the findings. They could never answer this question. The point to take from this story is to always know up front how you are going to be rated. Be friendly and cooperative to the auditing team, they can make you or break you. In our management comments to the audit report, we suggested they develop a better rating system that is objective and not subjective. We'll be ready next year."

You can pass the test, but only if you can guess what the questions are

"Although the auditors are quick to tell us what we did wrong this year, none of them have provided us with either best practices nor what additional work we should be doing to be proactively compliant. I am reasonably sure that we will continue to be slammed owing to the fact that the governance audits are being handled in the tradition of a general accounting audit - a review of an established process, with the assumption that we know what we're supposed to be doing, when in fact we are receiving only guidance on the focus of a given year's audit and have not idea of the *real* goals to strive for."

Auditing is an art, not a science

"When we were getting our company ready for sale to a larger, public company we hired [auditing firm removed] to do a 2 year audit. When we had our first review meeting of the draft of the results we had questions about some of the findings that did not match our operating results. Now, you have to remember we kept a tight ship and I counted every paper clip. The senior partner who was running the audit told us 'Don't worry auditing is an art not a science.' When my business partner heard this he went nuts and said it was *all* about numbers and numbers are math and that math is a science. Fast forward 2 years later when the partner left [auditing firm removed] and went to one of his big auditing clients to work as the VP of finance we find out that he was indicted for cooking the books. Some art!"

That's what we cared about **last** time, not this time

"The theme of the audits is changing, as if their were some rotating focus mechanism the auditors are using to drive the process. Last year the focus was on documenting policies and processes. This year it seems to be on record keeping, with a heavy focus on physical documentary records for application, infrastructure and security changes. No one told us this was going to be the focus of the 2005 audits, nor was this raised as a significant issue in the 2004 audit, so we did not keep these records at the level of detail that the auditors are requiring."

The just plain goofy category

You can lock the door, but not the hallway

"We did have a new (just out of college) corporate auditor who was appalled that we printed checks in a room that wasn't locked. He insisted that we needed to install a lock on the door, and ensure that it was locked when check stock was in the room. The fact that once we printed the checks we carried the printed checks and the remaining blank stock unescorted through a public hallway back to the accounting department on the floor above was fine with him, as long as we locked the door to the printer room while we printed the checks."

It's not the spirit of the law, it's the letter of the law

"We are a lean manufacturing business (in the General Electric model). This means that most of our employees (mine included) are doing multiple jobs - a foundation of the lean concept. For example, in my organization, Business Analysts perform analysis, project documentation and management, programming, and move of applications into production. This is of course governed by a control process that has multiple sign-offs and [staff] termination penalties for violating the process, and in the 4 years I have led this team, we have *never* moved something into production that was not authorized, on a volume of about 600 modifications during that period. Nonetheless, I am in a constant battle with the external auditors that this is not acceptable and that we must have a dedicated change management group.

In other areas of the business, we have small service offices, which take orders, build product and perform repairs. For this reason, the 3 people in the office must have access to Order, Customer, Vendor, Purchase Order and Item Master data to perform their duties. These are highly profitable offices, due to the lean design and quick response to the Customer base. This of course is a major bone of contention between us and the auditors, as they would essentially like us to hire more people so that we have complete separation of duties, an action which would sink the profitability and effectiveness of these satellite operations."

What does this button do?

"In last year's SOX audit our auditors brought in a junior consultant to audit our SAP security environment and we had to teach the young man how to sign-on to SAP! Obviously things went down hill from there. They 'tested' hundreds of transactions, spent thousands of dollars and hundreds of man-hours, to 'find' one issue of a misplaced transaction and that was the one created by our internal auditor! We remediated this grievous error immediately, so I suppose it was well invested time and money (this last should be read very tongue in cheek)."

No Mr. auditor, you **can't** automate a dinosaur

"The level of documentary evidence requested and some of the recommendations/requirements in some cases are over the top. For example, in our business system, which is 25 years old and never designed for security audits, has 4-5000 menu options. The auditors would have us review all user's access every month, a task which is unachievable. We have settled on quarterly, which we still get grief for, and which we are struggling to perform in a timely manner - its like painting a bridge. The challenge in all of this of course, is that when you have an onerous process to perform on a regular basis, human nature is to begin 'rubber stamping,' which defeats the intent of the control."

Internal auditors gone awry

The sky is falling, the sky is falling

"Our 2004 SOX review by our Internal Audit department was by my standards similar to the story of Chicken Little. They ran around for months literally yelling at many in IT that we were never going to pass our SOX 404 review. When our external auditors finally came in, they had a much calmer attitude with a 'don't worry' theme. They reviewed everything we did throughout the year and when they found something they did not like gave us until the end of the year to correct it. They even gave us suggestions on how to best remedy our issues. I actually enjoyed working with them more than my internal audit team."

Never trust Microsoft

"When asked if we did regular updates & security patches for our computer work stations by the auditor, we replied 'Yes!' Then he asked if we did a virus/worm scan on the download, did a test install off-line, backed up an image of the work station before we installed, then installed from a tested image disc created from this process. We all looked at each other and replied in unison, 'No - we just click the download button.' That still seems funny in extremes to me, we thought we had it covered. Of course this was only off of the Microsoft download site, but it still should be a regular practice just to be safe. Time does not always allow proper execution, and wouldn't you know it, that's when it goes bad (Murphy!)."

What data?

"Seen stories of local government agencies that are ratcheting down their retention to 5-7 days due to freedom of information act. They claim that on any slow news day, they can get a request asking for 'for city government employees, how much email is used for personal use' or something of that nature. If they have the data, they have to produce it. So, they actively delete instead!"

Catch-22

"Our internal auditor lectures the company that procedures are 'forward thinking' that the idea is to state your 'best practices' that you are trying to meet. He then sends out monthly audits of those same procedures, and if you are not 90% compliant you get dinged. I have had numerous LOUD arguments that he has created an impossible compliance situation. Either I dumb down the procedures and meet 90% compliance, or I lie and tell him I am compliant, or my boss gets named at the board meetings as a scofflaw."

The separation of internal and external auditors gone awry

We'll get back to you...

"Earlier this week I discovered a problem with some Separation of Powers issues on one of our Production boxes in Europe. When I discussed this with Internal Audit they told me it had to be fixed ASAP before my external auditors began their review. Now knowing that this was not an easy fix due to the nature of the problem and that we were going to need some time to remedy, I went to my external auditors and explained the situation. When I asked them what my time table for remediation was, they said 12/31. As a matter of fact, they were willing to come back in February of next year to review what we did as long as I documented we fixed it by 12/31."

What was the point supposed to be?

Whatever the point of auditing was supposed to be, it can't be found in *those* stories.

Business governance and information governance have to form a bond, a union. Each has to support the other in order not to void the warranty. Somehow in moving from this big picture that the regulators saw, to the minutiae of the auditors' view of picayune obscurity, the point got lost. The *real* point to all of this is supposed to be that the interweaving of business processes and governance matters.

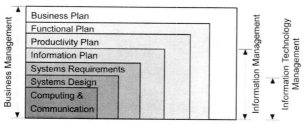

What matters to the regulators, to the business leaders, and therefore to the information services staff and auditors is that your organization has *institutionalized* the process of information governance. What *should* matter is that proper controls are a part of your established customs; that you have gained the cooperation for the use of appropriate controls by your groups *and* individuals as a part of the structure of organizational leadership. And what should matter *most* is that these information services controls fall *directly* in line with business processes, business governance, and therefore information governance. In other words, what should matter most is that **materiality** has been properly defined and that inconsequential controls are ignored.

And that's pretty much the same thing that was said during a business roundtable hosted by the SEC (Securities and Exchange Commission). During a six hour panel discussion on April 13th of 2005, many business people complained about the cost, scope, and complexity of the Sarbanes-Oxley audit process (which can be extended to most information compliance auditing). This led the SEC to issue a statement[23] on May 16th that advises (among other things):

- Value purpose over process – that is, exercise judgment in setting control scope – and the auditors need to respect this judgment in their assessments.

- Consider only those IS controls directly involved in financial reporting systems (which should be extended to other audit types and their relevance of IS to business processes).

- Auditors should respect management's judgment in their assessments.

- Auditors should offer advice to their clients *prior* to assessment.

"How will auditors react to the new guidance? This is the million-dollar question. After all, none of the recommendations changes the law or related auditing standards. They are suggestions, albeit strong ones, and auditors will ultimately determine how and how much they're executed in practice.[24]" wrote Cass Brewer, a field editor, and editorial and research director for the IT Compliance Institute. We agree wholeheartedly with her. Where the auditors understand the meaning of the law, *and* are able to put that into context and properly define materiality, *and* serve the customer instead of their monthly billing interests, the process works. Where the auditors have lost sight of what is really material, *or* get caught up in this month's newest auditing trend, *or* are more interested in keeping their monthly billable rate high, the company that pays for the auditing service gets fleeced.

What do we do about the fleecing?

The answer isn't to stop the auditing. All of these stories don't mean that our organizations are "clean" and that auditing is a waste of time. There is a general disconnect in many of our organizations between what the business units want, and what they are willing to pay for, in terms of information systems spending and the material need for information governance. And

---

23 Division of Corporation Finance Office of the Chief Accountant (2005). Staff Statement on Management's Report on Internal Control Over Financial Reporting, U.S. Securities and Exchange Commission. This was also covered and expanded on in Cass Brewer (2005). The Auditing Dilemma—Balancing Gullibility, Reasonability, and Liability under New Regulatory Guidance, IT Compliance Institute.

24 Ibid the Cass Brewer article.

that is the true spirit of the law – ensuring that there is transparency in decision making and professionalism in deployment and governance of organizational information controls that are needed for assurance of confidentiality, integrity, availability, and accountability.

If we are going to audit information processes, systems, and technology controls, we have to audit them within their proper context of business management in order to determine materiality.

As Paul Strassmann wrote in The Governance of Information Management, "Information management only has value within the context of business management. You cannot [audit] information management as an isolated activity.[25]" And the only way to ensure that we are auditing information management within the context of business management is for organizational leaders to establish a proper framework in which the audit function (both internal and external) can take place.

An audit framework that emphasizes the alignment of business governance to information governance can be depicted as we've done in the drawing that follows.

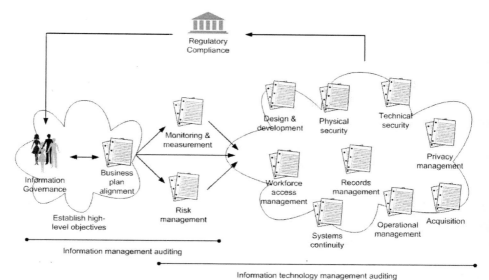

A framework for information governance and regulatory compliance

The first step is to establish a process of information governance – a process that creates consensus about your organizational principles and policies of who does what, and when, and how. These principles and policies have to

---

25   Previously cited, page 19. We changed the "justify" to "audit" to make our point.

extend from your business units through your information services teams and down to your internal (and hopefully, external) auditors.

Introducing the process of information governance allows you to make intelligent decisions about when and how to create proper control objectives and when to simply assume the risk of threat because it makes good business sense to do so. Because *that* is the essence of materiality, and *that's* the part that is missing in many of those stories of auditors gone awry.

Let's go back to one of the earlier stories, the one about the lean organization that didn't have (for the auditor) a proper separation of duties. The auditor's view was that the rule of the law specifies a separation of duties between analysts, documenters, testers, and administrators. The question framed as a definition of materiality is this – in this case, is the *separation of duties* relevant and therefore *the need for additional staff to perform those duties* important enough to properly control the information process and assure the confidentiality, integrity, availability, and accountability of the information system? The information management viewpoint is while that is all well and good for organizations who can *afford* to have a larger staff, *their* organization wasn't in the position to do so. Further, there were adequate alternate controls in place to ensure that any threats to the production environment would be mitigated by other means.

Citing information governance decisions, there is no reason that the information manager couldn't call those controls to light. The information management team could show how the current control methodologies were arrived at by demonstrating that information governance decisions were aligned with the business plan, thus demonstrating that they *do* understand the rules. However, based upon the organization's risk management plan and ability to monitor and measure this type of control objective using alternate means, the specified rule of employing different staff for a separation of duties is neither reasonable nor appropriate at this point in time and therefore not material. Furthermore, the organization has chosen to mitigate any potential threat using alternate means (the "multiple sign-offs and staff termination penalties" mentioned in the story) that *are* both reasonable and appropriate in this case. The process for the methodology would be something akin to our small diagram that follows.

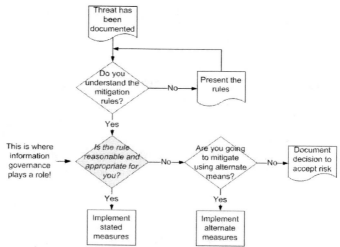

Information governance in the control objective decision making process

Without this key step, defining materiality, anything the auditor says might be what leads your compliance efforts and expenditures. You don't want *that*, do you?

To the IS staff, compliance is like picking a poison

Looking at the question of "why is compliance auditing such a pain" as we have just done from the business point of view is one thing. Looking at the question from the information systems' staff is something quite different. And it is not too far off the mark to say that to the IS staff, picking an audit methodology is akin to picking your "favorite" poison. You know you are going to get killed in the process one way or another.

Picking an audit methodology is like picking a poison – its going to hurt

The reason that compliance is so painful to the information systems staff is twofold: there's so *much* of it and the rules and frameworks that do exist *overlap*.

The proliferation of regulations and standards

When we began researching this work about two years ago, there were approximately 3 or 4 *major* regulatory organizations that you had to worry about. Sarbanes-Oxley, Gramm-Leach-Bliley, HIPAA, and for folks who take credit cards, VISA joined the group. With the addition of all of the new security, operational management, and privacy regulations there are over 150 security auditing guidelines that have to be taken into consideration, as well as more than 80 privacy auditing regulations (not counting the too many to count guidelines) that have to be taken into consideration.

Talking to one of our field editors, Charles Hibnick, I asked him what major regulations and guidelines he had to follow within the world of HIPAA.

Making short our discussion that threaded through several e-mails[26], here's the list of rule makers and auditors that we jointly came up with:

- Everything – HIPAA, the baseline federal regulation.

- Security – CMS/CSR (Centers for Medicaid and Medicare), FISMA (the Federal Government), DoD (for VA and military hospitals), HIT (Healthcare IT auditor group), AHCA (long-term care group), HCFA (Healthcare Financial Agency), NIST (National Institute of Standards and Technology audit manuals used by many auditors), CobiT (more audit guidelines used by auditors).

- Transactions – HEDIS (Healthcare EDI group), WEDI (same type of thing), and NIST again.

- Privacy – HHS/OCS (Office for Civil Rights), Social Security Administration

Q: Who has time to read all of this stuff?
A: The auditors. The IS staff is too busy.

And therein lies the problem. Below is small sampling of some of the regulations that a typical information services staff might have to deal with.

*Just **some** of the regulatory and standards guidelines for information governance*

---

26   Private communications between Charles Hibnick and Dorian Cougias, 9/16/2005 through 9/21/2005.

If you are wondering, because of the various rules that many organizations have to follow, they fall not just under a single regulation like HIPAA, but under *multiple* regulations. For example, the University of Delaware, where I serve on the advisory board, like most universities, falls under multiple regulations because of the student body, the research it does, student loans it grants, etc. Think about it, if over ten standards *bodies* are needed to support one *regulation*, how many standards bodies have to be supported by an organization that falls under multiple regulations? Too many, that's how many.

Add confusion and overlap to proliferation...

...and you have the full information services staff experience of regulatory compliance.

The overlapping nature of the previous diagram points to the overlapping nature of the control objectives (the policies and procedures the regulators want you to follow) set forth by the regulators and standards creators. Multiple rules point to overlapping sets of multiple standards (as one example, NIST is quoted by a great many rule makers and auditors for many types of audits). Multiple standards point to overlapping control objectives.

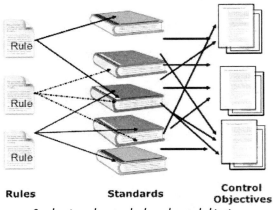

| Rules | Standards | Control Objectives |

Overlapping rules, standards, and control objectives

As a case in point, HIPAA *overlaps itself* in many areas. Section 164.310(b) and (c) deals with workstation use and security controls. This overlaps with facility access control policies, device and media control policies, workforce security, information access management, security awareness training and security incident procedures standards of the Security Rule § 164.310(a), (d), 164.308(a)(1), (3), (4), (5) and (6), respectively. Now, is this *one* all encompassing policy for workstation use and security, or is it *seven* overlapping, smaller rules for workstation use and security? As strange as it may seem, that depends upon who is auditing you at the time, say a few of our field editors who'd rather remain nameless here.

Here are two more audit questions for you, demonstrating how different regulations and standards overlap by asking *the same thing*.

- "Has a mission/business impact analysis (BIA) been conducted to include each business unit, process, and transaction?" Asked in NIST 800-26 Q 1.2.2, FFIEC Business Continuity Exam Q 4.1 & 2, ISO 17799 11.1.2, FISMA 1.2.2, NIST 800-30, CobiT DS 4.1, HIPAA 164.308(a)(7)(i) & 164.310(a)(2)(i) & 164.312(a)(2)(ii), OCTAVE App A: Contingency Planning/Disaster Recovery (SP6) pg. A-10, and CMS CSR § 5.2.7.

- "Are responsibilities for emergency procedures (to include recovery) assigned to specific individuals, including instructions for restoring operations?" Asked in NIST 800-26 Q 9.2.2 & 3, 9.3.2, FFIEC Operations Exam Tier II Q F.4, FFIEC Business Continuity Exam Q 2.1, NFPA 1600 § 4.1.3 and § 5.7.2.2, ISO 17799 11.1.3.b-c, FISMA 9.2.2 and 9.2.3, FISCAM 3.1, FISCAM SC 2.3, NIST 800-18, CobiT DS 4.3, HIPAA 164.308(a)(7)(ii)(A), 164.308(a)(7)(ii)(B), 164.308(a)(7)(ii)(C), 164.308(a)(7)(ii)(D), 164.310(a)(2)(i), & 164.312(a)(2)(ii), OCTAVE App A: Physical Security (OP1) Physical Security Plans and Procedures (OP1.1.5) pg. A-11 & App A: Information Technology Security (OP2) System and Network Management (OP2.1.3) (OP2.1.6) (OP2.1.7) pg. A-14 & App A: Contingency Planning/Disaster Recovery (SP6) pg. A-10, and CMS CSR 2.2.7 & 5.2.7 & 5.4.2 & 5.5.1.

Do ya *think* there's a bit a overlap there? If you had twelve auditors, you could face re-creating the same control objective (*and* associated documentation, *and* walking each auditor through the process) twelve times!

You can't handle the problem by creating a different compliance team for each regulation and standard. If your organization were to deploy multiple regulatory compliance teams, those teams would be dealing with multiple regulations, overlapping standards, and overlapping control objectives. Relying on the same budget and the same timeframe for completion. It can't work that way.

Other than just the numbers (personnel costs, equipment costs, time lost due to stupid audit tricks), the leadership implications of having multiple audit teams would be that the internal auditors would try to take charge of the situation or at least create havoc. And that doesn't work.

Leaders need to lead, not follow the direction of their audit teams

You have to take charge, define what is acceptable, and standardize the language, controls, and operating framework.

You have to set your direction & create your own framework

The first step in setting your direction and creating a framework that *works for you* is to ensure that you actually understand the rules that you are working with. What you need to understand is the underlying principles and high-level control objectives in order to determine *your* common ground[27].

The second step is to choose a framework, such as CobiT, ITIL, ISO, NIST, or as we propose here, a unifying framework of your own choosing that meets *your* needs and not the needs of this or that auditor. The problem with choosing CobiT *or* ITIL *or...* is that they **all** miss some aspect of compliance here or there. **None** of them is complete and whole. One thing is clear – you are going to need to consolidate your compliance efforts and unify your approach. Or you'll burn out your staff and expend your budget before you've ever fixed anything. In other words, you *have* to pick your poison, so pick one that works for *you*.

---

27   Interestingly enough, this is pretty close to the exact same conclusion that was arrived at in Dan Shoemaker, Gregory Ulferts, Jeanne David and Robert Otten (2005). Unifying the body of knowledge: why global business requires a single model for information security, National Standards Registration Board.

Is the regulatory world ready for a unified approach?

Can this be done? Is this pie in the sky? Let's take a look at a couple of independent projects to create a unified approach before we look at the best effort to date – the Unified Compliance Framework, a body of work that Network Frontiers, Latham Watkins, the IT Compliance Institute, over 500 field editors, and a host of others have been contributing to for quite some time.

CobiT

CobiT, the Control Objectives for IT, published by the IT Governance Institute and ISACA, is one of the most universal standards used by IT auditors today. They have begun 'harmonizing' their standard to others that are in existence. There are very well publicized efforts at CobiT harmonization including its harmonization across the "big three": ISO 17799, COSO, and ITIL (the IT Infrastructure Library). CobiT has also been harmonized within the security world across all known security standards. And the main auditing firms like Price Waterhouse Coopers and Deloitte have created harmonized control objectives for Sarbanes-Oxley and others.

HIPAA

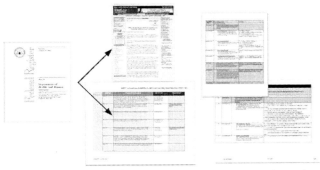

The problems of overlap and standards inflation within the healthcare world have not gone unnoticed. Along the same lines as the CobiT mapping, the world of Healthcare IT is doing its own harmonization that they are calling 'crosswalking.' HIPAA's control objectives have been crosswalked to cover their main standards bodies such as the Centers for Medicare and Medicaid's

Common Security Requirements as well as ISO's 17799. The WEDI electronic Data Interchange group has also crosswalked HIPAA with Carnegie Mellon's OCTAVE method, CobiT, and a few others.

The problem with these individual efforts is that they are just that – individual efforts within a given vertical market. Fortunately for us, Network Frontiers has joined efforts with Latham Watkins and the IT Compliance Institute to create and deliver a Unified Compliance Framework.

The Unified Compliance Project

The Unified Compliance Project (UCP) is a collaborative effort by the IT Compliance Institute and Network Frontiers. All of the information provided in the IT Impact Matrices and their associated summaries represents original research by Network Frontiers and Latham Watkins. The IT Compliance Institute (ITCi) provides complementary research, publishing media, formatting, and financial support for each of the IT Impact Zones that Network Frontiers has identified.

Development methodology and core findings

Our methodology began by defining key terms, and we'll list them here. They differ slightly from those published by other groups such as the ISACA, NSRB, and GAISP groups mentioned above.

Generally Accepted

The UCP's roots lie in many standardization projects already underway by a variety of organizations. As we've just sated above, ISACA calls its effort harmonization, WEDI calls it crosswalking, and ISSA calls it cross-referencing. This is where Network Frontiers started its research for the UCP. The unification documents from CobiT, ISSA, GAISP, CMS, WEDI, and a few others all reference ISO 17799.

We have drawn the line in the sand of what to accept into the framework and what not to accept into the framework through the definition of material that is "generally accepted" in practice and publication. In other words, we've not formalized a definition other than general usage and knowledge. This allows us to exclude individual authors' works (such as our own "Backup Book" and "Compliance Book") as authoritative sources, and therefore leaves us with the following:

- Regulations from countries, states, and regulating bodies (such as the case with VISA, MasterCard and American Express for the credit card industry).

- Documentation from expert practitioner groups (CobiT, COSO, ISO, BCI, AICPA, NSA's IAM/IEM project, the Center for Internet Security, or the IT Process Institute) that follow a due process procedure and broadly distribute their information for public or private group comment.

- Documentation from internationally recognized authorities, such as the United States' National Institute of Standards and Technology, or the Australian DIRKS committee for records management, or the ITIL group.

In limiting our document sources to these authoritative bodies, we cast the broadest net and eliminate having to chase after individual authors who fade into and out of the picture.

During the process of assimilating these documents, we have come to characterize several key definitions.

Information

Information applies to any *knowledge* asset such as facts, data, opinions, numbers, graphics, narrative forms, communications, video, reports, etc. maintained in any medium.

Information processing

An information system describes the organized collection, initial storage, processing, transmission, dissemination, and long term storage in accordance with defined procedures that could be automated or manual.

Information systems

Information systems describe the collected systems and technologies used in information processing.

Information technology assets

Information technology assets are the individual elements of an information system and are classified into the staff, documents and records, applications and databases, operating systems, storage components, firmware and hardware, network, power and cooling, and facilities.

The four properties of information assurance

Throughout the readings[28] we found that there are four basic properties of information, information processes, information systems, and information technology.

- Confidentiality is a characteristic of information only being disclosed to authorized entities, processes, or persons; at authorized times; in authorized manners.

- Integrity is a characteristic of information, information processes, and information systems being complete and accurate.

- Availability is a characteristic of information, information systems, and information technology being accessible and usable on a timely basis.

- Accountability is a characteristic of responsibly interacting at a level commensurate with the sensitivity and criticality of information, information processes, information systems, and information technology.

Furthermore, we found that in order for information *assurance* to be guaranteed, these four properties must co-support each other. Loss of one characteristic can lead to loss of the other characteristics.

Pervasive principles

Pervasive principles are aimed at information governance, information systems governance, and information technology governance. Pervasive principles address the four core properties or characteristics of information. We have found that there are seven pervasive principles[29] strewn throughout the corpus of the foundational documents:

1. **Awareness** – Everyone who has a need to know should have access to the framework, policies, and procedures that your organization is using as a basis for confidentiality, integrity, availability, and accountability.

---

28 This was best described in Gary Stoneburner (2001). 800-33 Underlying Technical Models for Information Technology Security, National Institute of Standards and Technology. The second best sources is GAISP Committee (2003). Generally Accepted Information Security Principles (GAISP) Version 3, Information Systems Security Association.

29 A slightly different viewpoint for this can be found at (2005). Principles of Information Assurance, National Standards Registration Board.

2. **Ethics** – Information should be used in an ethical manner. Security and privacy operations and management should be conducted in an ethical manner.

3. **Multidisciplinary** – Information governance from top to bottom should be addressed from the viewpoint of *all* interested parties and not just the interests of the information management department.

4. **Proportional** – Information security and privacy controls should be proportionate to the risks the organization faces. These risks should include risks to availability, integrity, confidentiality, and even risks to accountability.

5. **Integrated** – The organization's information framework should be coordinated and integrated between each stakeholder, policies and procedures coordinated with each other, and everything coordinated and integrated with third party stakeholders as well.

6. **Timely** – All stakeholders and everyone being held responsible and accountable needs to act in a timely (as well as integrated) manner to either prevent or respond to threats or actual breaches of availability, integrity, confidentiality, and accountability.

7. **Reassessment** – All threats and risks should be assessed periodically in order to ensure that the framework is up to date and as complete as necessary.

Broad functional IT impact zones

While it might be nice to understand the pervasive principles, they don't really help us to determine the scope of each of the audits we might be undergoing or the materiality of the controls being audited. For instance, CobiT and the ITIL library provide a massive span that covers a great deal of control objectives – everything from security through operational issues and even leadership objectives. Most of which can be ignored if the audit you are going through is an HR audit on hiring practices for your IS department. So for our first attempt to set boundaries for what should be "in play" during any particular audit, we searched for broad functional impact zones and came up with twelve of them, and we'll go through each in just a moment. These impact zones can be used to compartmentalize the audit process in order to filter out controls not materially important to that particular zone. By using cross-references as a key, we were able to build our first table of impact zones and summaries of requirements for control objectives within each Impact Zone.

The next step was standardizing the terms to be used within the key IS control objectives. For example, we use the common moniker confidential information to refer to HIPAA's electronic protected health information, VISA's and GLB's customer information, multiple privacy regulations' client information, and Microsoft's privileged information. Through this methodology we are able to determine when a yellow tomato and a red tomato should be simply referred to as tomatoes. And to ensure that we don't get confused ourselves, we maintain a full working glossary of all terms and their reference sources. You can find the glossary online at http://www.compliancebook.com.

The final step in the process was to examine the commonalities of major impact zones and unify control objective definitions and labels. CobiT divides the world into sections labeled PO, DS, etc. ISO 17799 divides its material differently, as do all of the other regulations and guidelines. While this might seem confusing, what they are all doing is really talking about the same 12 information management impact zones:

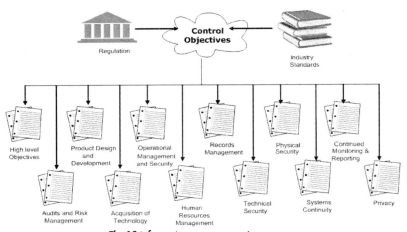

The 12 information management impact zones

1. **High Level Objectives** ensure that your organization's top echelon leadership is coordinating strategy with your IS staff's tactics.

2. **Audits and Risk Management** ensure that you are actively conducting threat and risk audits to assess your vulnerabilities and create a triaged gap plan to fix the problems that could turn threats into reality.

3. **Product Design and Development** deals with asking much tougher questions than most of us are used to asking when we are creating custom applications.

4. **Acquisition of Technology** asks the same type of questions when the organization is putting customized systems into place through acquisi-

tion. The complex equation of scoping, assessing, sourcing, and implementing acquired technologies are covered in this impact zone.

5. **Operational Management and Operational Security** is as it sounds, dealing with the day-to-day activities of most information management needs.

6. **Human Resources Management** focuses on the areas of identity management, background checks, separation of duties (and when it doesn't make sense), considerations for outsourcing, supervision strategies, team development and communication, budgeting, recruiting, job definitions, performance discipline, and more are covered here.

7. **Records Management** isn't thought of much by most information management leaders, but needs to be brought to the front burner. Paper records management has been professionally managed for years. But something happened when organizations moved to electronic records. We'd hazard a guess that most organization's electronic records management systems are no where near professionally managed as they should be. And that includes e-mails, instant messages, and unstructured information as well.

8. **Technical Security** has always been at the front burner of most IT staff members' minds and continues to play a dominant role in information governance. Access management, identity verification, data protection within and across networks, within databases and records archives, and down to individual computers and their software are all covered within this impact zone.

9. **Physical Security** is the touch-it-feel-it counterpart to technical security above.

10. **Systems Continuity** has evolved out of the disaster recovery world. Organizations today have learned that it is much better to ensure an organization's continuity rather than waiting for a disaster to happen.

11. **Monitoring and Reporting** is one of the *key* regulatory compliance impact zones as it is fundamental to being able to collect data and report on the condition of the systems being monitored.

12. **Privacy** is quickly becoming one of the most critical issues for information management – especially for organizations that are in multiple states or multiple countries.

By looking at the corpus of guidelines and regulations through the lens of unification along the lines of the 12 impact areas we just discussed, we created a unification matrix *for each impact zone* that can take into account all regulatory and guidelines bodies, doctrines, and language[30]. A small cross sampling of one of the matrices is shown below, demonstrating how the control objective of "establishing the need to define high level objectives" is defined in the SOX regulations and standards several times, as well as the NASD/NYSE standards. Each of the 12 impact zone matrices can be found ounline at http://www.itcinsitute.com/ucp.

	SOX					Combined Code		17 CFR (SEC)			NASD/NYSE		
Bold = Required Normal = Addressable Underline = Link	Sarbanes-Oxley	PCAOB Rel. 2004-001 Audit section	SAS 94	AICPA/CICA Privacy Framework	AICPA Suitable Trust Services Criteria	Combined Code on Corporate Governance	Turnbull Guidance	240.15d-15 Controls and Procedures	240.16a-3 Website Reporting	Public Companies Checklist	NASD	NYSE	240.17a-1 Recordkeeping Rule
Establish need and define high level objectives	Implied		¶8-13	P10	¶11	A.1	¶16			X	Implied	Implied	Implied
Analyze organizational objectives, functions, actvities, and tasks	Implied						Implied			X			

A sampling of one of the 12 impact zone matrices

Matrices segregate authorities by type (*Public Companies, Healthcare, General Standards*, etc.). Within each type, authorities are listed by name (*Sarbanes-Oxley, NIST, Basle II*, etc.), and, where appropriate, by specific publication (*SAS 94, AICPA/CICA Privacy Framework, NIST 800-14*, etc.). All relevant authorities are listed in a single row across the top of each matrix, and referenced against a hierarchical list of control objectives, set out in the leftmost column of the matrix. By looking at control objectives across the matrix, you can easily see which authorities require or provide recommendations for the objective. Moreover, we reference the specific section or paragraph that is relevant for each cited authority.

The next step was double checking our references. For each of the Impact Matrices within the 12 Impact Zones, we created a series of control-objective summaries. These helped us to check the context of each of the

---

30 We've started with the most obvious regulations and guidelines and will continuously add to, and update the matrices as we process information, changes are made to gudelines and regulations, or new guidelines and regulations emerge.

cross referenced items and rearrange accordingly. For each matrix, we re-read each of the references in each cell to ensure that the quoted selection truly fit the rest of the material present. If the material fit, the reference remained intact; if it did not, it was marked and referenced to a more appropriate position within the matrix.

Each Impact Matrix also contains original information: regulations and guidelines that were not a part of any other group's standardization project. The new material was read, indexed, and marked for matrix insertion. In most cases, we integrated the information into the existing list of control objectives. On rare occasion, it was added as a new row in the matrix.

Multiple editors within Network Frontiers reviewed and edited each proposed addition prior to insertion. When new terminology was encountered, it was added or assimilated into the existing glossary. The final step was integration of the new information into the Impact Zones' control-objective summaries.

Finally, once the master matrix, control-objective summaries, and glossary items were updated, the material was sent to the Network Frontiers' extensive field-editor list for vetting and approval.

This process gives us as complete a list of control objectives as we've found anywhere. What it doesn't provide is a way to decide which controls are material to *your* organization and which controls should be material to a framework that works for *you*.

Materiality

We're going to cover this again within the impact zone, but it is worth going over here in order to set the tone for the material that follows. Materiality is a legal term describing facts or items that would be important to a reasonable person in carrying out a task or understanding a situation. When applied to an information services audit, materiality means those things that are important and relevant to a reasonable person carrying out the audit.

When applied to creating a framework that works for your organization, materiality means the impact zones and control objectives that are important and relevant to carrying out the task of assuring that you have reasonable controls for confidentiality, integrity, availability, and accountability.

Properly defining the material controls to add to your framework (and the irrelevant and inconsequential ones to exclude from your framework) is what enables you to avoid the "stupid auditor stories" that we've previously written about. We cover the process you can use to define materiality below when we discuss your working methodology within the context of getting started and creating your own framework.

Has anyone adopted the Unified Compliance approach?

You bet. This approach has already been adopted by Emerson Network Power and Liebert Global Services for use in their Liebert Availability Assessment practice; as well as by Palo Alto Software in their Systems Continuity Plan Pro (SCPP) tool[31]; Symantec in their Systems Continuity Services offering; and service offerings from over 100 VARs and consulting firms worldwide.

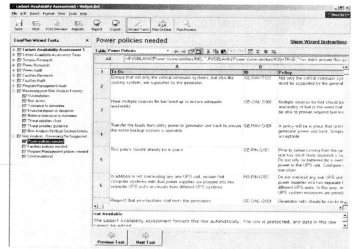

A screenshot from the Palo Alto software used by Symantec and Liebert

To learn more about the software, visit http://www.scplans.com.

Why *you* want to use this methodology as your starting point

Your staff needs to come to a consensus on information governance. You need to aggregate and align your control objectives in order to reduce the

---

31 As a reader of this material, you are entitled to a discounted version of Systems Continuity Plan Pro from Palo Alto Software (www.scplans.com). Just enter scp8cd30c into the discount code field for a 30% discount.

complexity and workload of compliance. And you don't want to reinvent the wheel.

Alignment and aggregation reduces the potential for confusion. Look at it this way – regulatory compliance is merely enforced assured protection from threats, such as deliberate actions by people wishing to do harm, accidental actions by people who are not paying enough attention, system problems caused by Microsoft Updates or viruses and the like, and natural or man-made disasters that strike without asking first. The idea is that we have to protect against all of these threats. Compliance isn't about having to make the control objectives and processes complex.

Protection isn't complex

So with all of this complexity out of the way, we in IS can do what we do best – hide from angry end users. Okay, just kidding about that part. With complexity out of the way, this methodology allows you to synthesize new and updated regulations and standards into your existing information governance program more easily, because chances are, there's already overlap between what you are doing in the way of information governance and what the new or updated regulations are asking for.

Because the Unified Compliance Project maintains a database of all known regulations and standards that are cross referenced, when new regulations or standards are added to the database, they can easily be compared to that which already exists and the new language and objectives can easily be aligned with the existing language and objectives. If the new regulations are similar to the existing regulations, there is bound to be a great deal of overlap. Which is good. Because a vast majority of the "new" issues won't really be "new" at all and will most likely be integrated into existing controls (making your job simpler), or as small additions to existing controls (which means that the burden isn't much at all).

How do you get started?

Read this section. Take the Unified Compliance Project's control objectives that we've presented and come to a consensus with regards to what works for *your* organization and what should be ignored. And then set your direction – your team *will* follow you.

Set the direction for the team to follow!

The steps we'll show you here are an abbreviated form of material we are swiping outright from the GAISP committee's Detailed Principles Cookbook[32]. This will get you moving in the right direction to create your framework complete with detailed principles.

Assemble your team

The working chair of the group should contact potential volunteers who want to join the team (or you could just volunteer them). You'll want to ensure that you have balanced representation on the team, including stakeholders from the various front line users and business units.

Orient according to your organizational direction

Review the mission, charter, and current project status of your organization to ensure familiarity with your business goals. If you already have high level objectives for information and information technology established, you'll want to include those in the orientation.

---

32   GAISP Committee (2003). Detailed Principles Cookbook, Information Systems Security Association.

Determine how your team wants to work together and identify the various responsibilities that each team member will have for producing your framework and tying that to your policies and procedures.

If your team is large enough and you are going to break it down into working groups (we are assuming you'd break them down according to the 12 IT impact zones), you'll want to determine how each team will be addressed and what each will comprise.

Your working methodology

Sequester everyone in the group for whatever uninterrupted period you need to deliberate which regulations you fall under, and followed by that, which frameworks (CobiT, ITIL, etc.), guidelines (NIST, BCI, etc.), and standards (ISO, BS, DIRKS) you want to include as foundation references[33]. As you read through this material, you'll see that we've broken down foundational references into different groupings (such as putting all of the NIST documents into a NIST grouping). If a grouping doesn't apply to you, you can ignore that whole section. If a grouping does apply to you, then as you read the material you'll see that when we reference the particular foundation document (such as NIST 800-14) we **boldface** the reference to make it easy to pick out. This should help you skim the material and pick out the parts that are relevant to you.

You'll also want to decide if you are tackling *all 12* of the impact zones at once, or if you are tackling them one at a time[34]. Each of the chapters in the book is broken down by IT Impact Zone. We did this so that if you want to completely skip a whole impact zone, you can do so quickly and easily.

Once you have your list of foundation documents and your list of impact zones, you'll then move your group through the process of determining which of the control objectives apply to you in your situation – i.e., you'll be defining the materiality of the controls you are going to use to construct your framework.

---

[33] If you have licensed the UCP database from us, the above step can be done through the database interface by simply selecting "all" or each individual foundation document. For more information about licensing the document, send an e-mail to UCPInfo@netfrontiers.com.

[34] Again, the UCP database will allow this type of selection.

All of your decisions hinge on the very first question – does the control objective apply in this situation? And when defining your situation, you have to set the boundaries of your scope[35]. Your scope will be different based upon the level of information governance you are focusing your framework on.

- If you are creating a framework for assuring a single IT asset, you'll need to ensure the scope covers its baseline setup controls, change management controls, and entitlement (usage and privilege) controls with respect to confidentiality, integrity, availability, and accountability.

- If you are creating a framework for assuring an IT system (multiple assets that must function together such as the financial system) you'll need to add the scope of assurance for each IT asset, as well as a scope of assurance for the transactions between the assets.

- If you are creating a framework for assuring an information process (such as the payroll process that leverages the financial system) you'll need to add to your scope the business rules, accuracy testing, process change management and process entitlements.

Once you've defined the nature of your framework and defined what you are protecting, you'll need to populate your framework with individual controls. There are five decisions you'll need to make in order to determine the materiality of controls for your framework.

1. **IF** the control objective does not apply to your organization **THEN** document your decision not to implement the specifications for this control objective **AND** document how the overall standard and goal is being met otherwise **OR** that your organization isn't taking part in the activities covered by the control objective.

2. **IF** the control objective applies to your organization *and* the specification is both reasonable *and* appropriate *and* it is entirely unique, **THEN** it should be implemented.

3. **IF** the control objective applies to your organization *and* the specification is both reasonable *and* appropriate *but* it is not entirely unique, **THEN** document how it matches a specification you are already using **AND** document how you made the decision that the specification matches another already in existence.

---

[35] As with materiality, scope will be covered again in more detail within the impact zone sextions.

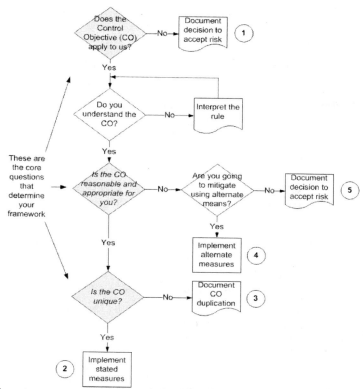

The information governance process as applied to deciding which rules to add to your control objectives

4. **IF** the control objective applies to your organization *and* the specification is unreasonable or inappropriate, but you want to mitigate the threat through alternate means **THEN** implement an alternate measure that accomplishes the same goal (albeit not within the specification's guidance) **AND** document the decision *not* to implement according to the specification **AND** document why the specification is either unreasonable or inappropriate **AND** document how the overall standard and goal is being met otherwise.

5. **IF** the control objective applies to your organization *and* the specification is unreasonable or inappropriate and you are going to decide not to mitigate the threat **THEN** document your decision not to implement the specification **AND** document why the specification is unreasonable or inappropriate **AND** document how the overall standard and goal is being met otherwise.

Here's a sample. Let's say that your organization has decided right now all you need to do is comply with a VISA regulation, and you also want to ensure that you are following the rules of ISO 17799. One of the control objectives is *registry control monitoring*. Registry control monitoring asks the question "are systems monitored to detect deviation from access control policy and record monitorable events to provide evidence in case of security incidents?" [VISA CISP § 10.6; ISO 17799:2000 § 9.7].

- If the control objective applies to your organization (you might even want to state explicitly the types of systems it applies to),

- and the control objective is reasonable and appropriate,

- and you don't already have this as a part of your repertoire,

- then you'll want to create a control statement (also known as a policy statement) for it.

Drafting your control objectives

Once you have selected all your control objectives and turned them into policy statements, you will have what we refer to as compliance templates. You can see sample templates at ITCi and we even have an area for readers to contribute templates. In addition, they can be obtained through a partner organization of ours that writes and maintains the SCPP software[36]. A few starter templates (and a blank one) are included as a part of this material. Each high level control objective should follow the same outline as we show in the example control objective here:

1. **Registry control monitoring**

Control ID PM-TIN-A101			
Control guarantor	Email	Modification Date	Next Revision Date
Joe Blow	jblow@acme.com	1/18/2006	7/18/2006

2. **Control Objective Statement**

   Systems will be monitored to detect deviation from access control policy and record monitorable events to provide evidence in case of security incidents.

3. **Purpose of Control Objective**

   Registry control monitoring will show you which applications are accessing your Registry, which keys they are accessing, and the Registry data that they are reading and writing.

---

36   For more information on the software, go to http://www.scplans.com. Each of the templates can be filled out, shared, and edited within SCPP. SCPP can also import and export these files to Microsoft Word 2000 or greater.

When a user-mode component makes a privileged system call, control is transferred to a software interrupt handler in NTOSKRNL.EXE (the core of the Windows NT operating system). This handler takes a system call number, which is passed in a machine register, and indexes into a system service table to find the address of the NT function that will handle the request. By replacing entries in this table with pointers to hooking functions, it is possible to intercept and replace, augment, or monitor NT system services.

When the monitoring application sees an open, create or close call, it updates an internal hash table that serves as the mapping between key handles and registry path names. Whenever it sees calls that are handle based, it looks up the handle in the hash table to obtain the full name for display.

The list of registry calls can then be parsed for any unauthorized change attempts.

4. **Compliance**

Regulations and frameworks

- VISA CISP § 10.6; ISO 17799:2000 § 9.7

Microsoft reference documents:

- http://support.microsoft.com/support/kb/articles/Q286/1/98.ASP

- http://support.microsoft.com/default.aspx?scid=KB;en-us;327657

- http://support.microsoft.com/default.aspx?scid=kb;en-us;555069

5. **Control Objective Scope**

5.1 **Control Objective Coverage**

This control objective applies to all servers and workstations marked as

- mission critical
- holding privacy-sensitive data
- holding integrity-sensitive data

5.2 **Assignment**

The technical security team will automate the capture of all registry change information during the system's initial hardening and rollout.

The security monitoring team will ensure initial and continued monitoring of all registry changes.

The security incident team will react to all potential and real unauthorized registry changes.

5.3 Pre-requisite Knowledge

Prerequisite knowledge includes training in the organizational technical security standards, registry control monitoring software to be used, monitoring applications and processes, and incident response processes.

5.4 Pre-requisite Tools

- Registry control monitoring applications
- Monitoring reporting applications
- Helpdesk and trouble ticket system

Isn't that a lot of writing?

If you noticed, the control objective that we listed above shouldn't be far from the type of documentation you *already have* – your procedures manual. If you *have* a procedures manual, then most of what you'll be doing is copying and pasting from your procedures manual so that you can call it your "regulatory compliance control objective" manual. If you *don't have* a procedures manual, then yes, you are in for a bit of work. But don't worry. We have over 1,000 controls you can use to jump start the process.

Gaining consensus

Any time more than one person works on a project, consensus has to be gained and politics will play a role. That's fine, because that is what ensures that due diligence has taken place and a better product has been created. Here are some rules to use when creating your detailed control objective documents:

Internal consensus

Based upon the UCP control objectives tables and citations that we've provided, prepare a working draft of the control objective statement to at least point 5.4 as shown here (you might want to leave out any specific applications and just mention generic ones).

Discuss and send the UCP working draft control objectives to each of the other members working on the project (and if subdivided, working on that particular IT Impact Zone). Use whatever discussion and consensus building methodologies you want to bring the working draft of the control objectives to a format that the entire group can vote on. This might mean that the working draft is routed through the group for comments and review several times before final revisions are made and it is ready to be voted on.

The working drafts will then need to be officially voted on by the working group. Whether you want to have a simple majority or a $2/3^{rd}$ majority for your vote is really up to you. Anyone who continues to hold reservations about the control objectives should be attended to, and those reservations should be addressed and any revisions to the working draft should be made accordingly.

If the working draft is voted down, it should be voted down with specific re-work recommendations in mind. And those re-worked recommendations should be made accordingly and the working draft resubmitted for a vote.

If the working draft is accepted, it should be guaranteed as accurate by a specific owner (including current contact information such as an e-mail address). Once the working draft has been accepted and guaranteed, it should be released as an "exposure draft" that you are going to test in the real world, and run by your internal and external auditor team for vetting.

External consensus

Once the exposure draft has been released, you'll need to review the control for accuracy and comment from the audit team(s). The comments should be sent back to the original groups through the guarantor of each control objective (hence why the e-mail contact info should be added to the document).

Each working group should be given about 30 – 60 days to organize and consolidate all of the comments and incorporate them into a working list, or directly into the documents if necessary. A revised draft should then be prepared and subjected to the same review process as before.

After achieving final consensus, you should have an insanely strong set of control objectives, and a framework that is broad and strong.

Defining Information Governance

As a support mechanism for the organization, there are three levels of information services that we are concerned with from here on out – information management (which enjoys the largest purview), information systems management, and information technology management (which has the most limited horizon). These three information services roughly map out according to the generally accepted layers of organizational management as shown in the following diagram.

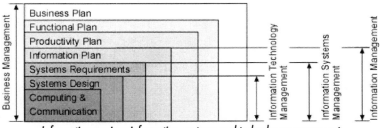

Information services; information, systems, and technology management

The management of the *technology* that creates, houses, manipulates, and stores information is concerned with providing technical solutions for specific business needs. Think of this as individual IT assets such as drive arrays, CPUs, applications and databases, hubs, routers, switches, etc.

The management of information *systems* focuses on aspects of confidentiality, integrity, and availability as information moves through combinations of IT assets, such as the application server communicating with the database server over the organiztaioal subnet (which together form one *system*).

The management of *information* is concerned with the use and effectiveness of information processes (whether those processes are computerized or not). These are the procedures that users follow when entering or outputting information, or the routines the applications and databases use during computing operations.

The regulators and standards creators are calling for our organizations to provide the appropriate level of governance in *each* of these three arenas. This section deals with the management and governance of information as opposed to the management and governance of the supporting systems or underlying technology.

Because others have intermingled the terms information governance and information technology governance to mean more or less the same thing, we are going to begin with a clear definition of *all three* layers of information services governance before we dive into what the regulators are saying about the highest layer of the three – information governance.

Definitions of information governance

This could also be titled "why your organization is different than my organization." Or if you were French, "Vive la différence."

Essential to our definition of information governance is the reach we give our terms. Too many authors have extended, and therefore co-mingled, their definitions. Our aim here is to scale back the span of those definitions to something much tighter, and therefore more clearly defined.

In this chapter we define the following:

What decisions need to be made.

The level within information services that those decisions need to be made.

How *your organizational structure* will affect both *who* and *how* those decisions are made.

The Main Thing

What we want to point out here is that however you slice it, the act of governing, even in a corporation determines:

- how power is exercised,
- how the users are given a voice in the process (or not),
- how decisions are made (and conflicts brought to resolution) on issues that concern all of those involved,
- how those decisions become policy within the organization, and
- how those policies and the actions of the staff are monitored[37].

In the above description, the act of governing defines the "how" portion of the definition. *What* must be governed within the world of information services and regulatory compliance is broken down into three levels of granularity:

1. Information governance at the highest level that leverages the information per se, as well as the methodologies for information processing.

2. Information systems governance that focuses on maintaining the confidentiality, integrity, and availability of the arrangement of IT assets that process the information.

3. Information technology governance that includes the computerized support assets of the information systems.

Who makes these decisions in the organization is determined by the lifecycle that the organization has developed into. The "who" can range from a single individual to a committee or the board.

---

[37] For one of the best definitions of corporate governance, see OECD.org (2004). OECD Principles of Corporate Governance. Organization for Economic Cooperation and Development. A perfect example of our point.

The scope of how we use the term "governance"

Governance is the people, policies, and processes that provide the framework within which those who are authorized to do so make decisions and take actions in order to optimize outcomes related to their spheres of responsibility[38].

Governance is the process of setting of policies for others to follow

Arranged more appropriately and simply, governance addresses three basic issues of "what," "who," and "how."

1. What decisions need to be made?
2. Who should make those decisions?
3. How will the decisions be made and monitored?

What decisions need to be made, who makes those decisions, and how they are made and monitored are decided by the level of information services you are working within (your viewpoint within the organization), as well as the type of leadership in effect within the organization. We're going to spend the rest of this chapter talking about how your organizational viewpoint affects addressing "what," "who," and "how" within the three levels of information services governance. Let's take a second and look at the various general forms of governance that can be found within today's organizations.

Governance is different than direct control – just as a military dictatorship is different than civilian politics. Without going into too much depth, here's the difference looking at four different types of organizational structures.

---

38   If you'd like to find other definitions, it is always interesting to load Google's search page in a browser and type a definition for a term. In this instance, enter the following into the Google search field (without the quotes): "define:governance".

- A military leader or dictator can command that a direction be set because the *authority of command* authorizes the power to do so.

- Democracy is completely the opposite and is derived from two ancient Greek words, demos (the people) and kratos (strength). Hence, the power to set direction in a democracy is *exercised by the people.*

- A bureaucracy is typified by formal processes, standardization, hierarchic procedures, and written communication found within most large organizations. Hence, power to set direction in a bureaucracy is found within the *administrative structure.*

- At the complete other end of the spectrum, and at odds with all of the above, is an anarchy – the complete absence of all governance and rule or formal processes. There is *no base of power* because there is *no structure.*

The *power* to govern is dictated by the *structure of the organization* in all of these instances. And don't tell us that you don't see all of these structures at work in everyday business life. Startups are usually democratic anarchies filled with bright and energetic people arguing for "the best idea to win" as a form of governance. Jack Welch doesn't come across as a leader who would like *either* the democratic *or* the bureaucratic approach, but rather, the benevolent dictator model. And while small groups within Daimler-Chrysler, Ford, or General Motors might be otherwise, we'd argue that for the most part those large, complex organizations are bureaucratic. And having survived the "dot com meltdown," we've seen our share of anarchies as organizations dissembled themselves. What accounts for the difference in organizational structures? Many leadership gurus would argue that what we presented here is just a part of the natural cycle of organizational development.

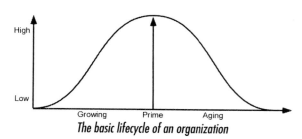

The basic lifecycle of an organization

The basic premise is this; all organizations move through a process of being born, growing, aging, and then dying. During this process, the organization is at it's "high" during the prime of it's life, as depicted in the previous diagram. Who makes information governance, or any other major decisions, and how those decisions are made, is based upon the organization's progress in the lifecycle.

How to skip over the rest of this section

If you want to skip over the next section and save yourself some time, think about the "who and how" of governance like this: babies think like babies, adolescents like adolescents, grown-ups like grown-ups, and really old folks are just set in their ways and think however they want. Just like dealing with people of different age groups, you have to relate to and work with these organizations in a way that makes sense for *them*. If you get this point, you get the whole next section of this chapter. If you want to know more about this point, and how to assess where your organization might be in its lifecycle, then by all means, read the following section *Understanding organizational character – the rise of the wave.*

If you want to just pick up the bullet points for which regulatory compliance impact zones fit into information, systems, and technology governance, then go straight to the table we present in *Putting governance in perspective* and you'll get the picture. If you want the detail, then read all three sections starting with *The scope of information technology management & governance.*

Understanding organizational character – the rise of the wave

We present a rather lengthy diatribe here about the wave-cycle theory of organizational development for a couple of reasons;

- Your organization is at some point of development in this wave.

- How decisions are made, and who makes them, is determined by how far along your organization has developed.

- In order to move your compliance project forward, you have to understand and leverage the group dynamics that surround you.

The reason for the length is that we present three views of the same topic; Lawrence Miller's which is the simplest, Ichak Adizes' which is more complex, and William Bridges' which is the most complex and the most up-to-date. Each of them describe organizational dynamics as a wave-form. We aren't espousing one above the other. Pick one.

Contrary to popular belief, "the wave" wasn't originated at a Bears football game. The fist historian to document the stages and styles of history as a wave-like form was Oswald Spengler back in 1926 when he wrote the following:

> Over the expanse of the water passes the endless uniform wave-train of the generations... But over this surface, too, the great Cultures accomplish their majestic wave-cycles. They appear suddenly, swell in splendid lines, flatten again and vanish, and the face of the waters is once more a sleeping waste.[39]

This same thought pattern was picked up by the great historian Alfred Toynbee[40] wherein he wrote about the successive rises and falls of the primary and secondary civilizations as an example of the same type of rhythm that moves towards a goal much as a wave moves toward the shoreline. In

---

[39] Oswald Spengler and Charles Francis Atkinson (1926). The decline of the West. New York, A. A. Knopf. Page 106.

[40] Arnold Joseph Toynbee and Edward D. Myers (1948). A study of history. London, New York,, Oxford University Press. Volume 8 contains the basis of his rhythmic theory that matches Spengler's.

1986 Arthur Schlesinger picked up the same rhythmic theme when focusing on American history[41]. However, there's one important (at least for us) point that Schlesinger made. Unlike the cycles of civilization that built upon each other's understand to create forward movement (as Toynbee pointed out), Schlesinger's waves of motion are merely repetitive. Schlesinger argues that there is a continuing shift "between public purpose and private interests.[42]" As you'll see in our arguments here, that theory fits the corporate wave-cycle like a glove.

Roughly within the same time period that Schlesinger was writing about the cycles of American history and Paul Kennedy was writing the same thing about the rise and fall of great national powers, Ichak Adizes and Lawrence Miller were penning the same wave-form theories about corporations.

A simple theory of corporate wave-cycles and organizational character

Lawrence Miller defines seven stages of corporate life that are tied to seven leadership styles dominant during each stage[43]:

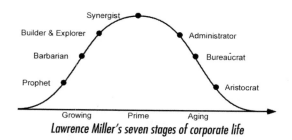

Lawrence Miller's seven stages of corporate life

1. **The Prophet:** The visionary who creates the break-through and the human energy to propel the company forward.

---

[41] Arthur Meier Schlesinger (1986). <u>The cycles of American history</u>. Boston, Houghton Mifflin.

[42] Ibid, page 27. Paul Kennedy argues much the same thing about the rise and fall of powerful nations in Paul M. Kennedy (1987). <u>The rise and fall of the great powers : economic change and military conflict from 1500 to 2000</u>. New York, NY, Random House.

[43] Lawrence M. Miller (1989). <u>Barbarians to Bureaucrats: Corporate Life Cycle Strategies, Lessons from the rise and fall of civilizations</u>. New York, NY, Fawcett Columbine. Page 2 – with a slight reordering to move the synergist to the middle.

2. **The Barbarian:** The leader of crisis and conquest who commands the corporation on the march of rapid growth.

3. **The Builder and Explorer:** The developers of the specialized skills and structures required for growth, who shift from command to collaboration.

4. **The Synergist:** The leader who maintains the balance, who continues the forward motion of a large and complex structure by unifying and appreciating the diverse contribution of the Prophet, Barbarian, Builder, Explorer, and Administrator.

5. **The Administrator:** The creator of the integrating system and structure, who shifts the focus from expansion to security.

6. **The Bureaucrat:** The imposer of a tight grip of control, who crucifies and exiles new prophets and barbarians, assuring the loss of creativity and expansion.

7. **The Aristocrat:** The inheritor of wealth, alienated from those who do productive work, who is the cause of rebellion and disintegration.

He then goes on to delineate each of the seven leadership characteristics and their matching organizational characteristic, pointing out the specific business challenges faced at each stage. Miller points out that at each stage and leadership style, leaders and the organization itself respond different to conflict and resolution. During growth, leaders are creative, love a challenge, and are forward looking. During decline, responses are mechanistic, challenges eschewed, and past history is relied upon for future direction.

We've all been there (well, most of us anyway). How many of us *can't* compare and contrast the dynamic energy of small, growing organizations versus the waste of human (and other) resources in dying and bureaucratic dinosaurs?

The point here is that if you want to get something done in your organization, you have to tailor your action-taking methodology to meet the organizational dynamic that surrounds you. You'll have a hard road to hoe for sowing the seeds of regulatory compliance if your leadership are "barbarians" versus "administrators."

A more complex theory of organizational character

Roughly the same time that Miller was applying wave-cycles to organizations, Ichak Adizes was doing the same thing, however in much greater depth[44]. Where Miller has seven stages, Adizes' theory has ten basic stages (with five additional quick-death stages that we'll omit here). Adizes also has the organization moving toward death at the *stable* stage, even before it reaches its high-point of growth. Also omitted here, Adizes goes into greater detail in defining the organizational attitudes and mores than does Miller.

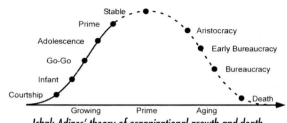

Ichak Adizes' theory of organizational growth and death

Broken down and simplified by Inc. Magazine[45], the ten stages of an organization's birth, growth, and death are as follows:

1. **Courtship:** Would-be founders focus on ideas and future possibilities, making and talking about ambitious plans. Courtship ends and infancy begins when the founders assume risk.

2. **Infancy:** The founders' attention shifts from ideas and possibilities to results. The need to make sales drives this action-oriented, opportunity-driven stage. Nobody pays much attention to paperwork, controls, systems, or procedures. Founders work 16-hour days, six to seven days a week, trying to do everything by themselves.

3. **Go-Go:** This is a rapid-growth stage. Sales are still king. The founders believe they can do no wrong. Because they see everything as an opportunity, their arrogance leaves their businesses vulnerable to flagrant mistakes. They organize their companies around people rather than functions; capable employees can--and do--wear many hats, but to their staff's consternation, the founders continue to make every decision.

4. **Adolescence:** During this stage, companies take a new form. The founders hire chief operating officers but find it difficult to hand over the reins. An attitude of us (the old-timers) versus them (the COO and his or her supporters)hampers operations. There are so many internal conflicts, people have little time left to serve customers. Companies suffer a temporary loss of vision.

---

[44]   Ichak Adizes (1988). <u>Corporate Lifecycles: How and Why corporations grow and die and what to do about it</u>. Englewood Cliffs, NJ, Prentice Hall.

[45]   (1996). <u>The 10 Stages of Corporate Life Cycles</u>, Inc. Magazine.

5. **Prime:** With a renewed clarity of vision, companies establish an even balance between control and flexibility. Everything comes together. Disciplined yet innovative, companies consistently meet their customers' needs. New businesses sprout up within the organization, and they are decentralized to provide new life-cycle opportunities.

6. **Stability:** Companies are still strong, but without the eagerness of their earlier stages. They welcome new ideas but with less excitement than they did during the growing stages. The financial people begin to impose controls for short-term results in ways that curtail long-term innovation. The emphasis on marketing and research and development wanes.

7. **Aristocracy:** Not making waves becomes a way of life. Outward signs of respectability – dress, office decor, and titles--take on enormous importance. Companies acquire businesses rather than incubate start-ups. Their culture emphasizes how things are done over what's being done and why people are doing it. Company leaders rely on the past to carry them into the future.

8. **Early Bureaucracy:** In this stage of decay, companies conduct witch-hunts to find out who did wrong rather than try to discover what went wrong and how to fix it. Cost reductions take precedence over efforts that could increase revenues. Backstabbing and corporate infighting rule. Executives fight to protect their turf, isolating themselves from their fellow executives. Petty jealousies reign supreme.

9. **Bureaucracy:** If companies do not die in the previous stage--maybe they are in a regulated environment where the critical factor for success is not how they satisfy customers but whether they are politically an asset or a liability--they become bureaucratic. Procedure manuals thicken, paperwork abounds, and rules and policies choke innovation and creativity. Even customers--forsaken and forgotten--find they need to devise elaborate strategies to get anybody's attention.

10. **Death:** This final stage may creep up over several years, or it may arrive suddenly, with one massive blow. Companies crumble when they cannot generate the cash they need; the outflow finally exhausts any inflow.

Of even more significance for our needs in understanding how the organization's point in its wave-cycle affects information governance, Adizes outlines the differences in form versus function between growing companies and aging companies. As you read through this list[46], think about how these

---

46   For our purposes, we are going to present an abbreviated form of the list that Adizes presents in Ibid pages 87 through 109.

differences affect your ability to create a successful information governance and regulatory compliance posture.

Growing	Aging
Personal success stems from *taking* risk.	Personal success stems from *avoiding* risk.
Emphasis on function over form.	Emphasis on form over function.
People are kept for their contributions in spite of their personalities.	People are kept for their personalities in spite of their contributions.
Everything is permitted, unless expressly forbidden.	Everything is forbidden, unless expressly permitted.
Political power is with the marketing and sales departments.	Political power is with the accounting, finance, and legal departments.
The front line leaders call the shots.	Corporate staff calls the shots.
Responsibility is not matched with authority.	Authority is not matched with responsibility.
Management drives the momentum.	Management is driven by the inertia.
The focus is on valued added (profit) goals.	The focus is on political gamesmanship.

Form versus function in growing and aging organizations

The most complex theory of organizational character

Along the same lines as Miller and Adizes, and roughly still within the same timeframe, William Bridges developed much the same concept[47]. With a few key differences which will help us to further understand how organizational character affects information governance and our ability to create a regulatory compliance stance within the organization.

Bridges' wave stops at the crest, and has the organization developing from the dream "inside the dreamer" through the venture which *extraverts* the dream, to getting organized, "making it," and becoming an institution.

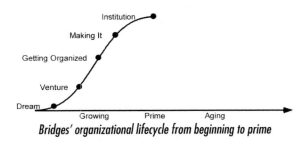

Bridges' organizational lifecycle from beginning to prime

---

47   William Bridges (1992). <u>The Character of Organizations: Using Jungian Type in Organizational Development</u>. Palo Alto, CA, Davies-Black Publishing.

There's no great need to detail each of these definitions as Bridges doesn't spend much time with them either. What makes Bridges' theory both more complex *and* interesting to us is that he adopted the Myers-Briggs 16-point personality matrix to explain organizational and leadership characteristics.

For those that need a refresher (or don't know about) Myer-Briggs, here's a quick rundown. About the same time that Toynbee was working on his history, Isabel Myers created a self reporting personality assessment system based on Carl Jung's theory of psychological types. Her work spawned the Myers-Briggs Type Indicator and an industry of professional "type practitioners who apply the theory to everything from being a Mom to running international organizations.

The theory is that the psychological "types" of people and organizations can be broken down into a *world attitude* that is either extraverted (E) or introverted (I). How *information is gathered and perceived* can be broken down into sensing (S) that leverages the concrete and experiential, or the intuiting (N) that leverages symbolic awareness. How *organization, evaluating and judging is handled* is either by thinking (T) through the objective assessment of multiple criteria, or through feeling (F) through subjective assessment based on values and an idea of "worth." The fourth preference is how the *outer world* is viewed, which is either through judging (J) as indicated by planning and then following the plan or by perception (P) as indicated by adaptability through keeping options as open as possible.

Pairing these four basic dichotomies of extravert vs. introvert and sensing vs. feeling, we can create a 16-point matrix of personal and organizational "types" that Myers-Briggs present[48].

| | | Sensing | | Intuiting | |
		Thinking	Feeling	Feeling	Thinking
Introvert	Judging	ISTJ	ISFJ	INFJ	INTJ
	Perceiving	ISTP	ISFP	INFP	INTP
Extravert	Perceiving	ESTP	ESFP	ENFP	ENTP
	Judging	ESTJ	ESFJ	ENFJ	ENTJ

The 16 Meyers-Briggs personality types

48   Isabel Briggs Myers (1987). Introduction to type : a description of the theory and applications of the Myers-Briggs Type Indicator. Palo Alto, CA, Consulting Psychologists Press. This is a republishing of the original work conducted in the 1940s.

While its "kinda neat" to learn a person's or organization's style, just knowing the type indicator doesn't do much for us in terms of putting information governance into perspective. That is, until you start arranging these little acronyms into an order that fits the wave-cycle theory we've been writing about today. A researcher by the name of Linda Berens organized the 16 types in order to display the affiliative vs. pragmatic, and abstract vs. concrete interaction styles of the 16 types[49]. The interaction styles that Berens points out are arranged in a matrix that describes their similarities and things in common.

		Directing		Informing	
		Abstract	**Concrete**	**Abstract**	**Concrete**
	Affiliative	INFJ	ISTJ	INFP	ISFJ
Responding		*Chart the course*		*Behind the scenes*	
	Pragmatic	INTJ	ISTP	INTP	ISFP
	Affiliative	EHFJ	ESTJ	ENFP	ESFJ
Initiating		*In-charge*		*Get things done*	
	Pragmatic	ENTJ	ESTP	ENTP	ESFP

Berens' Interactions styles

The left and right side of the matrix displays the communication types, with a *directing* and *time and task* focus on the left. The right side displays the *informing* communication style with a *process and motivation* focus.

The top and bottom displays the interaction methods, with types that take a *responding* and reactive role to interactions on top. The bottom displays the types that take an *initiating* role to interacting.

A diagonal plot of lower left to upper right quadrants show the control (decision making) methods. The diagonal plot of the upper left-hand quadrant to the lower right-hand quadrant shows how forward movement is accomplished.

How organizational character & information governance fit

Let's bring this back into the perspective of information governance and regulatory compliance. If you are working on information governance, and your organizational type is an ENTJ, they'll love you for initiating the project and taking control of the situation by directing the actions that need to

---

49   Olaf Isachsen and Linda V. Berens (1988). <u>Working together : a personality-centered approach to management</u>. Coronado, CA, Neworld Management Press.

take place – because the organization is pragmatic that way and will at least understand in the abstract that you are trying to help. However, you are dead meat if you run in and take the bull by the horns in an ISFJ organization that values team-building affiliations who focus on concrete plans (and about 40,000 memos before action can be taken).

And we aren't the only ones who are thinking along these lines. Paul Strassmann touched on this very topic in his seminal work regarding information politics that we've drawn repeatedly from[50] when he wrote about how he's observed organizational structures moving from the elitist view, through a populist reaction, theocracies, hierarchies, alliances, and democracies. Within each phase, Strassmann points out that decisions are made within the context of the phase. As an example, the democratic decision making process *couldn't* happen in an elitist environment.

Peter Weill and Jeanne Ross[51] build on this same principle in their recent work on IT governance. They point out how information governance decisions – and who in the organization have "input rights" to those decisions – are dependent upon the *type* of organization in question. They list a total of six governance (and hence, organizational) archetypes that range from anarchy through a monarchy and federal outlook, and whether the information group, executives, or business unit leaders drive those decisions and rules for input.

Yee gads, does this mean that we have to become organizational specialists or psychologists just to be compliant? *No. Sort of.*

But it also doesn't mean that just because the auditors are coming, you are going to get the right budget at the right time with the right staffing behind you – if you don't know how to play the game. You *have* to understand who you are working with – both those on your information governance team *and* those within the organization who have to be a part of the decision making process.

One of the great things about having the field editors that we have, is that we can *see* this very concept in action. Without naming last names, here are two responses regarding the "getting it done" of information governance that have come up during the writing of *just the introduction* to this book.

---

[50] Paul Strassmann (1995). The Politics of Information Management: Policy Guidelines. New Canaan, Ct., The Information Economics Press. Chapter 16 – History.

[51] Peter Weill and Jeanne W. Ross (2004). IT Governance: How Top Performers Manage IT Decision Rights for Superior Results. Boston, MA, Harvard Business School Press.

Richard, a former CEO of a public company and now a CEO of a new company in the "venture" mode, wrote in after reading the introduction and stated "you know, this is all just a bit complicated. I'm passing this down to Don (his name is changed here) to handle. I just want to know what I need to sign and fund to get this done." Clearly his organization doesn't care much about being "affiliative."

David, another field editor, took a completely different, and *highly* affiliative approach. He wrote "There must be something for everyone. Creating a plan that supports strategic corporate goals and enhances strategic corporate values grabs client interest. Well defined activities leading to measurable goals tied back to strategic goals and values gives every 'team member,' no matter what 'role,' their place in the sun. Designed, contractually specified deliverables; even if only a suggested further training list, provide a sense of accomplishment and enhances professional status (and keeps you cash flow positive)."

Our advice to *you*

If you are a business leader reading this to help your IS staff cope with regulatory compliance, you already know about corporate politics and how to leverage the organization and get things done. Because you "get it" doesn't mean that your IS staff does. Bring your IS staff into the loop of how decisions are made. Give them the insight they'll need into the organization's point of development in order to guide them through the appropriate channels and memoranda trails that it takes to obtain forward movement of projects.

If you are in the IS staff and you are saying "cripes, *that's* why I haven't gotten much done," then go back and figure out the organizational type that you are in. We've put a self-administered Organizational Character Index online at the Compliance Book's blog site[52]. Once you understand the nature of the organization that you are in, you'll be able to target how your organization communicates, interacts with new ideas, and makes decisions.

If you are an auditor looking in from the outside, apply what you've learned here to helping you write your audit report. What the CISA or IIA exam teach you about decision making and what happens in the real world can be quite contradictory at times. You might be looking for clearly defined procedures for creating policies based on governance principles that just might

---

52   Dorian J. Cougias (2005). <u>What is your organizational character index?</u>, Network Frontiers.

not exist, or even be capable of existing, within the organization you are auditing.

At the end of the day, it isn't *how* or *who* makes the right decisions. Its that they get made.

And that's precisely what we are going to talk about next – the decisions that you need to make with regards to regulatory compliance and information governance.

The scope of information technology management & governance

Information technology management is the most granular of our three levels of governance. Information technology includes all computerized *support* of information systems, and includes all IT assets from documents through the facility as shown in the diagram below.

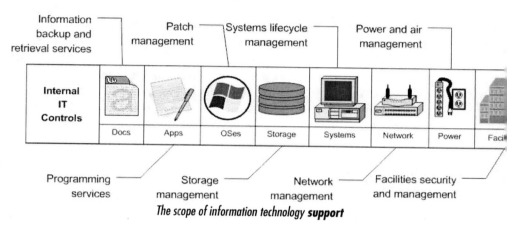

The scope of information technology **support**

Information technology is also concerned with the *design* of the information systems, to include all engineering, architectures, designs, and configuration management as shown in the diagram below.

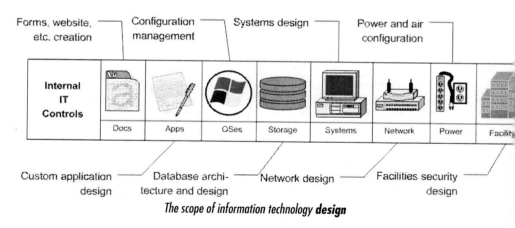

The scope of information technology **design**

This scope is extended to software and hardware purchasing, maintenance services, any outside contract programming or consulting services (such as external patch management services, etc.), systems continuity, and technical integration between systems for the exchange of information. In short, information technology focuses on the solutions for fitting together and maintaining the *pieces and parts* of information systems. Therefore, our "what," "who," and "how" of governance would be very tactical indeed:

- **What decisions** need to be made must focus on designing and maintaining individual components of a larger system. Thus, the decisions here spotlight two aspects of "what."

  Records Management – Records management is a pillar of compliance, explicitly required by many regulations and extensively described by many governance standards. And, like technical security, records management offers many opportunities for organizations to recognize sweeping benefits from compliance-based projects. In a Unified Compliance environment, records managers can reduce costs and increase the effectiveness and scope of records management programs by leveraging both centralized and point solutions across multiple systems. This IT Impact Zone focuses on identifying these opportunities, aligning records management requirements and governance standards with specific control objectives that can provide holistic business benefits.

  Technical Security – Focusing on the availability, integrity, and confidentiality of networks, computers, and data, technical security is perhaps the most critical and universal goal in IT compliance and governance. Approaches to technical security are as diverse as information systems. In general, however, all technical security practices should encompass data protection, as well as individual accountability for policy compliance and assurance that control objectives are being met. Often, security efforts can be efficiently leveraged across multiple corporate divisions, systems, and distributed access points. In a Unified Compliance environment, technical security managers have many opportunities to reduce costs and increase the effectiveness and scope of security programs by leveraging both centralized and point solutions across multiple systems. Since many federal regulations are based on a common standards (the 800 Series of Special Publications from the National Institutes of Standards and Technology), a single compliant security solution is likely to meet the requirements of multiple regulations.

  Physical Security – Physical security is generally the first line of defense against unauthorized data access and the physical theft of records. Organizations must understand the need for physical security, conduct thorough risk assessments, and implement physical and environmental controls as required by HIPAA, Gramm-Leach-Bliley, and a raft of other laws. The National Institute of Standards and Technology (NIST), CobiT, HIPAA, the Internet Security Forum (ISF), and ISO 17799 each provide robust guidance on physical security; however, it falls to the organization to assess its unique physical security needs and decipher which or which parts of these and other governance standards are most applicable. Aligning disparate standards with particular control objectives and legislation is the goal of this IT Impact Zone.

- **Who makes** those decisions is squarely within the realm of the information technology staff with input from those directly affected by the decisions (hopefully). Business unit managers are not usually involved in deciding how a web page should be coded.

- **How the decisions are made** are based upon anything from "that's the way I've always done it" through best practices such as those presented by the ISO committees, organizations such as IT Governance Institute, or found within the ITIL libraries[53].

---

53   We cover all of these and more in our in-depth discussions regarding regulatory and standards guidelines. We'll save the discussions about how these fit until then.

The scope of information systems management

Information systems focuses on the confidentiality, integrity, and availability of – you guessed it – the *systems* that *process information*. Let's break down these two terms ("systems" and "process information") further to better understand what we mean.

Information processing

Information processing denotes a formal procedure for accurate and confidential completion[54]. You jotting down figures from a meeting on a sticky-note is not information processing. Your warehouse workers completing a clipboard form is information processing. You sending an e-mail about the office football bet is not information processing. You routing a document for approval is information processing. Information processing denotes a defined organizational methodology and defined organizational procedures that must be followed.

Information systems

Information systems include personnel as well as equipment (the equipment doesn't have to include computers) and the scope therefore extends from the people involved in the processing of information that use the system all the way through the facility in which the system is housed.

To emphasize this point of what constitutes a *system*, we are going to return to well used discussion of ours about a national restaurant chain's supply ordering system. We'll define the *system* in two ways, one without the user of computer technology, and the other with the use of computer technology so that you can understand that the *system* is more or less the same in both instances.

---

54   We've added the concepts of confidentiality and accuracy – which implies integrity – to Paul Strassmann's definitions. Originally formulated in Paul Strassmann (1995). The Politics of Information Management: Policy Guidelines. New Canaan, Ct., The Information Economics Press. He then updated his thesis in Paul Strassmann (2004). The Governance of Information Management, The Information Economics Press. (pages 26-27).

In the first instance, without computer technology, the information process is comprised of the following steps (as always, this is completely oversimplified but serves our purpose):

1. The individual restaurant managers take an inventory of that which they need to order.

2. They then phone in the order to the central office.

3. The orders from all restaurants are aggregated into regional ordering and delivery lists.

4. The aggregated orders are placed with each regional supplier.

5. The supplier then creates a delivery manifest for delivery.

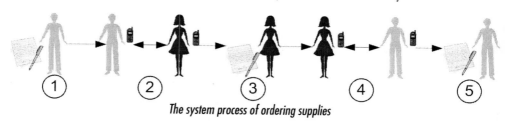

The system process of ordering supplies

The information system here is comprised of the people, documents, applications (in this case the procedure manuals), equipment (phones, note pads, filing cabinets), services (phones, contract systems, ordering forms), and facilities (the building they sit in) associated with the processing of this information. It would also be comprised of the trainers, support staff, etc., employed to sustain the system.

Internal Systems Controls								
	Docs	Apps	OSes	Storage	Systems	Network	Power	Facility

The technological components used in the manual ordering system

The automated information processes and system uses the same principles, except that it substitutes a computer interactions, checks, and balances for those that were done by people in the manual method – but the overall information processing portion is still very much the same. In the automated process, the number of steps are reduced to three:

1. The individual restaurant managers interact with the system and post their requests for supplies for their restaurants.

2. The requests are then automatically transferred to the central ordering system where checks and balances are applied, orders are regionalized and aggregated.

3. The regionalized orders are then communicated directly to the suppliers' order system via an EDI link to the suppliers' computers.

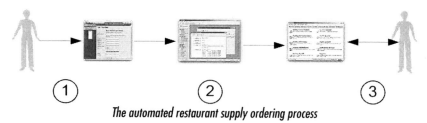

The automated restaurant supply ordering process

The technological portion of the information system then comprises everything from documents through the applications, OSes, and on down through the facilities that house everything.

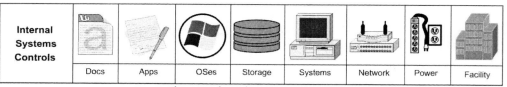

The scope of an information system

The management of the system must therefore focus on confidentiality (ensuring that only those who have access to the records and applications are allowed in, keeping everyone else out), integrity of the data being sent back and forth, and the availability of the system for processing the orders. As with the information technology that supports the system, the decisions about management here are also of the tactical nature.

- **What decisions** need to be made are about the tactical implications of accountability through confidentiality, integrity, and availability management of the system. At the local business unit level, the "what" decisions must include;

  Operational Management – Under Sarbanes-Oxley, the Turnbull Report, HIPAA, and other guidance, executives and line-of-business managers have major compliance responsibilities. Management must promote a positive control environment that addresses issues of integrity and ethical values and the competence of staff, management philosophy, operating style, and accountability. Moreover, operational leadership is responsible for setting and communicating policies that support compliance and business efforts. The Unified Compliance Project (UCP) IT Impact Zone for Operational Management provides the tools strategic leaders need to understand their specific responsibilities under various authorities.

Systems Continuity – In order for an organization to be in business, it must do business – even in the face of natural disasters, terrorism, technological failure, or human error. To protect customers and investors, legislation including HIPAA, Gramm-Leach-Bliley, and the Turnbull guidance call for companies to create continuity plans for the potential of business interruption. Correspondingly, COSO and CobiT, NIST, ISO 17799, and other standards offer guidance and frameworks for the design, execution, and testing of comprehensive – or at least compliant – continuity plans. Helping companies draw meaningful lines among these requirements and standards is one of the major goals of the Unified Compliance Project (UCP).

Product Design and Development – IT compliance strategy is just so much sound and fury without design and implementation. Because regulations are by design prescriptive, rather than descriptive, most laws assume or imply the need for proper implementation. On the standards side, FFIEC Development and Acquisition, DIRKS, CobiT Control Objectives, and the Standard of Good Practice for Information Security from the Internet Security Forum offer heavy guidance on project roles, management, and quality control, as well as systems design, development, testing, and implementation. And several authorities offer more limited guidance. Exploring to what degree and by what law specific design and implementation practices are required, and relating them to resources that provide best system design and implementation practices, is the goal of this impact zone.

Acquisition of Technology – In increasingly automated and integrated business environments, acquiring systems can be as risky as it stands to be beneficial. Accordingly, Sarbanes-Oxley, Turnbull, and other authorities ask companies to understand both the functional and organizational impact of systems acquisition. Covering controls for feasibility, disruptiveness, user acceptance, and third-party service commitments, standards such as CobiT and the Internet Security Forum (ISF) can help companies to develop holistically beneficial acquisitions practices. Outlining a complete set of systems-acquisition controls and indexing them with regulatory guidelines and standards guidance is the focus of this impact zone.

- **Who makes those decisions** now not only encompass the technology staff, but also the organizational unit staff that the system supports *and* the audit staff who must ensure accountability and compliance.

- **How the decisions are made** begins to become a federal issue[55] because now we aren't just looking at how a computer behaves. Now we have to look at how the computer behaves as a part of a system that must function within the organization as a whole.

Both the "who and how" aspects introduce the need to balance the impact of decisions across group "territories" and across departments within an organization. Call it what you will, we are going to call it "local politics."

---

[55] Double entendre intended.

The scope of information management

The scope and purpose of information management is of making effective use of all *information itself* and *information processes* – whether those processes are automated or not[56]. This usually implies the use and leveraging of information and information processes across the whole organization, and therefore sets information governance decisions within the top leadership realms of the organization.

In our restaurant example from the first section of the book, *information* management could be used to reduce the costs of guacamole by changing the ordering of the ingredients for manual assembly (storing them until just-in-time assembly for freshness) to just-in-time ordering of already-prepared guacamole. By analyzing the information, the decision can be made.

Also in our restaurant example, *information process* management could be used to insert each restaurant's Point-Of-Sale (POS) systems report in order to provide a check-and-balance against what was actually sold (and therefore inventory depleted) against what the manager said he or she needed during ordering. By changing the process, more thorough checks and balances can be obtained, and therefore better information can be obtained.

Both examples above affect people, processes, systems, and individual applications across *multiple* groups (store ordering, central processing, supply-chain management) within the organization. Information management, therefore, should be thought of as covering employees, contractors, supplier coordination, reporting, record-keeping, etc. Everything except the physical handling of production and delivery of goods. If you think about information management this way, you would then have to expand the scope of all three questions regarding "what," "who," and "how" governance is conducted.

- **What decisions** are made at this level should focus on leveraging the information *and* the processes by which the information is created.

  Principles and high level objectives – While many regulations assume the establishment of high-level objectives, several standards and regulations provide either broad or specific objectives. Regulations such as Sar-

---

56   Again, we are dealing with Strassmann's definition as our base here, because it diverges from many of the other views. We think he's right in his definition.

banes-Oxley, HIPAA, and California privacy laws imply control objectives related to security, records management, and privacy. Other regulations and standards provide more specific guidance; for example, information security controls outlined by the Federal Financial Institutions Examination Council (FFIEC) and records management controls indicated by ISO 15489. These inconsistencies challenge compliance managers to ferret out, and in many cases deduce, broad responsibilities related to defining objectives. Simplifying this task is the goal of this impact zone.

Audits & Risk Management – From an information governance perspective, audit and risk management are watch fires of compliance. Auditing guards compliance efforts, making sure they stay on a sound path towards their stated goals; risk management measures and sets the path. And, in reality, many of these paths can lead to a common goal of compliance – with one or multiple regulations. As part of the Unified Compliance Project, the Audit and Risk Management impact zone aims to help information compliance managers understand common requirements – such as those among HIPAA, Sarbanes-Oxley, Basel II, and FISMA – and commonalities between the standards that support their fulfillment – including COSO, CobiT, the Standard of Good Practice for Information Security (from the Information Security Forum), and others. Understanding how these regulations and standards align is the foundation of sustainable, efficient, and effective compliance.

Human Resources (for IS) Management – Many compliance failures – including most security breaches – are the result of human error or human error in conjunction with technical malfunction. Particularly in information compliance, a too-narrow focus on technical security controls tends to eclipse human factors, which can have serious compliance implications. Providing insight into disparate regulatory requirements and guidance for staff management is the goal of this impact zone.

Privacy – Privacy is one of the most growing regulatory concerns, especially for organizations that are multi-national or global in scope. Many privacy regulations around the world are at odds with the monitoring and measurement regulations created in the United States. Understanding what can be collected, and how, sets the precedent and "tone at the top" of an organization's privacy stance. Those higher-order principles are then passed down to information systems governance rules and information technology governance rules with respect to confidentiality and integrity controls for data privacy.

Monitoring & Reporting – In order for a company to assess how well it is functioning, it must frequently test internal controls. Most public-company regulations address monitoring and measurement to some degree: Sarbanes-Oxley provides general guidance, while PCAOB and SAS 94 are more specific. Basel II, the Turnbull guidance, HIPAA, and Gramm-Leach-Bliley (GLB) also include reporting requirements. To support compliance and other governance efforts, COSO, CobiT, and other standards cover measurement and reporting extensively—if not always congruently. Finding alignment between the diverse requirements and standards for monitoring, measurement, and reporting is the focus of this impact zone.

- **Who makes those decisions** now becomes a matter of the governance arrangements within your organization. For the purposes of regulatory compliance (remember, that's what the book is really about), your "who" needs to include everyone from the board that ratifies the decisions through those that understand their implications for information processing control objectives and the underlying technological control objectives.

- **How those decisions are made** will be a matter of policy control, distribution of power, and everything else that surrounds the governance arrangements that your organization has established.

Putting governance in perspective

The following table is only a representation of how we've seen governance decisions being made in our clients' organizations. It doesn't mean that it is the *right* thing to do, nor is this meant to be the "final answer" for a pattern of information governance. It just means that this is what we've seen and heard.

The target symbols show where the impact zones originate. The arrows denote the direction of influence the decisions take. Hence, high level objective decisions are made in the arena of information governance and flow downward to information systems and technology.

	Information Governance	Systems Governance	Technology Governance
High Level Objectives	◎	⇒	⇒
Audit and Risk Management	◎	⇒	⇒
HR for Information Staff Management	◎	⇒	⇒
Monitoring and Measurement	◎	⇒	⇒
Privacy Management	◎	⇒	⇒
Operational Management	⇐	◎	⇒
Product Design & Development	⇐	◎	⇒
Acquisition of Technology	⇐	◎	⇒
Systems Continuity	⇐	◎	⇒
Records Management	⇐	⇐	◎
Technical Security	⇐	⇐	◎
Physical Security	⇐	⇐	◎

Governance focal points and directional "pushes"

The regulations and standards

The Main Thing

Defining Objectives and Leadership

While many regulations assume the establishment of high-level objectives, several standards and regulations provide either broad or specific objectives. Regulations such as Sarbanes-Oxley, HIPAA, and California privacy laws imply control objectives related to security, records management, and privacy. Other regulations and standards provide more specific guidance; for example, information security controls outlined by the Federal Financial Institutions Examination Council (FFIEC) and records management controls indicated by ISO 15489. These inconsistencies challenge compliance managers to ferret out, and in many cases deduce, broad responsibilities related to defining objectives. Simplifying this task is the goal of this IT Impact Zone.

The Main Thing

Beyond addressing the need to establish high level objectives, there are three directives our organizations must follow regarding the defining of objectives and leadership within information governance:

❏ **Defining Rules that govern information technology:** the organization will identify and implement the rules and regulations (external requirements) that govern information, information systems, and information technology before implementing any policies or procedures surrounding control objectives.

❏ **Create a high-level strategic IT plan:** the organization will create a high-level strategic IT plan, information security policy, and other high-level IT policies, plans, and programs that take into account the business requirements and objectives of the organization, and that form the basis for requirements and controls as part of the organization's long-term plans.

❏ **Analyze organizational objectives, functions, activities, and tasks:** the organization will examine its business objectives, functions, activities and tasks to ensure they are being carried out as efficiently and successfully as possible. Analysis will be documented and any findings will be acted on immediately.

Have you established need and defined high-level information governance objectives?

The highest level objectives for information governance, as far as both regulators and standards creators are concerned, are the objectives of maintaining information confidentiality, integrity, availability, and accountability. Consider the following control objective on the subject:

> *The organization will establish information confidentiality, integrity, and availability through absolute accountability in keeping with the organization's overall mission, objectives, and principles. These objectives will then extend downward and apply to organizational systems and individual technology controls.*

Take time and care in creating your list of needs and your objectives – they will be used as a foundation for all other work that goes on within your organization.

Guidance from the regulations and standards

Public Companies

While some of the standards and regulations for public companies provide specific objectives, for the most part establishment of high-level objectives are already implied.

AICPA/CICA Privacy suggests that organizations should define and document privacy policies with respect to Notice, Choice and Consent, Collection, Use and Retention, Access, Onward Transfer and Disclosure, Security, Quality and Monitoring and Enforcement.

NASD/NYSE

NASD, NYSE, and **SEC** regulations imply pre-existing objectives that member organizations, brokers or dealers already have in place to confront the compliance issue.

Banking/Finance

While the **FFIEC Information Security handbook** states broad objectives for an entity to follow, most of the regulations and standards in banking and finance imply previous definition of high-level objectives with respect to the specific compliance issue.

FFIEC Information Security requires an organization to meet business objectives by implementing business systems that take into account information technology related risks to the organization, business and trading partners, technology service providers, and customers. There are five basic objectives to be met (as stated in pages 2 through 5):

- Availability – ongoing availability of all systems processes, policies and controls used to maintain appropriate access and security.

- Integrity of Data or Systems – processes, policies and controls used to ensure that information is not modified in an unauthorized fashion and that systems are free from manipulations compromising accuracy, completeness and reliability.

- Confidentiality of Data or Systems – processes, policies, and controls used to protect information of customers and the institution against unauthorized access or use.

- Accountability – processes, policies, and controls necessary to trace actions to their source, this area supports non-repudiation, deterrence, intrusion prevention/detection, recovery and legal admissibility of records.

  - Assurance – processes, policies and controls used to develop confidence that security measures work as intended, this objective includes elements of availability, integrity, confidentiality and accountability.

US Federal Security

The **Clinger-Cohen Act**, § 5123, indicates that an organization should *"establish goals for improving the efficiency and effectiveness of agency operations and, as appropriate, the delivery of services to the public through the effective use of information technology."*

Records Management

The discovery and records management standards generally state the need for objectives to be set by the entity involved, but do not give any further insight into the process.

Page 12 of **ISO 15489-1** calls for creating useful, integrity protected records through the use of a comprehensive records management program. The program includes deciding how records are to be created and captured, what info goes in the records, what metadata is created to link and manage data, how to determine requirements for retrieving using and transmitting records, organization of records, assessing risks of the record system failing, preservation of records, availability of records over time, compliance with legal and regulatory requirements, ensuring a safe maintenance environment for records, ensuring proper length of retention and identifying and evaluating opportunities for improving the effectiveness, efficiency or quality of the system.

NIST Special Publications

NIST 800-14 § 3.1.1 calls for the creation of a program policy that does the following:

- Create and Define a Computer Security Program
- Set Organizational Strategic Directions
- Assign Responsibilities
  - Address Compliance Issues

General Guidance

For general standards, the definition of objectives most commonly takes the form of a plan, policy, or set of objectives that the organization must create before implementation of control objectives.

Pg. 8 of **COSO ERM** lists 4 categories of objectives for your organization to consider:

- Strategic – relating to high-level goals, aligned with and supporting the entity's mission/vision.
- Operations – relating to effectiveness and efficiency of the entity's operations, including performance and profitability goals. They vary based on management's choices about structure and performance.
- Reporting – relating to the effectiveness of the entity's reporting. They include internal and external reporting and may involve financial or non-financial information.
  - Compliance – relating to the entity's compliance with applicable laws and regulations.

CobiT 3 PO1 suggests strategic planning processes should be created that give rise to long term plans that can be used to create operational plans with concrete short-term goals. These plans should take into consideration:

- enterprise business strategy

- definition of how information and information services supports the business objectives

- inventory of technological solutions and current infrastructure

- monitoring the technology markets

- timely feasibility studies and reality checks

- existing systems assessments

- enterprise position on risk, time-to-market, quality

  - need for senior management buy-in, support and critical review

From regulation to reality – sure signs you are complying

As you can clearly see, the regulations and standards are all over the board with respect to what constitutes establishing high level objectives and standards. If you want to boil it all down, you can think of it this way. Your organization has set out its mission or vision and established strategic objectives, which are the high-level goals that align with and support the mission. You've documented your mission (hopefully) in a mission statement. Flowing from this mission statement you've established a strategy for achieving your mission's strategic objectives. Your organization has also set related objectives it wants to achieve, which in turn flow from the strategy, cascading to organizational units and processes. In setting these objectives, have you also documented that you've taken into consideration the regulatory compliance objectives that *must match* your process objectives?

At a *minimum*, you know that you are complying with this control objective if within whatever executive committee, management committee, or board meeting, you actually *are* bringing the topic of regulatory compliance into the discussion. If someone were to read your committee or board minutes or notes, would they see discussion surrounding the issue of information confidentiality, integrity, or availability discussed as a part of organizational initiatives? Or would there be nothing documented because it isn't even a topic of discussion. Think about that.

Who is assigned to represent regulatory compliance within your organizational steering committees?

Is your CIO a glorified IT director, or have you actually given your CIO oversight authority and a seat (and a vote) at the leadership table?

If you are talking about acquiring a new organization, has anybody asked about the confidentiality, integrity, or availability record of the organization to be acquired? If called upon to produce them, would you have any documentation that shows this type of thinking is even a part of your acquisition strategy?

When talking about instituting a new program for one of the organizational units, who is the person – or who belongs to the committee – that is tasked with ensuring that the information meets regulatory privacy standards, or that the financial transactions and information handling processes meet integrity rules? What are the objectives that your organization has set for analyzing the compliance posture of new (or even existing) initiatives?

You *know* you are complying with this unified control objective if you answered in the positive to the questions we've posed above. If you aren't certain, your compliance might be in question.

Have you analyzed organizational objectives, functions, activities and tasks?

You can build amazing organizational IT defense, IT systems, business processes, train staff so they are incredible, and still not have done enough to ensure efficiency and security within your organization. That's because over time, people and systems have a tendency to stop working as swiftly and effectively as they did at first. To correct the slowing over time process, you need to know what's causing the slowing. If it's an employee, does he need a swift kick in the butt (purely for motivational purposes) to get moving again? If it's a system, does it need to be revamped, redesigned? To help you answer these questions, consider the following control objective:

> The organization will examine its business objectives, functions, activities and tasks to ensure they are being carried out as efficiently and successfully as possible. Analysis will be documented and any findings will be acted on immediately.

Analysis will point you towards the things you need to fix. Be sure to document your findings extensively – later when you conduct another analysis, you can compare your new findings to your old ones to determine trends and patterns.

Guidance from the regulations and standards

This addresses the need for an organization to analyze its own objectives, functions, activities and tasks as part of a planning process in order to determine how best to implement control objectives. As we stated in the scope of information governance, who your organization assigns to the task and how the task is carried out will be determined by your organization's character and charter.

Banking/Finance

The **FFIEC Information Security handbook**, Pg. 2 and 5 requires the definition of security objectives. They should be matched with the business objectives of the organization as much as possible. A solid plan will include objectives such as ensuring system availability, data and system integrity, confidentiality of data or systems, accountability and assurance that everything is working as intended.

The **FFIEC Business Continuity handbook**, Pg. 3 and 4 discusses business continuity planning. In general the organization will develop a plan that they can prove will maintain, resume and recover their business in all aspects, not just technology. To accomplish this, business impact analysis and risk assessment should be conducted prior to the construction of the business continuity plan. The plan should ALWAYS be tested, and it should be periodically updated as the organization changes and its needs change with it.

The **FFIEC Development and Acquisitions handbook**, Pg. 5 states that the roles and responsibilities for corporate management, senior management, technology steering committee, project managers, project sponsors, technology department, quality assurance, user departments, auditors and security managers must be outlined. It gives brief descriptions of what each area might be held responsible for to get you thinking.

The **FFIEC Audit handbook**, Pg. 3 and 5 says that you must create a board of directors who will oversee the audit function in your organization. They will also provide resources for making the process run smoothly and assign any important roles for the work. They will review recommendations made as the result of an audit, though audit and IT staff will likely have more authority in terms of understanding what must be done and implementing it.

The **FFIEC Management handbook**, Pg. 5 and 17 call for the creation of a board that will oversee IT work. They should also be responsible for creating policies and procedures for IT work , ensure that IT staff is competent, and create a project management structure for others to use. This document also talks about strategic IT planning. The idea is to create a plan that spans across 3 to 5 years and incorporates IT needs and the plans for the business's growth and development. Address long and short term goals in the plan. Good planning will have strong senior management participation, role of IT thoroughly defined, impact of IT laid out and an accurate scorecard of prior performance.

US Federal Security

In the standards mentioning this (**FISCAM, GAO**), the control required is the auditor's analysis of an organization's business than an analysis by the organization itself.

The **Clinger-Cohen Act** § 5125(b2) describes the role of the chief information officer. One aspect of the job which is relevant here is that this officer must develop, maintain and facilitate the development of an information technology architecture for the entire organization. It should be stable and have good security.

FISCAM calls for an auditor to gain an understanding of an organization's operations by reviewing all systems, applications and documentation pertaining to the items and systems to be scrutinized.

The **GAO Financial Audit Guide** has this to say about analysis:

"The auditor should obtain an understanding of the entity sufficient to plan and perform the audit in accordance with applicable auditing standards and requirements. In planning the audit, the auditor gathers information to obtain an overall understanding of the entity and its origin and history, size and location, organization, mission, business, strategies, inherent risks, fraud risks, control environment, risk assessment, communications, and monitoring. Understanding the entity's operations in the planning process enables the auditor to identify, respond to, and resolve accounting and auditing problems early in the audit."

Records Management

In controls regarding records management, several standards require the analysis of business activity as a principle stage (**ISO 15489, DIRKS**).

ISO 15849-1 § 4.1b says this about analysis: *"Collect information from documentary sources and through interviews; identify and document each business function, activity and transaction and establish a hierarchy of them, that is, a business classification system, and identify and document the flow of business processes an the transactions which comprise them."*

ISO 15849-2 3.2.3B says this about analysis: *"The purpose of this step is to develop a conceptual model of what an organization does and how it does it. It will demonstrate how records relate to both the organization's business and its business processes. It will contribute to decisions in subsequent steps about the creation, capture, control, storage and disposition of records, and about access to them. This is particularly important in an electronic business environment where adequate records will not be captured and retained unless the system is properly designed. This step provides the tools to undertake and document the business analysis in a systematic way and to make best use of its results."*

DIRKS breaks down analysis of business activity into a series of simple steps. In section B.4, it discusses a detailed process. Organizations are advised to collect information from documentary sources and interviews, identify and document each business function, activity and transaction, develop a business classification scheme, assess risk and record the findings, then review the findings.

NIST Special Publications

NIST 800-18 Guide for Developing Security Plans for Federal Information Systems 2.1 states that information resources should be clearly assigned to an information system. Doing this creates clear boundaries for all information systems. Methods for grouping resources are provided. Generally a group of resources should serve the same function or meet the same objective and reside in the same general operating environment. 2.2 gives a definition for major applications in an organization. They are applications that are critical to an organization's success and require special management in order to be properly maintained. System owners should be notified if they oversee a major application and provided with a copy of the application's system security plan. The plan should contain a reference to the general support system security plan. 2.3 defines a general support system as an interconnected set of information resources under the same direct management control that shares common functionality. It often includes hardware, software, information, data, applications, communications, facilities, people and provides support for a variety of users and applications. 2.4 defines minor applications as those applications not selected as major applications. It is important to be sure security controls are covering these applications, and that the minor applications are documented in the system security plan as an appendix or a paragraph.

Section 1.7 says an organization must be aware of it's system security plan responsibilities. Organizations should develop policies on how to develop a system security planning process. The chief information officer should be responsible for developing and maintaining an agency-wide information security program. Information system owners should be held responsible for procuring, developing, integrating, modifying, operating and maintaining the information system. Information owners should establish controls for generation, collection, processing, dissemination and disposal of specified information. The senior organizational information security officer is responsible for serving as a CIO's primary liaison to an organization's information system owners and information system security officers. The information system security officer is responsible for ensuring appropriate operational security postures for information systems and programs. More detail about responsibilities for each of these roles is provided in the NIST 800-18 document.

Section 1.8 calls for an organization to clearly delineate responsibilities and behaviors of individuals with access to information systems. Consequences of behaving inappropriately should also be clearly stated and where possible, employees should be made to sign a document stating that they understand how to behave and the consequences of violating rules.

1.9 requires that organizations have a policy that clearly defines who is responsible for system security plan approval. This may be an individual or a board that convenes to determine if system security plans are appropriate.

NIST Special Publications

NIST 800-14 states in § 2.1 that managers must work to understand their organization's goals and how the systems within the organization support or hinder those goals. Ultimately, this understanding is to be used to create high quality security that can be defined in terms of the organization's goals. In § 3.1.1, how to define a program policy is discussed. NIST 800-14 calls for creating and defining a computer security program, setting organizational strategic directions, assigning responsibilities and addressing compliance issues. In § 3.2.1. a central security program is called for. In general, the idea is to include a stable program management function, existence of policy, published mission and functions statement, long-term computer security strategies, compliance program, intra-organizational liaison and liaison with external groups. Each item is defined if the names are not self-explanatory enough.

General Guidance

COSO ERM Framework p. 5, 9 and 35 discuss defining high level objectives. It says an organization should create a strategy laying out all its business objectives and apply this strategy across the entire organization for best results.

CobiT 3 provides in-depth information on this topic. In PO 1.1, it calls for developing a plan for your organization that includes IT short range and long range plans. Including IT in plans for your organization's development ensures that as you grow, you will not accidentally outgrow your IT capacity, in terms of security, storage or anything else. In PO 2.1-4 multiple high-level objectives are discussed. First, you need an information architecture model – this describes how your IT system will be built, how you will add to it, or remove from it if need be. Next you need a corporate data dictionary and data syntax rules. This is a file or document that contains a definition for each of your organization's data syntax rules. A data classification scheme is also important, it is a framework that explains where different information classes will be placed, who owns them, and who gets to access them. Finally in this section, security levels are reviewed. Security levels are for different types of data. Data with low sensitivity likely is paired with low-level security, while very important data will have high-level security. The next section of CobiT, PO3.2-3.5 covers the IT systems more directly. It calls for monitoring your systems to uncover positive and negative trends which you can then use to improve security or daily business processes. Along with monitoring, regular assessment of plans such as your contingency plans for your systems should be examined. Check them to be sure they are appropriate, bounce back quickly and allow for growth and development. Other plans to examine are your hardware and software acquisition plans. These plans describe how you will determine if software and hardware is compatible with your systems, its efficiency when paired with your systems, and how it will be implemented.

Finally, technology standards are important in this section. Your organization must determine what constitutes 'normal' on your systems and work to bring all systems to meet your definition of normal. The last relevant section of CobiT for this topic, PO4.1, requires that you create a planning or steering committee for IT. Their job is to ensure the IT functions are running smoothly, and report on their findings to senior management.

CobiT 4 PO2-2.4 talks about requirements for defining an information architecture. PO2.1 calls for the establishment of an information model that enables application development and decision-supporting activities. PO2.2 requires organizations to create a data dictionary that incorporates the organization's syntax rules. This dictionary is meant to enable sharing of data elements amongst applications and systems and promote a common understanding of data among IT and business users. PO2.3 states that organizations should create a classification scheme for data based on criticality and sensitivity. The scheme should be used across the organization and include details about data ownership, definition of appropriate security levels and protection controls, and a brief description of data retention and destruction requirements, criticality and sensitivity. PO2.4 says procedures for ensuring integrity and consistency of all data stored electronically must be defined and implemented.

PO3-3.5 talks about planning and organizing technological infrastructure. PO3.1 recommends that organizations analyze existing and emerging technologies and plan what direction they will take using these to achieve an appropriate IT strategy for their organization. PO3.2 suggests creating and maintaining a technological infrastructure plan that is in accordance with IT strategic and tactical plans. This plan is based on the technological direction and includes contingency arrangements and direction for acquisition of technology resources. PO3.3 requires organizations to establish a process for monitoring future trends in industry, technology, infrastructure, legal and regulatory environment trends. PO3.4 states that organizations should create technology guidelines for selecting and using technology which is compliant and offers secure technological solutions. PO3.5 recommends creating an IT architecture board to provide guidelines for the way technological infrastructure is designed with an emphasis on designing in compliance with appropriate regulations and standards.

PO4.2 calls for forming an IT strategy committee. Their job is to ensure that IT governance is properly addressed throughout the organization, and to provide advice on strategic direction and spending for IT projects and resources.

ME4.2 is about enabling board and executive understanding of strategic IT issues such as the role of IT, technology insights and capabilities. Special care should be taken to ensure that there is a shared understanding between business and IT within the organization. This may potentially be accomplished by creating committees to review strategies and make recommendations for aligning them.

From regulation to reality – sure signs you are complying

If the first step in the category of establishing high level compliance objectives was to ensure that compliance flows as directly from your mission statement as does any other organizational objective. And the second step was to ensure that you have an up-to-date listing of all regulations and standards you are going to comply with. And the third step was to create your high-level information strategic plan that serves as your overall compliance objective roadmap. Then the fourth step (and the bottom of the diagram from the beginning of this chapter) is to ensure that you are correctly matching the right people, processes, activities, and tasks to meet your compliance objectives.

For some regulations and standards, this means that you are solely focusing on one aspect of compliance (business continuity, or physical/technical security), and for others such as HIPAA or the FFIEC, your focus must be more encompassing. In fact, it's the FFIEC Audit Handbook that says it best when it said "the roles and responsibilities for corporate management, senior management, technology steering committee, project managers, project sponsors, technology department, quality assurance, user departments, auditors and security managers must be outlined."

What are the sure signs that you are complying? How about the fact that you are incorporating the development of your policies and procedures in your executive board reports? Nobody, not one regulation says that everything has to be completed. They all, in one way or another, say that you have to be on your way.

Have you created a high-level strategic IT plan?

As you will see in this book, plans are essential to compliance. A plan is an indispensable tool that will guide an organization to achieving its goals. Plans are not set in stone; they change when you discover what is working and what is not. They are tested and time-tested, to create a working document. In this case, the IT plan is a strategy. It uses your organizations business requirements and goals, as well as the rules that govern IT for your organization, and becomes the control objectives your organization will seek to reach in the years ahead. This plan is a roadmap, an essential tool for driving your organization forward. The control objective for this section is:

> *The organization will create a high-level strategic IT plan, information security policy, and other high-level IT policies, plans, and programs that take into account the business requirements and objectives of the organization, and that form the basis for requirements and controls as part of the organization's long-term plans.*

This plan will vary depending on what your organizational goals are and what type of organization you are. But, there are constants, which we address in the battle plan. There are also specifics, which are touched on in the regulations below.

Guidance from the regulations and standards

Public Companies

Standards on public companies do not directly address the need for a high-level strategic IT plan. Financial auditors may make use of this plan or policy depending on how it relates to the activities of the organization.

Banking/Finance

GLB and FFIEC call for an information security policy relating to controls surrounding the use of information technology and internal control.

Specifically, the **FFIEC Information Security handbook**, Pg. 13-14 discusses development of a strategy that defines control objectives and establishes an implementation plan. *"The information security strategy is a plan to mitigate risks while complying with legal, statutory, contractual, and internally developed requirements."* The security strategy should include: cost comparisons, layered controls with multiple control points, and policies that guide officers and employees in implementing the security program.

The **FFIEC Management handbook**, Pg. 17 explains that *"strategic planning focuses on a three to five year horizon and helps ensure that the institution's technology plans are consistent or aligned with its business plan. If effective, strategic IT planning can ensure delivery of IT services that balance cost and efficiency while enabling the business units to meet the competitive demands of the marketplace.*

Strategic planning should address long-term goals and the allocation of IT resources to achieve them. Tactical plans outline specific steps and timetables to achieve the strategic goals. These should include hardware and software architecture, end-user computing resources, and any processing done by outside vendors. The strategic plan should address the budget, periodic board reporting, and the status of risk management controls."

There is much more information on this topic in the FFIEC Management Handbook, starting on Pg. 17, but you should get the idea from what we've presented here.

US Federal Security

While most government regulations do not call for an overall IT plan, the **Clinger-Cohen Act** calls for executive agencies to have a plan for the use of IT and an information security policy in place.

NIST Special Publications

NIST 800-18 Guide for Developing Security Plans for Federal Information Systems 1.5 requires that all information systems be covered by a system security plan and labeled as a major application or general support system. Minor applications do not require system security plans because the general security system often covers them already. If they are not covered, then they should be briefly described and receive a security plan.

NIST 800-14 § 3.1 states that an organization should have a computer security policy. A computer security policy allows senior management to create a computer security program, establishing goals and assigning responsibilities. Policy is also defined to refer to the specific security rules for certain systems. There are also other policies, such as managerial policies created to control certain job functions, like an email policy. NIST 800-14 does state that organizations should have three different types of policies: program, issues specific, and system specific.

International Standards Organization

ISO 17799 § 3.1.1 explains that a policy document should be created which includes a definition of information security, including its overall objectives and scope, a brief explanation of security policies, a definition of responsibilities and roles with regard to information security, and references to documentation that supports the policy.

General Guidance

Nearly all general standards require the need for a high-level plan that stems from business objectives and considers the role of information technology in information security. The plan or policy defines the use, procedures, review and assessment of information technology as a basis for creating controls that govern the use of IT in relation to the organization's mission and objectives.

CobiT 3 PO1 explains that *"senior management is responsible for developing and implementing long- and short-range plans that fulfill the organization's mission and goals. In this respect, senior management should ensure that IT issues as well as opportunities are adequately assessed and reflected in the organization's long- and short-range plans. IT long- and short-range plans should be developed to help ensure that the use of IT is aligned with the mission and business strategies of the organization."*

CobiT 4 PO1-1.6 provides recommendations for creating a strategic IT plan. PO1.1 suggests working to integrate IT with business needs. It also explains that IT processes and services should be effective and efficient. PO1.2 makes it clearer that business and IT must be aligned in their goals and objectives to achieve success. PO1.3 says organizations should assess current performance of IT functions in the organization before developing the strategic plan. PO1.4 specifically recommends creating a strategic plan that contributes to the organization's strategic objectives and related costs and risks. PO1.5 calls for the creation of tactical IT plans derived from the IT strategic plan. PO1.6 suggests actively managing IT projects with business needs in mind. Good management includes clarifying desired business outcomes, ensuring that program objectives support the achievement of outcomes assigning accountability and defining projects.

First, there are some do's and don'ts for creating your information governance strategic plan. These closely mirror a really great article we read a few years ago[57]. The first "do" is to ensure that when creating the strategic plan that you are planning *both* from the information governance down through the information systems and technology viewpoints *and* at the same time you are planning up from the technology, through the system, and ultimately back to the information governance viewpoint. Top down planning gives you the executive board's viewpoint. Bottom up planning gives you a rubber-meets-the-road execution viewpoint. Having both will make it a good plan.

The strategic plan *is not* the detailed plan. That's actually the next step in this chapter. The strategic plan allows enough wiggle room to change implementation details without re-writing the plan and is written *so that non information services staff can understand it.* In our office we call this the "dad" edit. If our fathers can understand the plan (most are in their 70s and 80s), then it's a good plan. If they can't it needs to be re-written.

The next is a don't. Don't let the plan become like the family history book which is taken from the shelf only to be updated when a family member is born, married, or dies. A great IT strategic plan is one that the University of California at San Francisco posted *in 2000*[58] and hasn't updated since. It was a good plan *then*, but we haven't the faintest idea if it is a good plan *now.*

Our companion website, www.compliancebook.com[59] has some great links for further research if you need help in deciding what needs to go into your strategic plan. We've listed planning guidance tools, articles, and some great examples of plans to get you started.

---

[57]   Derek Slater (2002). Strategic Planning don'ts (and do's), CIO Magazine.

[58]   (2000). IT Strategic Planning, University of California, San Francisco.. And they aren't the only university of have a good, but outdated plan. Another two are (2002). Univesity of Colorado, Boulder IT Strategic Plan, University of Colorado, Boulder., & (2002). University of Memphis, Tennessee, IT Strategic Plan, University of Memphis, Tennessee.

[59]   Dorian J. Cougias (2005). Strategic planning online resources, Network Frontiers.

Your Audit and Risk Management program

The Main Thing

Below is a checklist that you'll need to address regarding your internal audit program.

❑ If you don't have one, you *will* need to create an internal audit program (you can outsource this if you need to).

❑ You will need to clearly define the roles and responsibilities for the members of your organization in terms of their participation in your internal audit program. This means from the top down.

❑ You will need to conduct regular business risk assessments.

❑ Because you will need to conduct a regular business risk assessment, you'll therefore need to adopt some type of formalized risk assessment approach.

❑ As a part of your risk assessment, you'll need to conduct regular IT asset inventories.

❑ Once you have your current list of assets (gathered during your inventory process), you'll then need to identify the threats and vulnerabilities (risks) associated with those assets.

❑ You'll also need a method of analyzing your risk assessments so that you can

❑ score and weight them properly.

❑ Once you have your weighted risks in hand, you'll either need to choose to mitigate the risks (i.e., fix the problem which costs money), or accept the risks and gamble that your organization won't succumb to the threats. This means that you'll want to have a documented acceptable risk level that you can base your judgments on.

❑ Once you've decided which risks you are going to accept and which risks you are going to mitigate, you'll need to have an action plan that tracks your progress toward mitigation.

❑ Because you can't do everything at once, you'll also have to have a prioritization scheme that is a part of your risk action plan. You don't want to be spending your time fixing low priority problems when high priority problems are temporarily being ignored.

And finally, you'll want to show that you are demonstrating an ongoing a commitment to continual risk assessments as a part of your normal operating procedures.

Have you defined materiality?

The objective of any audit is to determine whether the organization has complied with the provisions of the applicable laws and regulations through assessing the effectiveness of internal control through control tests that are coordinated with other tests. To achieve these objectives, the organization and auditor will have to create a methodology to

- design and perform compliance and control tests;

- design and evaluate audit samples; correlate risk and materiality with the nature, timing, and extent of substantive tests;

- and design multipurpose tests that use a common sample to test several different controls and specific accounts or transactions.

In other words, what the auditors are looking for are material weaknesses in information controls. Auditors are looking for weaknesses – in either the design or the operation of those controls – that are significant enough to be greater than the risk the organization is willing to take. The key here is correlating risk and what the auditors call "materiality". The question for your organization is have you defined materiality, material changes (to processes, systems, and assets), and what constitutes a material weakness?

The organization will work with the audit team to clearly define materiality as it applies to information processes, information systems, and IT assets. Along with this definition, the organization will define the threshold for material changes as they relate to accountability, availability, integrity, and confidentiality.

Think of materiality as a measurement of impact. Your definitions will have to classify what is both relevant and important when it comes to the controls to be inspected, the changes to be monitored, and the weaknesses which *have* to be overcome. Because your auditors are going to label the problems they've found as either material, reportable (not as bad as material, but important nonetheless), or "other." If you don't have a working definition of these terms, you will immediately be at odds with the auditors and the auditing process.

Guidance from the regulations and standards

Financial auditors ordinarily measure materiality in monetary terms, since what they are auditing is also measured and reported in monetary terms. However, financial auditing is now a very small part of overall information management auditing. Within the larger scope of information management auditing, information processes, systems, and technical assets are audited for their baseline compliance as well as changes to baseline compliance that are either authorized or unauthorized. Therefore, we'll need to understand financial materiality in order to discern guidance on how materiality should be assessed outside of the financial realm, such as assessing the organization's ability to cope with material changes to their information processes, systems, and IT assets.

Public Companies and Banking/Finance

The reason for audits (as mentioned in **PCAOB Audit Standard No. 2 ¶ 4**) is to determine whether material weaknesses exist in the control structure of the organization's information management program. The reason for this is found in the **Sarbanes Oxley Act** itself. In § 302, when the reason for a change in internal control over financial reporting is the correction of a material weakness, management has a responsibility to determine whether the reason for the change and the circumstances surrounding that change are material information necessary to make the disclosure about the change not misleading. And in § 404, management is precluded from concluding that the organization's internal control over financial reporting is effective if there are one or more material weaknesses. In addition, management is required to disclose all material weaknesses that exist as of the end of the most recent fiscal year.

As defined in the **PCAOB Audit Standard No. 2 ¶ 123-132**, and **Basel II** Part 4, § 2, ¶ 636, materiality represents the magnitude of an omission or misstatement of an item in a financial report that, in light of surrounding circumstances, makes it probable that the judgment of a reasonable person relying on the information would have been changed or influenced by the inclusion or correction of the item. The PCAOB's Auditing Standard No. 2 ¶ 10 states that a "*material weakness is a significant deficiency, or combination of significant deficiencies, that results in more than a remote likelihood that a material misstatement of the annual or interim financial statements will not be prevented or detected.*" But as the **FFIEC Audit Booklet** suggests on page 23, financial statements are not the only indicator of materiality, as material weaknesses "*could affect the institution's reputation or compliance with laws and regulations without a direct impact on the financial statements.*"

NASD/NYSE

NASD Rule 3510(b) and **NYSE** Rule 446(b) require each member to update its plan in the event of any *material change* to the member's operations, structure, business, or location. **NASD** Rule 3520(b) requires members to provide NASD with emergency contact information and to update any information upon the occurrence of a material change.

While these rules don't define material change per se, the implication is that material change has to be defined.

Healthcare and Life Sciences

Within the **HIPPA** regulation, organizations are required to revise and distribute their privacy policy notice whenever they make material changes to any of their privacy practices according to 164.520(b)(3), 164.520(c)(1)(i)(C) for health plans, and 164.520(c)(2)(iv) for covered health care providers with direct treatment relationships with individuals.

US Federal Security

The **Clinger-Cohen Act**, Appendix III, § 5 states that the organization must report all material weaknesses within their reporting mechanism. **FISCAM**'s Appendix VII, which is the glossary, identifies a material weakness the same way that the PCAOB auditing standard does.

Materiality in the definitions found within US federal security guidance, whether financial or otherwise, is based on the concept that items of little importance, which do not affect the judgment or conduct of a reasonable person, do not require auditor investigation according to **FISCAM** § VI.2. Materiality has both quantitative and qualitative aspects. The **GAO Financial Audit Manual** ¶ 230.02 points out that even though quantitatively immaterial, certain types of misstatements could have a material impact on or warrant disclosure in the financial statements for qualitative reasons.

But what defines the threshold for materiality? According to the regulatory guidelines followed by the Sarbanes-Oxley auditors, it is the judgment of the auditor. They state that *"consideration of materiality is a matter of professional judgment and is influenced by [the auditor's] perception of the needs of a reasonable person who will rely on the financial statements"* (§ AU 312.10.).

In order for an organization to develop materiality thresholds, the project team should consider materiality concepts in developing a strategy and approach for documenting and evaluating an overarching framework and the control objectives within it. In ¶ 230.05 the GAO's audit manual goes on to describe 3 classifications of materiality for planning and performing an audit (which can also be used for deciding an organization's overall control framework):

- **Planning materiality** is a preliminary estimate of materiality, in relation to the financial statements taken as a whole, used to determine the nature, timing, and extent of substantive audit procedures and to identify significant laws and regulations for compliance testing.

  In further defining the classification of planning materiality, the GAO guide ¶ 230.08 states that the "*auditor should estimate planning materiality in relation to the element of the financial statements that is most significant to the primary users of the statements (the materiality base).*" And that planning materiality "*generally should be 3 percent of the materiality base*" in ¶ 230.11.

- **Design Materiality** is the portion of planning materiality that has been allocated to line items, accounts, or classes of transactions (such as disbursements). This amount will be the same for all line items or accounts.

  The GAO guide ¶ 230.12 then defines design materiality for the audit at 1/3rd of planning materiality "*to allow for the precision of audit procedures.*"

- **Test materiality** is the materiality actually used by the auditor in testing a specific line item, account, or class of transactions. Based on the auditor's judgment, test materiality can be equal to or less than design materiality. Test materiality may be different for different line items or accounts.

  And finally, the GAO guide ¶ 230.13 then defines test materiality as generally the same level as design materiality or lower if testing for items of a sensitive nature.

As to the question of identifying and classifying a material weakness, the GAO guide states in ¶ 260.55 that the organization has to have a clear methodology for identifying material weaknesses, and then goes on to define what constitutes a material weakness in ¶ 580.33 which we've paraphrased the definition as a condition in which the design or operation of one or more of the internal control components does not reduce to a relatively low level the risk that misstatements would be material in relation to the financial statements, or a performance measure or aggregation of related performance measures may occur and not be detected within a timely period by employees in the normal course of their assigned duties.

US National Institute of Standards and Technology

According to NIST 800-26, a material weakness as a "*very specific term that is defined one way for financial audits and another way for weaknesses reported*" *under the Federal Managers Financial Integrity Act of 1982. Such weaknesses may be identified by auditors or by management.*" Not a lot of help there.

General Guidance

According to **COSO ERM** on page 5, determining whether an organization's risk management is "effective" is a judgment resulting from an assessment of whether the a control framework is present and functioning effectively. For the framework to be present and functioning properly there can be no material weaknesses, and risk needs to have been brought within the organization's risk appetite.

The Information Systems Audit Control Association's **IS Standards, Guidelines and Procedures for Auditing and Control Professionals** § 2.1.3 – 2.1.5 states much the same thing when they write that "assessment of what is material is a matter of professional judgment" on the part of the auditor. While general guidance isn't as specific in their categories as public company or banking and finance guidance, there are rough definitions of planning materiality, *design materiality*, and *testing materiality*.

Within the world of IT, ISACA defines **planning materiality** as the "*aggregate level of error acceptable to management.*"

The ISACA definition that most closely fits **design materiality** would assign this the value of the "*potential for the cumulative effect of small errors or weaknesses to become material.*"

The ISACA equivalent to this is defining relevant **test materiality** and control objectives and determining, based on design materiality, which controls to examine. In their definition "*a material control is a control or group of controls without which control procedures do not provide reasonable assurance that the control objective will be met.*" They then list several measures which should be considered to assess materiality:

- Criticality of the business processes supported by the system or operation
- Cost of the system or operation (hardware, software, staff, third-party services, overheads, or a combination of these)
- Potential cost of errors (possibly in terms of lost sales, warranty claims, irrecoverable development costs, cost of publicity required for warnings, rectification costs, health and safety costs, unnecessarily high costs of production, high wastage, etc.)
- Number of accesses/ transactions /inquiries processed per period

- Nature, timing and extent of reports prepared and files maintained
- Nature and quantities of materials handled (e.g. where inventory movements are recorded without values)
- Service level agreement requirements and cost of potential penalties
- Penalties for failure to comply with legal and contractual requirements
- Penalties for failure to comply with public health and safety requirements
- Consequences to shareholders, organization or management of irregularities going unresolved

The only mention of material changes in **CobiT 3** is in PO8.6 which mentions "*informing the insurers of all material changes to the IT environment.*"

US State Laws

The **CA 1386** § 22577(a) requires an organization to determine the nature of material change in their privacy policies so that they can describe how the operator notifies consumers who use or visit its web site or online service of any material changes to the privacy policy. The **CA Office of Privacy and Policy Recommended Practices on Notification of Security Breach Involving Personal Information** Part 1 ¶ 10 calls for organizations to define a material change in business practices that may reasonably implicate the security of personal information.

United Kingdom and Canadian Guidance

The **Turnbull Guidance**, § 24, discusses how a sound system of internal control provides reasonable, but not absolute, assurance that a company will not be hindered in achieving its business objectives, or in the orderly and legitimate conduct of its business, by circumstances which may reasonably be foreseen. And in this context they mention both material fault and material error, and how there can never be absolute certainty of avoiding both. The key here, though, is reasonable assurance.

From regulation to reality – sure signs you are complying

Determining whether a deficiency is material requires qualified judgment and the consideration of various factors. In making the judgment as to which information control deficiencies are material, the audit team must consider various factors, such as the size of operations, complexity and diversity of activities, organizational structure and the likelihood that the control deficiency could result in problems with high impact to the organization. In all cases, materiality is the relevance of the information to the situation. In information systems, data, devices, and processes possess materiality if they do one of two things:

1. Provide reports by which decisions are made. For example, if the data in a report was the basis for future business direction, it is most certainly material. Thus, the data and processes must ensure accuracy.

2. Provide a critical business function. Criticality can range from loss of life to loss of significant revenue. If the absence of an information process, system, or IT asset would result in loss of revenue that exceeded operating costs, the process is most certainly material.

For a simple scenario we'll look at a website that nets $2 million in sales per year, spread across 200 "cycle" or actual selling days with an average of a 12 hour "cycle day" (because the website only supports US traffic which means it isn't busy 24 hours per day).

Materiality	3%
Cycle Days	200
Cycle Hours	12
Net per year	$ 2,000,000
Net per day	$ 10,000
Net per hour	$ 833
Material Loss	$ 60,000
Aggregate hours of downtime	72
Aggregate days of downtime	6

Materiality for an ecommerce website

The *aggregate* days and hours of downtime that could accumulate over the year come to 6 days (remember these are 12 hour "cycle" days), or a total of 72 hours. From there, you'd examine the operating deficiency materiality of the system to determine the maximum allowable downtime for *each* asset within the system (the database, the application, the OS, the storage array, the CPU, etc.). In this scenario, materiality would be reached at 24 hours of downtime due to lack of discrete operations, such as a drive array dying.

In summary, the IT department is informed by business leadership as to what business functions are material. In addition, finance may provide limits as to what can be spent on ensuring the availability and integrity of IT assets that possess materiality. With this knowledge, IT management can go about the business of doing their best to ensure that relevant data, devices, and processes perform at the level dictated prior to an event becoming material.

Material deficiency (failure, fault, error, loss, breach, weakness, unauthorized change)

The best definition we can think of at this time for a material weakness of your information management controls would be classifying it as a condition in which the design or operation of one or more of the internal control components does not reduce to a relatively low level the risk that a performance measure or aggregation of related performance measures may occur and not be detected within a timely period by employees in the normal course of their assigned duties. Which means that you have to classify both *design* and *operating* deficiencies.

Design deficiency

A design deficiency exists when a vital control is *missing* or an existing control is *not properly designed*, so that even when the control is operating as designed the control objective is not always met.

Operating deficiency

An operating deficiency exists when a properly designed control either is *not operating as designed* or the *person performing the control* does not possess the necessary entitlements or qualifications to perform the control effectively.

Have you created a scope for your audit and information management framework?

Have you developed your organizational strategy for developing your information management control reviews? If you don't have a strategy, you will fall prey to auditing anything and everything – whether the control items have relevance, significance, or not. Therefore, creating an organizational strategy to scope your audit boundaries will provide a means to create an audit framework within a reasonable expenditure of resources and time.

> *The organization will define the scope of its information processes, information systems, and IT assets. It will also define the scope of protection in the form of a suitable framework of information management controls.*

Remember, *you* set the definition for materiality and therefore *you* need to define the scope for your audit framework and planning strategy as well. At the end of the day, it is *your* organization and not your auditor's organization that is being protected.

Guidance from the regulations and standards

There isn't a whole lot of material written about scoping your overall strategy within the regulations and standards. The regulations don't normally drill down that far into the process, and most of the guidelines such as CobiT and ITIL assume that *they are* the boundaries of the scope.

Banking/Finance

Page 11 of the **FFIEC Audit Booklet** (and then in more detail in the glossary) describes the scope of the audit as a *"description and schedule of audits to be performed in a certain period of time (ordinarily a year). It includes the areas to be audited, the type of work planned, the high-level objectives and scope of the work and includes other items such as budget, resource allocation, schedule dates, and type of report issued."*

US Federal Security

Appendix VI.1 of **FISCAM** is a great source for defining the scope of an audit – even if their definition is for a review of control objectives in support of financial statements. Drawing from the first part of their overall audit planning strategy material, there are four steps to consider (the numbering of these steps is ours).

1a. Identify significant information processes, systems, and IT assets. Then document the relation of materiality to those information processes, information systems, and IT assets.

1b. Analyze for input, output, master files, rejected transactions within the information processes. Then document those processes, the information systems supporting those processes, and individual IT assets that support the information systems.

1c. Perform an assessment of the framework and general controls already in place.

1d. Assess whether the controls are likely to be effective (i.e., are there controls that are lacking?). If they are not thought to be effective, then document the assessed deficiencies in the framework and reassess the framework itself or the individual controls.

As the **GAO Financial Audit Manual** points out in § 210, one of the keys to a quality audit is planning. The explicitly point out that "*planning requires the involvement of senior members of the audit team.*" They also point out that scoping and planning is an *iterative process* performed throughout the audit. The example they use is that findings from the internal control phase could directly affect planning the substantive audit procedures.

Records Management

As a part of defining a records management project, **DIRKS** Step A, page 11 suggests that as a part of scoping the project, a general canvas of all issues, options, and recommendations are reported.

General Guidance

CobiT 4 PO9.1 calls for integrating IT governance, risk management and the control framework with the organization's risk management framework. This should include alignment with the organization's risk tolerance level. ME4.1 expands on this idea, requiring that an IT governance framework be created by defining and establishing leadership, processes, roles and responsibilities, information requirements and organizational structures to ensure that the organization's IT program is aligned with business objectives. Ideally, the framework should clearly link the organization's business strategies with IT investments, strategies and projects.

Scoping your information management framework is, after defining materiality, the most fundamental aspect of your overall program. This is where aligning the information services group with the organizational strategy really takes root and builds the foundation upon which everything else rests.

Remember that we are limiting our discussion here about audit scoping to the point where information services plays a part. A lot of auditing has nothing to do with the information services group as it is about auditing manual design and operational controls of financial and other matters. The overall scope of your audit framework will probably fall into something akin to the four area diagram we present here.

During the first phase of the scoping process, your organization will need to define significant information processes, systems, and IT assets so that you can analyze their input and output, master files, and transactions. Doing this should produce a list of general controls (read policies and procedures here) that are in place for protecting confidentiality, integrity, and availability. Your control list should be matched up against any regulatory or contractual agreements to ensure the control lists match.

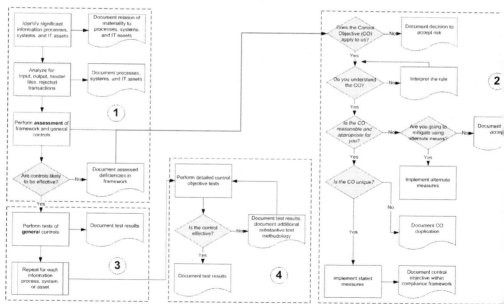

Overall Audit scope's four major areas of concern

Your second phase is crucial to determining your overall framework and filling out your policy and procedure books. We've talked about this phase in several places in our writing because it helps your organization determine the controls that *fit the way you work* as opposed to having a complete list of controls supplied by an outside auditor or simply imported from some organization's framework template – even ours. During this phase you'll go through *each and every* list of controls that your regulators, your staff, and your auditors are presenting. You'll check that list for a general understanding first (if you and the auditors can't agree on the interpretation, the control won't do either of you any good). You'll then proceed through the tasks of ensuring that the control is both reasonable and appropriate for your organization, or whether or not you are going to mitigate the threat through other means. Finally, you'll check to make sure that the control is unique and either isn't already in place or a duplicated control. This is the point where the Unified Compliance Framework can come in handy. We've already done one heck of a lot of checking for both unique and overlapping controls. A quick trip to the ITCI website at http://www.itcinstitute.com/ucp will bring up all of the tables for all of the controls that we could find – over 1,000 unique controls that have been consolidated down from well over 15,000 controls in over 250 regulations, standards, and guidelines.

You'll move to phase three once you've gotten your control list documented. This is the phase where you'll determine which general controls should be tested. And then for each information process, information system, and key IT asset you'll move into phase four where you'll perform your detailed control objective tests.

The auditors are looking for transparency

They key to creating both a sustainable and defendable scope for your information management framework is transparency. Can you show your organizational management and external auditors that you've moved through this kind of process in determining your controls? Can you show that you've done the research, and defend why you have chosen to apply certain controls and not others? Can you show continuous testing of your controls – whether the auditor is looking or not? If you can do these things, you are well on your way to defining your own scope for your information management framework.

Have you defined rules that govern information technology?

There is a whole Olympic-sized swimming pool filled with laws, regulations and standards governing information technology. Wading through this swimming pool is a tedious task, we should know, we've done it to bring you this book. Knowing what rules apply to your organization, how they apply and what this means for information compliance is a job that belongs to you. It is not a glamorous task, but it is absolutely necessary. The first step is to follow this control objective:

> *The organization will identify and implement the rules and regulations (external requirements) that govern information, information systems, and information technology before implementing any policies or procedures surrounding control objectives.*

Once you have accepted the task as yours and resolved to define the rules that govern information and information services, the next step is to look at what these regulations have to say and what the rules pertain to. Below is a sampling of this information, a summary of important passages from the rules that govern information and information services.

Guidance from the regulations and standards

Public Companies

In the case of a financial audit, auditors must be aware of various regulations and standards that apply to the use of information and information services – these standards make mention of this or imply it through their verbiage.

SAS 94 ¶ 8 does not specifically mention the rules governing information technology, however, it does have this to say about defining objectives, which can be applied to information and information services rules. *"There is a direct relationship between objectives, which are what an entity strives to achieve, and components, which represent what is needed to achieve the objectives. In addition, internal control is relevant to the entire entity, or to any of its operating units or business functions."*

Similarly, the **Turnbull Guidance** ¶ 20 doesn't specifically mention the rules governing IT. However, it does mention this important piece of information. *"An internal control system encompasses the policies, tasks, behaviors* *and other aspects of a company, that, taken together: facilitate its effective and efficient operation by enabling it to respond appropriately to significant business, operational, financial, compliance and other risks to achieving the companies objectives; help ensure the quality of internal and external reporting; and help ensure compliance with applicable laws and regulations and also with internal policies with respect to the conduct of business."*

NASD/NYSE

SEC regulations comprise recordkeeping and records retention rules that contribute to this process as requirements. Since we go into greater depth about records retention in the recordkeeping section, we'll skip over these rules for now.

Banking/Finance

Banking and finance do not directly address defining rules that govern information technology, aside from the FFIEC. The **FFIEC Management handbook**, Pg. 17 includes it as part of strategic IT planning, similar to **CobiT**, **NIST** and other general standards. FFIEC Management explains that as part of strategic IT planning, the organization will consider a variety of factors, including regulatory requirements and technology standards.

The **FFIEC Information Security handbook**, Pg. 3 states that financial institutions that are developing or reviewing their information security controls, policies, procedures, or processes have a variety of sources to draw on. These include federal laws and regulations, security industry best practices from outside auditors, consulting firms, and information security professional organizations. Also, international standard-setting organizations are working to define information security standards and best practices for electronic commerce. There is no list of formally accepter standards. Instead, there are several regulations and standards institutions can draw on to define the rules that govern information technology.

Healthcare and Life Sciences

Both **HIPAA** and **21 CFR Part 11** comprise rules that govern privacy of records and rules for electronic records and signatures, and thus contribute to this process as requirements.

US Federal Security

Though **DOD 5015.2** is, in itself a standard of rules that govern information technology (and thus contributes to this process), most of the governmental standards refer to organizational compliance with external requirements.

For example, **FISMA** § 11331 discusses compliance with the National Institute of Standards and Technology Act as mandatory, but advises that the heads of agencies have the discretion to apply stricter standards.

NIST Special Publications

NIST 800-53 recommends that organizations use the document as the minimum standards for the organization and a starting point for information security controls and plans for information systems. Specifically, NIST 800-53 § 1.3 states that *"building a more secure information system is a multifaceted undertaking that involves the use of: (i) well-defined system-level security requirements and security specifications; (ii) well-designed information technology component products; (iii) sound systems/security engineering principles and practices to effectively integrate component products into the information system; (iv) appropriate methods for product/system testing and evaluation; and (v) comprehensive system security planning and life cycle management."*

US State Laws

California privacy laws are inherently rules that govern information and information services, and thus contribute to this process as requirements. The credit card regulations do not directly address this issue.

From regulation to reality – sure signs you are complying

As we mentioned above, there are more information and information services regulations and standards that one knows what to do with. There are laws, regulations, standards, industry best-practices, and the list goes on. While they may all be relevant, or at least have meaningful principles, they are not all applicable to your organization. Rules exist that govern credit card organizations, financial institutions and government. There are different rules for records management than there are for SOX compliance. More than just categories of regulations, there are categories of the rules themselves. There are rules that govern records privacy, rules that govern security breaches, rules that govern financial reporting documents, rules that govern automatic transactions, and the list goes on.

Figuring out where your organization fits on the spectrum of information and information services rules is a threshold job that must be completed before you can begin to be compliant. After all, you have to know what you are complying with before you attempt to comply with it.

Where can you find a list of all regulations that fit your organization? Start with this table at the Unified Compliance Project website over at the IT Compliance Institute[60] and you'll see everything that we've listed here in more detail than we can present on paper. From there, the IT Compliance Institute also has the capability to let you enter in regulations you know you have to follow, as well as the industry segment you are in, in order to create a custom information and information services impact zone list of control objectives[61]. These two should get you started. If you have other questions, you can always contact us and we'll give you a hand.

Once you have sorted out the tongue twister, you understand that you need to retrieve all the laws, regulations and standards that apply to you. This may be a job for your legal department or general counsel. But, this does not mean that this person (or group of people) is the only one who should know what those laws are and what information they contain. The information and information services manager, CIO, CTO and anyone who has a managerial role in information and information services governance should be familiar with these laws. In fact, the more people who know, the easier it will be to become compliant because everyone will be on the same page.

And if you want a gold star on your report card, you'll follow suit with a simple posting of the regulations and standards you are following, as did the University of Salford, in Manchester England[62]. Their website documents all of the legislation that they fall under, with click-through definitions to each of the acts and standards that they are following so that the reader can easily grasp the information being presented. If a student wants to know why their request for information under the Freedom of Information Act will be successful or not, they merely need to follow the links to understand the process and parameters the university follows. Nicely done.

---

60   Dorian J. Cougias, Erikka Innes and Paige Tomaselli (2005). Leadership and High Level Objectives Impact Matrix, IT Compliance Institute.

61   Dorian J. Cougias, Erikka Innes and Paige Tomaselli (2005). Custom IT Impact Matrix, IT Compliance Institute. Check this out online at http://www.itcinstitute.com/ucp

62   David Goodman (2005). University of Salford, Information Services Division, Information Governance Legislation index, University of Salford.

Legislation

Data protection

The Data Protection Act 1998, The eight principles of the Act, Further facts about the Act, Policy, Useful links.

Freedom of Information

The Freedom of Information Act, The University publication scheme, Requesting information, Dealing with requests for information.

Environmental information regulations

Find out about the new Environmental information regulations due to come in to force on 1 January 2005.

Other legislation

The Human Rights Act 1998, The Computer Misuse Act 1990, The Copyright, Designs and Patents Act 1988, The Regulation of Investigatory Powers Act 2000, The Waste Electrical and Electronic Equipment (WEEE) Directive.

Page maintained by David Goodman on 13/09/05

The compliance posting page for the University of Salford in Manchester, England

If your organization can provide this level signage that you understand and can communicate the rules that you fall under, you are *definitely* on the right track and compliance *is* a reality for your organization.

Can you identify key information processes, applications, and documents?

The purpose of describing your organizational functions is to develop a conceptual model of what the organization does and how it does it *by examining the business activities and purposes*. The objective of this step is to establish the model representation of the business activities that are carried out by the organization.

> *The organization will identify and map all information process and applications that are significant to the organization.*

The simplest representation will come in the form of a tree structure that begins with the organizational goals and structures and then develops out through the functions, activities, and transactions of the organization as shown in the following diagram. It doesn't matter if that tree structure is a simple table or an elaborate Visio diagram or relational database.

Guidance from the regulations and standards

Combining the information in the DIRKS records management guidelines with the information found in NIST 800-14 and CERT's OCTAVE program should give you more than enough material for developing an organizational standard when identifying key information processes, applications, and documents.

Banking/Finance

The **FFIEC Information Security Booklet**, pages 8 and 9, detail the information gathering steps necessary for understanding systems' risk. A key part of this information gathering is the listing of all information systems and breaking those systems down by their IT assets classifications (documents, applications & databases, OSes, storage, system, network, power & cooling, facilities). The **FFIEC Operations Booklet** goes into more detail on pages 6 through 11 where they cover gathering information system information under the rubric of an environmental survey and technology inventory. The operations material actually blends into another control objective we cover about gathering system specific information.

DIRKS § B.4 suggests two types of analysis; hierarchical- (top down) and process-based (bottom up). Whichever method is used, DIRKS suggests that the interview identify:

- *"your organization's goals and the strategies to achieve these goals;*

- *the broad functions the organization undertakes to support its goals and strategies;*

- *the activities that contribute to the fulfillment of the organization's functions; and*

- *the groups of recurring transactions or processes that make up each of these activities."*

Section B.4.2 of DIRKS further defines the differences between function, activity, and transaction as such:

- *Functions are the largest unit of business activity in an organization. They represent the major responsibilities that are managed by the organization to fulfill its goals. Functions are high-level aggregates of the organization's activities.*

- *Activities are the major tasks performed by the organization to accomplish each of its functions. Several activities may be associated with each function.*

- *Transactions are the smallest unit of business activity. They should be tasks, not subjects or record types. Transactions will help define the scope or boundaries of activities and provide the basis for identifying the records that are required to meet the business needs of the organization. The identification of transactions will also help in the formulation of the records description part of a records disposal authority.*

In order to create a common *language* that everyone in the organization can use when talking about what it is they *do* all day and how they are going to categories what they do, DIRKS suggests, in § B.4.2.1 to assign specific terms to functions and activities. The choice of terminology should depend upon the way in which the organization has defined its functions, activities, and transactions. By choosing and documenting terminology, you will be able to create an unambiguous and integrated business classification scheme[63].

---

63   This classification scheme will go a long way in defining the structure in which you will be storing and locating your evidentiary records.

Section B.4.2.2 of DIRKS takes this further and then asks the analyst to create a glossary entry for each of the terms, much like the glossary entry we use for our writing purposes. Below is a typical glossary entry that we are using for our compliance book. First is the title of the entry, which is then followed by a detailed description of what the glossary entry means according to the authorities who we drew the term from. The authorities are listed at the end in brackets.

Authentication NIST 800-33 would say that verifying the identity of a user, process, or device, often as a prerequisite to allowing access to resources in a system is the definition of authentication. All systems that store, process or protect regulated data need to implement access controls in order to manage where this information is allowed to flow and who is allowed to create, view or change it. If the authentication attempt fails then access has to be blocked. For HIPAA, all attempts to gain access to a system containing ePHI have to be logged for later investigation. See also Identification, Key Management, and System Access Control. [HIPAA and NIST 800-33]

DIRKS would have the analyst produce much the same thing, using documentary sources or interviewees as the authority sources and the interview or research material as the basis for the definition of the term being described.

Section B.4.2.3 of DIRKS takes this one step further by asking the analyst to document dates for functions and activities. These dates *"establish a time frame, which will be useful for the development and application of the linked recordkeeping tools such as a thesaurus and disposal authority"* states DIRKS. In practical terms, it provides more metadata that you can feed into your recordkeeping system

NIST Special Publications

NIST 800-14 § 3.3.1 states that prior to conducting a risk assessment, the system under consideration must be identified and analyzed, documenting the system's level of detail and formality. **NIST 800-18**, Appendix A lists all of the key information that must be recorded for a system within the System Security Plan:

1. **Information System Name/Title**: Unique identifier and name given to the system.

2. **Information System Categorization**: Identify the appropriate FIPS 199 categorization.

3. **Information System Owner**: Name, title, agency, address, email address, and phone number of person who owns the system.

4. **Authorizing Official**: Name, title, agency, address, email address, and phone number of the senior management official designated as the authorizing official.

5. **Other Designated Contacts**: List other key personnel, if applicable; include their title, address, email address, and phone number.

6. **Assignment of Security Responsibility**: Name, title, address, email address, and phone number of person who is responsible for the security of the system.

7. **Information System Operational Status**: Indicate the operational status of the system. If more than one status is selected, list which part of the system is covered under each status.

8. **Information System Type**: Indicate if the system is a major application or a general support system.

9. **General System Description/Purpose**: Describe the function or purpose of the system and the information processes.

10. **System Environment**: Provide a general description of the technical system. Include the primary hardware, software, and communications equipment.

11. **System Interconnections/Information Sharing**: List interconnected systems and system identifiers (if appropriate), provide the system, name, organization, system type (major application or general support system), indicate if there is an ISA/MOU/MOA on file, date of agreement to interconnect, FIPS 199 category, C&A status, and the name of the authorizing official.

12. **Related Laws/Regulations/Policies**: List any laws or regulations that establish specific requirements for the confidentiality, integrity, or availability of the data in the system.

13. **Minimum Security Controls**: Provide a thorough description of how the minimum controls in the applicable baseline are being implemented or planned to be implemented. The controls should be described by control family and indicate whether it is a system control, hybrid control, common control, scoping guidance is applied, or a compensating control is being used.

14. **Information System Security Plan Completion Date**: Enter the completion date of the plan.

15. **Information System Security Plan Approval Date**: Enter the date the system security plan was approved and indicate if the approval documentation is attached or on file.

General Guidance

Carnegie Mellon's **CERT OCTAVE** approach is a 1200+ page document that centers almost entirely on the methodology of identifying information processes and information systems as well as their threats and vulnerabilities. **Process 1** of CERT's OCTAVE defines how to document information processes and information systems. **Process 6** defines how to evaluate those processes and systems and is therefore a good read as well as the two tie directly together.

Section B.5.a(i) and (ii) of the **Business Continuity Institute's Standards of Professional Competence** point out that a key to defining business continuity is being able to identify and confirm the processing and documentation critical to the organization's key business activities. Their point is that you can't determine which processes and systems should be replicated off site unless you can place them into their context within the organization's day-to-day business activities.

CobiT 3 and 4 PO 2.1 both detail the need for defining an organizational information architecture model. **CobiT 3**'s PO 8.5 and **CobiT 4**'s ME 3.1 cover the identification of laws and regulations having a potential impact on information technology. This also *assumes* that the organization can properly *define* the information processes, systems, and IT assets that are being affected by those rules and regulations.

US Federal Privacy

FISCAM Appendix VI.1.1 states the need for organizations to identify computer applications significant to the financial statements of the organization. Significant applications are those with auditable line items and accounts under investigation or that are material to the organization.

United Kingdom and Canadian Guidance

BS 15000-2:2003 § 5.6.1 documents the need for a service provider to maintain an inventory of the information assets that are necessary to deliver services such as information processing, and that those assets should be classified according to their level of criticality. Section 8.1.1 deals with configuration management planning, but also stresses the need to understand the configuration of information processes as those processes are they key to integrating the system overall.

From regulation to reality – sure signs you are complying

There are a lot of ways to document the information services operational scope of your audit framework. We'll present three different approaches here and leave it up to your imagination how to proceed from there. However you *do* decide on proceeding, what you need to make clear in your documentation is the mapping of your organizational business units, functions, processes, tasks, and documents to the information systems and supporting IT assets. For our exercise, we'll map the Network Frontiers' processes of creating a custom document for a client or a book project (we consider each book project a client). Why this process? As writers, our written objects, whether articles, reports, analysis, or books, are *material* to our organization. It took a year to create the Backup book and a couple of years to create the database for the Unified Compliance Framework.

Creating a simple table

The information you could put in a basic information process mapping table can be as simple as the five column table we'll show here, or it can be as complex as a relational table that ties this information to the full information gathered and presented for a federal systems security plan as discussed above in the NIST documentation.

Business Units	Business Function	Key Tasks	Documents Created	Applications used
Writing Department	Project Management	Time & expense reporting	Time and expense card	Outlook & Excel
	Client communication	Information sharing	messages, support documents	e-mail, Sharepoint
	Product creation	Online material research	Research bibliography	Endnote/Browser
		Writing and editing	client files	Microsoft Office
Design Team		Document design and layout	client files	Creative Suite CS
		Time & expense reporting	Time and expense card	Outlook & Excel
Management Team	Project Management	Statement of Work creation	SOW document	Microsoft Office
		Project creation	Client record set	AccPac
		Time & expense reporting	Time and expense card	Outlook & Excel
	Project Billing	T&E Reporting	Billing record update	Excel & AccPac
		Invoice creation	Invoice Report	AccPac
IT Services	IS	Backup and replication	Backup and replication files	EMC, Symantec
		Records Retention	Archive File	EMC

Information process table

139

Creating a Visio diagram

Another popular method of documenting information processes is through flowcharting. Flowcharts, can become *quite* extensive and time consuming if you let it. However, if you stick to high level flowcharts such as the one below which maps the same processes as in the table, you'll be fine.

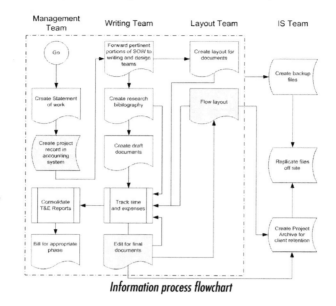

Information process flowchart

The beauty of using Visio to create your high level information process flow is that you can now tie your information process flow diagram directly in to your information asset database (covered in the next control objective) that you can *automatically* discover using the Visio tie in with Neon's LANsurveyor.

You Need to Gather Information about your systems

A risk assessment is only as good as the information you collect for that assessment. If you collect inappropriate information, or too little information, you will be unable to accurately determine potential risks your organization faces. To avoid this, use the following control objective when gathering information:

> *Prior to risk identification, the organization will gather information on the information systems environment, including inventories of all hardware, software, networking and media assets, and information on the handling of information, employee training, and existing incident response procedures.*

Once you've collected information properly, the organization can then proceed with identifying threats and vulnerabilities associated with this information.

Guidance from the regulations and standards

Banking/Finance

Both **GLB** § (b)(2) and FFIEC call for an environmental (IT) survey, technological inventories and information gathering on handling, training and incident response procedures prior to risk identification.

FFIEC Operations Pg. 6 calls for: *"an inventory of all computing software; and inventory of all computing hardware; network topologies or other diagrams that detail the internal and external connectivity of voice and data communication networks; data flow and business process diagrams that depict operational interdependencies; and a comprehensive, holistic view of how technology operations support the strategic business goals of the institution."*

Records Management

ISO 15489 calls for an assessment of existing systems for records that could be integrated into the risk assessment control objective.

NIST Special Publications

NIST 800-14 § 3.3.1 *"calls for asset valuation, which includes the information, software, personnel, hardware, and physical assets (such as the computer* *facilities.) The value of an asset consists of its intrinsic value and the near-term impacts and long-term consequences of its compromise."*

International Standards Organization

ISO 17799 § 5.1.1 calls for an inventory of all assets including information assets, software assets, physical assets and services. It also contains provisions on information handling, specifying the importance of creating procedures for information labeling and handling.

General Guidance

Though COSO and CobiT 3 do not directly address the need for information gathering, ISO 17799 and other standards call for asset management as a precursor to identifying risk.

CobiT 4 PO9.2 says that when determining risks, establish the context the risk is in before assessing it – where context is meant to describe the context of the information system or IT assets.

The **ISF Standard** § SM 4.3.6 calls for hardware and software inventories which specify the location, version, and unique identifier of each asset, and are protected against unauthorized change, checked periodically against physical assets, kept up to date and reviewed independently.

United Kingdom and Canadian Guidance

BS 15000-2 § 5.6.1 calls for the *"identification and classification of information assets (including hardware, software, network and media), maintaining an inventory of the assets, classifying each asset according to its criticality, and nomination of asset owners for accountability."*

From regulation to reality – sure signs you are complying

Once you lay out the details of the approach you will take to risk analysis, you must gather as much information about your organization as possible so you can conduct an effective risk analysis. Thorough information gathering includes inventorying all software and hardware, collecting network topologies or other diagrams that detail the internal and external connectivity of voice and data communication networks and collecting data flow and business process diagrams that depict operational interdependencies. Each inventoried item or data collection should have the following information about it specified:

- Location
- Version
- Unique identifier

Once the inventory is gathered, all items and data should go through an asset valuation that includes determining intrinsic value as well as the short and long term impacts of an item or data being compromised. During the asset valuation process, items should be classified according to their criticality, and if a particular asset is highly important, an owner should be nominated for it. The owner will take responsibility for the care of the selected asset.

In doing these things you prepare for the next step of the auditing process and also ensure as little compromise to important assets as possible.

Have You Defined Roles and Responsibilities?

As we discussed in the section about the definition of information governance, there are plenty of seats at the table, you just have to ensure you know where everybody is going to sit, especially during the audit process. God forbid you don't define clear roles for your audit staff. The unified control objective for ensuring auditing roles and responsibilities would read as thus:

> *In order to promote the integrity, confidentiality and availability of information systems, our organization must determine roles and responsibilities for auditing controls of the IT environment, thus ensuring the preservation or improvement of the organization's strategies for risk management and internal control. Roles and responsibilities for board members and senior management, internal auditor management and staff, IT operations staff and external auditors must be considered.*

When you know what tasks make up each role, it's easier to find problem spots in your IT environment. It's also easier to deal with them because you'll know who to assign the fixing of a problem spot to.

Guidance from the regulations and standards

Again, many of the regulations and standards are a bit vague as to what the roles and responsibilities in the organization should be regarding the audit process. And again, the FFIEC Audit guide is very specific in its guidance. Just as specific, the GAO's audit manual provides great detail on the roles and responsibilities of the key players in the internal audit process. But that's getting ahead of ourselves. Let's start with public company regulations and standards as we always do.

Public Companies

Most standards for public companies call for internal or external auditors to assess what components of the organization's risk management and internal controls for IT are relevant to an audit of financial statements. The Combined Code additionally calls for the board of directors or senior management to assess the organization's own internal audit function.

SAS 94 ¶ 2 calls for the auditor to obtain an understanding of internal control sufficient to plan the audit by performing procedures to understand the design controls relevant to an audit of financial statements and determining whether they have been placed in operation. The auditor should consider how an entity's use of IT and manual procedures may affect controls relevant to the audit.

The Combined Code § C.3.1 &2 calls for the board to establish an audit committee, with one member of the committee having established experience. The Code goes on to list the roles and responsibilities of the audit committee including: monitoring the financial statements and any other formal announcements or judgments involving finances of the organization; reviewing the companies internal financial controls and internal control and risk management systems; monitoring and reviewing the effectiveness of the company's internal audit function; making recommendations to the board concerning the appointment, re-appointment or removal of the external auditor; reviewing and monitoring the external auditors independence and objectivity, and the effectiveness of the audit process; developing and implementing a policy on the engagement of the external auditor to supply non-audit services.

Banking/Finance

Banking and financial institution standards and regulations require specific roles and responsibilities regarding an IT audit. The FFIEC Audit manual, in particular, addresses responsibilities for all levels of management and staff.

Basel II ¶ 405 calls for an internal audit or an equally independent function to review (and document) at least annually the bank's rating system and it's operations. Areas of review include adherence to all applicable minimum requirements.

Appendix of 12 CFR 30 § III.C calls for regular testing of the key controls, systems and procedures of the information security program. The tests should be conducted or reviewed by independent third parties or staff independent of those who develop and maintain the security programs.

The FFIEC Audit Manual Pgs 3-6 explains:

- *The board of directors has overall responsibility for the effectiveness of the audit function.*

- *The board of directors and senior management are responsible for providing the audit function with sufficient resources to ensure adequate IT coverage and audit function independence.*

- *Senior management is responsible for supporting IT audit by establishing programs defining and requiring compliance with IT planning practices, operating policies, and internal controls.*

- *The manager of internal audit is responsible for implementing board approved audit directives.*

- *Internal IT audit staff is responsible for independently and objectively evaluating the institution's technology activities to improve the efficiency and effectiveness of its risk management, internal controls, and corporate governance.*

- *Operating management is responsible for promptly and effectively responding to IT audit recommendations.*

Healthcare and Life Sciences

HIPAA § 164.308 defines the responsibility for management to create an audit function for IT but does not address further specific responsibilities.

US Federal Security

For the most part, government standards and regulations call for the same roles and responsibilities as financial institutions—however, in the case of **GAO**, responsibilities for the audit only concern the relevance of risk management and controls related to financial statements.

FISMA § 3544(a)(2)(D) calls for *"periodic testing and evaluating information security controls and techniques to ensure that they are effectively implemented."* In addition, according to § 3545(a), each year an *"independent evaluation of the information security program must be performed"* to determine the programs effectiveness. This will include: *"testing the effectiveness of information security procedures, policies, and practices"*; a compliance assessment; and an evaluation of information security relating to national security systems. Section 3545(a)(2)(A)-(C) FISMA also calls for an independent auditor, but does not define the roles and responsibilities of this function.

GAO § 100.26 provides detail on the roles and responsibilities of every person involved in the audit function:

- *The assistant director is the top person responsible for the day to day conduct of the audit.*

- *The audit director is the senior manager responsible for the technical quality of the financial statement audit.*

- *The reviewer is the senior manger responsible for the quality of the auditors reports.*

- *The statistician is the person the auditor consults for technical expertise in areas such as audit sampling, audit sample evaluation, and selecting entity field locations to visit.*

- *The data extraction specialist is the person with technical expertise in extracting data from agency records.*

- *The technical accounting and auditing expert advises on accounting and auditing professional matters and related national issues, and reviews reports on financial statements and reports that contain opinions on financial information.*

- *The office of general counsel provides assistance to the auditor in (1) identifying provisions in laws and regs to test, (2) identifying budget restrictions, and (3) identifying and resolving legal issues encountered.*

- *The special investigator unit investigates specific allegations involving conflict-of-interest and ethics matters, contract procurement irregularities, official misconduct and abuse, and fraud in federal programs or activities.*

- *Finally, the internal auditor is ultimately responsible for assessing inherent and control risk, and assessing the effectiveness of IS controls requires a person with IS audit technical skills.*

Records Management

Roles and responsibilities for auditing records management systems are addressed briefly by **DIRKS** and **ISO 15489** but do not define any specific roles other than that of the individual performing the audit.

NIST Special Publications

NIST 800-53 § AU-2 calls for the organization to decide "which events require an auditing on a continuous basis, which events require auditing in response to s specific situation, and which events are adequate to support after-the-fact investigations of security incidents."

General Guidance

Although most of the general standards do not define specific responsibilities other than that of the internal or external auditor, COSO and CobiT define responsibilities for senior management with respect to providing adequate resources or delegating responsibility for the audit. COSO further defines the roles and responsibilities of internal and external auditors.

COSO ERM explains that the *"board of directors may use committees to carry out certain duties. The audit committee, for example, has a direct role in the reliability of external reporting, and the nominating committee identifies and considers qualifications of prospective board members"* (COSO ERM Pg. 93). Internal auditors evaluate the effectiveness of and recommend improvements to enterprise risk management (COSO ERM Pg. 97). The external auditor gives an opinion on financial statements, not on the internal control system (COSO ERM Pg. 98-99).

CobiT M 4.1 calls for senior management to establish a charter for the audit function. *"This document should outline the responsibility, authority and accountability of the audit function. The charter should be reviewed periodically to assure that the independence, authority, and accountability of the audit function are maintained."*

International Standards Organization

ISO 17799 § 4.1.7 calls for management to create a security policy included in which should be the policy and responsibilities for information security. *"The implementation of this policy should be reviewed by the internal audit function, an independent manager or a third party specializing in such reviews."*

United Kingdom and Canadian Guidance

BS 15000-2 § 4.3.1 calls for management to "make use of internal audits and other checks. When deciding frequency of the internal audits, risk and past history of problems should be taken into consideration. Internal audits should be planned, carried out completely, and recorded."

From regulation to reality – sure signs you are complying

Glancing through all the different regulations available on the subject of auditing can make the task seem daunting, but it's easier than you think. As we can see, a good audit program begins with good planning. The first step is to outline the roles and responsibilities of staff involved with the auditing process. Depending on the size of your organization, roles and responsibilities will vary, but there are six key roles to be sure to establish:

- Board of Directors

- Senior Management

- Internal IT Audit Manager

- Internal IT Audit Staff

- IT Operations Staff

- External Auditors

If at all possible, it is best to have a different person for each role, but in a small organization this may not be possible. In the case where roles need to be doubled up, use your best judgment when assigning the responsibilities.

Board of Directors

The most important set of roles to assign is the board of directors. This is because the board is responsible for the overall effectiveness of the audit function. They will create an audit committee among themselves that includes at least one member with established experience doing audit work. This committee is responsible for making recommendations to the board regarding the selection of auditors, determining whether auditors are appropriately independent and objective and creating and implementing a policy for handling non-audit services that may be provided by an external auditor. The committee will also monitor the financial statements and any other formal announcements or judgments involving finances of the organization.

The rest of the board's role regarding the committee is to provide necessary equipment and support for their work, and ensure that the quality of the audit is maintained at an acceptable level. It is absolutely necessary that the board be supportive of what the committee is doing otherwise the audit will not be able to get off the ground. In general, for most departments security is not the number one priority—getting workers to do their work counts for more. Thus the audit committee must have high-level staff supporting their endeavors so that they can push through with some of the more challenging aspects of their work such as collecting information or conducting interviews with staff.

Senior Management

The primary role of senior management is to demonstrate their awareness of the auditing process by creating programs for their staff that define and require compliance with IT planning practices, operating policies and internal controls. Ideally, senior management should write a charter for the audit process that contains details defining the roles and responsibilities of their staff during an audit. This makes it easier to support the audit staff in their endeavors. Periodically, senior management should review the charter to ensure that workers are complying with its requirements, and that the charter is current.

Internal IT Audit Manager

The internal IT audit manager is responsible for implementing any audit directives that the board has approved.

Internal IT Audit Staff

Internal IT audit staff is responsible for evaluating the organization's technology activities and determining where the efficiency and effectiveness of risk management, internal controls and corporate governance may be improved. To effectively carry out their assigned tasks, the organization should ensure that all audit staff is independent from the functions they evaluate, so they may be objective in their assessments.

IT Operations Staff

This group has the task of responding to IT audit recommendations. Responses should be prompt, and can involve implementation of a recommendation or discussions about how best to use a recommendation.

External Auditors

If an organization chooses to have audits conducted by an external staff, that staff inherits the roles and responsibilities otherwise held by the internal IT audit staff. If external and internal audit staff are used, the internal staff has authority in determining how the two groups will coordinate activities.

Have You Created an Internal Audit Program?

Internal auditing programs help you identify problem spots with your IT environment and controls. When creating an internal audit program, a good control objective to keep in mind is:

> In order to promote the integrity, confidentiality and availability of information systems, the organization will establish an internal auditing program or function for auditing controls of the information services environment, thus ensuring the preservation or improvement of the organization's strategies for risk management and internal control.

Once you establish a regularly recurring audit program, you will be able to detect issues with your IT environment and equipment before they become full blown problems. Solving IT issues before they become massive problems saves you time and money.

Guidance from the regulations and standards

Most regulations and standards aren't very specific about how to create an internal audit program. The FFIEC Audit guide, as you might expect, is the *most* specific in terms of what should be included within the internal audit program.

Public Companies

As relevant to financial reporting controls, Sarbanes Oxley and SAS 94 imply the *existence* of an internal audit *program* and Turnbull and the AICPA call for an internal audit *function* or at least a review of the need for one.

Banking/Finance

Both Basel II and FFIEC call for an internal audit program or function. FFIEC details the creation of an audit charter and plan that integrates risk assessment and internal controls.

FFIEC Audit Pgs. 11-12 call for *"management to develop and follow a formal internal audit program consisting of policies and procedures that govern the internal audit function, including IT audit."* This should include:

- *A mission statement or audit charter outlining purpose, objectives, authorities and responsibilities;*

- *A risk assessment process to describe and analyze the risks inherent in a given line of business;*

- *An audit plan detailing internal audit's budgeting and planning processes;*

- *An audit cycle that identifies the frequency of audits;*

- *Audit work programs that set out for each audit area the required scope and resources, including the selection of audit procedures, the extent of testing, and the basis for conclusions;*

- *Written audit reports informing the board and management of individual department or division compliance with policies and procedures;*

- *Requirements for audit work paper documentation to ensure clear support for all audit findings and work performed, including work paper retention policies;*

- *Follow-up processes that require internal auditors to determine the disposition of any agreed upon actions to correct significant deficiencies;*

- *Professional development programs to be in place for the institution's audit staff to maintain the necessary technical expertise.*

Healthcare and Life Sciences

HIPAA calls for an "information system activity review" – the equivalent of an internal audit program. Specifically, HIPAA§164.308(1)(ii)(D) calls for health care organizations to "implement procedures to regularly review records of information system activity, such as audit logs, access reports, and security incident tracking reports."

Credit Card

The credit card regulations call for an internal audit function with respect to information security – Visa and Amex explicitly state the need for a program, while MasterCard merely implies the need.

US Federal Security

FISMA calls for government agencies to adopt strict internal audit programs – GAO implies, but does not explicitly provide for the creation of an internal audit program as audits are relevant to financial statements.

Records Management

DIRKS and ISO 15489 call for the establishment of an internal audit program as relevant to recordkeeping controls.

ISO 15489-1 §10 calls for internal auditing to ensure that the organization is in compliance with its policies and procedures.

ISO 15489-2 §5.1 calls for the internal audits to "take place regularly at intervals agreed and set down in the organization's records management policy."

DIRKS § G.4.1.5 calls for the audit program to "cover all aspects of records keeping; specify performance indicators used to analyze efficiency and effectiveness; assign responsibility for the conduct and reporting of the audit; specify methods for collecting information; specify the period and frequency of reviews; and provide a secure report that can be used for comparative purposes over time."

NIST Special Publications

NIST 800-53 § AU-1 offers some guidance as to the components of the internal audit program. *"The organization should develop, disseminate, and periodically review/update: a formal, documented audit and accountability policy that addresses purpose, scope, roles, responsibilities, and compliance; and, formal, documented procedures to facilitate the implementation of the audit and accountability policy and associated audit and accountability controls."* In addition NIST 800-53 calls for government agencies to adopt strict internal audit programs.

General Guidance

As with financial institution standards, general standards call for an internal audit program or function that assesses controls for IT and ensures the preservation and improvement of risk management and internal controls through the organization.

COSO ERM (Pg. 80) calls for regular *"management and supervisory activities, variance analysis, stress testing, comparisons, reconciliations and other routine actions."* On Pgs 80-82, it additionally discusses scope and frequency, documentation and responsibilities.

CobiT § M4 calls for the *"establishment of an internal audit plan to ensure that regular and independent audits a re obtained regarding the effectiveness, efficiency, and economy of security and internal control procedures, and management's ability to control the IT function activities."*

International Standards Organization

ISO 17799 § 4.1.7 addresses independent reviews of information security by stating that *"an information security policy document should set out responsibilities."* The implementation of this policy should be reviewed by the internal audit function.

United Kingdom and Canadian Guidance

BS 15000-1 § 4.3 calls for an *"audit program to be planned, taking into consideration the status and importance of the processes and areas to be audited, as well as the results of the previous audits."*

BS 15000-2 § 4.3.1 explains that the following should be audited: *"achievement of goals against defined service targets; customer satisfaction; resource utilization; trends; major non-conformities; and results of reviews."*

From regulation to reality – sure signs you are complying

Once you select the staff and form the committee and board of directors that will be responsible for various aspects of an audit, it's time to design the audit program itself. More or less, this fits within the policy creation phase of your compliance program because you are creating the program itself. The key to making the program a success is to create a formal program that covers audits of all controls in the IT environment and ensures the preservation or improvement of the organization's strategies for risk management and internal control. You begin by creating the policies and procedures that will govern the internal audit function. Then, depending upon your organization's needs you can add a variety of additional elements. Here's a list of some of the elements you may wish to consider making a part of your audit program:

- A documented statement of purpose, goals, authorities and responsibilities

- A policy addressing compliance

- A policy addressing scope and frequency or internal audits

- The audit's budget and planning process

- An audit cycle

- Specifications for *each area* to be audited including the procedures, extent of testing, and resources for that area

- Written audit reports

- Documentation for all findings and conclusions

Senior management should periodically review the internal audit program to ensure that the program remains effective and efficient. Elements can be added or discarded to continue to meet the changing goals of the organization.

What is Your Risk Assessment Approach?

Deciding how you will approach risk assessment is vital to its success. You can think of approach as a road map – it's there to help you see where you're going clearly and prevent you from getting off course. While keeping that metaphor in mind, consider the following control objective:

> *As part of initial risk assessment, the management of this organization will define an approach to risk assessment, including a methodology, responsibilities, and the required skills.*

Once you define your approach, the risk assessment becomes simple – you know what you will do and how it will be accomplished.

Guidance from the regulations and standards

Banking/Finance

For financial institution risk assessment, FFIEC calls for a risk assessment approach methodology that points to responsibilities and required skills.

FFIEC Business Continuity Planning Pg. 9 states that a risk assessment should consider: "the impact of various business disruption scenarios on both the institution and its customers; the probability of occurrence based, for example, on a rating system of high, medium, and low; the loss of impact on information services, technology, personnel, facilities, and service providers from both internal and external sources; the safety of critical processing documents and vital records; and a broad range of possible disruptions, including natural, technical, and human threats."

Healthcare and Life Sciences

HIPAA addresses the need for risk assessment but does not outline a risk assessment approach.

US Federal Security

Several government regulations address the need for an auditor's understanding of agencies' risk assessments.

FIPS-PUB-191 has a lot to say about risk assessments. In 3.3 it indicates that threats and vulnerabilities should be identified, then measured to determine likelihood of occurrence. According to 3.4.2, an early step in a good risk assessment is identifying and valuing each of an organization's assets. This process is subjective as it requires determining both the cost of an item and what it means to organizational operations. 3.4.3 goes more in depth on describing how to determine the likelihood of a threat's occurrence. Assigning measurements from 1 to 3, with 3 being highest likelihood of a threat becoming a problem is suggested. 3.4.4 says that while a quantitative approach may be useful, qualitative approaches can also be just as good. Striking a balance between the two is considered to be ideal.

12 CFR Part 748 pg. 81 calls for organization to create a risk assessment approach that includes preparing to handle *"reasonably foreseeable internal and external threats that could result in unauthorized disclosure, misuse, alteration, or destruction of member information or member information systems"* by examining the likelihood and potential damage of threats and ensuring that policies, procedures and systems are sufficient enough to control risks. Pg. 82 continues, stating that once risks are identified and prioritized, a program must be implemented to deal with them. Recommended security measures include access controls on member information systems, authentication devices, background checks for employees with special access privileges and incident response programs.

NIST Special Publications

NIST 800-14 § 3.3.1 calls for the determination of the risk assessments scope and methodology. This includes identifying *"the system under consideration, the part of the system to be analyzed, and the analytical method including its level of detail and formality."*

NIST 800-53 § RA-1 states that the *"organization should develop, disseminate, and periodically review and update: (i) a formal documented risk assessment policy that addresses purpose, scope, roles, responsibilities, and compliance; and,(ii) formal, documented procedures to facilitate the implementation of the risk assessment policy and associated risk assessment controls."*

NIST 800-61 Computer Security Incident Handling Guide 3.1.2 talks about preventing security incidents from happening frequently by conducting a risk assessment. It offers a list of remedies for handling some of the problem spots an organization might uncover during an assessment. Items included in the discussion are patch management, host security, network security, malicious code prevention and user awareness training.

The IT Infrastructure Library

ITIL Best Practice for Security Management 2.2.4 calls for conducting a risk analysis to best determine how to spend money and resources defending the organization against potential risks.

General Guidance

COSO, CobiT, NIST and other general standards call for a risk management approach to define a methodology, responsibilities and required skills for performing a risk assessment – for example, COSO's risk management philosophy.

COSO ERM Pg.19-20 discusses roles and responsibilities of everyone in the organization, as well as the use of the risk assessment procedure.

CobiT 3 PO 9.2 provides that *"management should establish a general risk assessment approach which defines the scope and boundaries, the methodology to be adopted for risk assessments, the responsibilities and the required skills. Management should lead the identification of the risk mitigation solution and be involved in identifying vulnerabilities. Security specialists should drive the control selection. The quality of risk assessments should be assured by a structured method and skilled risk assessors."*

CobiT 4 PO9.4 states that risk assessments should be done on a regular basis to determine the likelihood and impact of all identified risks. Methods used to measure risks should be qualitative and quantitative. PO9.6 calls for maintaining and monitoring any risk action plan you do create to ensure it is effective and up-to-date. PO6.2 talks about fitting risk assessments into an IT risk and internal control framework. This framework should define an organization's approach to handling risk and defending important IT assets. This framework should be implemented with the quality management system, and comply with overall business objectives.

The **ISF Standard** § SM 3.3.4 calls for risk analysis methods to be determined by: *"defining the criticality of the information and systems; assessing vulnerabilities due to control weaknesses and by special circumstances that heighten vulnerability; identifying accidental and deliberate threats to confidentiality, integrity and availability of information; taking into account known incidents; and evaluating the likelihood and business impact of a threat materializing."*

International Standards Organization

Finally, **ISO 17799** § ix calls for the assessment of security risks, *"balancing the expenditure on controls against the business harm likely to result from security failures."*

From regulation to reality – sure signs you are complying

A significant portion of any audit program is how you plan to assess the risks turned up by the audit.

Prior to doing a risk assessment, define the approach you will use in handling risks, including a methodology, scope, responsibilities, and required skills. The quality of risk assessments is assured by a structured approach using skilled assessors. When determining the right risk assessment approach for your organization, have management consider the following factors:

- Assess the risks to security
- Define sensitivity of information and systems
- Assess known and potential vulnerabilities
- Consider known incidents
- Identify threats to confidentiality
- Identify possible technical, natural, and human threats
- Consider the roles of staff and their relative skill

Other details include deciding how you will prioritize any risks you encounter during the audit, and what levels of risk your organization is comfortable having. Management's involvement in the risk assessment approach is vital to a smoothly functioning risk assessment system. Management's oversight and participation in the identification of a risk mitigation solution and identification of vulnerabilities helps ensure a quality risk assessment. Skilled security assessors also play a vital role in the process. The organization's creation of a risk assessment methodology, carefully outlining the scope of the assessment, and the skills and responsibilities of the assessors will facilitate a well-balanced risk assessment procedure.

Have You Identified Risks?

Risk identification is a way of determining what potential attacks and problems your organization must be prepared to address. You can't plan for absolutely everything, so a large part of risk identification involves choosing what risks are most likely to happen, and how you will combat them. The control objective for this section is:

> *In order to effectively address and mitigate risk, our organization will analyze information gathered to identify threats to the organization, and the vulnerabilities inherent in the information systems environment itself.*

When you compile a list of potential risks, you can then easily begin to create plans and solutions for dealing with each of them.

Guidance from the regulations and standards

Public Companies

Public standards do not directly call for a risk identification control objective, but as with SAS 94 ¶ 38, they do tend to mention the process of risk identification as it relates to an auditor's understanding of risk assessment within an organization.

Banking/Finance

FFIEC Operations Pg. 12 calls for the identification of threats and vulnerabilities based on information gathering. A variety of techniques can be used for risk identification, including *"performing self assessments, incorporating concerns identified in internal and external audits, reviewing business impact analyses prepared for contingency planning, assessing the findings of vulnerability assessments conducted for information security purposes, and understanding the concerns identified by insurance underwriters for establishing premiums."*

Appendix of 12 CFR 30 III.B.1 calls for the *"identification of reasonably foreseeable internal and external threats that could result in unauthorized disclosure, misuse, alteration, or destruction of customer information or customer information systems."*

Healthcare and Life Sciences

HIPAA mentions the need to identify threats and vulnerabilities in its risk assessment requirement, but there is nothing beyond that.

US Federal Security

Though government regulations address the need for an auditor's understanding of agencies' risk assessments, the National Strategy to Secure Cyberspace is the only standard that suggests requiring a risk identification control objective to identify threats and vulnerabilities.

General Guidance

COSO, CobiT, NIST and other general standards call for a risk identification control objective to identify threats and vulnerabilities of an organization.

COSO ERM Pg. 38-43 calls for management to identify potential events affecting an entity's ability to successfully implement strategy and achieve objectives.

CobiT 3 PO9.3 explains that the *"risk assessment approach should focus on the examination of the essential elements of risk and the cause/effect relationship between them. The essential elements of risk include tangible and intangible assets, asset value, threats, vulnerabilities, safeguards, consequences, and likelihood of threat."*

CobiT 4 PO9.3 requires organizations to identify any events that have the potential to impact the goals and operations of the organization, including business, regulatory, legal, technology, trading partner, human resources and operational aspects.

NIST 800-14 calls for a vulnerability analysis, a safeguard analysis, a likelihood assessment, threat identification, and a consequence assessment.

Finally, The **ISF Standard** § SM 3.3.5 calls for identification of accidental and deliberate threats to the confidentiality, integrity and availability of information.

From the information collected during the information gathering process, go through and determine where your organization has the biggest weaknesses and therefore the greatest amount of risk.

The question becomes, how do you do this? High quality risk identification can be accomplished by using a variety of techniques, such as:

- Performing self assessments
- Incorporating concerns identified in internal and external audits
- Reviewing business impact analyses
- Assessing the findings of vulnerability assessments
- Investigating the likelihood of accidental and deliberate threats
- Looking at possible safeguards and consequences

Do you conduct a Business Risk Assessment

Risks to your organization aren't just about fire hazards or attacks on your systems or problems with staff. They're also about cost. How much does it cost you to deal with a fire? Unruly staff? An attack on your systems? How much time do you lose, and what is the overall loss of profit? Use the following control objective to answer these questions:

> During the risk assessment an organization must assess risk in terms of overall business objectives and strategy, forming a framework as a basis for determining what information risks should be assessed as they impact business within the organization and forming a general definition of acceptable risk to the organization.

Knowing your technological exposure to risk, as well as how much you're willing to tolerate in terms of loss, makes it easier to prioritize the severity of each risk encountered.

Guidance from the regulations and standards

Each of the major regulations is clear on the point that you should absolutely be conducting a risk assessment – period. This control objective is more of a "we should do this" sort of thing than a "how to" piece of advice. That comes in the next control objective.

Banking/Finance

FFIEC requires a business risk assessment in the form of a BIA (Business Impact Analysis) as an initial business risk assessment.

According to the **FFIEC Business Continuity Handbook** Pg. 6, a business impact analysis should include: *"identification of the potential impact of uncontrolled, non-specific events on the institutions business processes and its customers; consideration of all departments and business functions; and estimation of maximum allowable downtime and acceptable levels of data, operations, and financial losses."*

Healthcare and Life Sciences

While **HIPAA** requires a risk assessment process, it does not directly address the need for business risk assessment control objective.

US Federal Security

Though government regulations address the need for an auditor's understanding of agencies' risk assessments, they do not directly address this risk assessment control objective.

General Guidance

CobiT, NIST and other general standards call for a business risk assessment, taking into account global and system-level risk as they relate to the business of the organization.

CobiT PO9.1 calls for management to *"establish a systematic risk assessment framework. Such a framework should incorporate a regular assessment of the relevant information risks to the achievement of the business objectives, forming a basis for determining how the risks should be managed at an acceptable level. The process should provide for risk assessments at both the global level and system specific level, for new projects as well as on a recurring basis, and with cross disciplinary participation. Management should ensure that reassessments occur and that risk assessment information is updated with results of audits, inspections and identified incidents."*

The **ISF Standard** § SM 3.3 and 3.3.4 explains that *"business risks associated with the enterprise's information and systems should be analyzed using a formal risk analysis methods, which should be: documented, approved by management, consistent across the enterprise, reviewed periodically to ensure that they meet business needs, applicable to systems of various types and sizes, and understandable by business managers."*

International Standards Organization

ISO 17799 § 11.1.2 calls for a business impact analysis, identifying events that can cause interruptions to business processes.

From regulation to reality – sure signs you are complying

With all the risks identified, it's time to assess each risk by how it impacts business in terms of business objectives and strategy. For example, what if the physical integrity of the building where your organization is centered is compromised? Say Mr. Koolaid busts through the wall – aside from boosting staff morale by providing delicious beverages, how will this affect your organization's ability to function? Or what if your server goes down, bringing down your website and your organization deals with e-commerce? Will customers still be able to purchase your products? How much does it cost to deal with these situations, and what impact does it have on business? In the case of an e-commerce organization, how much money do you lose if your site is down? Information collected from such an assessment should be used to construct a definition of what level of risk is acceptable to the organization.

To be sure you have a high quality procedure for conducting a business risk assessment, be sure your impact analysis includes the following:

- Identification of the potential impact of uncontrolled, non-specific events on the institutions business processes and its customers

- Consideration of all departments and business functions

- Estimation of maximum allowable downtime and acceptable levels of data, operations and financial losses

- To ensure effective business impact analysis, management should establish formal analysis methods for risks such as documenting them, making certain they are approved by management, consistent across the enterprise, reviewed periodically to see that they meet business needs, examined for applicability to systems of various types and sizes, and understandable by business managers.

How Do You Analyze your Risk Assessment?

Part of conducting a risk assessment is figuring out what all the information you collect means. When you set out to analyze your data, keep the following control objective in mind to ensure the proper analysis of the risk assessment:

> Once threats and vulnerabilities are identified, an organization must analyze risks to estimate the likelihood of threats and the consequence of continued vulnerabilities to them.

Estimating the likelihood of threats lets you determine how best to use your resources so you can defend the most against the worst of them.

Guidance from the regulations and standards

Public Companies

Public standards do not directly call for a risk analysis control objective, but as with SAS 94, they do tend to mention the process of risk analysis as it relates to an auditor's understanding of risk assessment within an organization.

Banking/Finance

FFIEC and other financial standards call for a risk analysis to estimate the likelihood of threats and the consequences of continued vulnerabilities.

Appendix of 12 CFR 30 § III.B.2 calls for organizations to *"identify reasonably foreseeable internal and external threats that could result in unauthorized disclosure, misuse, alteration, or destruction of customer information or customer information systems."*

FFIEC Operations Pg. 12 states that it should be management's responsibility to analyze the environment and inventory of technology resources available for IT operations. Their analysis should involve identifying threats and vulnerabilities to IT operations and include:

- Internal and external risks
- Risks associated with individual platforms, systems, or processes as well as those of a systemic nature
- The quality and quantity of controls

As much as possible, the assessment process should quantify the probability of a threat or vulnerability and the financial consequences of such an event.

Healthcare and Life Sciences

HIPAA mentions the need to analyze risk in its risk assessment requirement. When conducting a risk analysis, it is not specifically required that a covered entity perform one often enough to ensure that its security measures are acceptable enough to provide the level of security required by 164.306(a). However, it is recommended that a covered entity make the effort to keep their security measures current. The best way to do this is through periodic risk analysis, reassessment and update of any security features that need it.

NIST Special Publications

NIST 800-14 § 3.3.1 suggests that risk analysis is composed of a few sections:

- Determine the Assessment's Scope and Methodology
- Collecting and Analyzing Data
- Interpreting Risk Assessment Results

Determining the assessment's scope and methodology includes identifying the system under consideration, the part of the system that will be analyzed, and the analytical method including its level of detail and formality.

Collecting and analyzing data involves examining the multiple components of risk to see which are most pertinent. Components include asset valuation, consequence assessment, threat identification, safeguard analysis, vulnerability analysis and likelihood assessment.

Interpreting risk assessment results involves reviewing the results of assessment to determine what risks are of most concern to the organization.

NIST 800-53 § RA-3 states that a good risk assessment takes into account all that is known about vulnerabilities, threat sources, and security controls planned or in place to determine the resulting level of residual risk posed to organizational operations, organizational assets, or individuals based on the operation of the information system. During the course of analyzing risks, it should be determined what risks are greatest, which are most likely to occur and how to deal with each of them.

General Guidance

COSO, CobiT, NIST and other general standards call for an analysis of threats and vulnerabilities and an estimation of the likelihood of threats and the consequences of continued vulnerabilities.

COSO ERM Pg. 47-51states that frameworks for enterprise risk management are relevant and applicable to all organizations, but the manner in which management applies enterprise risk management varies greatly from organization to organization. To perform high-quality risk management an organization should take into account their business model, risk profile, ownership structure, operating environment, size complexity, industry and degree of regulation, among others. Based on these factors, management should determine the best methods and techniques for risk management across the organization.

To determine if risk management is effective, management should ascertain whether they have appropriately taken into account all the factors necessary for good risk management as described above. If any factors are missing, they should be included to ensure maximum effectiveness.

CobiT PO 9.3 calls for the risk assessment approach to include the following elements: tangible/intangible assets, asset value, threats, vulnerabilities, safeguards, consequences and likelihood of threat. When identifying specific risks, they should be ranked qualitatively and quantitatively, with input included from management brainstorming, strategic planning, past audits and other assessments.

From regulation to reality – sure signs you are complying

Once you have inventoried your organization's assets, and determined what risks exist in your organization and how these risks impact the business, you must then analyze this assessment. The goal of a risk analysis is to prioritize identified threats and vulnerabilities based on the likelihood of occurrence and the consequences of being confronted with one of them.

There are three basic steps to a good risk analysis process:

- Determine the assessment's scope and methodology
- Collect and analyze data
- Interpret risk assessment results

The first step involves planning out the assessment, what threats and vulnerabilities will be reviewed and how you plan to examine them. Figure out what equipment is necessary for a good analysis, what type of data you need to collect and what kinds of tests you plan to run.

The second step of a top-notch assessment, "collect and analyze data," will take into consideration everything that is known about threats, vulnerabilities and available security controls, then prioritize bigger threats and vulnerabilities over smaller ones. All factors such as your organization's business model, risk profile, ownership structure, operating environment, size complexity, industry and degree of regulation should be taken into account so that the prioritization of threats and vulnerabilities is as accurate as possible.

The third step "interpret risk assessment results" involves taking what you learned in the course of testing and prioritizing risks in the second step and implementing or suggesting solutions for all threats and vulnerabilities above the acceptable risk level. Whether solution implementation occurs is left up to the audit committee or whoever else has the authority to give the go ahead for an implementation.

What is Risk Measuring and Scoring?

Risk measuring and scoring gives you a quantitative way of telling how big and scary each risk to your organization is. The unified control objective for ensuring risks are measured and scored properly would read as thus:

> *The organization will measure risk identification and analysis in a quantitative or qualitative form to best determine the mitigation of risks, acceptable levels of risk and the creation of a gap analysis.*

Once each risk has been measured, you'll be able to see clearly what needs the most attention.

Guidance from the regulations and standards

Public Companies

Public standards do not directly address risk measurement and scoring, but the auditor's role in relation to risk assessments by the organization will provide important audit information.

Banking/Finance

Financial standards call for the measurement of risk based on analysis. FFIEC Audit suggests a scoring system to rank risk quantitatively.

FFIEC Audit Pg. 16 states that scoring systems help ensure successful risk-based IT audit programs. A good scoring system is easy to understand, avoids subjectivity as much as possible and considers all relevant risk factors. Scoring systems can take into consideration a wide variety of factors including:

- The adequacy of internal controls
- The nature of transactions
- The age of the system or application
- The nature of the operating environment
- The physical and logical security of information, equipment and premises
- The adequacy of operating management oversight and monitoring

- Previous regulatory and audit results and management's responsiveness in addressing issues

- Human resources, including the experience of management and staff, turnover, technical competence, management's succession plan, and the degree of delegation

- Senior management oversight

In addition to considering these important factors, auditors should develop written guidelines for the use of scoring systems and other risk assessment tools. Sophistication of guidelines depends on the organization.

Records Management

Records management standards do not directly address risk measurement and scoring, although **DIRKS** Step D does address the creation of a gap analysis as it relates to records management—risks associated with records could result in a similar gap analysis.

General Guidance

COSO, CobiT and NIST call for a quantitative or qualitative measurement of risks following risk analysis. For example, COSO suggests using a benchmarking process or probabilistic models to represent risk analysis.

COSO ERM Pg. 49-51 calls for risk assessments to have a methodology comprised of two parts: qualitative and quantitative techniques. Qualitative techniques should be employed when quantitative techniques cannot be used, or when data necessary for good quantitative assessments are not available, or when obtaining the data is not cost-effective.

Quantitative tests require a high degree of rigor, are dependent upon the quality of supporting data and assumptions, and may include some of the following techniques:

- **Benchmarking**: This process involves multiple organizations coming together to create a common system of metrics to measure how well each of them is doing by. Data on events and processes is measured and compared and benchmarking may be used small scale, or even to predict potential events across an entire industry.

- **Probabilistic Models**: Such models associate a range of events and the impact of these events with the likelihood that they will occur based on certain assumptions. Likelihood and impact are assessed based on historical data or simulated outcomes reflecting assumptions of future behavior. In general, probabilistic models can be used with different time horizons to estimate outcomes such as the range of values of financial instruments over time, etc.

- **Non-probabilistic Models:** These models use subjective assumptions to estimate the impact of events without quantifying an associated likelihood. Event impact assessments are based on historical or simulated data and assumptions of future behavior. Examples of this type of model include sensitivity measures, stress tests and scenario analyses.

CobiT PO 9.4 states that a good risk measurement system includes qualitative and quantitative measurement of risk to which each examined area is exposed. The risk acceptance capacity of the organization should also be assessed.

NIST Special Publications

NIST 800-14 § 3.3.1 calls for risk measurement to include asset valuation, consequence assessment, threat identification, safeguard analysis, vulnerability analysis and likelihood assessment.

From regulation to reality – sure signs you are complying

After you have interpreted risk assessment results, the next step is to measure and score organizational risk. Risk must be measured and scored both qualitatively and quantitatively to best determine the mitigation of risks, acceptable levels of risk and the creation of a gap analysis.

Quantitative methods are formulaic and should be employed before qualitative methods are introduced. Use qualitative methods when quantitative methods are unavailable, when there is not enough quality data available for a complete quantitative assessment, or when it is not cost effective to obtain the necessary data. Since quantitative tests are more rigorous, they are highly dependant on quality data and assumptions. Some examples of quantitative techniques are:

- Benchmarking
- Probabilistic Models
- Non-probabilistic Models
- Scoring Systems

Benchmarking

To create an adequate "benchmarking" system, a variety of organizations must resolve to participate in the process. These organizations collectively create a common system of metrics. Once available, you compare your organizational data against the common system. Benchmarking can be used on a small scale or in a giant effort to predict potential industry wide events.

Probabilistic Models

These models associate a range of events and the impact of these events with the likelihood they will occur based on certain assumptions. Likelihood and impact can be based on historical data or simulated outcomes reflecting assumptions of future behavior. Probabilistic models can be used with different time horizons, to measure outcomes over a certain time frame.

Non-probabilistic Models

Non-probabilistic models use subjective assumptions to estimate the impact of events without quantifying an associated likelihood. Event impact assessments are based on historical or simulated data and assumptions of future behavior. Examples include: sensitivity measures, stress tests and scenario analyses.

Scoring Systems

Scoring systems should be easy to understand, objective and take into consideration all relevant risks. They can take into consideration a variety of factors, including:

- The adequacy of internal controls
- The nature of transactions
- The age of a system or application
- The nature of the operating environment
- Physical and logical security
- The adequacy of operating management oversight and monitoring
- Previous audit results
- Management's responsiveness in addressing issues
- Human resources
- Senior management oversight

No matter what system your organization chooses to use, management should create written guidelines for the use of risk assessment tools. The system is then applied using the written procedures to ensure accuracy and consistency.

The final step in the risk measuring and scoring process is to undertake a gap analysis. A gap analysis studies the difference between projected outcomes and the desired outcomes. The gap analysis naturally flows from benchmarking and other assessments. Once the expected industry performance is known, then it is compared with the organizations current capabilities, becoming the gap analysis.

Do You Have a Risk Action Plan?

Once you know what risks you face, the next step is to figure out how to deal with them. What's your game plan when you come face to face with the biggest of your risks? Hopefully it's not hiding under the covers and hoping it goes away. If you want a more robust plan, the unified control objective for ensuring actually takes action on the risk assessment's gap analysis would read as thus:

> *The organization will develop a risk action plan that identifies a strategy for mitigation, avoidance or acceptance of each assessed risk.*

If your plan identifies each of these areas, you'll be well prepared when it comes time to deal with a risk.

Guidance from the regulations and standards

Banking/Finance

Though these standards do not call directly for a risk action plan, banking and finance standards (most notably FFIEC) imply developing a strategy for mitigation of risks through consideration of security measures.

FFIEC Operations Pgs.13-14 calls for risk mitigation actions to be prioritized based on the probability of occurrence and the magnitude of the financial, reputational or legal impact to the institution.

Healthcare and Life Sciences

HIPAA does not call for a risk action plan. **HIPAA** § 164.308(a)(1)(ii)(B) states that while an action plan is not directly called for, HIPAA does mention that an organization must implement security measures sufficient to reduce risks and vulnerabilities to a reasonable and appropriate level to comply with 164.306(a).

General Guidance

COSO, CobiT, and other general standards call for either a risk action plan or strategies to determine the mitigation of the risks assessed. Most notably, COSO provides four risk response categories: avoidance, reduction (mitigation), sharing, and acceptance.

CobiT 4 PO9.5 calls for developing and maintain a risk action plan that ensures cost-effective controls and security measures are used to handle risks. The plan should also identify risk response strategies such as avoidance, reduction, sharing or acceptance.

The **ISF Standard** § SM 3.3.6 calls for risk analysis methods to include a process ensuring that the results are documented, with documentation containing a clear identification of key risks, an assessment of the potential business impact of each risk and recommendations for actions to reduce risks to acceptable levels.

From regulation to reality – sure signs you are complying

You may be asking why you need a risk action plan. Basically, it is a guide to dealing with risks. The action plan takes the details of the risk analysis and scoring and determines how each assessed risk will be dealt with. The plan should implement solutions based upon the prioritizations given to each risk, and document all decisions thoroughly for later review.

Do You Know What Your Organization's Acceptable Level of Risk is?

Your organization's acceptable level of risk is all about boundaries. What will you tolerate across your organization and what won't you tolerate? The unified control objective for accepting certain levels of risks would read as thus:

> *Following the development of a risk action plan, the organization will determine an acceptable level of risk to its business and information security — i.e., residual risk — and offsets the risk by appropriate means.*

Determining risk tolerance can save you time and money—there may be some risks you don't need to address because your organization decides they don't step over its defined risk threshold.

Guidance from the regulations and standards

Public Companies

Though this is implied in the process of risk assessment, public standards do not directly address the acceptance of risk.

Banking/Finance

FFIEC addresses the need for consideration of an organization's risk tolerance when determining mitigation of risks, but there really isn't much meat to the information presented there.

Healthcare and Life Sciences

HIPAA implies that risks must be reduced to an "appropriate level", which assumes risk acceptance by the organization.

General Guidance

COSO, CobiT, and other general standards address the need for a formal acceptance of risk. COSO goes one step further in suggesting that a risk assessment be applied to remaining residual risk, as well.

CobiT 4 ME4.5 calls for working with the board that works to establish IT policies to determine an organization's risk tolerance levels. Responsibilities for risk should be defined and assigned to employees. Part of creating the risk action plan should involve provisions for ensuring that IT management follows up risks the organization is exposed to and finds out their actual and potential business impact.

The **ISF Standard** § SM 3.3.6 calls for risk acceptance to be implied by the phrase "recommendations for actions to reduce risks to acceptable levels."

From regulation to reality – sure signs you are complying

Once you have developed a risk action plan, your next task is to determine the acceptable level of risk to your business and information security systems. This is often called residual risk. Once you have determined he risk, prioritize this risk from high to low. Then, address the risks in the order of priority.

Risks must be offset by appropriate means, to bring the risk to the "acceptable level" for your organization. This requires that you first determine what the acceptable level of risk is for your organization. This can be described as your organizational risk tolerance.

Document a list of actions that will reduce risks to acceptable levels. Include mitigation techniques and procedures and a variety of suggestions in case one or more options is not practical. A plan to attack residual risk can also be included in this document. These actions will then be formally recommended to management.

When selecting safeguards, do you prioritize them?

Before you rush out and start defending your organization from all the world's harms, figure out what needs the most protection. If money grew on trees you could probably skip this step, but as it doesn't, prepare yourself to make some difficult choices. You likely can't defend everything at the same level, if not for monetary reasons, then because sometimes it's just not feasible. For example, you could prevent attacks coming in from the internet by disabling internet altogether for employees. However this likely isn't going to work if people need to do web research or send emails. For best results, employ the following control objective when trying to decide what safeguards are most important to you:

> *Following the development of a risk action plan, the organization will prioritize the mitigation of risk—in other words, the organization will designate priority levels for all controls and security measures that will be implemented as a result of risk assessment.*

Once you define priority levels, you'll be able to defend yourself from the biggest threats first. Covering the smallest threats is at your organization's discretion and is likely based on your risk tolerance levels.

Guidance from the regulations and standards

Banking/Finance

In general, FFIEC Operations calls for a prioritization of risk mitigation actions and the security controls associated with them.

FFIEC Operations Pg. 13-14 specifically lists a set of safeguards banks should consider to manage and control risk. Safeguards include:

- Designing an information security program to control identified risks commensurate with the sensitivity of the information and the bank's activities.

- Adding access controls to customer information systems such as authentication, controls to prevent employees from providing customer information to unauthorized individuals.

- Access restrictions at physical locations containing customer information such as buildings, computer facilities and records storage facilities.

- Encryption of electronic customer info. including while in transit or storage on networks/systems to which unauthorized individuals may have access.

- Procedures designed to ensure that customer information system modifications are consistent with the bank's security program

- Dual control procedures, segregation of duties

- Monitoring of systems and procedures to detect actual and attempted attacks on or intrusions into customer information systems

- Response programs that specify actions to be taken when the bank suspects or detects that unauthorized individuals have gained access to customer information systems

- Measures to protect against destruction, loss or theft

- Training for staff to make them aware of security issues

- Regular testing of key controls, systems and procedures

FFIEC Information Security Pg. 11states that after collecting information about risks and threats the organization should prioritize them by importance. The importance of each item is determined by comparing it to the threshold set in the organization's security requirements and seeing whether it meets or exceeds that threshold. It is up to management to decide on each risk and the appropriate response.

FFIEC Operations Pg.13-14 further states that once risk and threat data has been collected, management should prioritize risks based on their probability of occurrence and their financial, reputational or legal impact to the institution. Organizational impacts include lost revenue, increased cost of insurance premiums, loss of market share, etc. When management prioritizes risks, they should consider which impacts are most important to the organization.

General Guidance

Most general standards call for safeguard selection and prioritization. For instance, CobiT calls for control measures with a high ROI to receive first priority.

The **ISF Standard** SM 3.3.7 states that when selecting safeguards management should consider all special security controls necessary for particular environments, then evaluate the cost of implementing security controls. Finally management should determine the limitations of the security controls selected and ascertain whether further controls or security is necessary.

When choosing safeguards for your organization, look at the way risks have been prioritized. The more risk, the sooner these risks need to receive attention. For instance, the highest-level risks require the most immediate attention, while lower-level risks can be addressed once the high-priority risks have been resolved.

It's management's responsibility to decide what security controls are necessary. This involves determining the cost of implementing and maintaining them and whether additional controls must be added to prevent certain risks or vulnerabilities.

A solid system of safeguards is possible when organizations take the time to consider the following safeguards:

- Adding access controls to customer information systems such as authentication, controls to prevent employees from providing customer information to unauthorized individuals.

- Access restrictions at physical locations containing customer information such as buildings, computer facilities and records storage facilities.

- Encryption of electronic customer information including while in transit or storage on networks/systems to which unauthorized individuals may have access.

- Procedures designed to ensure that customer information system modifications are consistent with the bank's security program.

- Dual control procedures, segregation of duties.

- Monitoring of systems and procedures to detect actual and attempted attacks on or intrusions into customer information systems.

- Response programs that specify actions to be taken when the bank suspects or detects that unauthorized individuals have gained access to customer information systems.

- Measures to protect against destruction, loss or theft.

- Training for staff to make them aware of security issues.

- Regular testing of key controls, systems and procedures.

Have you made a commitment to continual risk assessments?

Commitment isn't easy. But it is vital that you commit to continual risk assessments in your organization. If you don't do this, you will not have a good grasp of how the threats and vulnerabilities your organization faces are changing. As a result, you will not be able to adequately prepare to deal with them. Thus, the unified control objective for ensuring that risk assessments (and mitigation) are a continuous process within the organization reads:

> The organization will make a commitment to risk assessment as a regular tool for all business and security considerations, including implementation of controls and security measures, creation and definition of high-level IT plans, and in monitoring and evaluating mechanisms.

By making risk assessment dynamic, you become more readily able to adapt to any changes to risks that occur over time.

Guidance from the regulations and standards

Public Companies

Public standards do not directly address an ongoing commitment to risk assessment, but do define the auditor's role in relation to risk assessment.

Banking/Finance

FFIEC calls for an ongoing risk assessment process all business processes and the control measures associated with them.

FFIEC Management Pg. 15calls for a commitment to an excellent risk assessment program to be demonstrated by those organizations that ensure that they have:

- An effective planning process aligning IT and business objectives

- An ongoing risk assessment process

- Technology implementation procedures including appropriate controls

- Measurement and monitoring efforts that identify ways to manage risk exposure

Risks associated with IT environments should be assessed from multiple perspectives:

- If the IT department is a centralized function, management should centralize risk management efforts

- If the IT function is decentralized, and business units manage the risk, then management should coordinate risk management efforts through common organization-wide expectations

International Standards Organization

ISO 17799 § ix calls for a commitment to good risk assessment that involves not only carrying out a risk assessment but committing to making them periodic occurrences. Each new assessment should take into consideration the findings of previous assessments alongside new discoveries.

In general, an assessment should involve determining the business harm likely to result from a security failure, taking into account the potential consequences of a loss of confidentiality, integrity or availability of the information and other assets. It should also involve examining the realistic likelihood of such a failure occurring in the light of prevailing threats and vulnerabilities, and the controls currently implemented.

General Guidance

COSO and CobiT both call for a commitment to risk assessment. Risk assessment should be an iterative process built into an organization's infrastructure, and utilized whenever possible to mitigate and manage risk effectively.

The **ISF Standard** § SM 3.3.3 states that a commitment to high quality risk assessment means an organization will ensure that risk assessments are performed periodically and involve representatives from key areas, IT specialists, key user representatives and experts in risk analysis and information security.

From regulation to reality – sure signs you are complying

Make a commitment to risk assessment as a regular tool for all business and security considerations. This includes implementing controls and security measures, creating and defining high-level IT plans, and monitoring and evaluating mechanisms.

Commitment is demonstrated by those organizations that have established:

- An effective monitoring process aligning IT and business objectives

- An ongoing risk assessment process

- Technology implementation procedures including appropriate controls

- Measurement and monitoring efforts that identify ways to manage risk exposure

A commitment to risk assessments also includes involving representatives from key areas, such as IT specialists, key user representatives, and experts in risk analysis and information security. Additionally, risks associated with IT environments need to be assessed from multiple perspectives. Each new assessment should take into consideration the previous findings and look at them alongside new findings and discoveries

Continuous Monitoring and Measurement

This is the last chapter in this saga, and now that you've gotten this far its time to lay one last story on you about the best technology every invented. Carl Reiner and Mel Brooks, two of the funniest comedians to ever live, do a skit about a 2,000 year old man being interviewed. Carl Reiner is the interviewer and Mel Brooks is the 2,000 year old man.

Reiner: "In your 2,000 years of life, what's the greatest technological invention you've ever seen?"

Brooks thinks for a moment, and then looks up with great enthusiasm "The Thermos!"

"The *thermos*" Reiner questions? "How could the thermos be the greatest technological invention? We've sent men to the moon. We've cured Polio. We've mapped the human genome. How does the thermos compare to these?" he asked.

"Simple" replied Brooks. "The thermos keeps hot things hot, and cold things cold" he said matter-of-factly.

"So **what**" quizzed Reiner. "What's so great about that?"

Brooks looked at him with a wry deadpan, his face then grew with excitement "how does it *know?*" he exclaimed.

The Main Thing

The Main Thing for regulatory compliance is that *we know*. It's one thing to build a ship and ensure that it will be seaworthy. It's another to continually monitor it once its in the water to ensure that there aren't any leaks or breakages. Your IT staff will more than likely be very good at building their systems. But in all of the years this authoring team has spent being a part of the IT world, what we know is that the collective "IT we" haven't been that great at continuous monitoring and measurement because it can (and does) get tedious. But it has to be done. Here's the checklist for this chapter.

❏ Establish the need for continuous monitoring and measurement within IT's systems and all business systems IT manages.

❏ Begin actively collecting monitoring data if you aren't doing so already.

❏ Ensure that your security testing program (and the associated ongoing monitoring) is in place.

❏ If you aren't collecting compliance monitoring and auditing data, you'll need to identify it and begin collecting it.

❏ You'll also need to conduct risk monitoring as a part of your overall monitoring and logging program.

❏ If the regulations you fall under call for it, you'll need to collect customer satisfaction monitoring information.

❏ Your monitoring and logging operations won't be worth a plugged nickel unless you formalize your performance assessment framework.

❏ Evidential weight of information and technology: the organization will assess the evidential weight of information, information processes, and information technology, and will ensure that all data files recording access, unwanted access, and daily use of your systems are tamperproof. The organization will regularly inspect the material in these files for accuracy, and keep track of daily information processing functions to ensure these are not being corrupted either.

❏ The job isn't finished unless you are creating your management reports in a way that management can understand them and take action on them.

❏ Finally, you'll need to report your monitoring statistics and follow-up activities to the Board of Directors or leadership of the organization if you don't have a board.

Why do you need monitoring and measurement?

We all want our IT organizations to function like a well-oiled machine – they should be in excellent working order, producing high-quality services for our business units with little or no downtime or corruption. So how do you ensure your IT organization is the well-oiled machine of which we speak versus a broken down old rust heap? You monitor it. You monitor for risks, threats, vulnerabilities, and for compliance. You measure the input and output of business transactions. You test all of the inputs and outputs to ensure that your processes are as efficient as possible. Therefore, the control objective for this section is:

> *In order to promote accuracy and integrity in information systems and business functions, the organization must monitor and measure these functions to ensure they are up-to-date and working effectively. Continuous monitoring should be instituted to ensure compliance with regulations and organizational policies.*

And if it turns out your organization needs a little fixing up, never fear. We can rebuild it. We have the technology. Okay, bad play on words there.

Guidance from the regulations and standards

Public Companies

Monitoring measurement is addressed by nearly all of the public company regulations. **Sarbanes-Oxley** § 104 specifically requires the Board to "conduct [a] program of inspections to assess the degree of compliance" for each public accounting firm. SOX is specific in addressing the requirement of a monitoring program, without stating why such a program is necessary. SOX also discusses monitoring in other contexts, such as monitoring staff compliance with internal ethics standards, and reporting monitoring results to the board.

PCAOB § 49 addresses the need for monitoring and measurement by stating that management conducts monitoring because it is necessary to detect material misstatements in accounts and disclosures and other related assertions of financial statements.

SAS 94 does not specifically address the need for monitoring and measurement but in §319.07(e) states that monitoring is a process that assesses the quality of internal control performance over time.

The **AICPA/CICA Privacy Statement**, §10, discusses monitoring in the context of privacy, stating that it is necessary for an organization to monitor compliance with its privacy policies and procedures. The **AICPA Suitable Trust Services Criteria ¶ 17 § 4.0** addresses the need for monitoring by stating that an organization should monitor the system and take action to maintain compliance with its defined system security policies.

NASD/NYSE

These regulations do not specifically address the need for monitoring and measurement, but the SEC regulations **17 CFR 240.17a-4 & Ad-7** address compliance monitoring and auditing as a necessary function. See the Compliance Monitoring and Auditing section of this Chapter for more information on this specific topic.

Banking/Finance

Once again, we find that the Banking and Finance Regulations have a plethora of information on the need for monitoring and measurement. Specifically, **Basel II ¶ 689** explains that a fundamental element of sound capital assessment is instituting a process of "internal controls, reviews, and audits to ensure the integrity of the overall management process."

The **Sound Practices of Operational Risk**, Principal 4, identifies the need for monitoring as a major component of risk management. This process includes self assessments and measurement using benchmarks and scorecards as indicators of where an organization is on the spectrum of risk.

Gramm-Leach Bliley's counterpart regulation, **16 CFR § 314.4(e)**, establishes the need for monitoring and measurement by stating that results of testing and monitoring are used to evaluate an information security program. In other words, in order to assess whether an information security program is effective, it first needs to be monitored and measurements must be taken so that accurate assessments of adjustments can be made.

All of the FFIEC Handbooks discuss monitoring and measurement in one way or another. But, only one specifically referenced the need for monitoring and measurement. **FFIEC Information Security**, Pg. 82 frames the need for monitoring and measurement as a tool that provides the basis for updating risk assessments, strategies, and implemented controls. Specifically, it states that a "static security program provides a false sense of security and will become increasingly ineffective over time (FFIEC Pg. 82)." Monitoring and updating is key in what is called a "cyclical security process." In this ongoing process, organizations should continuously gather and evaluate information regarding new threats and vulnerabilities, actual attacks, and effectiveness of existing controls.

FFIEC Management is also detailed on the topic of monitoring and measurement. While the need for monitoring and measurement is not specifically addressed, activities such as establishing benchmarks, reviewing business plan goals and strategies, and implementing a quality assurance program to monitor and test products and practices are encouraged (FFIEC Management Pg. 33).

Healthcare and Life Sciences

HIPAA touches generally on establishing a monitoring operation, but doesn't go into detail concerning the need for a monitoring and measurement program. It does require that procedures are implemented to "regularly review records of information security activity" (HIPPA 45 CFR 164.308(a)(1)(ii)(D)).

Credit Card

While the consumer facing standards have a great deal to say about monitoring and measurement, they do not specifically address the *need* for monitoring and measurement. **VISA CISP** § 9.2.1-7 has a great deal of information on collecting monitoring data, such as specifics on monitoring accesses to cardholder data, tracking invalid logging attempts, and reviewing accesses to audit trails. For more information on collecting monitoring data, see the Collecting Monitoring Data section in this Chapter.

US Federal Security

While FISMA does not establish the need for monitoring and measurement, **FISMA** § 3545 calls for annual evaluations of information security programs and practice.

The **Clinger-Cohen Act** § 5113(b)(4) states that periodic reviews are necessary in order to "ascertain the efficiency and effectiveness of information technology in improving the performance of the executive agency and the accomplishment of missions of the executive agency."

FISCAM does not address the need for monitoring and measurement specifically either, but it does state that compliance monitoring is an important part of management's role (FISCAM SP-3.1).

GAO 260.48 explains that monitoring is important because it is necessary for the assessment of internal control performance.

Records Management

ISO 15489-1 § 10 addresses the need for monitoring and measurement in the realm of compliance monitoring. Compliance monitoring is important because it ensures that "records systems procedures and processes are being implemented according to the organizational policies and requirements and that they meet anticipated outcomes" (ISO 15489-1 § 10). ISO 15489-2 § 5 also addresses the need for monitoring and measurement by stating that there are three reasons for monitoring and auditing records systems: "to ensure compliance with the organization's established standards; to ensure that records will be accepted as evidence in a court of law, should this be required; and to improve an organizations performance" (ISO 15489-2 §5).

DIRKS § G 4.1.5 establishes a monitoring and auditing strategy, necessary to assess recordkeeping performance. According to DIRKS, this kind of monitoring helps ensure organizational accountability.

NIST Special Publications

NIST 800-53 CA-7 states that an organization must monitor the security controls in the information system on an ongoing basis. These activities include ongoing assessments of security controls, security impact analyses of system changes, and status reporting.

International Standards Organization

ISO 17799 § 9.7 states that the reason monitoring and measurement is needed is to "detect deviation from access control policy and record monitorable events to provide evidence in the case of security incidents. System monitoring allows the effectiveness of controls adopted to be checked and conformity to an access policy model to be verified."

General Guidance

The general standards could not be left out of this discussion, as many of them address the need for monitoring and measurement. COSO ERM encourages monitoring the effectiveness of enterprise risk management in the ordinary course of running the organization. Some examples of monitoring activities include variance analysis, stress testing, comparisons, reconciliations and other routine actions.

The ISF Standard SM 7.1 suggests that monitoring and measurement is necessary to "provide individuals who are responsible for particular IT environments, and top management, with an independent assessment of the security condition of these environments."

EU Guidance

The **OECD Risk Checklist** I.14 states that monitoring and measurement is necessary to ensure that "adequate safeguarding controls exist over networks and customer data."

United Kingdom and Canadian Guidance

The **Combined Code** § C2 states the need for monitoring and measurement as the Board's responsibility to maintain a sound system of internal controls, including review and revision of these controls as necessary to maintain compliance. Finally, the Turnbull Guidance ¶ 21 states monitoring is necessary for the continued effectiveness of the system of internal control. **BS 15000-2** § 4.3 states that monitoring and measuring is needed to ensure that the service management objectives and plan are being achieved.

From regulation to reality – sure signs you are complying

We're at step one in the *understand* phase of your action plan right now. All you are trying to do at this point is determine how monitoring and measurement fit within your organizational strategy and how it aligns with your business and compliance goals.

You'll want to touch on the monitoring of all of your key applications, security monitoring, customer satisfaction monitoring, whatever it is that you are required to monitor and ask the simple question – are we *currently monitoring this*? If yes, you'll need to ascertain if your monitoring practices meet compliance standards (which we'll talk about next).

There's a ton of guidance from most of the regulations and standards for monitoring and measurement. Your action plan's first step is to sit down with your auditors and find out what it is *they* are looking for in monitoring and measurement.

Once you've checked the guidance, you are ready to move on to the next step.

Have you established overall monitoring and logging of key concepts?

Monitoring and measurement of operations should be continuous. Information gathering and analysis regarding new threats and vulnerabilities is key to proper information system upkeep and protection. You have to keep your eyes on operations to ensure that the existing security controls are effective and actual attacks are handled appropriately. The control objective for this section is:

> *The organization will establish overall monitoring and logging of key concepts. Ideally, the monitoring and measurement controls should include four key concepts — measurement, traceability, thoroughness and frequency.*

Each of these areas will be defined in greater detail in this section.

Guidance from the regulations and standards

Public Companies

Several of the public companies' standards address the key concepts. Sarbanes Oxley calls for a continuing program of inspections to assess compliance. Frequency depends on the number of issuers. **PCAOB** requires management to assess the effectiveness of the company's internal control and base this assessment on a control framework that permits reasonably consistent qualitative and quantitative measurements of a company's internal control and is sufficiently complete. **SAS 94** calls for the establishment and monitoring of internal controls. Management is to determine whether the controls are operating as intended and modify them appropriately for changing conditions. The **AICPA Suitable Trust Services Criteria** calls for monitoring of the system and maintained compliance with defined system security policies. The **AICPA/CICA Privacy Framework** calls for monitoring of privacy policies and procedures.

Banking/Finance

Basel II calls for a process of internal controls, reviews, and audit to ensure the integrity of the overall management process. The **Sound Practices for the Management** and **Supervision of Operational Risk** calls for the implementation of a regular monitoring process, and frequency should reflect the risks involved and the frequency and nature of changes in the operating environment.

The **FFIEC Information Security Handbook** explains that financial institutions should continuously gather and analyze information regarding new threats and vulnerabilities, actual attacks on the institution or others, and the effectiveness of the existing security control. They should then use the information to update the risk assessment, strategy, and implemented controls. Effective monitoring of threats includes both technical and non-technical sources.

The Handbook also addresses the four key concepts. In reference to measurement, it calls for institutions to design tests to produce results that are more logical and objective. Results that are reduced to metrics are potentially more precise and less subject to confusion, as well as being more readily tracked over time. Further, test results that indicate an unacceptable risk in an institution's security should be traceable to actions subsequently taken to reduce the risk of an unacceptable level. The scope of testing should be adequately thorough and encompass all systems in the institution's production environment and contingency plans and those systems within the institution that provide access to the production environment. Finally, testing should be frequent, based on the risk that controls are no longer functioning.

The **FFIEC Management Handbook** also provides detail on the key concepts and is consistent with the **Information Security Handbook**.

Healthcare and Life Sciences

HIPAA calls for implementation of procedures to regularly review records of information security activity.

NIST 800-66 An Introductory Resource Guide for Implementing the Health Insurance Portability and Accountability Act (HIPAA) Security Rule 4.15 is intended to match up with § 164.312(b) from the HIPAA Standard. This section discusses how to meet the HIPAA objective of implementing "hardware, software and procedural mechanisms that record and examine activity in information systems that contain or use electronic protected health information" by providing a series of key activities to handle. The material is very detailed, and should be reviewed directly.

Credit Card

Visa CISP calls for the establishment of a process for linking all data access activities to an individual user or system.

US Federal Security

Several of the government regulations address this topic area. **FISMA** calls for an annual independent evaluation testing the effectiveness of information security policies, procedures, and practices.

The **GAO Financial Audit Manual** calls for the construction of efficient tests, taking into consideration the nature, timing, and extent of the tests to be performed.

Records Management

ISO 15489-1, **ISO 15489-2**, and **DIRKS** all call for regular monitoring and auditing of the record keeping system to assess its performance.

NIST Special Publications

NIST 800-53 calls for the regular review and analysis of audit records for indications of inappropriate of unusual activity, and investigation of suspicious activity or violations.

International Standards Organization

ISO 17799 calls for monitoring system access and use, and the logging of events to ensure the effectiveness of controls.

The IT Infrastructure Library

ITIL Best Practice for Security Management 4.2.4.2 calls for monitoring and auditing information system access and use. Recommended measures include audit trails that warn of suspicious events, monitoring system use and generating warnings if established limits are exceeded, clock synchronization and setting up a procedure for staff to handle and communicate reports from anti-virus software that it has blocked an attempt at a virus infection.

General Guidance

COSO ERM calls for ongoing monitoring activities and evaluations to assess the presence and functioning of an organization's components over time. Evaluations of enterprise risk management vary in scope and frequency, depending on the significance of risks and importance of the risk responses and related controls in managing the risks.

CobiT 4 ME1.1 states that organizations should ensure that management creates a general monitoring framework and approach defining the scope, methodology and process to be followed for monitoring IT's contribution to the results of the organizations portfolio and program management processes.

The **ISF Standard of Good Practice for Information Security** calls for monitoring and security reviews to be conducted frequently and thoroughly to ensure that controls are effective enough to reduce risk to acceptable levels.

EU Guidance

The OECD Risk Checklist calls for identification, monitoring, measuring, and control of electronic security risks.

United Kingdom and Canadian Guidance

The **Combined Code of Corporate Governance** calls for maintaining a sound system of internal control with at least an annual review of the internal control system. The **Turnbull Guidance** explains that the system of internal control should be imbedded in the operations of the company and form part of its culture. Additionally, the internal control should be capable of responding quickly to evolving risks in the business and should be performed on a continuous basis.

BS 15000-2 includes the objective to monitor, measure and review to ensure that the service management objectives and plan are being achieved.

From regulation to reality – sure signs you are complying

Where we are in the action plan is a combination of risk assessment and policy creation – assessing whether or not our monitoring program is capturing the right information, determining where the gaps are in what you are capturing, and then creating the policies that will enable your team to capture the correct data.

There are four key logging and monitoring concepts; Measurement, Traceability, Thoroughness, and Frequency. Your action plan is now in the "risk assessment" phase because you are going to want to analyze if your logging and monitoring processes and procedures correctly include each of these four concepts. You'll want to examine every monitoring operation you have for their measurement, traceability, thoroughness, and frequency.

Measurement

You must measure and interpret test results and activity logs as a crucial step in monitoring. Base your assessment of internal controls on a control framework that permits reasonably consistent qualitative and quantitative measurements. Reducing test results to metrics is advised in order to facilitate ease of tracking, simplicity and accuracy. Based on these tests, management can monitor the effectiveness of internal controls and make changes accordingly.

Traceability

You don't want to conduct logging operations or tests if the result will not show you where a particular action occurred and, if applicable, by whom. In other words, test results and logging should be traceable to actions taken by a particular user or program. Further, test results that indicate an unacceptable level of risk in security should be traceable to actions subsequently taken to reduce the risk.

Thoroughness

It doesn't make much sense to conduct tests if you are not going to be thorough. In fact, the scope of testing and logging should be adequately thorough. All systems in your organization's production environment and contingency plans and those that provide access to the production environment should be tested regularly. It is not enough to test some aspects of your system. Instead, you must test everything that contains potential risk.

Frequency

The frequency of testing will vary, depending on the significance of risks and importance of the risk responses and related risk management controls. Testing frequency will also vary for different organizations with different needs. At a very minimum, testing must occur every time a change is instituted. Establish procedures with concrete testing intervals based on organizational needs and system risk.

Do you actively collect monitoring data?

Monitoring data, if collected properly, enables you to see whether your log files are secure, identify and respond to security incidents quickly, and enforce IT compliance across your organization. What makes collecting monitoring data difficult is deciding what you want to monitor, and what to do with the information once you collect it, which means that you are going to need to create a "normal" benchmark of what your organization deems to be acceptable performance so that you can see both upward and downward trends. The control objective for this section is:

> *The organization will collect monitoring data. This includes determining the key areas of an organization's system that require monitoring, as well as the benchmarks each area must meet in order to be operating smoothly. The benchmarks enable the organization to use the collected monitoring data effectively.*

The best benchmarks are created using internal and external sources. As a simple case in point, we had a publishing client awhile ago that we collected application speed performance data for. Each month, around deadline time, many of the staff would complain that the system wasn't functioning properly and was "slow." Because we had all of the performance data, we were able to pinpoint the problem. It wasn't with the system. It was in the users' delusional head. It seems that their idea of the system being slow was proportional to the amount of time they were behind in their deadlines. The system was performing normally – it was only because they were trying to rush tasks that they thought it was slow. Drawing on criteria from both internal benchmarks and industry practice benchmarks gives you the chance to see what's directly important to your organization versus what other organizations find useful.

In terms of security monitoring, the "benchmarks" we're talking about are called "attack signatures." Your staff's ability to see which attacks are hitting them is directly based on their ability to define the attack against known signatures.

Guidance from the regulations and standards

Public Companies

SAS 94 calls for assessing the design and operation of controls by monitoring ongoing activities and through separate assessments. Much of the monitoring data is produced through the entities information system.

Banking/Finance

The **FFIEC Information Security Handbook** instructs financial institutions to identify the system components that warrant logging, determine the level of data logged for each component, and establish policies for handling and analyzing log files. Financial institutions should take reasonable steps to ensure that sufficient data is collected from secure log files to identify and respond to security incidents and to monitor and enforce policy compliance. Appropriate logging controls ensure that security personnel can review and analyze log data to identify unauthorized access attempts and security violations.

The **FFIEC Management Handbook** also discusses collecting monitoring data. Financial institutions should establish performance benchmarks or standards for IT functions and monitor them on a regular basis.

Credit Card

VISA CISP calls for implementation of automated audit trails to reconstruct the following events: all accesses to cardholder data; all actions taken by any individual with root administrative privileges; access to all audit trails; invalid logical access attempts; use of identification and authentication mechanisms; initialization of audit logs; and, creation and deletion of system level objectives.

US Federal Security

NIST 800-53 calls for a plan of action and milestones for the information system that documents the organization's planned, implemented, and evaluated remedial actions to correct any deficiencies noted during the assessment of the security controls, and to reduce or eliminate known vulnerabilities in the system.

The **Clinger-Cohen Act** requires the means to be provided to senior management to obtain timely information, including a system of milestones for measuring progress, on an independently verifiable basis, in terms of cost, capability of the system to meet specified requirements, timeliness, and quality.

FISCAM calls for access to audit trails and the logging of invalid **access** attempts.

Records Management

The records management standards generally do not address collecting monitoring data. However, **DIRKS** calls for the specification of objective, verifiable and quantifiable performance indicators used to analyze efficiency and effectiveness.

NIST Special Publications

NIST 800-14 requires access to all audit trails be made available.

General Guidance

CobiT 3 is instructive on the subject of collecting monitoring data. It explains that for the IT and internal control processes, management should ensure relevant performance indicators (benchmarks) from both internal and external sources are being defined, and that data is being collected for the creation of management information reports and exception reports regarding these indicators. Controls should also be aimed at validating the propriety and integrity of both organizational and individual measures and indicators.

CobiT 4 ME1.2 recommends ensuring that IT management work to define a balanced set of performance objectives, measures, targets and benchmarks in accordance with business goals and objectives.

EU Guidance

The **OECD Risk Checklist** calls for the logging of all invalid access attempts.

United Kingdom and Canadian Guidance

BS 15000-2 calls for the monitoring and measurement of achievement against defined service targets.

From regulation to reality – sure signs you are complying

You are now at the implementation stage of your action plan. You should now be focused on the active collection of monitoring data.

Collecting monitoring data includes the use of audit trails. An audit trail will collect and log the data to be reviewed by your IT staff and appropriate management. The first thing you need to do is determine the system components that warrant logging. The following events are examples of the system components that should be logged:

- All accesses to customer or sensitive data.
- All actions taken by an individual with root administrative privileges.
- All accesses to the audit trails themselves.
- Any invalid logical access attempts.
- Use of identification and authentication mechanisms.
- Initialization of the audit logs.
- Creation and deletion of system level objectives.

Let's go back a minute to the introduction, wherein we discussed the network of systems that your organization is employing, Collecting data on every device within the network would only provide a cacophony of reports, drowning out the key information that you really want to hear about. What you'll want to do is work with the IT staff to possibly split up their monitoring tasks into reporting groups, for instance a security reporting group that would monitor such things as firewalls, intrusion detection devices, and anti-virus measures on one hand, and key applications on the other. In the sample network diagram immediately below, we show five key security points for monitoring information. This list isn't meant to be the "be-all-to-end-all" list, merely a discussion point for you and your IT staff.

Security monitoring points of interest

1. The most outside devices you have, your border routers (whether they are connected to the Internet or they are WiFi routers), will provide key security information as it is the first to be able to detect incoming attacks.

2. Your border and interior firewalls will also provide key monitoring information as they provide a hefty security role.

3. Anti-virus software is crucial to monitor in all locations as it will tell you where infections are starting and where they've spread to.

4. Your managed hubs and switches can also be monitored for performance and problems.

5. And finally (for this list anyway), your intrusion detection systems need to be monitored for any attacks, whether they be from the external world or from your own folks.

You'll also need to plan on monitoring your key applications. Again, for discussion purposes here, we'll show the sample network diagram and list a few of the applications that you might want to consider monitoring.

Monitoring key applications

1. Of course you'll want to monitor all of your key front, middle, and back office applications. As the regulations suggest, you'll want to monitor them for activity, input, and output to ensure that they are working properly.

2. Your mail server should be monitored if you are sending critical or secure information through it, or if the regulations require you to do so.

3. Same thing for your web server.

4. Many organizations are also using intranets and workgroup application servers such as Microsoft's Sharepoint. A great many Sarbanes-Oxley, HIPAA, and 21 CFR-based workflow systems are being built to work with these types of servers. So if you have them, you should be adding them to your monitoring list.

5. Another key server you should be monitoring is your directory server. This can take the form of LDAP (lightweight directory access protocol), DNS (domain name server), or your Microsoft Active Directory server. The reason that you'll want to check and ensure that they are being monitored is to ensure that they have the right listings (people and services attributed to your company) and especially that they are removing the wrong listings (people and services that are *no longer* attributed to your company).

6. Finally, you might even want to monitor your patching and update servers to ensure that your folks are actively keeping up with the most current patches and security updates.

In addition to choosing what to monitor, you need to identify performance indicators for each system. A performance indicator gives meaning to your monitoring data— it tells you what to analyze collected data for. Each performance indicator, or benchmark, should be defined using both internal and external sources. Once the data has been collected, use both the data and the benchmarks to create management information reports. This kind of detailed monitoring and cross-referencing will help your organization identify potential problems areas as well as provide assurance that objectives are being met. We'll delve deeper into the security monitoring and compliance monitoring aspects in the next two sections.

Is your security testing program in place?

Having a security program in place is not enough. Just like every other aspect of an information system, your security program must undergo ongoing tests and monitoring as well. Your security program is what keeps everything else in the organization safe from outside attacks and inside blunders. Letting it deteriorate due to lack of monitoring and assessment will only ensure harm comes to the organization. Don't make any assumptions about whether your risk mitigation strategy and implementation is working. Instead, follow this control objective and rest assured knowing your security program is in prime form:

> *In order to promote the integrity and availability of security devices and to validate security systems, the organization will make a continuous assessment of the risks to the system. Because tests only measure a security posture at one time, frequent testing is recommended.*

Creating a security testing program is what this section is all about. So read on for tips and guidance to ensure that your security testing program is up to par.

Guidance from the regulations and standards

Public Companies

The **AICPA/CICA Privacy Framework** calls for the periodic undertaking of threat and vulnerability testing. This includes security penetration reviews and Web vulnerability and resistance testing. The **AICPA Suitable Trust Services Criteria** requires that the organization's security system is periodically reviewed and compared with the defined system security policies. The information security team monitors the system and assesses the system vulnerabilities using proprietary and other tools. Potential risk is evaluated and compared to service level agreements and other obligations of the organization.

Banking/Finance

The **FFIEC Information Security Handbook** has an abundance of information on security testing. It explains that financial institutions should gain assurance of the adequacy of their risk mitigation strategy and implementation by: basing their testing plan, test selection, and test frequency on the risk posed to systems by non-functioning controls; establishing controls to mitigate risks posed to systems from testing; and using test results to evaluate whether security objectives are met.

The Handbook calls for the use of both penetration testing and assessments. The benefit of penetration testing is that it allows the administrator to identify the extent to which a system can be compromised before the attack is identified and assess the response mechanism's effectiveness. Penetration tests are generally of a comprehensive test of the system's security and should be used along with other tests, such as assessments and audits.

Credit Card

VISA CISP calls for the establishment of a process to identify newly discovered security vulnerabilities, and standards should be updated to address new vulnerability issues. VISA requires testing of security controls, limitations, network connections, and restrictions routinely to make sure they can adequately identify or stop any unauthorized access attempts. Internal vulnerability scans should be run at least quarterly. Finally, security and firewall logs should be reviewed daily.

MasterCard SDP calls for penetration testing on a quarterly basis to confirm that the system is operating at adequate security levels.

US Federal Security

FISMA calls for the periodic evaluation and testing of information security controls and techniques to ensure that they are effectively implemented.

The **Clinger-Cohen Act** encourages reviews of security controls, due to the fact that the security system will degrade over time. Reviews should ensure that management, operational, personnel, and technical controls all function effectively. This can be done by an independent audit or by a internal self-review. Technical tools such as virus scanners, vulnerability assessment products, and penetration testing can be used.

FISCAM explains that management should periodically assess the appropriateness of security policies and compliance with them. Periodic assessments are an important means of identifying areas of noncompliance.

US Internal Revenue Service

The **IRS Revenue Procedure 97-22** and **98-25** require periodic checks to make sure that security standards are maintained.

NIST Special Publications

NIST 800-53 requires an assessment of the security controls in the information system to determine if the controls are implemented correctly, operating as intended, and producing the desired outcome with respect to meeting the security requirements for the system.

International Standards Organization

ISO 17799 requires regular review by management of security systems. Information systems should be regularly checked for compliance with security implementation standards. Compliance checking also covers penetration testing. This is useful for checking for vulnerabilities in the system and for checking how effective the controls are at preventing unauthorized access.

US State Laws

CA 1386 requires periodic penetration testing to determine the effectiveness of systems and staff procedures in detecting and responding to security breaches.

EU Guidance

The **OECD Risk Checklist** calls for both vulnerability testing and penetration testing. The penetration tests should assess both external and insider threats. The ISF Standard calls for a comprehensive assessment of the security of the enterprise. Additionally, penetration tests should be performed.

From regulation to reality – sure signs you are complying

A good monitoring and measurement program cannot be implemented without security testing. As we have mentioned in other chapters, IT security is crucial to the functioning of your organization. You have to know the strengths and weaknesses of your system in order to make the system stronger and less vulnerable to attacks.

Include procedures for assessment tests and penetration testing in your security-testing program. An assessment test is a study to locate vulnerabilities and identify corrective actions. This can include testing security controls to make sure they are functioning and effective. Security controls need to be tested, because even the best security systems can degrade over time. Based on the results of the assessment test, standards should be updated to address these vulnerability issues.

Penetration testing is also crucial to the effectiveness of your security system. A penetration test will actually simulate an attack on the system, to see if it is possible for a hacker to get through. These tests are simulations of real world attacks, but they are conducted and monitored by security personnel. If your security can be penetrated, this is an indication that you have security weaknesses that need to be fixed.

Include policies in your security-testing program about the frequency of testing as well as the distinctive kinds of tests to use. Specifically determine how often to test and what kinds of tests to use. Also document the results of previous tests and risks posed to the system. Schedule testing as frequent as is necessary for your organization to maintain optimal security. Once you have evaluated whether or not security controls are being met, you can adjust the program accordingly.

Do you conduct compliance monitoring and auditing?

Compliance with regulations and standards is what this is all about. And this book exists to help make compliance less painful. But it is not enough to just be compliant during one audit, say on a Tuesday at 2:00 in the afternoon. You have to monitor for compliance *continuously* to avoid liability and unnecessary regulatory sanctions. Take a look at the following control objective for starters:

> The organizations will maintain an adequate internal control structure. This includes an assessment of organizational and employee compliance with the security policy and other laws, regulations, and controls on a regular basis. Internal monitoring as well as external auditing should be provided for.

Compliance is about more than regulations and standards and getting by with as little as possible. Okay, so maybe there's a lot of that last part there. Compliance also involves adhering to organizational policies of internal control measures for critical systems. Keep reading for insight into compliance monitoring and auditing.

Guidance from the regulations and standards

Public Companies

Most of the public companies' standards at least touch on compliance monitoring and auditing. **Sarbanes Oxley** calls for management assessment of internal controls, including both maintaining an adequate internal control structure and assessing the structure annually. **PCAOB** calls for the monitoring of internal control activities. **SAS 94** explains that control activities are policies and procedures that help ensure that management directives are carried out and discusses the effectiveness of monitoring the internal control structure.

The **AICPA/CICA Privacy Framework** calls for compliance with privacy policies and procedures, commitments and applicable laws, regulations, service agreements, and other contracts. This compliance is reviewed and documented and the results of such reviews are reported to management.

NASD/NYSE

17 CFR 240.17a-4 and 240.17Ad-7 call for an audit system to be in place providing for accountability regarding inputting of records required to be maintained. The results of the audit system must be available and preserved.

Banking/Finance

Basel II explains that the bank's internal structure is essential to the capital assessment process. Effective control of the capital assessment process includes independent audit review, and where appropriate, the involvement of internal and external audits.

The Appendix of 12 CFR 30 calls for regular testing of key controls, systems and procedures of the information security program. The FFIEC Audit Handbook calls the IT audit staff to independently and objectively assess the controls, reliability, and integrity of the institution's internal IT environment. Both day-to-day controls and plans and procedures should be assessed.

The FFIEC Management Handbook also addresses compliance monitoring and auditing. Financial institutions should develop, implement, and monitor a process that measures IT compliance against their established policies, standards, and practices. In addition to internal audits, financial institutions should perform self assessments on a regular basis. The scope and frequency of self assessment should depend on historical performance.

Credit Card

VISA CISP calls for securing and preservation of audit trails. Additionally, audit trail history should be retained for a period that is consistent with its effective use, as well as legal regulations. MasterCard SDP requires the assessment of organizational and employee compliance with security standards on a regular basis.

US Internal Revenue Service

The IRS Revenue Procedure 97-22 calls for taxpayers' electronic storage systems to be in compliance with recordkeeping regulations.

US Federal Security

GAO Audit Manual requires compliance with applicable laws and regulations. Transactions are to be executed in accordance with laws, regulations and government policies identified in the audit guidance.

NIST Special Publications

NIST 800-14 calls for audit trails to be protected from unauthorized access.

General Guidance

CobiT has an abundance of information on compliance monitoring and auditing. First, an assessment if internal agency control adequacy must be accomplished. This includes internal control monitoring, the timely operation of internal controls, internal control level reporting, and operational security and internal control assurance. Next, independent assurance must be obtained. Finally, an independent audit must be provided for. Audit results are to be made available in the form of a report.

The **ISF Standard of Good Practices** calls for frequent monitoring and auditing of security controls.

EU Guidance

CA 1386 calls for the promotion and awareness of security and privacy policies.

United Kingdom and Canadian Guidance

The **Combined Code on corporate Governance**, the **Turnbull Guidance**, and the **Smith Guidance** all call for internal audit or other monitoring process, so that the company may assure itself and the board that the system of internal control is functioning as intended.

From regulation to reality – sure signs you are complying

To determine how compliant your organization is with your policies and procedures as well as laws, regulations and controls, you need to assess them on a regular basis. Hence, this action plan is smack in the middle of the implementation phase. Thorough assessments include internal monitoring and having an external audit of your compliance controls performed. The results of monitoring and auditing should be preserved and provided to management for review. In the event that changes need to be made, management can implement them.

An internal control is nothing more than a policy or procedure that will be examined during management's assessment or an audit to determine if it complies with your organization's policies and procedures and the appropriate laws and regulations. Each control is assessed on the way it supports the overall internal control structure and how compliant it is. The internal control structure itself, which involves the processes for how new controls are created and how existing controls are maintained or removed, is also examined to determine how compliant it is with privacy policies, procedures, commitments, applicable laws, regulations, service agreements and other contracts.

Along with examining your organization's policies and procedures, you will want to review your system monitoring logs and audit trails to ensure they have not been tampered with, and that they too are compliant with appropriate laws and regulations.

Reports made on everything, from the functioning of internal controls, to system monitoring, audit trails and operational security must also be reviewed to ensure they are written up correctly and contain accurate information.

Determining how often to review your controls, systems and documentation for compliance depends upon your past performance. If you've always done well with compliance, you may not need to run checks as often as an organization that hasn't done well in the past. Then again, you may do so well with compliance because you put in the effort to check up on your organization regularly. Decide what works best.

Do you conduct risk monitoring?

It is one thing to do a risk assessment. It is a whole other thing to actually monitor risks and determine which risks pose immediate threats, which risks are being eliminated, and which risks are in between. In order to effectively monitor risks, we recommend you create a risk monitoring program as well as apply the following control objective:

> To ensure that established controls are functioning properly, the organization will institute regular risk monitoring. Self-assessments of the control environment can lead to an early solution to any potential problems.

Risk monitoring will help you manage risks more efficiently. This section will guide you through the risk monitoring process, beginning with the regulations and standards.

Guidance from the regulations and standards

Public Companies

PCAOB calls for management to identify the risks of material misstatements in the significant accounts and disclosures and implement controls to prevent or detect errors or fraud that could result in material misstatements. **SAS 94** explains that risks can arise or change due to circumstances such as changes in the operating environment, new personnel, new or revamped information systems, rapid growth, or new technology. Management could use information technology as an important element in the identification and management of risks.

Banking/Finance

Basel II calls for periodic reviews of the risk management process to ensure its integrity, accuracy, and reasonableness. The **Sound Practices of Operational Risk** call for the development of a viable operational risk monitoring and control system. Internal and external factors that could adversely affect a banks achievement of objectives should be considered.

The **FFIEC Business Continuity Planning Handbook** has an extended amount of information on risk monitoring. Risk monitoring is the final step in the internal control process. It should ensure that the institution's internal controls are viable through testing each control at least annually, subjecting each control to an independent audit and review, and updating the controls based upon changes.

Specifically, an overall testing strategy should be developed, detailing the frequency of testing for each internal control. Management should evaluate the risks and merits of various types of testing and develop the testing strategy based upon the needs of the organization and the sensitivity of each internal control. The test strategy should include the test objectives, scripts, and schedules as well as provide for review and reporting of test results.

Management should define what controls are to be tested and what constitutes a successful test. Management should develop a test plan and review the test plan prior to each test to identify weaknesses that could lead to unsatisfactory or invalid tests. The test plan's assumptions should be validated to ensure they are appropriate for each control, and all documented data should be checked for accuracy. Test procedures should be checked for completeness, and appropriate testing methods should be used. A variety of testing methods exist, and the appropriate methods are to be chosen by management based on a variety of factors.

FFIEC Operations also has a wealth of information on risk monitoring. Management should monitor IT operations risk and the effectiveness of established controls. Regular risk monitoring provides management and the board with assurance that established controls are functioning properly.

Credit Card

MasterCard SDP calls for the reassessment of the security of applications and the production environment on a regular basis.

NIST Special Publications

NIST 800-14 calls for risk management to be an ongoing process. Plans should be tested and revised as needed for efficient risk monitoring.

International Standards Organization

ISO 17799 calls for the testing, maintaining, and reviewing of business continuity plans to ensure they are up to date and effective.

US Federal Security

The **Clinger-Cohen Act** calls for an assessment of the major factors of risk management: the value of the system or application, threats, vulnerabilities, and the effectiveness of current or proposed safeguards. **FISCAM** explains that when significant weaknesses are identified, related risks should be reassessed, appropriate corrective actions taken, and follow-up monitoring performed to make certain that corrective actions are effective. In addition to modifying written policies, testing strategies should be reviewed and modified as needed.

General Guidance

COSO states that ongoing risk monitoring should occur due to the natural outdating of risk responses. Risk responses that were once effective may become irrelevant; control activities become less effective, or not longer can be performed; or organization objectives may change.

The **ISF Standard** instructs that business continuity arrangements are to be tested periodically, using realistic simulations, to demonstrate whether services can be resumed with critical timescales.

United Kingdom and Canadian Guidance

The **Turnbull Guidance** explains that it is management's responsibility to implement board policies on risk and control. In fulfilling its responsibility, management should identify and evaluate the risks faced by the company for consideration by the board. Management should also design, operate and monitor the system of internal control, which requires an understanding of the risks the company faces.

From regulation to reality – sure signs you are complying

We discussed measuring risks in an earlier section. But, measuring risks once and then moving on will not get you to where you want to be. This would be like checking to see if you had enough gas before you began your trip, and then never checking again until after you've completely run out. Instead of waiting for a disaster to happen, you have to monitor risks continuously, to ensure that the established controls are functioning properly. Hence, this portion of your plan is within the implementation phase of compliance.

The first step in risk monitoring is to develop an overall testing strategy. This strategy will provide details on the frequency of tests and monitoring. Frequency will vary for different controls. Some may require annual testing, while others may require testing once a month, and yet others continuous monitoring. This is heavily influenced by how critical the control is to the operation of the system and the risks placed on the control in the initial risk analysis. Besides the frequency of tests, your test strategy must include test objectives, scripts, schedules and procedures concerning review and reporting.

Next, create a test plan. Before the risk monitoring begins, management needs to define what exactly a successful test would look like, so that the testers have something to compare the results to. Add this information into your test plan, and review it before every test. Look at results from pervious tests, so that you know whether you are improving, or if drastic measures must be taken to get you back on track. Keep some previous results in your test plan as well, to refer to during the testing. Identify any weaknesses that could lead to invalid test results and include them in the plan. Testing procedures also belong in the plan. Before each test, check the procedures for completeness and accuracy. It would be a major setback to find you used inaccurate testing methods, because all of the data just gathered would be useless.

If and when you find significant weaknesses, don't stop there. Instead, test all of the related risks, looking for the same or similar weaknesses. One weakness could provide a trail of breadcrumbs to other more significant weaknesses. Follow the clues that the monitoring provides.

The final step is to constantly update your risk monitoring strategy and testing plan. Every time you test, build on it to provide more significant tests for the next round. This will help your organization formulate the tightest internal controls imaginable.

Do you assess customer satisfaction?

To determine how well your organization is functioning, you need to know what your customers think. It's not enough to use your own opinion, because there is every chance that what you think is great, your customers have complaints about, or ideas for improvement. Therefore, you should follow this control objective:

> In order to protect and promote customer relations, the organization will assess customer satisfaction. By taking into consideration what others have to say, the organization is given the opportunity to find out what customers like and dislike about the organization.

Once you know how your customers feel about everything, you can build on the positive feedback, and correct the negative aspects of your company.

Guidance from the regulations and standards

Public Companies

The **AICPA Suitable Trust Services Criteria** calls for the use of a feedback questionnaire to confirm customer satisfaction with completion of service or delivery of information to the customer.

Banking/Finance

The **Sound Practices of Operational Risk** requires bank management to ensure that the expectations and obligations of each party are clearly defined, including customers, and that any interaction with third party providers should be monitored closely for the possible negative effect on customers.

The **FFIEC Management Handbook** calls for focusing IT resource decisions on specific objectives such as improved customer satisfaction or customer retention. The **FFIEC Operations Handbook** calls for management to review customer satisfaction metrics.

General Guidance

COSO ERM explains that conversations with customers, suppliers, regulators, and personnel often provide critical information needed to identify risks and opportunities.

CobiT calls for assessing customer satisfaction at regular intervals. Management should measure customer satisfaction regarding the services delivered by the IT function to identify shortfalls in service levels and establish improvement objectives.

United Kingdom and Canadian Guidance

BS 15000-2 leads the way on assessing customer satisfaction. BS 15000-2 explains that customer satisfaction should be measured to enable the service provider to compare performance with customer satisfaction targets and previous surveys. The scope and complexity of the survey should be designed so customers can respond easily and without excessive time being required to complete the survey accurately.

After assessing the customer satisfaction levels, if management finds significant variations in customer satisfaction, the reasons should be investigated and understood. Trends or other comparisons should only be made on comparable satisfaction questions and across comparable sampling methods. BS 15000-2 also advises that the results and conclusions of customer satisfaction surveys should be discussed with the customer.

From regulation to reality – sure signs you are complying

Within the realm of Monitoring and Change Management, assessing customer satisfaction will help your organization become more effective by giving you a different perspective on what works and what doesn't. There are several ways you can assess customer satisfaction. You can send out surveys, call your customers and ask questions, or simply ask them after a transaction if there is anything that they think your organization can do better. Whatever you choose, it should be designed so that customers can respond easily, without requiring an excessive amount of time. You want your customers to actually complete the survey or interview, not decline to do so because it seems burdensome.

Once you have collected a number of customer suggestions, complaints, and feedback, you should organize it into a report for management to review. Figure out how many people feel the same way about one aspect of your service, or if only one customer found the service inadequate. The more people who complained about or praised a certain service, the more likely it is to be true. This is not to say that if one customer complained about something you shouldn't do something about it, but it is likely to be an isolated incident.

Management should take this report and measure customer satisfaction specifically regarding IT services, to identify any shortfalls in service levels and establish improvement levels. Any variations in customer satisfaction should be investigated and understood. As we indicated above, it is possible for a single customer to have had a problem, and it is extremely important management find out why this problem occurred so that it can be prevented from happening again.

Any results of a survey or interview should be discussed with the customer. This could be as simple as sending out a flyer with the next mailing explaining the results, or speaking with customers individually the next time they call in or are contacted. Customers will feel more confident knowing that you have identified the problems and are working to fix them, instead of feeling like they participated in the survey for no reason.

Do you monitor the performance of critical systems and processes?

Assessing performance is one way to see whether or not you are on track. And for continued insight on performance, we recommend frequent monitoring. Start with the following control objective:

> *The organization will monitor performance of critical systems and processes to ensure, amongst other things, efficiency, security, and customer satisfaction. Performance monitoring involves measuring operational activities, analyzing the resulting metrics, and comparing them to established industry benchmarks. This process will help assess the effectiveness and efficiency of a system.*

Merely instituting a control objective to monitor critical systems isn't enough. You are going to have to define **business** metrics behind *what* you are monitoring. That means that you are going to have to define **business** performance factors such as capacity, usage, response time, uptime, etc. Take a look at the regulations, standards and the battle plan for more insight into monitoring performance.

Guidance from the regulations and standards

Public Companies

These standards do not have much to say with regards to performance monitoring. However, **SAS 94** calls for performance reviews as one control activity relevant to auditing.

Banking/Finance

The **FFIEC Operations Handbook** discusses performance monitoring at some length. Performance monitoring and management involves measuring operational activities, analyzing the resulting metrics, and comparing them to internally established standards and industry benchmarks to assess the effectiveness and efficiency of existing problems. Performance factors may include: resource usage, operations problems, capacity, response time, and personnel activity.

The Handbook recommends the use of capacity planning, which involves the use of baseline performance data to model and project future needs. The **FFIEC Management Handbook** calls for financial institutions to conduct periodic reviews to determine if plans, goals and expectations are on target. Failure to perform such measurements could put the institution at risk.

US Federal Security

FISMA calls for testing of management, operational, and technical controls. The **Clinger-Cohen Act** requires performance and results based management. The **GAO** calls for the use of controls to provide reasonable assurance that the organization achieves its mission, maintains quality standards, and does what management directs it to do. Performance measures are those designed to provide reasonable assurance about reliability of performance reporting. Performance measures are included in the GAO controls, as well as an established monitoring and reporting of performance standards. The **IRS Revenue Procedure 97-22** also calls for performance monitoring.

Records Management

ISO 15489-2 requires performance monitoring. Performance monitoring requires organizations to establish agreed expected and/or required performance levels in such matters as procedural responsibilities, work quantity and quality, and system process security and integrity. Operation of the resulting system has then to be regularly and routinely measured against these benchmarked expectations or requirements.

NIST Special Publications

NIST 800-41 Guidelines on Firewalls and Firewall Policy 5.4 recommends that firewalls offer logging functionality. Most of them are equipped with advanced logging functionalities. It is suggested that organizations not only ensure they have firewall logging, but a suitable software package for analyzing the logs when they are passed to their centralized logging server.

General Guidance

CobiT 3 has a wealth of information on performance monitoring. Some of the highlights are that CobiT calls for management to implement a process to ensure that the performance of IT resources is continuously monitored and exceptions are reported in a timely and comprehensive manner. Capacity management of resources and workload forecasting should be addressed as well as a variety of additional performance monitoring controls. Similarly, quality should be managed through a series of detailed control objectives including quality assurance planning and coordination and communication.

CobiT 4 ME1.4 calls for periodically reviewing performance of assets against targets. If there are problems encountered, root cause analysis should be performed along with remedial actions to address whatever the cause of poor performance is. DS3.5 calls for continuous monitoring of assets to ensure that not only are they performing well, but that they have appropriate capacity for day-to-day tasks, or potential upgrades. If assets are monitored and found to be lacking appropriate capacity, provisions should be made to bring them up to the required levels.

The **ISF Good Practices Standard** calls for the performance of systems associated with computer installation to be monitored, and system availability should be measured.

From regulation to reality – sure signs you are complying

As a part of your implementation plan, monitor the critical applications and systems within your organization to ensure that they are functioning as designed. Good performance monitoring involves measuring operational activities, analyzing the resulting metrics and comparing them to established industry benchmarks.

To make useful measurements, decide ahead of time what expected and required performance levels should be for procedural responsibilities, work quantity and quality and system process security and integrity. Whenever you examine performance, it should be compared against these levels.

How do you assess performance of the audit data collected?

Monitoring and logging data is only as useful as you make it. So how do you get the most out of your monitoring data? By using it to assess your systems or security and anti-virus performance. Its one thing to collect data and benchmark data, and then something completely different to make a judgment call and say "this is working" or "it isn't working" as you'd thought. Performance assessment will act as an indicator of what is going well, and what needs to be changed. The control objective for this section is:

> In order to protect the accountability of business functions the organization will assess performance. Everything an organization collects should be examined to determine whether the organization is meeting defined organizational performance objectives.

This work of assessment and judgment calls is critical – without it you won't know whether your organization's performance is progressing forwards, backwards or sideways. And that's not good.

Guidance from the regulations and standards

Public Companies

PCAOB calls for management to base its assessment of the effectiveness of the company's internal control over financial reporting on a suitable, recognized control framework.

Banking/Finance

The **FFIEC Information Security Handbook** calls for financial institutions to review performance reports to identify trends, new threats, or control deficiencies. The **FFIEC Management Handbook** calls for identification of performance benchmarks to be monitored on a regular basis.

US Federal Security

The **Clinger-Cohen Act** calls for performance and results-based management techniques. Performance measurements should be prescribed and agency performance should be quantitatively benchmarked in terms of cost, speed, productivity, and quality of outputs and outcomes.

Records Management

DIRKS calls for the use of benchmarks to assess performance as well as any monitoring reports to establish performance indicators.

General Guidance

CobiT requires that services to be delivered by the IT function should be measured by management and be compared with target levels. Assessment of the IT function should be performed on a continuing basis.

From regulation to reality – sure signs you are complying

Your action phase is now squarely within the Monitoring and Change Management realm. To successfully use your monitoring and logging data you'll need to establish performance indicators with which to measure, and base those indicators on a formal framework (not some framework you or your IT department made up). An indicator is generally defined as a level of efficiency you expect from each system or system component in your organization for which you collect data. Once you establish indicators, use the data collected to determine whether or not you are meeting these goals.

Conducting performance assessments helps management establish the need for modification of particular functions. If you find that something is out of whack, you can fix it to get the organization back on track. Ideally, your performance assessments should be a continuous function. Things are always in motion with your organizational machine, so you must ensure that the machine is inspected all the time to determine whether it is in working order.

To organize the results of each assessment, generate performance reports. These reports should be viewed by management to identify trends, new threats, or control deficiencies.

Do you create management reports?

Management reports exist to inform senior management of how well the systems are functioning, or that they aren't functioning well at all. Of course these reports have to be written slowly because management can't read that fast (that's a joke by the way). As President Bush would say "is we teaching our students to write good?" Aside from the irony, the management reports have to be objective, to the point, and results oriented. The great news is, once upper management gets wind of what's ailing the organization's compliance efforts, they *have* to either formally take action to mitigate the problems or document that they are accepting the inherent risk and exposure the report brings forth. Therefore, the control objective for this section is:

> The organization will create management reports regularly to aid senior management in determining what types of corrective actions, improvements or maintenance activities need to be carried out.

Well written, regularly submitted reports create a strong chain of communication between the lower and upper levels of management, increasing the swiftness with which action can be taken on a given initiative.

Guidance from the regulations and standards

Public Companies

The **AICPA/CICA Privacy Framework** calls for documentation of periodic reviews, such as internal audit plans, audit reports, compliance checklists, and management sign-off sheets. The results of the compliance review and recommendations for improvement should be reported to management.

Banking/Finance

Basel II requires banks to establish an adequate system for monitoring and reporting risk exposures. The senior manager or Board of Directors should, on a regular basis, receive reports allowing the senior manager to effectively evaluate trends, risks, assumptions and goals.

The **Sound Practices of Operational Risk** calls for senior management to receive regular reports from appropriate areas such as business units, group functions, the operational risk management office, and internal audit.

The **FFIEC Management Handbook** provides for progress reports to be sent to management on an ongoing basis. The **FFIEC Operations Handbook** points out that effective monitoring and reporting help identify insufficient resources, inefficient use of resources, and substandard performance.

US Federal Security

FISMA calls for agency evaluations to be submitted to the director by the head of each agency. The **Clinger-Cohen Act** calls for reporting to the head of the agency of the progress made in improving information resource management capability.

Records Management

ISO 15489-1 calls for system compliance monitoring to be documented and reports to be maintained. **DIRKS** requires assignment of responsibility for a structured report to be provided that can be used for comparative purposes over time.

General Guidance

In answering the question "what should be reported," **COSO ERM** explains that it is necessary to look at the implications of the findings. It is essential not only that a particular transaction or event be reported, but also that potential faulty procedures be identified and re-evaluated. Information generated in the course of operating activities should be reported to immediate superiors. Communication to a higher level of management for needed support or oversight for taking corrective action will be necessary one way or another.

CobiT explains that management reports should be provided for senior management's review of the organization's progress toward identified goals. Status reports should include the extent to which planned objectives have been achieved, deliverables obtained, performance targets met, and risks mitigated. Upon review, appropriate management action should be initiated and controlled.

CobiT 4 ME1.5 requires that management reports be provided covering senior management's work reviewing the organization's progress towards IT-enabled investment programs, service levels of individual programs and IT's contribution to performance.

The **ISF Good Practices** standard calls for security audit/review activity to be controlled by monitoring and logging the activities of the audit/review team.

United Kingdom and Canadian Guidance

The **Turnbull Guidance** calls for a system of internal control which includes procedures for reporting immediately to appropriate levels of management any significant control failings or weaknesses that are identified together with details of corrective action being undertaken.

From regulation to reality – sure signs you are complying

Ahh, the compliance reporting phase. When employees report to management, the worst thing the managers can do is sit on that information. IT has the duty to go beyond, and create reports for senior management or the board of directors, depending on the structure of your organization. Yes, management **has** the authority to institute changes and to fix problems, this is why they are management. That and they golf better than you. And now with regulatory compliance, not only do they have the authority, they **have the responsibility** to either take action or document that they are accepting the risk and exposure.

Creating reports for senior management involves taking all the logging and monitoring data and reports they you received, and turning them into a report that can be read by somebody who doesn't give a rat's patoot about packets, firewalls, IDSes, or any IT procedures for that matter. It also has to include recommendations for improvements and the necessary resources that need to be allocated in order to accomplish these improvements. If you organization is on the ball, you'll also have a Business Impact Analysis and Risk report defining the costs of exposure to the problems you want mitigated. Your organization's management exists for oversight, and their approval and allocation of resources will be necessary.

Do you perform follow-up activities after an audit of your monitoring ?

What happens after an audit is in the hands of management. Whether or not the comments of auditors get applied depends on how aggressive management is in instituting necessary change. Further, the next time an audit takes place, auditors will look at previous results and compare them with new findings. Don't follow up just to please the auditors. Do it to improve your organization! Start with this control objective:

> In order to promote the integrity of the organization and its information systems, management will ensure that the recommendations of auditors are followed and changes are instituted in a timely manner. During each audit, auditors will request and evaluate appropriate information on previous findings, conclusions and recommendations to determine whether appropriate actions have been implemented in a timely manner.

Next, take a look at what the regulations and standards have to say about performing follow-up activities.

Guidance from the regulations and standards

Public Companies

SAS 94 encourages the consideration of previous audits to influence the designs of test controls. The Smith Guidance calls for the audit committee to review the effectiveness of the audit process, including changes in perceived audit risks and the work taken to address those risks.

Banking/Finance

The Appendix of 12 CFR 30 requires the monitoring, evaluating, and adjustment to the information security program in light of any relevant changes in technology, the sensitivity of customer information, internal or external threats to information, and changing business arrangements.

The FFIEC Management Handbook calls for an audit to verify that management has implemented effective control processes.

US Federal Security

FISMA requires the head of each agency to submit to the director the results of the agency evaluation.

NIST Special Publications

NIST 800-14 calls for audit trails to be reviewed in order to implement the appropriate controls.

General Guidance

CobiT requires the request and evaluation of appropriate information on previous findings to ensure that appropriate actions are being taken.

CobiT 4 ME1.6 calls for creating and initiating remedial actions based on performance monitoring, assessment and reporting. Other follow-up measures to be taken include reviewing, negotiating and establishing management responses, assigning responsibility for remediation and tracking of the results of actions committed.

EU Guidance

The **OECD Risk Checklist** calls for review and follow-up of internal audits.

From regulation to reality – sure signs you are complying

Once an audit has been performed, comments based on the auditor's findings are written up in a report along with his conclusions and recommendations. This report is handed off to management for review. Such a report is only useful though, if management follows-up by acting on the report's findings.

There are several ways to act on report findings. Management can choose items that need correction listed in the report and implement solutions. They can also review old audit reports to determine the designs for test controls for future audits. This is a highly recommended procedure, as it allows you to tailor tests to find problems more quickly that your systems may have had in the past. You can also review a current audit report with previous ones to make an assessment of how effective the audit process has been in the past compared to the current audit. This gives you ideas for what you may need to improve in an audit.

Do you report monitoring statistics and follow-up with the Board of Directors?

The Board of Directors is at the top of the ladder. There are many things that require Board approval before they can be done. Even when Board approval is not required, their expertise and consultation on matters is greatly beneficial to the workings of an organization. That is part of their advisory role. Therefore, use the following control objective to remind you to report to the Board:

> *In order to promote a top down management approach and ensure that changes are authorized and instituted as timely as possible, the Board of Directors will be updated on compliance monitoring and auditing.*

Reporting to the board will help you ensure that things get done. This section illustrates this point and guides you in the process.

Guidance from the regulations and standards

Public Companies

Sarbanes Oxley calls for periodic reports and an annual report to the Board. Reports may be required more frequently, as necessary to update the Board on progress or audits.

Banking/Finance

The **Appendix of 12 CFR 30** calls for reporting to the board or an appropriate committee of the board at least annually. This report should describe the overall status of the information security program and compliance with these guidelines. These reports should discuss material matters related to programs, addressing issues such as risk management and control decisions; security breaches or violations and management's responses; results of testing; and recommendations for changes in the information security program.

The **FFIEC Audit Handbook** calls for auditors to make recommendations to management about procedures that affect IT controls. In this regard, the Board and management should involve the audit department in the development process for major new IT applications. The Board and management should develop criteria for determining those projects that need audit involvement.

The **FFIEC Management Handbook** calls for the IT management department to report directly to the Board of directors or a designated committee of the board. Audit should verify that management has implemented effective control processes.

US Federal Security

The **GAO** calls for keeping the organization informed about problems and deficiencies, including the progress of corrective actions.

General Guidance

CobiT 4 ME4.6 requires organizations to report relevant portfolio, program and IT performance to the board and executives in a timely manner. These reports are to be used by to ensure IT functions are on track to meet specific goals. They are also used to assess risk in the organization.

EU Guidance

The **OECD Risk Checklist** calls for executive e-summaries to be produced for the Board on a monthly basis, or if not monthly, then frequently.

United Kingdom and Canadian Guidance

The Combined Code on Corporate Governance, the **Turnbull Guidance**, and the **Smith Guidance** all call for recommendations to be made to the Board by the audit committee.

From regulation to reality – sure signs you are complying

Periodically, your organization's board of directors should receive detailed updates on monitoring and auditing compliance. You can update them as little as once per year, but it is often best to have more frequent updates, such as once per board meeting, so they can remain informed of progress. Any updates you have can be submitted in the form of reports and address internal control decision, risk management, testing, security violations, audit results and other material matters.

If necessary, the board should act on updates. If not enough progress is being made to maintain compliance in a certain area, the board can push through an initiative to make it a top priority. They can also delegate new projects to improve compliance within the organization. Keeping your board informed makes important changes easier to make and improves the chances of maintaining compliance continuously.

IT Staffing

The Main Thing

Have you established an IT organizational structure?

IT today is one of the most important aspects of your organization. Whether your organization is large or small, processes must be in place allowing you to select IT solutions and procedures in a structured, organized fashion. If you're not sure how important good IT management is, grab a copy of "2001: A Space Odyssey" and review it. Lousy IT management that doesn't provide for procedures under all conditions – good, bad or emergency – can be disastrous. In order to prevent an event as catastrophic as the hostile computer takeover in "2001: A Space Odyssey", we recommend you follow this control objective:

> *In order to promote the integrity and availability of IT systems, the organization will define an IT organizational structure. This structure will include general oversight, roles and responsibilities, measurement of risk, monitoring and testing of systems, reporting incidents and issues, and establishing acceptable levels of risk.*

Take time and care in creating your structure – it is the frame upon which everything else your IT department does will build.

Guidance from the regulations and standards

Public Companies

While most public standards do not have much to say with regards to IT organizational structure, the **AICPA Suitable Trust Criteria** contributes much with its principles for security services. The Criteria calls for a QA program and information security management, as well as appointment of data and system ownership. The Criteria frequently mentions the role of the IT steering committee and address IT staffing and job description needs. It also calls for a definition of critical personnel for disaster recovery procedures. The AICPA Privacy framework requires job descriptions be created and maintained for personnel responsible for the privacy and security of personal information. And **SAS 94** mentions the segregation of duties as an essential control for financial auditors to consider.

NASD/NYSE

Rules **3520 (NASD)** and **446(g) (NYSE)** require that the business continuity plan define emergency contact personnel roles in the event of a significant business disruption. These personnel must be a registered principal and member of senior management. Rule 3520 calls for a minimum of two such personnel.

Banking/Finance

The **FFIEC Handbooks** all pretty much cover IT organizational structure. Though not comprehensively linear, most of the considerations for IT staffing, segregation of duties, and roles and responsibilities are reiterated throughout these standards. Since Graham-Leach Bliley concentrates primarily on the integrity of financial information, most of the guidance is in relation to information security, but FFIEC does a pretty good job of defining the IT function and requirements.

FFIEC Information Security Pg. 5-6 discusses roles and responsibilities for everyone in the organization. Of chief importance is the board of directors, which provides management with guidance, receives reports on the effectiveness of management's response regarding information security and provides management with expectations and requirements in the areas of central oversight and coordination, specific assigned areas of responsibility, measuring risk, monitoring and testing, reporting and acceptable risk levels.

FFIEC Business Continuity Appendix E-1 places staffing requirements into a series of questions you should be able to answer about your workers and their environment. These questions include:

* If management is lost, who will stand-in to do decision making?

* Who is responsible for acting as the leader for different key teams, such as Crisis/Emergency, Recovery, Technology, Communications, Facilities, Human Resources, Business Units and Processes and Customer Service?

* Who is assigned the responsibility of security, both information and physical?

In terms of environment, how workers will operate in an alternative facility should be considered for multiple scenarios.

Credit Card

With respect to personnel operating as e-commerce merchants or in the Member Service program, the **MasterCard SDP** calls for an information security officer to delegate security responsibilities regarding cardholder information. The Program also calls for job descriptions and responsibilities and a proper segregation of duties.

Government

Government standards and regulations do not address most aspects of IT organizational structure except for when referring to use of IT or acquisition of IT solutions. The **OMB Circular A-130** requires owners of information systems be held accountable and also calls on the Office of Personnel Management to periodically evaluate information resource staffing needs. NIST and **FISCAM** address the requirement of organizations to identify and define critical personnel needed for disaster recovery. The National Strategy to Secure Cyberspace, FISCAM and the **GAO Financial Audit Manual** mention segregation of duties, and FISCAM specifically addresses roles and responsibilities and ownership of systems as auditor concerns.

FIPS Publication 191 § 3.2 suggests an organizational structure for managing LAN security. It offers five points to cover. The first is LAN Management, which is responsible for conducting risk assessments, providing proper LAN configurations including hardware, software, data and functionality mapping. The second point in the structure offered is Organizational Management. This group is responsible for supporting LAN security policies by providing funds to implement security services and achieve compliance with policy goals. This group will also assess longterm consequences to the organization if a threat is realized. The next group is Security Personnel, which ensures that security policies are developed and adhered to. Data and Application Owners are the next group. These people are responsible for ensuring that data and applications are appropriately protected and available to users. Finally LAN users themselves are responsible for providing accurate information about their applications, data and LAN usage.

Records Management

Insofar as records management is considered a facet of information technology, **ISO 15489-1** and **15489-2** call for senior management to define records roles and responsibilities. ISO 15489-1 also requires that roles and responsibilities be defined in job descriptions.

The IT Infrastructure Library

ITIL Best Practice for Security Management § 2.4 calls for recognizing that there are many relationships between IT security management processes and other IT management processes. When establishing IT organizational structure, it is important to determine how different groups will relate to one another. 3.1.1 says that security management should have clear goals. The first goal is to meet external security requirements. These come from various SLAs. The second goal is to meet internal security requirements, which are necessary for an organization's own security and continuity.

4.2.1.2 talks about ensuring that all of an organization's important assets are assigned to a specific group or person so that they may be accounted for. 4.2.1 echoes this.

4.2.3.2 calls for organizing roles within an organization so that there is segregation of duties. Tasks should be shared among more than one person. This reduces the possibility of security incidents due to human error, and reduces the possibility of misuse or fraud.

4.2.2.2 suggests creating job descriptions that include security roles and responsibilities for each staff member.

3.5 requires organizations to think about the relationship between proper security and management. It shows a triangular chart, point down. This chart places incident control/help desk at the base (up top), followed by problem management and finally, change management. Another way to think of these areas is discovery of a problem, handling a problem and finally, modifying systems so that they won't be susceptible to that problem in the future.

International Standards Organization

ISO 17799 addresses various elements of organizational structure, though mostly with respect to information security and risk management. CobiT is the only general standard that addresses all the above objectives in their entirety

General Guidance

CobiT is the standard to follow here for establishing an IT organizational structure. COSO, the ISF Standard for Good Practices of Information Security,

CobiT 4 has a lot to say about establishing an IT organizational structure. PO4.5 explains that organizations must develop an internal and external IT organizational structure that reflects business needs. PO4.3 requires organizations to establish an IT steering committee. The committee should have executive, business and IT management staff all working to prioritize IT programs and projects, follow the status of ongoing projects and monitor service levels and improvements. PO4.4 calls for placing the IT function within an organization into the overall organizational structure so that it can be aligned with business models. PO4.6 recommends defining and assigning roles and responsibilities for all employees with regards to information systems. PO4.7 says responsibility for quality assurance should be assigned to a group along with appropriate quality assurance resources. PO4.8 tells us that ownership and responsibility for IT-related risks should be embedded within the business at an appropriate senior level. Associated roles and responsibilities should be assigned. PO4.9 states that the organization should provide the necessary tools and procedures for addressing ownership of data and information systems. PO4.10 suggests implementing supervisory practices in the IT function to ensure that assigned roles and responsibilities are properly exercised. PO4.11 calls for segregating duties so one employee does not have too many roles and responsibilities. This helps organizations avoid having a single individual with the ability to subvert a critical process. PO4.12 talks about regularly evaluating staffing requirements to ensure that the IT function has a sufficient number of competent staff. PO4.13 says organizations should define and identify key IT personnel. Care should be taken to avoid over reliance on them. PO4.14 requires that organizations define and implement policies and procedures for working with consultants and other contract personnel by the IT function. PO4.15 asks that organizations work to ensure good communication between the IT function and other departments within the organization.

EU Guidance

The **OECD Risk Checklist** all address various elements of organizational structure, though mostly with respect to information security and risk management. CobiT is the only general standard that addresses all the above objectives in their entirety

From regulation to reality – sure signs you are complying

Good IT functionality begins with good management. Senior management within the organization should appoint a board of directors. This board is to be assigned the responsibility of providing IT management with guidance, receiving reports of management's responses to security incidents involving IT and providing management with requirements for IT in the following areas:

- Coordination and central oversight

- Tasks for assigned areas of responsibility

- Measurement of risk

- Monitoring and testing systems

- Reporting incidents and issues
- Acceptable risk levels

Senior management should see to it that management assigned to work with the board of directors has sufficient tools and authority to implement recommendations from the board or any other IT solutions that are approved. The healthiest IT structures include creating a relationship with upper management to increase their awareness, understanding and skill in identifying and resolving IT issues.

None of the management structures described thus far will be any use without delegating roles and responsibilities to all involved parties. Decide who has the authority to do what, how different managers must interact with one another and how staff will be made aware of their duties. There are a few key roles to choose during the delegation process. One is the position of information security manager. This person's role will be to oversee and enforce logical and physical security controls for IT functions. The information security manager will have an active part in defining roles and responsibilities for workers, as well as delegating some of the tasks depending on what privileges the information security manager is assigned by the board and senior management.

One of the roles of the information security manager is assigning system owners. The method for selecting these owners should be created and documented by the board, then passed on to the information security manager. Appointed system owners will have the job of making decisions about asset classification, access rights and delegating day-to-day custodianship. Each owner is to be held accountable for any security measures required for the systems and data they govern.

Equally important to assigning daily and emergency IT job roles is quality assurance for all work being done. Senior management should assign quality assurance tasks to IT staff and ensure that they have the expertise to perform their jobs. If possible, quality assurance procedures should be worked in as regularly expected responsibilities along with general procedures for daily workloads.

An overarching requirement of task delegation at the board or information security manager levels involves making certain that no one person has control over all key aspects of a process or project. This improves security within your organization by making it more difficult for a worker to sabotage your systems. It also makes it easier to continue operations if jobs are spread around instead of concentrated in one person, who then must always be present to handle any problems that crop up.

To prevent the possibility that a crisis arises and the appropriate people are not on hand to solve the problem, determine who in your organization comprises critical IT staff. These are the people who will be essential to recovery and restoration in the event of a disaster or significant business disruption. The group may include people with specialized skills, or ownership responsibilities for sensitive applications and systems. When you are developing IT functionality and determining staffing requirements, consult these people.

For the IT organizational structure to run smoothly, more must be done than simply assigning tasks, responsibilities and job titles. Standardize work for different positions by creating specific job descriptions for each desired staff member of IT. This serves three purposes. First, it gives you a list of criteria to compare incoming resumes to so that you can hire staff with appropriate job skills. Second, it allows you to be sure that you are hiring essential staff. In a disorganized IT department, you may have people with skills and roles that overlap so much that they aren't adding much value to your organization. The third purpose is to create a base description that can grow as your organization grows. Update job descriptions annually, and assess staff to see if they are maintaining the appropriate level of skill to continue in their job functions. If new skills become necessary, you can determine if it is best to hire new workers, or train existing ones.

IT management can also help the IT structure function smoothly by implementing communication procedures and coordinating their actions within the department and all external parties, both within and outside the organization. If certain systems need to be taken down for awhile, IT management should endeavor to schedule this at a time when other workers will be least affected by the lack of the selected system. This helps streamline IT activities and integrate IT function into the overall organizational structure.

Finally, senior management should institute a framework for reviewing the IT organizational structure to ensure it is effective, current and meets the organization's goals and objectives.

How do you recruit and promote employees appropriately?

All organizations are different. Within each organization, distinct work ethics and environment exists. While some people may thrive in one kind of environment, others may not. This is not necessarily based on a potential employee's education or skills, but the type of person they are in general and what work environment will produce the best results for that person. It is for this reason that your organization must create hiring criteria that address both skills as well as personality. This will help you decide whether to promote an employee when the time comes, because you can determine if this person is thriving in the organizational environment. To help you out with this process, we recommend you follow this control objective:

> *In order to employ and retain competent and trustworthy personnel, the organization will implement and regularly assess quality recruitment and promotion processes. Practices surrounding hiring, orientation, training, promotion, compensation, evaluations and discipline will all be based on objective criteria and consider education, experience, compatibility and responsibility.*

The creation of appropriate recruitment requirements and procedures helps you choose people that suit your organization's culture. Benefits of good requirements and procedures include increased productivity and decreased interpersonal troubles between staff members.

Guidance from the regulations and standards

Public Companies

The **AICPA Privacy Framework** requires that qualifications of personnel responsible for the privacy and security of information be verified through quality hiring procedures.

Banking/Finance

The **FFIEC Operations Handbook** calls for a human resources plan that ensures a competent and motivated workforce. It calls for incentive programs for management personnel that meet performance goals.

General Guidance

CobiT calls for personnel recruitment and promotion processes as a major control objective for managing human resources. COSO discusses human resources practices in the same vein, but not as a requirement, only as guidance with respect to risk management

From regulation to reality – sure signs you are complying

To maintain the best staff, and bring in new staff that integrates well, develop strong promotion and recruitment procedures within your organization. Create criteria for hiring, orientation, training, promotion, compensation, evaluations and discipline. Document this criteria, and update it as information becomes available on what is and what is not working.

Determining whether a person is a good fit for the corporate culture within your organization is an essential part of the hiring criteria. You can choose the best match from a pool of qualified applicants by having a documented version of not only required skills, but also what personality traits are most appropriate for the job. To make it easier for applicants to determine if they belong at your organization, you can provide interviews and presentations on your organization's culture, history and operating style. This weeds out candidates that don't suit the structure, leaving the most qualified options, culturally and skill wise, available.

Within the organization, encourage good management by offering well-designed incentives for managers that reach specific performance goals, or motivate their teams well enough to attain a selected goal. Promotions may also be used to encourage staff to stay and to work hard for your organization. Before making a promotion, ensure that the selected individual has all the appropriate skills for the work, and has continually worked to meet organizational goals.

How do you hire qualified employees?

There is no doubt that an organization wants qualified personnel managing and running its operations. This process is about both hiring qualified employees and keeping them qualified. A person who was an IT expert five years ago won't still be an expert today without a continued effort to learn the newest technologies. All things change over time, and IT changes faster than most, so it is best to keep your employees on top of the latest advancements. Use the following control objective as a reminder that qualified employees help to make a successful organization:

> *Aside from doing its best to hire the most skilled professionals, the organization will take steps to confirm that its employees continue to be qualified to execute their specific responsibilities. Qualifications should continuously be reassessed on the basis of education, training and experience.*

Qualification tests not only help you weed out people who aren't appropriately skilled for their jobs, they also let you see what skills your staff needs training on.

Guidance from the regulations and standards

Public Companies

The **AICPA Privacy Framework** requires that qualifications of individuals who are responsible for the privacy and security of personal information be verified through training.

Banking/Finance

The **FFIEC Management Handbook** calls for programs to ensure that personnel have the appropriate expertise to carry out their duties.

General Guidance

CobiT calls for organizations to continuously verify that personnel carrying out specific tasks are qualified on the basis of education, training and experience. CobiT also recommends that managers encourage their employees to join professional organizations.

CobiT PO7.1 suggests developing personnel recruitment and retention procedures to help ensure the best employees are hired for the organization's needs. PO7.2 extends concepts in PO7.1 by suggesting that employees should regularly be tested to ensure they have the appropriate level of competency to fulfill their roles.

From regulation to reality – sure signs you are complying

The best way to hire qualified employees is to create a list of criteria for a specific job, then hunt for people that match your list. Once you hire people however, how do you continually ensure they remain qualified for their positions? It's key that workers, particularly in an area like IT, stay on top of new tools and technology pertaining to their job. This is not solely the responsibility of the worker. Management must provide the resources and tools for employees to do this. For instance, if there is a conference that will provide your employees with the latest information on a certain topic, don't hesitate to send them.

Keep track of your workers and ensure they are up-to-date in both knowledge and expected goals and milestones. The best way to do this is to regularly assess employee skill levels to see whether the skills are progressing as fast as expected. Regular assessments will help both you and your employees. Communicating with an employee about expected goals and where she is on the spectrum will help the employee gauge what she needs to do in order to meet the expected milestones. If it appears that an employee is not on track, it does not necessarily mean she needs to be fired right away. Instead, assess what it is that is holding her back and discuss it with her. Attempt to get her back before resorting to harsher situations.

Do you have clearance procedures for personnel?

Part of organizational security is about ensuring that new employees have appropriate backgrounds for hire and current employees have appropriate backgrounds for transfer or promotion. This helps you weed out dishonest or problematic workers before they can cause a lot of damage. The control objective for this topic is:

> Prior to hiring, transferring or promoting personnel, the organizations will make use of security clearance procedures. This includes verifying applicants' integrity through the use of background checks, investigating references, and confirming identity. Additional screening procedures may be required for positions dealing with especially sensitive information.

By making these procedures uniform across your organization, you can better ensure that you are not hiring or promoting someone who'd be better suited to a life behind bars or in a padded room.

Guidance from the regulations and standards

Public Companies

The **AICPA Privacy Framework** and Suitable Trust Services Criteria both call for background, reference and identity checks.

Banking/Finance

Federal Guidelines for Safeguarding Customer Information and **FFIEC Information Security** call for background checks. FFIEC elaborates further and requires additional screening measures such as reference and identity checks, and confirmation of previous experience and qualifications.

Healthcare and Life Sciences

NIST 800-66 § 4.3 addresses § 164.308(a)(3) of the HIPAA Standard. 4.3 indicates that policies and procedures should be implemented to ensure that all employees have appropriate access to electronic protected health information. Appropriate access means that employees who should not have access to information are prevented from obtaining access to that information. The method for implementing controls that allow appropriate access is detailed in a chart in this section. Due to the volume of information, it should be read directly.

Credit Card

VISA CISP calls for a screening of all potential employees but does not details specific clearance procedures.

NIST Special Publications

NIST 800-53 calls for personnel clearance procedures prior to authorizing access to an organizations' information systems. The standard refers to the Office of Personnel Management Policy and guidance as the appropriate source for screening procedures.

International Standards Organization

ISO 17799 recommends a credit check for employees who are being promoted or are gaining new access to sensitive information.

General Guidance

CobiT, and the **ISF Standard of Good Practices for Information Security**, require that personnel be subject to clearance procedures prior to employment. CobiT adds that the same should be done during transfer or promotion. **CobiT 4 PO7.6** says that when recruiting new employees, background checks should be completed. They should be regularly conducted while the person is working for the organization too if possible.

EU Guidance

The **OECD Risk Checklist** requires that personnel be subject to clearance procedures prior to employment. CobiT adds that the same should be done during transfer or promotion.

From regulation to reality – sure signs you are complying

Before you hire, transfer or promote someone, ensure the person is appropriate for the job you want to give him. This can be accomplished by putting each person through your organization's security clearance procedures. If you don't have such procedures, create them. If you have clearance procedures in place, make sure they are up-to-date and used each and every time they should be.

Solid security clearance procedures involve verifying applicants' integrity through the use of background checks, investigating references and confirming identity. Depending on the nature of the position a person is to be placed in, you may wish to include additional background checks. This may be especially necessary if the person is to work with sensitive information.

Background checks are essential if you wish to ensure confidentiality and organizational integrity. They should not be viewed as an inconvenience, but a necessary function of today's wok environment. Determining that someone is who she says she is, and has done what she says she has done is only fair when placing employees in an organization.

Do you have roles, responsibilities and a code of conduct?

It would be nice if everyone treated their responsibilities and one another well. The trouble is, even if everyone intended the very best, they could still screw things up due to misunderstandings of their jobs or one another. If you want people to work effectively with one another and understand how to carry out their responsibilities, you're going to need to tell them in detail. The following objective sums this up:

> *The organization will create and maintain a defined list of roles and the assigned responsibilities for each role. In addition, a code of conduct will be created and maintained documenting what kinds of behavior and ethics are acceptable to your organization and what kinds are not.*

A code of conduct tells everyone in your organization what they can and can't do. It presents ethical values to keep in mind while performing daily tasks and contributes to the health of your corporate culture.

Guidance from the regulations and standards

Public Companies

PCAOB Auditing Standards and **SAS 94** mention codes of conduct as an organization's method of ensuring ethical behavior and how an auditor should investigate it.

Banking/Finance

FFIEC Information Security and **Management** both require that management must define roles and responsibilities for personnel upon employment in job descriptions. They do not address the use of terms and conditions or codes of ethics or conduct.

Credit Card

VISA CISP requires that job descriptions include responsibilities for employees handling cardholder information.

Government

Much like public standards, the **GAO Financial Audit Manual** mentions codes of conduct as an organization's method of ensuring ethical behavior and how an auditor should investigate it.

Records Management

ISO 15489-1 calls for job descriptions *and other statements* to define records management roles and responsibilities for personnel.

General Guidance

CobiT calls for management to define roles and responsibilities for personnel at the time of employment. CobiT further calls management to define responsibility for employees to follow ethical standards and practices. Along with the ISF standard, both documents require that terms and conditions of employment define staff's responsibility for internal control and security. COSO discusses corporate codes of conduct as a method of ensuring integrity and ethical behavior.

CobiT 4 PO7.3 recommends defining, monitoring and supervising roles, responsibilities and compensation frameworks for employees. This includes employee ability to adhere to management policies and procedures and the organization's code of ethics and professional practices.

From regulation to reality – sure signs you are complying

A code of conduct does several things for your organization. First, it encourages cohesiveness when approaching solutions to business problems. With everybody operating under the same code, certain choices will be obvious, and certain choices will clearly be inappropriate based on the ethics of your organization. Second, during an audit, a written code that is constantly in use is easier for an auditor to examine and compare employees against to see how well they're doing at upholding its principles.

At hire, the code of conduct should be handed to the new employee. In addition, a description of the employee's job function, expectations for that job and daily acceptable behaviors should be handed in documented form to the new hire.

Do you train your staff?

Training your staff is a key component in creating a secure workplace with quality service. The following control objective covers what sorts of training you need to think about:

> To get the most out of training, the organization will include these four basic types when working with the staff: Orientation, Skill maintenance, Security awareness, and Cross-training

Orientation gets new staff acquainted with your work environment and employee hand book. Skill maintenance helps people maintain or improve key job skills. Security awareness teaches staff about appropriate procedures for work, handling of data, etc. so that they do not compromise important organization secrets. Finally, cross-training will help your organization deal with crisis more effectively – if someone leaves or is out sick, you will still have staff available to do the work of the missing person.

Effective training in each of these areas makes your organization a more secure, efficient work place for everyone.

Guidance from the regulations and standards

Public Companies

The **AICPA Privacy Framework** calls for qualifications of personnel through training programs related to privacy and security. The **AICPA Trust Services Criteria** also calls for training and development in security concepts and issues and requires procedures to provide alternate personnel for key security functions in case of an absence or departure.

Banking/Finance

Federal Guidelines for Safeguarding Customer Information and numerous FFIEC handbooks require appropriate education and training programs to be implemented to promote security awareness and knowledge and skills in the use of applications and information systems. **FFIEC Management** also calls for cross-training and back-up of key personnel.

Healthcare and Life Sciences

HIPAA calls for security awareness training for all personnel.

Credit Card

VISA CISP and **MasterCard SDP** call for employee awareness of card-holder information security. MasterCard specifically calls for a program that should be repeated annually.

US Federal Security

Most government standards call for a security awareness program for all agency employees. **The National Strategy to Secure Cyberspace** specifically calls for a "cyber-security" awareness program, while the **DoD 5015.2** criteria call for users of records management systems to be trained appropriately.

The IT Infrastructure Library

ITIL Best Practice for Security Management 4.2.2.2 calls for security awareness training for all personnel. Employees should be made aware of the importance of information security and equipped with the proper resources, knowledge and skill to maintain information security. Employees that do incident response should be trained in security procedures and techniques.

General Guidance

CobiT 4 PO7.4 requires organizations to train IT employees so they can maintain their knowledge and skills as pertains to internal controls and security awareness. PO7.5 recommends cross training so that it is not necessary to be dependent on any one individual for important work in the organization.

US State Laws

CA 1386 requires orientation and ongoing employee training in awareness of security policies and procedures.

From regulation to reality — sure signs you are complying

Training of staff will vary widely from organization to organization. Not all of these areas will be feasible for everyone. For example a small company may have an easier time cross-training than a larger one because a small company often requires everyone to wear different hats at the start. The goal of this list of four types of training is to give you an idea of what you should be considering for your organization, and you can tailor it as necessary.

Orientation

Orientation allows new hires to adjust more quickly and feel more at home in their new surroundings, which leads to more efficient work.

Skill Maintenance

Skill maintenance can either be refresher training for activities you have already trained employees for, or the addition of new skills necessary to keep up with the changing nature of an employee's job. New skills could include learning new software or new system configuration methods.

Security Awareness

Security awareness is vital to maintaining solid defenses against external and internal attacks on your system. This type of training reviews appropriate behavior and procedures for maintaining security in the organization. For example locking the screen of your computer if you step away from the desk. Making staff aware of their role in maintaining security improves the overall security of your organization by getting everyone involved.

Cross-training

Cross-training is for business continuity. The general idea is to provide inter-departmental training where you review emergency procedures with key employees for the work. Assignments should be rotated to improve business continuity possibilities. The more key personnel that know multiple aspects of emergency business continuity procedures, the more people you can safely rely on to keep your organization running in a time of crisis. If you allow just one person this type of training, you will become dependent on her to solve all emergency situations, which is bad for you if she can't be there when a problem strikes.

For each type of training, document what the training will include, what goals the staff should attain in terms of knowledge from a session, how often the training is conducted, whether there will be refresher training and what procedures will be used to conduct the training. This documentation will not only make it easier to see what training will encompass, but also allows auditors to more easily evaluate the programs you offer during an audit.

Do you perform employee job performance evaluations?

"If it ain't broke, don't fix it," is a great way of saying let stuff that's working keep on working. However, if you don't have a method of figuring out when things aren't working properly, you're in danger of finding a use for a lesser known saying that goes like this: "If you can't tell it's broken, you won't fix it." This saying is not only less catchy, but mildly disturbing in that if it applies to you, it could mean big trouble for your organization. One of the hardest places to look for problem spots can be with employees. People don't always tell you when they're not doing their work, or if they're having trouble. Try this control objective to help solve this problem:

> *By having regular performance reviews and performance review processes, the organization will ensure that the staff are working together efficiently.*

Good performance evaluations help ensure that staff are qualified for the work they are performing and capable of completing the tasks they are assigned.

Guidance from the regulations and standards

Public Companies

The **AICPA Privacy Framework** and Trust Services Criteria call for performance appraisals of personnel that assess their professional and development activities. The Privacy Framework considers this in the context of ensuring employee qualifications with respect to the privacy and security of information. **The Combined Code** on Corporate Governance calls for periodic performance evaluations of directors under Board supervision. **SAS 94** also mentions performance appraisals as it applies to the auditor's consideration of an organization's internal environment.

Banking/Finance

The FFIEC Management handbook lists one of the effective components of human resources management as performance reviews. It also suggests that management be provided with incentives contingent on meeting IT performance goals.

General Guidance

CobiT calls for employee performance evaluations as detailed in the above summary. **COSO** also address performance appraisals in terms of an organization's internal environment human resource standards. The **ISF Standard of Good Practices for Information Security** does not directly call for performance evaluations, but notes that appraisals should be linked directly to an individual's adherence to security policies.

CobiT 4 PO7.7 says that timely evaluations should be performed on a regular basis to determine the organization's goals, established standards and specific job responsibilities.

United Kingdom and Canadian Guidance

BS 15000-2 calls for service provides to review each individual's performance at least annually, and take action based on the results.

From regulation to reality — sure signs you are complying

There are a few elements to keep in mind if you want to get your performance review process up and running. First, figure out how frequently you will have performance evaluations. Second, base your evaluations on existing standards. Finally, provide incentive to management to complete the reviews regularly.

The frequency of performance evaluations will depend on the job function of a particular group of staff and the nature of the tasks they are performing. It is recommended that you create set intervals for performance evaluations, and if necessary add in additional evaluations for a particular project. The more sensitive a task is, the more checks you should institute to ensure that the staff working on the task are getting it right.

Base evaluations on existing standards and pre-defined job responsibilities and goals. The point of these evaluations is to ensure that the staff you hired are doing what you hired them for, and doing it well. Always reward your staff for positive work appraisals – this gives them incentive to continue on in the same fashion. The award system should be clearly defined and applied consistently. Once evaluations have taken place, you should discuss the performance with your staff. Staff should be counseled as to performance or conduct.

One of the most effective components of human resource management is the completion of performance reviews. This process includes providing management with incentives on meeting established IT performance goals. This will encourage them to motivate staff and run a tight ship with regards to projects and deadlines. Finally, make sure you address compliance with IT security requirements and policies in the evaluations. Ensuring security is an ongoing process and should be considered every step of the way.

How do you handle job change and termination?

It's not easy firing people or changing their job functions. Aside from potential emotional issues – such as liking an employee as a person but realizing they can't meet their job standards – there's procedure to worry about. If you don't have well defined procedures, you might fire someone, but discover three months later that you haven't gotten rid of the person – instead they've been logging onto your systems ever since termination! Avoid these tricky situations by using the following control objective:

> *To make job change and termination situations smoother, the organization will institute procedures for both circumstances, creating a protocol or checklist of steps to follow.*

Once you've defined your procedures and protocols, terminating someone becomes simpler – you will have a checklist of activities to carry out to ensure an employee is properly removed.

Guidance from the regulations and standards

Public Companies

The **AICPA Trust Services Criteria** call for processing integrity measures that provide for termination of user accounts when the human resources department informs system owners of termination.

Banking/Finance

The **FFIEC Management handbook** calls for management to establish a timely process for removing or changing access rights when an individual's job changes or is terminated.

Credit Card

VISA CISP and **MasterCard SDP** call for revocation of access privileges whenever an employee or contractor leaves the company.

Government

FISCAM addresses the need for revoking the access rights of employees who have left the organization and its applicability to financial statement audits.

NIST Special Publications

NIST 800-53 is actually the most detailed of any standard, and in addition to what is summarized above, calls for exit interviews and access to any stored records the employee created.

Much like NIST 800-53, **NIST 800-14** is the most detailed standard and stipulates provisions for both friendly and unfriendly termination. Friendly termination requires removal of access privileges, accounts and tokens, a confidentiality briefing, return of property, and any cryptographic keys should be made available to management. Unfriendly termination dictates that account and access privileges should be revoked as soon as possible, before notification of termination or immediately upon resignation.

General Guidance

CobiT states that management must ensure that appropriate and timely actions are taken whenever an employee job change or termination occurs, in order to protect internal controls and security. It does not detail any specific procedures. **CobiT** 4 PO7.8 tells us that when a job termination is to occur, knowledge transfer needs to be arranged, responsibilities reassigned and access rights removed so that risks are minimized and continuity of the function is guaranteed.

The **ISF Standard of Good Practices for Information Security** calls for a documented procedure requiring revocation of access rights for individuals who have been terminated.

US State Laws

CA 1386 call for revocation of access privileges whenever an employee or contractor leaves the company.

From regulation to reality – sure signs you are complying

Whether you are dealing with a termination or a job change, the most important element to keep in mind is access rights. If you're dealing with a termination, they need to be revoked immediately. If you're dealing with a change, they need to be modified to suit the person's new work. In either situation, clear, well defined procedures make the process much simpler.

For terminated employees, revoke access rights, accounts, tokens and keys immediately. Change any passwords that the employee may have known. Any system related property, such as keys or ID cards should be confiscated upon termination. If possible, management should have exit interviews with terminated individuals, briefing them on the continued obligation of confidentiality. Remember, termination can be friendly or unfriendly, so make sure you prepare accordingly.

When changing an employee's job function, make sure their access rights change to be consistent with the new job function. As we have mentioned several times before, access rights should always be the minimum amount necessary to perform the job function, no more, no less. Counsel the employee on the new job function, confidentiality of information from the previous job functions and changing access rights and passwords. Change any keys, tokens and ID cards to make them consistent with the new job function.

The most important thing is to ensure you have procedures in place for termination and job function changes, so that the transition will be as smooth as possible. For more information on access rights and user termination, see the chapter on Technical Security.

How do you manage third-party interaction and service?

In the former sections, we have discussed how important it is have standards for recruitment, qualifications, security and training of internal staff. Of equal or greater importance is applying these principles and additional controls when contracting for third-party services. Use the following control objective for best results:

> *Because third-party service providers are not bound by organizational employment contracts or confidentiality standards, separate contracts must be formed, addressing all issues of organizational concern.*

Good management of third-party interaction and service involves careful planning, so that miscommunications and inappropriate expectations may be avoided.

Guidance from the regulations and standards

Public Companies

The **AICPA Privacy Framework** and **AICPA Trust Services Criteria** require third party and outsourcing contracts cover the protection of personal information and bind third parties to information security commitment. AICPA Criteria call for non-disclosure agreements. Both standards also address the need for counterparty trust through auditor reports.

NASD/NYSE

SEC Rule 240.17ad-7 calls for third party escrow arrangements for electronically stored records.

Banking/Finance

Graham-Leach Bliley, the **Federal Guidelines for Safeguarding Customer Information** and all **FFIEC handbooks** all require due diligence when selecting third party service providers and also call for non-disclosure agreements.

FFIEC elaborates further and fully details considerations for auditing third parties, including full details on **SAS 70** reporting. FFIEC also addresses third party and outsourcing contracts and escrow agreements. Both the Safeguarding Guidelines and FFIEC Information Security also call for continuous monitoring of third parties for compliance with contractual agreements.

Credit Card

VISA CISP and **MasterCard SDP** both call for third party and outsourcing contracts to require adherence to security controls and confidentiality (through non-disclosure agreements).

NIST Special Publications

NIST 800-53 calls for non-disclosure agreements and requires organizations to establish security requirements for third parties and outsourcing.

International Standards Organization

ISO 17799 addresses all concerns for third party contracts, including non-disclosure agreements.

The IT Infrastructure Library

ITIL Best Practice for Security Management 4.2.3.2 requires organizations to take appropriate security measures when exchanging information across a network. The measures should be laid down in an Interchange Agreement.

General Guidance

CobiT provides the most comprehensive controls for managing the interaction and services of third parties.

CobiT 4 DS2.2 requires organizations to formalize their relationships with suppliers through the use of service level agreements and active management of the relationship. DS2.4 says processes should be established to monitor service delivery to ensure the supplier is meeting current business requirements and is continuing to adhere to the contract agreements and service level agreements.

EU Guidance

The **OECD Risk Checklist** requires assurance reviews of third party security (SAS 70). It also requires consideration of third party service continuity and call for the ongoing monitoring of third parties to ensure their adherence to contractual agreements.

United Kingdom and Canadian Guidance

The **Turnbull Guidance** on **the Combined Code** also addresses the need for audit reviews of third parties.

From regulation to reality – sure signs you are complying

As you may have guessed, the first step in managing third-party interaction and services is to create procedures. These procedures should first address the following three steps:

- First, consider supplier interfaces. Identify all required third-party services and document technical and organizational interfaces.

- Second, have management appoint a relationship owner who is responsible for ensuring quality interactions with third-parties.

- Third, assess third-parties' capability to deliver the required services with due diligence, before selecting any service providers.

Once procedures have been created for the above three steps, you can move on to contracts. Before entering into a contract with a third-party provider, management should sit down and establish what the organization needs to get out of the contract. Some questions you may ask are: What are rights and obligations of the organization? What are the obligations of the third-party? What kind of liability is the organization willing to absorb? What needs to be done to protect confidentiality and integrity? What standards and regulations is the organization required to comply with?

After establishing organizational needs, then it's time to sit down and create a contract with the third-party. Formal contracts must contain numerous stipulations, including required processing levels, security, monitoring, and contingency requirements. They must address regulations and standards, liability and so forth. All third-parties, including independent auditors, should be required to sign non-disclosure agreements to protect organizational integrity and confidentiality. To ensure continuity, your organization should take into account business risk and negotiate escrow agreements where appropriate.

Review third-parties just as you would an internal employee. This can take the form of using external auditors to conduct the evaluation, such as a SAS 70 auditing, or using the third-parties own internal audit reports. Either way is acceptable, but whichever way works best for your organization *and* the third-party should be agreed upon in advance.

Create controls that authenticate third party electronic instructions or transactions through trusted exchange of cryptographic keys, tokens or passwords. The same importance is placed on access controls with third-parties as it is with employees. Ensure that when the third-party service is complete, access rights, keys, tokens and passwords have been revoked and terminated.

The final step in the process is monitoring. Management should establish procedures for consistent and continuous monitoring of third-parties, to ensure that all obligations of the contract are being met. Additional audits, reviews, supervision, or contract negotiations can be used to test whether third-parties are adhering to all agreed upon terms.

Operational Management

The Main Thing

Have you determined roles and responsibilities for operations management?

You will never encounter the situation where you go to pick something up with your hand and suddenly have your pinky become confused and try to take on the thumb's job. That's because each one of your fingers has a defined, specific role for each task you plan to use your hand for. If you want your IT operations management to run with the precision and efficiency of a hand, you need to ensure that you define and document each individual role. To avoid ending up with management that's all thumbs, institute the following control objective:

> *The organization will define roles and responsibilities for the board of directors and all management with regards to operational management of information governance. From the CIO to IT line and business unit managers, everyone has some measure of responsibility.*

It takes more than instinct to create an efficient IT operations management team. In this section we will arm you with information to guide you in defining the roles and responsibilities of operations management.

Guidance from the regulations and standards

Public Companies

Public standards do not specifically isolate roles and responsibilities for operational management. For the most part, management responsibilities for operations are mentioned in relation to auditors' assessments and interactions with organizations. The **AICPA** documents discuss management responsibility for various operational activities, but do not isolate a section dedicated to the subject. These responsibilities will be detailed in further summaries.

Banking/Finance

The **FFIEC Operations and Management** booklets are the most detailed when it comes to defining management of operations. The board of directors and senior management are responsible for providing oversight of IT operations. This includes proper risk philosophies and assessments, determining operational objectives, and delegating responsibility to operations management. The board and senior management establish and communicate an appropriate control environment and policies and standards governing IT.

FFIEC Management provides more specific guidance, describing the duties of both the CIO (Chief Information Officer) and CTO (Chief Technology Officer). The CIO, a member of senior management, retains authority over the IT initiatives of the organization, implementing the board's policies and objectives through strategic IT planning and capital investment. The CIO oversees the IT budget, and maintains responsibility for performance management, IT acquisitions, professional development, and training. The CTO, on the other hand, reports to the CIO and is a more narrowly defined role, concentrating more on tactics and efficiency of IT operations.

The standards further define the roles of IT line and business unit managers. Reporting to the CIO, CTO or other senior management, line managers are responsible for specific IT functions or departments. They coordinate daily activities, monitor production, and ensure adherence to schedules and IT controls defined by management policies. Business unit leaders ensure IT operations are soundly integrated with the appropriate business line. They establish processes to ensure compliance with IT controls within the business unit, and in a decentralized environment, take on many of the responsibilities for IT investments and implementation.

US Federal Security

The **Clinger-Cohen Act** clearly defines roles and responsibilities for managing IT operations. The Director of the Office of Management and Budget is equivalent to the board and senior management and sets strategic objectives and establishes policies for the acquisition and use of IT in government agencies. The Director also, obviously, oversees the budgeting of resources. The Director delegates authority over IT acquisitions and operations to the heads of all executive agencies, ensures proper policy adherence and training, and reports to congress on the status of the use of IT from a government-wide perspective.

The Act also requires a CIO be appointed as the head of IT solutions for every executive agency. The CIO enforces the Director's policies and procedures, overseeing the acquisition and performance of IT within the agency. In addition, the CIO monitors and measures the performance and use of information technology within the agency and instructs the heads of the agency whether to continue, change, or terminate a particular program or project. The CIO also annually reviews business and personnel requirements and is responsible for developing strategies and specific plans for hiring, training and professional development.

The **OMB Circular** further defines responsibilities for the heads of agencies, and is essentially more of the same, but more narrow in scope. Essentially, the heads of government agencies are charged with establishing policies for the acquisition and use of IT resources in compliance with policies and procedures defined by the OMB. Agency managers are also charged with maintaining an appropriate inventory of major information systems, holdings and information dissemination products.

The It Infrastructure Library

ITIL Best Practice for Security Management 5.2.4 – 5.2.5 talks about the role of a security manager. A good security manager should have a strong sense of responsibility and be highly trustworthy. This person needs extensive knowledge of ICT, typical security knowledge and a knowledge of financial reporting. In addition, a sense of PR and tactical skills are required. The person should have previous experience at the senior management level. An organization should give their security manager the authority to issue instructions to the workforce during security incidents if necessary, without asking for senior management's permission.

These sections also differentiate between a security manager and a security officer. A security officer is different in the sense that it is a role that is part of the customer function. This person acts as an intermediary between the security manager and the business, co-ordinates escalation in the event of security incidents, co-ordinates security measures to be implemented on the user's side and acts as interpreter of the official corporate security policy.

General Guidance

General standards like **CobiT** and the ISF Standard do not specifically devote a section or control objectives focused on the roles and responsibilities of management over IT operations. Most operational controls refer to the management responsible for the activity and will be noted in further summaries.

From regulation to reality – sure signs you are complying

There is a potentially infinite number of roles and responsibilities you could assign IT operations management, but there are definitely a few mandatory things to include in this process. First, define the key staff, which includes:

- Board of directors/Senior management
- Chief Information Officer

- Chief Technology Officer
- Line and business unit managers

Then, define the roles and responsibilities for these staff members based on their job titles and descriptions.

Board of Directors/Senior Management

The board of directors and senior management are responsible for the overall flow of IT operations. They define the risk philosophies and assessments that will be applied to each new IT task, choose operational objectives, and delegate responsibilities to appropriate operations management staff. To make this process easier, the board of directors and senior management should create an appropriate control environment for workers along with policies and standards for governing each IT task and worker responsibility.

Sometimes, as in the **Clinger-Cohen Act**, the roles and responsibilities of the board of directors and senior management is referred to as the Director of the Office of Management and Budget. This is a position title for a single person who handles all the duties of the board and senior management. The Director has additional roles, such as delegating authority over IT acquisitions and operations to the heads of all executive agencies within the organization, ensuring proper policy adherence and training, and reports to congress on the status of the use of IT from a government-wide perspective. A Director is also responsible for overseeing budgets of resources, as the title suggests.

Generally, if you are a government agency, you will follow the **Clinger-Cohen Act** methodology and have a Director of the Office of Management and Budget. If you're not a government agency, you could still combine some of the responsibilities of a Director into the Board of Directors or Senior Management's job. Either way, defining the roles and responsibilities of those on top will affect the roles of other management and staff, so make sure you define the responsibilities in a clear and consistent fashion.

Chief Information Officer

The CIO acts as the head of IT solutions for every executive agency in the organization, and is required to support and implement the policies and procedures created by the Director or the board and senior management (which the CIO is part of). The CIO also reviews business and personnel requirements, develops strategies and plans for hiring, training and professional development.

The CIO must also examine the performance and use of IT in the organization and instruct senior management for various groups as to whether they are to continue, change or terminate a specific project based on her findings.

Chief Technical Officer

The CTO of your organization has a more narrowly defined role than the CIO. Her job is to concentrate on tactics that can be used to promote efficiency of IT operations. She reports on all her findings and her work to the CIO.

Line and Business Unit Managers

Line and business unit managers may report to a variety of people in your organization depending on how you are set up. One option is for them to report to the CIO or the CTO. However, they can also report to other senior management as you see fit. The only rule is to maintain clarity. Whoever your people report to, it should be clear who that person is, what they expect of their workers, and how reports should be made to him.

Average tasks for line managers include coordinating daily activities, monitoring production, and ensuring adherence to schedules and IT controls defined by management policies. Business unit managers have similar roles, but their work is more IT based. Such a manager is responsible for making certain that IT operations are properly integrated with the appropriate business line. This type of manager is also responsible for ensuring compliance with any existing IT security controls. In certain settings, where responsibilities for IT investments and implementation are not centralized, a business unit manager may take on this type of work as well.

As you can see, roles and responsibilities can easily vary depending on how your organization is structured. This is fine, after all, variety is the spice of life. Just don't try adding ambiguity and lack of definition of roles and responsibilities as seasonings too. However you decide to structure work in your organization, make sure everyone has a clearly defined, clearly documented role with described responsibilities that they can turn to. The end result is increased efficiency, since no one will be stepping on one another's toes as they try to figure out what they're supposed to be doing.

Have you established key policies?

Any organization that expects to have an ounce of direction and order should establish some key policies. Creating an internal control environment will enable both you and your staff to understand what direction the organization is heading as well as what is generally acceptable. Policies help an organization function smoothly. Therefore, the control objective for this section is:

> *Based on overall strategic objectives and plans, management will establish, develop, document, implement and maintain policies covering general aims and directives.*

A little bit of direction can go a long way. In this section, we will dive deeper and establish key policies.

Guidance from the regulations and standards

Public Companies

The PCAOB Auditing Standards and **SAS 94** both address the need for organizations to develop an internal control environment and the auditor's responsibility for assessment of related controls and policies. The **AICPA Privacy Framework** calls for organizations to delegate responsibility for the establishment, maintenance and review of a privacy policy, communication of the policy to all personnel, and procedures for ensuring employee compliance. It also charges management with the responsibility for developing and implementing privacy awareness and training. The framework also requires that resources are properly allocated for the implementation and support of privacy policies and that such policies are reviewed regularly. The **AICPA Suitable Trust Services Criteria** also calls for the establishment and communication of policies, and procedures for ensuring compliance. The criteria require that organizations define and document security policies and details the contents, also calling for a security awareness training program for all personnel.

Banking/Finance

FFIEC discusses the establishment of policies as a component of risk mitigation and provides examples of possible policies, such as business continuity, strategic planning, capital investment and security. In general, FFIEC covers the promulgation of policies as summarized above, further emphasizing that policies provide a basis for standards and should be relative to the complexity of the IT environment. The Information Security document calls for an information security strategy and a policy to support it. In addition, FFIEC calls for security awareness training for all employees. The Management handbook also calls for quality assurance procedures but no specific policy. The standard further addresses the need for a process to ensure compliance with organizational policies, standards and procedures.

Aside from the FFIEC standards, the **Appendix of Standards for Safeguarding Customer Information (12 CFR 30)** calls for management to implement an information security program and document it (as a policy, one would assume), and to train all employees in the implementation of the program.

Healthcare and Life Sciences

HIPAA calls for a security management process that consists of policies and procedures to preserve the security of electronic protected health information. It also requires a security awareness and training program be implemented for an organization's entire workforce.

Credit Card

The **VISA CISP, MasterCard SDP,** and **AMEX DSS** programs all call for an information security policy or plan that should be communicated to all employees, complied with, reviewed and updated as circumstances require. Both the VISA and MasterCard programs also require security awareness training for all members.

US Federal Security

The OMB Circular (of the **Clinger-Cohen Act**) and **FISCAM** both call for security programs that implement information security through policies. FISMA, NIST, OMB, the **National Cyberspace Strategy** and FISCAM all call for security awareness training or an associated program to make government employees aware of their security responsibilities.

Federal Information Processing Standards Publications 191 1.5.5(1) lists inadequate LAN management and security policies as a security concern because it contributes to risk associated with a LAN. A good security policy offers a clear statement of management's position on information values, protection responsibilities and organizational commitment. Such a policy is in place to provide direction and support from the highest levels of management. Appendix A, pg. 14-16 describes general policies for a LAN. It calls for assigning ownership and responsibilities for equipment as small as a single computer up to an entire network. Users are expected to know the security policy and follow all procedures for maintaining security of sensitive data. Functional Managers and other high-level management are to develop the policies that users will follow, and ensure that each user is aware of the policies. The appendix also calls for the LAN Management Division to be responsible for enforcing security policies, advising management on how to maintain policies in their departments, securing the network, responding to incidents, keeping security tools up-to-date and functional, determining when and where to improve existing technology and examining audit logs. Local Administrators are to be responsible for managing user access privileges, maintaining LAN server software, scanning LAN servers with anti-virus software, assigning and revoking user IDs and passwords and notifying appropriate groups of security incidents. While each organization may not assign these specific roles and responsibilities, all of these responsibilities should be assigned in some fashion so they are covered. In addition to roles and responsibilities, Appendix A pg. 13 describes general aspects of a good security policy. A good policy states management's position on the value of information, responsibilities for protecting the LAN and who they are assigned to, the organization's commitment to protecting information and the LAN and finally, what constitutes the LAN environment and what parts may be exempted. Appendix D pg. 17 adds to this by requiring that an organization train its staff to carry out the duties they are assigned by the security policy, and more generalized training to make everyone one aware of the security rules.

1.6 calls for creating a policy that achieves the basic goals of maintaining confidentiality and integrity of stored data, maintaining the availability of stored data, and ensuring the identity of a sender and receiver of a message.

NIST Special Publications

NIST 800-14 § 3.1.1 addresses the establishment of policies in broad terms. It calls for a security program composed of policies and procedures describing how to handle security incidents, and day-to-day maintenance of security systems, and improvements of systems.

NIST 800-61 2.3- 2.3.1 talks about creating incident response policies and procedures. Key elements include a statement of management commitment, purpose and objectives of the policy, the scope of the policy, a definition of computer security incidents and their consequences, a layout of organizational structure including roles, responsibilities and levels of authority, prioritization of incidents, performance measures and reporting and contact forms.

NIST 800-66 An Introductory Resource Guide for Implementing the Health Insurance Portability and Accountability Act (HIPAA) Security Rule 4.2 addresses § 164.308(a)(2). This section covers selection of an official who will be made responsible for development and implementation of policies and procedures for security. The information provided is not highly detailed—activities include selecting a competent person to manage security and documenting all of this person's responsibilities and privileges.

4.1 matches with § 164.308(a)(1) of the HIPAA Standard and describes how to implement policies and procedures that prevent, detect, contain and correct security violations. A chart provides a list of activities to aid an organization in implementing these policies and procedures. Due to the high level of detail, it is best to read the chart directly from the document.

4.5 addresses § 164.308(a)(5) of the HIPAA Standard. This section explains how to implement a security awareness and training program for all employees. A chart lays out all the activities an organization must take to implement a training program. The chart is too detailed to summarize here, so it is best to review it in the NIST 800-66 document.

The IT Infrastructure Library

ITIL Best Practice for Security Management 2.2.3 says that top management must support information security policies for them to succeed. A management framework should be in place to review security measures as well as ensure they are being effectively implemented. 4.2.3.2 discusses the creation of security policies and procedures to prevent the misuse of IT resources and ensure they operate correctly. This section recommends creating operational procedures and responsibilities and documenting them. It also calls for the creation of incident management procedures, segregation of duties, separation of development and production, provisions for external facilities management, handling and security of data carriers and provisions for network management and services.

4.3.1-4.3.2 talks about ensuring compliance with created security policies within the organization. Different ways to be sure of compliance are listed, such as conducting security reviews of IT systems and facilities and conducting EDP audits.

3.1.1 presents a detailed model of IT Security management. The model is set up to allow an organization to meet external and internal security requirements. This section should be reviewed directly.

4.2.2.2 calls for making staff aware of security through training.

International Standards Organization

ISO 17799 concentrate on security and internal control policies and also call for security awareness training or associated programs.

General Guidance

CobiT addresses establishment of policies in broad terms. CobiT pretty much covers everything summarized above, while the ISF Standard,

CobiT 4 PO6.3 states that organizations should develop and maintain policies that support the IT strategy. The policies should include policy intent, roles and responsibilities, exception process, compliance approach and references to procedures, standards and guidelines. Topics covered should include quality, security, confidentiality, internal controls and intellectual property. PO6.1 suggests defining the elements of a control environment for IT. It should be aligned with the organization's management and operating styles. In addition, elements such as expectations regarding the delivery of value from IT investments, risk tolerance, integrity, ethical values, staff competence, accountability and responsibility should be defined. PO6.4 calls for ensuring that IT policies are rolled out to all appropriate employees in a timely fashion, and enforced.

PO8.1 says that a quality management system that provides a standard, formal and continuous approach regarding quality management and is aligned with business requirements should be created. PO8.4 asks that the quality management system have a customer focus so that IT standards are aligned towards customer needs. PO8.5 calls for continually striving to improve the quality plan as well as ensure it is communicated across the organization. PO6.5 says that all IT security objectives and goals should be communicated clearly throughout the organization so all employees know their security responsibilities.

US State Laws

CA 1386 also calls for security and privacy awareness training and requires organizations to monitor employee compliance with security and privacy policies.

EU Guidance

The **OECD Risk Checklist** concentrate more on security and internal control policies calls for security awareness training or associated programs.

United Kingdom and Canadian Guidance

BS 15000-2 a concentrates on security and internal control policies and also calls for security awareness training or associated programs.

From regulation to reality – sure signs you are complying

Key policies are created by management in your organization and cover general aims and directives. Just as strong trees grow from strong roots, useful policies grow from a strong foundation. Before having management undertake the process of establishing, developing, documenting, implementing and maintaining key policies, you need to ensure you have the following:

- Overall strategic objectives and plans for your organization

- An appropriate internal control environment

You need an understanding of the goals your organization wishes to attain before you can develop policies that suit those ends. To make sure the team of managers assigned to create key policies is properly oriented, distribute the documentation describing your organization's strategic objectives and discuss them. If all is well, you can proceed to the second criteria you need to start working on making policies to create a good internal control environment.

Internal control environments indicate the way your organization deals with issues such as ethical values, integrity, competence of staff, management philosophy, operating style and accountability. How these things come into play in daily office life depends upon the framework that management creates to deal with these issues, and how clearly your organization describes the goals for each one. Key policies thrive in a positive control environment, and it is up to management to see that such an environment exists, is maintained, and that all employees are aware of it.

Once you're certain you have both criteria, you can begin creating key policies. These should cover three basic areas, information security, privacy and training. They should draw on the framework provided by the existing criteria we just discussed so that staff can easily understand and comply with them.

Your information security policy should address internal control over IT resources and systems as well as your organization's overall approach to security. The goals of this policy are to protect integrity, availability and confidentiality of your organization's information. This is a lot to cover, but keep in mind this particular policy is high-level. It defines security purposes and objectives, management structure, scope, assignment of responsibilities for implementations at all levels and the consequences of not complying with the policy. In general, much of this policy will draw on existing processes and procedures within your organization. You should reference any documentation that describes security features, controls and procedures. The final aspect of this policy to consider is maintenance. Determine how often it will be reviewed, and define the criteria for indicating its effectiveness and how to update it.

The next policy to consider is your organization's privacy policy. Some aspects of it might seem simple, for example, employees should not tell competitors what they are working on. However, in the long run, it's not that obvious what needs to be kept private, what doesn't, how to decide which is which, and how to maintain effective privacy. Poorly defined privacy policies that rely on 'common sense' or 'everybody should know' bases lead to information leaks to the wrong places and can even trickle down to involve mistakenly showing customer information to the wrong pairs of eyes. Customer information is a much bigger problem for you than leaks to competitors since multiple regulations have a lot to say about how to preserve the privacy of data you take in from customers.

Fortunately, there's a simple solution to all your privacy woes. Define a clear-cut policy that touches on how to handle customer data, what procedures an employee must go through to release information, what topics are classified within the organization and what the consequences of breaching privacy are. Again, for ease of use, this policy should build on existing frameworks. Not just because it's easier for management to create, but because it's easier for everyone to follow. If you write a policy that is completely different from your company culture, philosophy and existing procedures, you will end up with a lot of people scratching their heads trying to figure out what to do, which means a lot less work is getting done.

The final policy you need to put together ties back into the first two policies we've discussed, and that is training. Without training the other two policies describing procedures and rules are utterly useless. Just as a product with no advertising will not sell, a policy that no one is aware of will not work. Training policies have several components you need to plan for. The first component is deciding what training you will offer employees. You may need to offer specialized sets of training. Employees working with customer data will need to know how to handle that data. Employees dealing with IT security will need to know how to use certain applications or analyze materials for different kinds of security breaches. Everyone will need to be made aware of general security and privacy principles. With a team of managers, write out a plan describing who needs to know what special information for their work, and what general awareness everyone needs to know about.

The next step for training is to schedule it into employee's daily workloads. Take the time to coordinate training with worker schedules by speaking with their managers. Be aware that when you schedule training will have everything to do with how enthusiastic and ready to absorb information your employees will be. For example, if you schedule four hours of mandatory all-staff training and it begins at 7a.m., many people will be annoyed about getting up early and probably tired. They won't retain as much as if you'd scheduled the same meeting beginning at say, 10 a.m. Another example has to do with employee workloads. If you schedule training during a crunch time, those employees will be stressed and may either try to avoid the training to do work, or attend and be unable to focus since they will be thinking about what they need to get done outside the meeting. We're going over all this because security and privacy awareness training is some of the most important training your organization will do. The more training fits into employee schedules without being a nuisance, the more they will benefit from the information included in the sessions.

The final aspect of training is a commonly neglected area. Everyone likes to start new things, but nobody really likes maintenance much. It's absolutely vital though, that your training policies include mandatory refresher courses and update sessions whenever your information security and privacy policies change in some way. Lack of maintenance will lead to outdated training, which can ultimately lead to compromise of privacy and security across your organization.

Have you documented all your policies and procedures?

Policies and procedures govern every systems development, acquisition, implementation, modification and maintenance. And, it is incredibly important that these policies and procedures are documented. Therefore, the control objective for this section is:

> *In order to effectively enforce and ensure adherence to policies and procedures, management must provide commensurate documentation. Operational requirements and service levels must be defined, user procedures and operations manuals must be developed, and training materials must be provided.*

In this section we will explore the need for documenting all of your policies and procedures.

Guidance from the regulations and standards

Banking/Finance

The **FFIEC Development and Acquisitions handbook** addresses documentation in broader terms, as documentation standards. It mentions documenting non-technical policies and procedures as well as operating and user instructions.

Healthcare and Life Sciences

HIPAA calls for policies and procedures relating to electronic protected health information to be maintained in written form.

NIST 800-66 § 4.22 addresses § 164.316(b)(1) of the HIPAA Standard. This section calls for documenting policies and procedures for management, operational and technical controls. It also covers how long to retain documentation, how often to update it, and how to make it readily available to employees who need to review it.

Credit Card

VISA CISP briefly calls for training materials in the form of posters, letters and memos.

NIST Special Publications

NIST 800-14 addresses the need for training materials as part of an overall employee training program.

International Standards Organization

ISO 17799 calls for defined and documented operational requirements as well as documented operating procedures.

The IT Infrastructure Library

ITIL Best Practice for Security Management 4.2.3.2 asks that organizations document their operating procedures for management of operations with specific attention paid to segregation of duties and security incident handling.

General Guidance

CobiT frames these documentation requirements in terms of the software development lifecycle methodology. It calls for all the above documentation for every systems development, implementation or modification project.

United Kingdom and Canadian Guidance

BS 15000-2 requires a service catalogue be developed that contains definitions of service levels and other details.

From regulation to reality – sure signs you are complying

Policies and procedures aren't very useful until you put them on paper. You can argue about how things are supposed to go with a person, but it is well nigh impossible to argue with a paper covered with words. To ensure clarity throughout your organization the best thing you can do is document everything. Collect policies and procedures for every systems development, acquisition, implementation, modification and maintenance project you can find. If there aren't documents for all these things, have them written up. If you find yourself in the position where you cannot write them up, then implement a procedure for writing up such projects in the future. Written documentation improves your organization's ability to organize, plan, spot weaknesses and adjust for greater efficiency. It also makes everyone's life a lot easier when it comes time for an audit. Handing an auditor a stack of neatly organized documents that's been properly maintained and updated is much easier than having each manager in each department verbally describe their processes and procedures.

There are many other uses for documenting policies and procedures across your organization. You can use documents to record operational requirements, service levels and provide training to people who use your products or your own employees. Documentation also comes in handy for matters of compliance. Most regulations want to see that you've documented your policies and that you provide instructions to users on how to operate your products. You'll find it much easier to align yourself with the objectives set forth by nearly any standard if you are in the practice of carefully documenting all your work.

What are your standards?

Policies and standards are closely linked. Whereas policies are generally high-level and broad in nature, standards are more narrow in scope and establish measurable controls and requirements to achieve policy objectives. Just as a organization must have policies, it must also have standards. Therefore, the control objective for this section is:

> *Organizations should standardize hardware, software and the operating environment with respect to the IT infrastructure, business decisions, and risk analysis.*

Standardization creates a sharper focus that organizations can use to streamline operations, security, development, acquisitions and maintenance and provides a basis for detailed procedures and regulation. Technology standards will inevitably provide interoperability, simplify risk management, and allow for more timely restoration and recovery of critical systems.

Guidance from the regulations and standards

Public Companies

The **AICPA Suitable Trust Services Criteria** calls for processes to follow standards but does not specifically call for the establishment of standards or go into detail concerning them.

Banking/Finance

The **FFIEC Operations handbook** goes into the most detail about standards, primarily from a technological perspective. It discusses the role and benefits of standardization as detailed above. The document also warns that organizations that have standardized software and hardware should still be aware that standards may need to be waived for certain applications or hardware configurations.

US Federal Security

The **Clinger-Cohen Act** calls for the establishment of standards and guidelines, designating the Secretary of Commerce as the primary authority. It also allows for heads of agencies to develop more stringent standards and includes a clause permitting the Secretary to waive standards as needs require. Though the standards cover "the efficiency of operation, security and privacy of federal computer systems", the Act does not offer any additional details about the standards other than that they are based on NIST regulations.

Records Management

ISO 15489-2 recommends the development or adoption of recordkeeping standards in addition to policies and procedures but does not provide details on the nature of standards.

DIRKS Step E is more detailed and discusses "standards tactics" for designing a recordkeeping system, citing interoperability, maintainability, portability, extensibility and possible focuses of standards within an organization.

NIST Special Publications

NIST 800-14 mentions that standards may be developed due to the broad nature of policies, but does not offer any further details. The ISF Standard tends to list most of its control objectives with respect to "policies, standards, and procedures", implying the existence of standards, but does not provide for the development of standards.

General Guidance

CobiT does not address standardization universally, but does call for technology standards that define technology norms based on the IT infrastructure.

CobiT 4 PO8.2 requires that IT standards, procedures and quality practices for key IT processes be identified and maintained with the goal of meeting quality management system objectives.

From regulation to reality – sure signs you are complying

Because policies and standards are closely linked to one another, it's easy to confuse what they are. A policy states at a high-level what you need to accomplish. A standard is like a policy, but at a more detailed level. It tells you how you will do what the policy says must be done and defines a way of quantifying how well you achieve the goal by creating measurable controls and requirements. A common problem with creating standards is having multiple well written, detailed requirements that don't overlap with one another. At the risk of sounding redundant, you need to avoid this issue by standardizing your standards. Come up with a method for creating and documenting procedures for operations, security, development, acquisitions, maintenance as well as a basis for detailed procedures and regulation.

Important standards to prioritize are technology standards and recordkeeping standards.

Technology standards include the efficiency of computer systems as well as privacy, operation and security. You should also expect to include hardware, software, operating environment, business decisions and risk analysis, all with respect to your organization's IT infrastructure. Recordkeeping standards should describe the way you store records classified at different security levels, how you transfer them, how long you keep them for and how you will maintain their integrity.

What's your policy on acceptable use?

Does your organization have a policy on acceptable use? Well, if not, you should. To start, take a look at this detailed control objective:

> *In addition to the key policies of the organization, management will develop acceptable use policies (AUPs) for any users who will be accessing internal systems. Users will range from the organizations own developers to end-user customers. The AUP will detail permitted system uses, user activities, and the consequences of non-compliance. Authorized internal users will receive a copy of the policy and appropriate training, and signify their understanding and agreement with the AUP before management grants access. For external customers, Web site disclosures (terms-of-agreement) will function as AUPs.*

But don't stop with the control objective. We provide detailed information acceptable use policies in this section.

Guidance from the regulations and standards

Banking/Finance

The **FFIEC Information Security handbook** addresses acceptable use policies within the framework of logistical access rights. It details AUPs thoroughly, and includes examples of elements of AUPs, such as bans on attempting to break into accounts, crack passwords, or disrupt service. The FFIEC Management booklet calls for management to require periodic acknowledgement of AUPs.

NIST Special Publications

As part of personnel security, **NIST 800-53** requires personnel to comply with various access agreements, including acceptable use policies, but does not provide any further details on them.

International Standards Organization

ISO 17799 details access control policies that contain similar elements.

EU Guidance

The **OECD Risk Checklist** includes use policies under personnel security. Also like NIST, the Checklist only seems to be referring to internal user access.

From regulation to reality – sure signs you are complying

Does it bother you when people place coffee on their desks next to their laptop because you think it could potentially spill and wreck it? How about if an employee decides his tower makes a great paperweight? What if someone likes writing their password on a post-it note and attaching it to the monitor so they can easily type it in each morning, just like anyone else who happens by? The point of these questions is, if you don't do something to let everyone know what acceptable use of internal organization systems is and isn't, the sky's the limit on how stupid or how anal retentively security conscious people can get.

The first part of an acceptable use policy is figuring out who uses what in your organization. Not everyone needs to know every last procedure for every last system you have. Organize users into groups that denote their use privileges. All privileges should be based on whether users need to access certain materials for their work. Once you have identified your users, you can proceed to the next part of developing your policy.

An acceptable use policy (AUP) should be created by management and distributed to anyone who accesses internal systems. There may be multiple AUPs tailored to the different systems and privileges of your staff. A good policy will detail what users cannot do, such as try to break into an account, crack a password, or disrupt a certain service. It will also detail what they ought to do. For example your policy might include explaining to a user that he needs to lock his computer before stepping away from it.

A highly effective AUP will not only describe the dos and don'ts of system use, but will describe the consequences of errors or malicious attacks. The consequences are as much a warning to users as they are a way of regulating and standardizing response to violations of AUPs within the organization.

Do you have operations procedures in place?

You may be thinking, more procedures? But procedures are key to a well functioning organization. Especially when it comes to IT operations. Procedures should be developed and documented to ensure that IT operations are handled in an effective manner. Take a look at the following control objective:

> Based on pre-established policies and standards, management must develop and document procedures for IT operations and processing. Management should ensure that personnel are adequately familiar and confident with the system start-up and close-down process, back-up, and other operations procedures. Furthermore, continuous scheduling of jobs, processes and tasks should be organized efficiently. Procedures should also require processing continuity during operator shift changes, providing for formal handover of activity, status updates and reports on current responsibilities. All procedures should be reviewed, tested, and updated regularly.

Now, turn to the regulations and standards for guidance on IT operations procedures.

Guidance from the regulations and standards

Public Companies

The **AICPA Trust Services Criteria** call for documented computer operations and job scheduling procedures consistent with documented processing integrity policies and standards.

Banking/Finance

The **FFIEC Operations handbook** discusses the development and documentation of procedures governing IT operations. The standard covers a wider basis, including incident, problem, configuration, change, database management and other procedures that have been detailed in previous or further summaries. It does not go into detail regarding job scheduling or remote operations.

US Federal Security

The **OMB Circular A-130** calls for authorization in writing of the use of each general support system before beginning or changing processing in the system. This seems to imply that operations procedures must be documented and approved.

International Standards Organization

ISO 17799 calls for documentation of operations procedures, but does not detail job scheduling, processing continuity, or remote operations procedures.

The IT Infrastructure Library

ITIL Best Practice for Security Management 3.4.2 discusses the importance of maintaining the technical availability of IT components. Reliable, resilient systems that are maintainable are ideal.

General Guidance

CobiT calls for the development and documentation of operations procedures as detailed in the summary above.

CobiT 4 DS13.1 states that organizations should create procedures for IT operations and ensure that all operations staff is familiar with procedures necessary for their daily jobs. DS13.2 calls for organizing and scheduling jobs, processes and tasks into the most efficient sequence while still meeting business requirements. All job schedules should be authorized prior to initialization.

From regulation to reality – sure signs you are complying

Operations procedures should be built based on pre-established standards and policies. Management develops these procedures for documenting IT operations and processing. All procedures should include a mechanism for processing continuity during operator shift changes, formal handover of activity, status updates and reports on current responsibilities. For remote operations, specific procedures should ensure that the connection and disconnection of links to the remote site or sites are defined and implemented.

In general, you create procedures to make it clear what needs to be done, how it needs to be done and above all, to ensure continuity. Each procedure should be placed in writing and made available to staff that works with them. In addition, management should see to it that all their employees are familiar and confident with any operations procedures they are responsible for. If necessary, provide training for crucial procedures. Such procedures definitely include system start-up, shut down and back-up. Having a staff that is comfortable with these procedures means having a staff that can guarantee systems continuity should anything go wrong.

Ideally, training should be offered to at least make staff aware of procedures, and if possible demonstrate the procedures. All training should be repeated to ensure it is not forgotten, and to allow for the dissemination of modifications or updates to any processes the employees are accustomed to doing.

Do you have service level agreements?

When IT provides services to other departments within your organization or to customer outside the organization, generally a service level agreement is recommended. Creating a generalized service level agreement, that lists the internal needs of the organization, is useful. Once you know the service needs of the IT operations staff, then you can create service agreements with others. The control objective for this section is:

> *During the creation of documented policies, senior management has defined operational requirements and service levels to be met by the IT function. Consequently, management must establish a framework for service level agreements (SLAs).*

In this section we will take a detailed look at service level agreements so that IT operations can get exactly what they need out of a service level agreement.

Guidance from the regulations and standards

Public Companies

The **AICPA Privacy Framework** does not address the development of SLAs, but does include SLAs and contracts as documents required for annual review. The **AICPA Suitable Trust Service Criteria** goes a little bit further and calls for user requirements to be documented in service level agreements and that SLAs be reviewed annually. It also implies monitoring of service performance by requiring that risk be evaluated against SLAs during security reviews.

Banking/Finance

While the **FFIEC Management handbook** does not detail SLAs thoroughly, it does cover the main requirements. The standard calls for the establishment of SLAs with both in-house and outsourced providers and discusses measures for monitoring and reporting levels of service. It discusses using outcome-based measurements and performance benchmarks to monitor levels of service against baseline expectations.

The IT Infrastructure Library

ITIL Best Practice for Security Management 2.3 says that IT Security management should define the security demands for IT. These are referred to as security service level requirements, and are reflected in the Service Level Agreement (SLA) between the customer (the business) and the IT service organization. The service organization must detail all generic security service level requirements with specific security measures per system and/or organizational unit within their organization. 2.3.1.2 mentions that SLAs are refined in Operational Level Agreements, which define IT support requirements internally. 4.5.2 talks about offering reports including information about SLAs. For example it mentions creating a report that indicates how much security plans conform to the SLA.

International Standards Organization

ISO 17799 covers third party contract services extensively, but only mentions SLAs with respect to cryptographic services.

General Guidance

CobiT devotes an entire section to SLAs and addresses all aspects and procedures surrounding them as summarized above. CobiT does not get very specific concerning the review process or service improvement program. The ISF Standard covers the basics of SLAs, including key aspects and review requirements.

CobiT 4 DS1.3 calls for defining and agreeing to service level agreements for all critical IT services based on customer requirements and IT capabilities. DS1.1 recommends creating a service level management framework. This framework should include processes for creating service requirements, service definitions, service level agreements, operating level agreements and funding sources. DS1.2 says organizations should base definitions of IT services on service characteristics and business requirements. DS1.5 indicates that organizations should continuously monitor specified service level performance criteria to ensure everything is going as planned and agreed. DS1.6 requires organizations to regularly review and update service level agreements and underpinning contracts to ensure they are still appropriate.

United Kingdom and Canadian Guidance

BS 15000-2 is a standard that deals primarily with service management, and is therefore quite informative on the subject. It addresses SLAs in great detail and also provides a process for continuous improvement of service.

Though it does not call for a service improvement program, it does require a similar policy or plan.

From regulation to reality – sure signs you are complying

For any service there is a service provider and a customer. When documented policies are being created for your organization, senior management defined operational requirements and service levels to be met by the IT function. As a result of their work, direct management for IT must create a framework for handling service level agreements (SLAs). For our purposes, we define a service level agreement as a contract between the service provider and the user of the service. Users are often from other departments within your organization, but they may also be customers outside your organization, depending on the services you offer. While external customers can be more problematic and require more careful agreements, it is best to have a solid SLA put together that works well for your in-house and external needs.

A service level agreement must cover the following aspects of service to be useful:

- Availability
- Reliability
- Performance
- Capacity for growth
- Levels of support provided to users
- Continuity planning
- Security
- Minimum level of satisfactorily delivered system functionality
- Restrictions (limits on workloads)
- Service charges
- Central print facilities and distribution
- Change procedures

For each of these points, define the responsibilities of the service provider and the users. If you have different service providers and user groups, come up with a break down of roles and responsibilities for each grouping with clear labels. That way, each type of service, the roles and requirements for all parties involved are documented for ease of use.

An ideal service level agreement lists what the IT function offers, what quality the offering is, and how much of the service is available. The user end also has limits defined so that users cannot make too many demands upon the IT function. Additional elements of a service level agreement may include non-disclosure agreements if some technology or information is being displayed that should not be passed around, as well as codes of conduct. Good codes of conduct make it easy to weed out problematic users. For example on yahoo, if you use an email address to purposely send other addresses viruses, you would be violating user responsibilities outlined in the code of conduct. Yahoo could then shut down your account.

Beyond actual agreements, a framework for monitoring SLAs should also be implemented. A service level manager should be appointed to monitor and report on the achievement of service performance and criteria, as well as any problems encountered during processing.

In addition to monitoring service levels, management can ensure they are being met by creating an annual SLA review process, and a service improvement program. The SLA review process includes examining any underpinning contracts with third party service providers. The review process ensures quality, and helps the organization spot weaknesses in maintaining service levels. This is where the service improvement program comes into play. Whatever problems are uncovered during the review can be fixed with this program. To avoid fixing every last little glitch that's found, which can be a big waste of time if the glitches aren't big enough, compare processes against a service level baseline. You can then easily see what service targets are being directly reached, are improving as planned, and what needs work. Combined with the information gathered from the review, you can implement plans for improvement. Please note that this process is only effective if you base service targets and improvements on business and operational requirements that are communicated to all affected users and providers in the form of a policy or a plan. If you skip this part, it will be difficult to improve service or hit targets, because no one will be sure of what to expect.

For all programs involving creating, maintaining and reviewing SLAs, take the time to determine their successes and failures so that you can replace, update, develop or maintain them as needed.

Do you have a help desk available for user support?

Users will need support. That is certain. The sun will shine somewhere tomorrow, the dogs will bark at the gardener and users will need IT help. That's OK; you want to help them. That is why you have a help desk. Therefore, the control objective for this section is:

> *Management will institute a user support process in the form of a help desk function. Users to be supported include end-user customers, clients, and anyone who utilizes the organization's IT services.*

If you are not convinced you need a help desk yet, just think about users banging on your door every time something freezes or crashes and then you will understand. IT help is a job all in itself, and you don't want other folks with other responsibilities wasting their valuable time trying to fix IT problems. Leave it to the experts. Leave it the people who get paid to provide IT help. And free up all the other IT staff's time so that they can do the things they were hired for.

Guidance from the regulations and standards

Public Companies

The **AICPA Suitable Trust Service Criteria** call for users to be provided with instructions for communicating issues to the help desk or customer service center. The criteria also require that procedures exist to escalate issues that cannot be resolved by the help desk.

Banking/Finance

The **FFIEC Operations handbook** is the most detailed in its description of user support services. Though it does not address trend analysis and reporting, it does thoroughly detail methods for submission of queries and strategies for help desk functions.

Records Management

DIRKS briefly mentions help desk systems as being recipients of information on new or modified recordkeeping systems.

The IT Infrastructure Library

ITIL Best Practice for Security Management § 3.3.2 describes the role of the help desk. It is a single liaison point of contact for end-users of services. All incidents are registered and monitored with the help desk. Incidents should be categorized, handled and resolved as quickly as possible. When an incident prevents employees reporting the problem from working, the goal is to get them back to working as fast as possible.

§ 3.3.2.2 describes when to escalate a reported incident. This section indicates that escalation is required whenever solving the security incident exceeds the authority of the organizational unit.

§ 3.3.2.3 states that incident registration is so important that it deserves its own section. A list of information to record when registering an incident is provided. The list of data to record includes the date, time and report serial number, the date and time of the security incident, details of the reporter, a descriptive title for the incident, a detailed description of the incident, an estimate of damage done, urgency of need to resolve, the organizational unit where the incident occurred, the system affected, a point of contact that can be questioned about the incident, the escalation status and the solution to the incident when one is achieved.

NIST Special Publications

NIST 800-14 calls for user support in the form of a help desk but do not elaborate.

General Guidance

CobiT covers what is summarized above, though as usual it is not very detailed in methods for implementation.

The ISF Standard of Good Practices for Information Security calls for user support in the form of a help desk but do not elaborate.

United Kingdom and Canadian Guidance

BS 15000-2 is fairly detailed but labels user support as incident management.

A help desk makes life easier for users. It gives them a place to go and ask questions about IT problems that they do not know how to handle. Most help desks will serve a variety of users. Thorough support includes end-user customers, clients and anyone else who uses your organization's IT services.

To ensure high quality help desks, there are a few basic principles to adhere to. First, the desk is not a static function. People will not consistently have the same problems. Thus, the desk needs to be flexible and kept update with the latest technologies and solutions to the problems users are likely face at any given time. Work done at the desk should also be tightly integrated with problem management procedures and service level agreements. More specifically, work should be defined based on user requirements. Determine what help services the desk will and won't provide, what qualifications the staff needs, and then provide the appropriate tools and training for them to help users effectively.

Another key element of the help desk is the way service issues are recorded. Determine what kind of systems are needed to track incoming queries. Most of the time, queries will come into the office by telephone, internet or intranet. Some storage systems can be automated, for example email exchanges might be stored without manual user input.

The purpose of storing all help queries is many-fold. First, if there is a problem the help desk can't solve, the problem can be placed on record and prioritized for review so that it is solved as quickly as possible instead of getting lost. Second, management can look through a catalog of incoming queries to see how fast the help desk staff turns around each problem. Inefficiencies can be easily spotted and corrected. In addition, if a help issue is left unresolved for too lengthy a time period, these can be investigated and corrected.

To make it easier for you to store incoming records, as well as easier for users, provide instructions to all users on how to use the help-desk function. This can be as simple as listing the phone number for your organization's help hotline, or offering a web-based form for a user to fill out and submit. Providing instructions also helps standardize the way you receive help questions, which in turn makes it easier later to analyze them and figure out what inefficiencies in the help desk support process can be improved upon.

How do you deal with problem management and handle incidents?

Incident handing can be a sticky situation. That's why you create procedures for dealing with problem management and incident handling. The way you handle an incident should be organizational policy, not your bright idea, and trust us, you will be happier with it that way. Therefore, the control objective for this section is:

> *In order to promote the integrity and availability of information systems, an organization must effectively handle incidents and manage problems. Procedures should be in place to ensure that problems and incidents are identified in the most efficient way possible, prioritized according to risk, and resolved in a timely manner.*

Take a look at the regulations and standards for more guidance on how to handle incidents and problem management techniques.

Guidance from the regulations and standards

Public Companies

Sarbanes-Oxley and associated auditing standards do not address the need for a problem management system specifically, but do call for controls to detect and prevent errors or fraud that could result in faulty financial statements. The **AICPA Suitable Trust Service Criteria** provides more detailed problem management requirements. It calls management to implement procedures for reviewing, documenting, escalating, and resolving availability, processing, confidentiality and online privacy problems and incidents.

Banking/Finance

The **FFIEC Operations handbook** calls for organizations to implement an event and problem management process. It mostly focuses on operations processing problems (and provides examples) but also addresses security incidents and training of personnel in recognizing and reporting such incidents. For the most part, the standard addresses everything summarized above except for emergency access authorizations and processing priorities.

Healthcare and Life Sciences

HIPAA calls for the development of policies and procedures regarding security incidents and a process for mitigating the harmful effects of such incidents.

NIST 800-61 § 4.6 addresses § 164.308(a)(6) of the HIPAA Standard. The goal of this section is to implement policies and procedures to address security incidents. Activities to carry out in order to implement these policies and procedures are provided in a chart. They are highly detailed and worth reading directly. 4.7 addresses § 164.308(a)(7) of the HIPAA Standard and requires organizations to create policies and procedures for responding to emergencies. A highly detailed chart describes how to create a contingency policy among other things. This chart is worth reading through directly because it is so detailed.

Credit Card

VISA CISP and MasterCard SDP programs both call for incident response plans that address security breaches. VISA is a bit more specific, but basically both programs require incident response teams, a reporting mechanism and communication with affected parties.

US Federal Security

Government standards and regulations address problem management primarily with regards to information security incidents. FISMA calls for a security incident center that provides assistance and guidance to government agencies for responding to security incidents. The National Strategy to Secure Cyberspace concentrates primarily on incident management of cyber-security breaches and calls for similar processes. FISCAM refers to NIST and the OMB Circular's guidance on security incident response procedures for the benefit of auditor understanding. FISCAM also details controls on emergency access authorization and emergency processing priorities, though not specifically within the realm of problem management.

NIST Special Publications

NIST 800-14 is probably the most inclusive of all general standards, but it focuses mainly on computer security incident handling, not universal problem management.

NIST 800-53 pretty much covers what is summarized above but only with respect to security incidents (not processing problems or errors). The OMB

Circular calls for security incident response capability procedures and complementary training for agency personnel.

International Standards Organization

ISO 17799 calls for incident response procedures with respect to security.

The IT Infrastructure Library

ITIL Best Practice for Security Management 3.3.2.2 touches on the notion that establishing a problem management and incident handling system is important. Requirements for this system include being able to process incidents in a timely manner, being able to receive and act on incident reports efficiently and knowing when to escalate a security incident.

§ 3.3.3 talks about problem management, which is about establishing links between incidents, and following up with measures to prevent the incidents from reoccurring. 3.3.3.1 covers what to do when a problem arises from a security incident. Recommended issues to consider when resolving the problem include determining who was involved with the incident, figuring out what people are essential to finding a solution for a security incident and ensuring that no new security problems occur as a result of the solution.

General Guidance

CobiT generally covers most of what is summarized above, but does not require much in the way of incident reporting.

COSO ERM tends to lump everything into risk management, but does cover a great deal of the reporting process, primarily referring to incidents or problems as "events."

The **ISF Standard of Good Practices for Information Security**, calls for incident response procedures with respect to security.

US State Laws

CA 1386 also calls for an incident response plan for breaches of personal information. It requires procedures to contain, control and correct security incidents. The document requires organizations to identify and notify appropriate affected parties.

United Kingdom and Canadian Guidance

BS 15000-2 details program management procedures for most problems arising from service incidents or errors.

From regulation to reality – sure signs you are complying

Problem management and incident handling are terms that cover a broad spectrum of activity within your organization. There are a variety of alternative names for these terms, including event management, incident management, incident response and the popular but vague 'fixing broken stuff management'. Whatever you decide to call it within your organization, be consistent with the label as well as what activities the terms are meant to encompass. A good problem management and incident handling program will include identification of problems, containment of problems and the correction of each problem. Finally, you will want to record what went wrong and how you dealt with it for review later by management and auditors.

There are a number of ways you can implement a successful problem management and incident handling program. You can appoint individuals to an incident response team, elect a management official to oversee all major incidents, or disseminate responsibility throughout the organization role by role. To ensure appropriate staff are appointed in whatever configuration you elect, take the time to write out the roles and responsibilities for managing different types of problems and incidents. You will need to think about what skills are required for these jobs, from IT operations, management and internal auditors to fraud, loss prevention and information security incident response teams.

In addition to appointing appropriate staff to run your program, you will need procedures that ensure problems and incidents are identified in the most efficient way possible, prioritized according to risk, and resolved in a timely manner. For problems that affect your organization's ability to run continuously, design an escalation procedure in place that triggers the activation of your business continuity plan.

In the procedures you create, include a well-defined system for how each incident is to be reported and written up. Design the reporting capability in such a way that it is easy to use and personnel feel comfortable reporting incidents without fear of attribution. For each incident, create a mechanism for determining what user groups need to hear about it. Possible groups could include customers, service providers and officials.

For emergency problems, create procedures indicating what the differing priorities and access rules are. You may need temporary authorizations or a change in the order of priorities to fix certain issues. Document and approve these ahead of time so that when the problem occurs, the appropriate staff can take swift action to correct it. Immediately revoke any privileges that are granted for the emergency situation once a problem is solved.

When you are done, you will have roles and responsibilities for staff, a clear, easy way for them to report problems, a method of recording and storing each issue and response capabilities with provisions for emergency situations. Make sure management periodically reviews and redefines the entirety of this program.

How do you manage the current IT configuration?

Wouldn't it be nice if your IT operations ran smoothly and efficiently, all the time, without anyone ever having to lift a finger? Wake up and smell the impossibility. In order for IT operations to run as smoothly as you would like, someone has to manage them. Therefore the control objective for this section is:

> *In order to promote the availability and accountability of IT systems, the organization will manage the current IT configuration. Configuration management is a vital process that ensures an organization's IT assets and configurations are recorded, maintained, and accounted for.*

But don't take our word for it. Look at what the regulations and standards have to say about managing IT configuration.

Guidance from the regulations and standards

Banking/Finance

The FFIEC handbooks do not address configuration management as an isolated process, but rather tend to combine it with change management. However, the standards do make mention of configuration baselines, and thoroughly discuss library controls that maintain and track software versions and changes. In its discussion of contracts, the **FFIEC Development and Acquisitions handbook** calls for programs that scan for unauthorized software on internal systems. The **FFIEC Operations handbook** also contains a very detailed section on conducting an environmental survey of IT resources (including configurations), which is more or less the same as a process for identifying configuration items (although the handbook includes the process as part of risk assessment).

Credit Card

Although the **VISA CISP** and **MasterCard SDP** programs call for the installation of virus software on systems, the requirements are not placed within the context of configuration management.

NIST Special Publications

NIST 800-14 mentions configuration management but only as a control to ensure system security.

NIST 800-53, much like FFIEC, integrates configuration management with change management. The regulation does, however, call for configuration baselines of the organization's information systems and constituent components.

International Standards Organization

ISO 17799 addresses software licensing and checks for unauthorized software and details library controls but does not address configuration management as a process.

The IT Infrastructure Library

ITIL Best Practice for Security Management 3.3.1 explains that a prerequisite for security management is a well constructed process for configuration and asset management. Goals for this type of management are a clear way to see what configuration items make up the IT infrastructure being managed, who is responsible for which item, where the items are, and the status of and relationship between items. Finally configuration and asset management should verify whether registration correctly reflects the situation in reality.

General Guidance

CobiT is the most detailed standard with regards to configuration management. Together, both standards cover what is summarized above. CobiT is generally less detailed, while BS 15000-2 provides more examples of configuration items and also discusses configuration management reporting.

United Kingdom and Canadian Guidance

BS 15000-2 covers configuration management and provides more examples of configuration items and also discusses configuration management reporting.

From regulation to reality – sure signs you are complying

The first step in successfully managing your current IT configuration is to establish procedures to define and control all configuration items. Configuration items are the critical components of the IT infrastructure, including:

- Software
- Hardware

- Systems
- Services
- Documentation
- Licenses
- Software libraries
- Security components

Defining procedures provides consistency in the management process. Procedures will help your organization maintain a current, complete and accessible configuration. This has more benefits than you think. Configuration management supports development, change management, business continuity and numerous other processes.

What kind of procedures should be instituted to create a well-rounded configuration management program? What makes for good change management policy? The following is a list of just some of the change management procedures we recommend you institute:

- Record all authorized identifiable configuration items into a configuration database. Catalog them by their functional and physical characteristics. Record the identification method you use, and make sure it is used consistently throughout the process.

- Develop procedures for tracking changes to configuration items throughout their lifecycle.

- Create a status accounting of configuration items. Configuration records should reflect the actual status of configuration items and include historical data detailing changes. Ensure that current configuration information is accessible to users, suppliers and providers. You will want to periodically check the existence and consistency of the IT configurations and institute procedures regarding adding, deleting or changing a configuration item.

- Develop policies restricting the development and use of personal and unlicensed software. Check your organization's computer systems for unlicensed software, and install virus software. Make sure you are in compliance with software and hardware licensing agreements.

- Maintain software libraries. Segregate libraries of information according to each phase of the SDLC. Monitor library management by using audit trails or other means of tracking access and maker sure you put someone in charge of the library, such as a custodian.

Have you identified and allocated costs?

It's been said that money makes the world go round. As it turns out, money also plays a key factor in determining whether your IT operations and infrastructure go round, or round the bend. If you prefer the former to the latter, there are three things you need to keep in mind: the establishment of an IT operating budget; the establishment of a cost monitoring process; the establishment of a cost justification process. Therefore, the control objective for this section is:

> In order to promote the integrity and accountability of IT operations, management will identify and allocate costs. This includes establishing an IT budget, establishing a cost monitoring process, and establishing a cost justification process.

We will discuss all three of the cost identification and allocation steps in this section.

Guidance from the regulations and standards

Public Companies

SAS 94 provides control activities relevant to audits, including performance reviews that compare actual performance to budgets. The **AICPA Suitable Trust Service Criteria** requires that system performance and capacity analysis and projections be completed annually as part of the IT budgeting process.

Banking/Finance

The **FFIEC Management handbook** includes budgeting in its section on IT operations planning and investment. It concentrates heavily on integrating budget decisions with strategic IT planning and provides detailed guidance, though it does not directly call for an annual IT operating budget. The **FFIEC Development and Acquisitions handbook** calls for project management to implement cost-monitoring and cost-justification processes during and at the completion of systems development projects.

US Federal Security

FISMA requires that the heads of each agency submit annual reports to various committees including annual agency budgets. The **Clinger-Cohen**

Act requires the Director of the Office of Management and Budget to develop a budgeting process. The process covers the life of each information system and includes explicit criteria for analyzing the projected costs, benefits, and risks associated with the investments. The Director is also responsible for reporting the program performance benefits achieved and how they relate to the goals of executive agencies.

The **GAO Financial Audit Manual** does not specifically address agency management of IT costs, but calls for the auditor to gain an understanding of the budget formulation process.

The IT Infrastructure Library

ITIL Best Practice for Security Management § 3.4.5 requires that organizations understand and monitor costs and charge the costs to the customers of IT services. To do this, organizations must make the effort to identify, allocate, predict and monitor costs involved in delivering IT services. Then organizations must determine how much to charge customers based on their internal costs.

General Guidance

CobiT calls for an IT operations budgeting process, cost/benefit-monitoring and cost/benefit justification as summarized above.

CobiT 4 PO5.1 talks about establishing a financial management framework for IT. The goal of this framework is to drive the budgeting for IT through prioritization of IT projects. The prioritization should be based on the results of cost/benefit analyses for each potential project or IT investment. PO5.2 asks that organizations implement a process for coming to decisions on how to prioritize the allocation of IT resources. PO5.3 continues in this vein, suggesting that organizations create a process for budgeting. It should include the costs of any current projects as well as potential costs for future projects. PO5.4 calls for managing actual costs of projects compared to assigned budgets. PO5.5 says that a method for monitoring the benefits of selected IT projects and processes should be created. Deliverables from this should be reports describing IT's contribution to the organization.

United Kingdom and Canadian Guidance

BS 15000-2 details cost monitoring and justification with regards to budgeted IT services.

When Spinal Tap was short on cash, they wrote a little ditty to all the women out there entitled "Gimme Some Money". Because you don't have this luxury you'll need to do better – you'll need to create a budget. In an organization, a budget is the glue holding everything together. Have senior management create a process that ensures that an annual operating budget is established and approved. Like most things, make sure the budget reflects the organizational objectives and IT short and long-range plans. Finally, dedicate a section of the budget to funding alternatives.

Creating the budget is just the first step. If you want to keep things running smoothly you'll also need to follow your budget. Doing a good job following it means monitoring and comparing costs against your overall budget. Management should institute a process that compares the actual costs to the budget, and determines possible benefits derived from IT activities. Make use of the organization's accounting system in this process. Routinely record, process and report IT activities and monitor high-level performance indicators.

Finally, you don't want to get ripped off, so come up with a process for justifying the cost of services and products, making sure that the costs are in line with industry standards. This includes considering the total cost of ownership (TCO) for acquisitions of IT resources. TCO includes procurement, configuration, installation, support, upgrading, repairing and maintaining a resource.

Have you conducted the initial systems hardening process?

Adding a new system or system component can be tricky. If you add it without testing, it might introduce new vulnerabilities to all of your systems. Therefore, you must follow this control objective:

> *In order to promote the integrity and availability of information systems, the organization will conduct systems hardening. Hardening will ensure security and efficiency of information systems.*

Since hardening is a detailed concept with a wealth of information, we will provide an overview of hardening in this section.

Guidance from the regulations and standards

Public Companies

The **AICPA Privacy Framework** and Trust Services Criteria do not specifically address hardening of acquired, off-the-shelf systems and software, but do call for secure communications protocols, such as VPN. The Privacy Framework also calls for penetration testing as part of its overall security program, and the **AICPA Suitable Trust Services Criteria** requires that all unneeded network services (such as Telnet, HTTP, etc.) be disabled on the organization's servers.

Banking/Finance

The **FFIEC Information Security handbook** calls for hardening of systems when organizations procure off-the-shelf systems and software. The standard details all procedures as summarized above. The handbook further discusses penetration testing as one of many diagnostics tests run on systems to test for security.

Credit Card

The **VISA CISP** and **MasterCard SDP** programs require steps to harden systems before installation. Aside from FFIEC, the MasterCard program is the only document that refers to the process as hardening. The procedures summarized above are covered by both programs, although MasterCard does not focus much on network component configuration.

US Federal Security

The **OMB Circular** calls for penetration testing, but for all systems, not just for new software. Both the **National Strategy to Secure Cyberspace** and **FISCAM** require organizations change vendor-supplied default IDs and passwords. FISCAM also refers to the OMB Circular's guidance on penetration testing as a method for testing security controls.

NIST Special Publications

NIST 800-14, the Risk Checklist, and the ISF Standard all require penetration testing, with the Checklist providing the most details on penetration and vulnerability testing.

NIST 800-53 requires that the default configuration of security settings be as restrictive as possible for all IT products consistent with information system operational requirements. It also calls for organizations to define network protocols and services that a prohibited for the systems, as well. It is important to note that this control is considered part of configuration management by NIST.

NIST 800-41 § 5.2 recommends tailoring the hardening procedure used during installation of a firewall to the specific operating system undergoing hardening. It lists important issues to be aware of while conducting the hardening such as removing unused network protocols from the firewall operating system build, disabling unused network services and applications, removing unused user and system accounts and applying all relevant operating system patches.

General Guidance

The **ISF Standard of Practices for Information Security** devotes the most attention to the hardening of systems, although it does not make a distinction between acquired systems and newly developed systems.

US State Laws

CA 1386 also calls for periodic penetration tests to determine the effectiveness of systems.

EU Guidance

The **OECD Risk Checklist** calls for organizations to change vendor-supplied defaults and disable unnecessary services and network protocols.

From regulation to reality – sure signs you are complying

Newly acquired software and systems need to be treated a little differently than those that have been designed and developed specifically for your organization. There is absolutely nothing wrong with purchasing off-the-shelf products. However, these products have more functions than your organization will likely use. Further, administrators or system owners don't monitor the unused software or systems in the same manner as they would with in-house operating software. This is risky business because of potential security weaknesses in the systems where software is installed. There is a solution to these potential problems; newly acquired software must be properly installed, configured and secured before being deployed within the organization. As you may have guessed, this process is called hardening.

There are many procedures involved in system hardening; so many that we could not include them all here. Instead, we can include an overview of the hardening process, to give you an idea of how hardening works and what kinds of questions you should be asking. Speaking of questions, the first thing you need to ask is: have you instituted system hardening procedures? They are the cornerstone of your operations and provide guidance and consistency in delicate tasks. They should require that all vendor-supplied defaults be changed, including: passwords, community strings, unnecessary accounts, and so on. Additionally, system configuration standards should exist for all network components, addressing best practices and known vulnerabilities.

Another component of the system hardening procedure is to ensure the security settings are configured properly. This includes:

- Setting parameters to allow activity and disable unauthorized functions
- Configure access so that a user has the minimum access necessary
- Disable all unnecessary services
- Remove all unnecessary functionality
- Encrypt internal non-console administrative access to systems.

You want to ensure that independent security personnel conduct penetration tests *before* installing the system or software into production or operations. They will generate a series of real world attacks on the system or software, to identify to what extent it will be compromised before the attack is identified and whether any response mechanisms were activated.

One final key point to remember is this: The degree of protection is based on the criticality of the system or software you are looking to protect. System hardening procedures should address this point, ensuring that critical systems and software receive more protection than those that are less critical to IT operations.

Do you conduct preventative maintenance for hardware?

So you've gone out and purchased that corvette you have always wanted. You drive her around, and man, does she purr. Then, that first little reminder card comes in the mail, the first maintenance check-up. Do you say to yourself, well, no biggie, I'll get it looked at later? Of course not, this is a Corvette; this car is a finely tuned machine. This is the same attitude you need to have with preventative maintenance for your hardware. Granted, the hardware may not look like a corvette, but it is delicate, it is part of a finely tuned machine, and man, can it purr. The control objective for this section is:

> In order to promote the integrity and availability of information systems the organization will conduct preventative maintenance on all system hardware. Maintenance should occur at designated intervals.

If your treat your hardware like it is a corvette, you will get a lot more life out of it. Keep reading for tips on how to make that possible.

Guidance from the regulations and standards

Public Companies

The **AICPA Suitable Trust Services Criteria** contain a small clause that calls for preventive maintenance agreements and schedule maintenance procedures for key system hardware components.

Banking/Finance

The **FFIEC Operations handbook** provides the most detailed guidance on preventive maintenance, and includes all requirements as summarized above.

US Federal Security

FISCAM calls for routine periodic preventive maintenance of hardware. It does not discuss maintenance agreements but does pay special attention to the need for maintenance schedules to interrupt operations as little as possible.

International Standards Organization

ISO 17799 requires preventive maintenance for hardware and somewhat detailed, including a recommendation that additional controls be implemented for equipment taken off premises for maintenance or repair.

General Guidance

CobiT requires preventive maintenance for hardware and provides a general requirement with very few details.

CobiT 4 DS13.5 indicates that organizations should implement procedures that ensure timely maintenance of infrastructure.

From regulation to reality – sure signs you are complying

The integrity and performance of your hardware is a priority in operational management. This is what houses your systems and software. In order to keep this hardware operating at top performance levels, you have to institute a preventative maintenance procedure. Think of it just like the maintenance check you get for a car, it comes at certain intervals, at a set number of miles. Your hardware maintenance program should be the same way, scheduled at certain intervals. This procedure and schedule should be documented to ensure it is accurately followed.

The procedure should also include a list of all the warranties and liability disclaimers that correspond to the existing hardware. Organizational staff may not be authorized to conduct maintenance on certain pieces of equipment without causing the organization to lose rights or incur liability. Vendors and suppliers should conduct maintenance where necessary, and staff should conduct maintenance only where specifically authorized. Staff should, however, conduct general checks and cleaning of tape heads, printers and work areas.

Where staff is not authorized to conduct the maintenance, you should have agreements in place with vendors, manufacturers, or maintenance contractors. The agreements should detail the following items:

- Equipment repair services
- Routine maintenance
- Schedules for maintenance
- Problem management and conflict resolution

When you draw up the maintenance schedule, you have to make sure that it is coordinated with operational management. You do not want to interrupt workflow, or cause operational difficulties. Operational staff should act as custodians and ensure that maintenance personnel have the appropriate authorization to access systems.

The same basic access principles apply to maintenance personnel as would apply to any other member of the organization. First, make sure they only have access to the minimum amount of software needed for them to complete the maintenance. Keep all access activity logged. The logs should be on all the time, detailing activity, and they should be documented and stored as required. Logged information should periodically be generated into a report and given to management for review. This will help gauge future maintenance procedures.

What is Change Management?

It's often said the only thing constant in life is change. Which in a way is lucky for you, because now you know what to plan for. Part of planning for changes is dealing with change management. The control objective for this section is:

> *In order to promote the integrity, accountability, and availability of information systems, the organization will institute change management procedures. Change management covers changes to all software, hardware, systems, services and associated documentation and procedures. Additionally, change management will be used to monitor the system or supplier maintenance we discussed in the previous section.*

You'll need good change management if you plan on altering anything within your organization at any time. In this section we'll take a look at how to deal with staff and create the procedures that make change management great within an organization.

Guidance from the regulations and standards

Public Companies

The **AICPA Suitable Trust Services Criteria** address change request procedures for change management, as detailed above. The criteria also require that emergency changes be logged daily by IT management and reported to appropriate business line management.

Banking/Finance

The **FFIEC Handbooks** call for organizations to develop and implement change management standards and procedures. Most of the information on change control is discussed in the Development and Acquisitions handbook, though Information Security and Operations both briefly address the process. As previously pointed out, FFIEC merges configuration and change management into a single process, which does nothing more than to further reinforce their relationship. FFIEC details procedures for patch management in the Development and Acquisitions handbook, but also briefly addresses patch management in the Information Security and Operations handbooks. FFIEC does not address change procedures for software releases and distribution or maintenance (although the section on preventive maintenance certainly implies such procedures).

Healthcare and Life Sciences

NIST 800-66 § 4.8 addresses § 164.308(a)(8) of the HIPAA Standard. This section discusses an important aspect of change management – performing a periodic technical and non-technical evaluation in response to environmental and operational changes affecting the security of electronic protected health information. A chart provides a list of tasks to complete in order to conduct a thorough evaluation. The chart provides a lot of information and is worth reviewing directly.

Credit Card

The **VISA CISP** and **MasterCard SDP** programs both require the installation of patches. VISA offers more detailed controls, calling for merchants to keep up with vendor changes to security patches, install them within one month of release, and to test all patches before they are deployed. The MasterCard SDP requires that both system software and network software patches be installed, but does not offer any procedures other than requiring merchants to keep them up-to-date. While neither program provides change management procedures, VISA requires that organizations follow change control procedures for system and software configuration.

US Federal Security

FISCAM provides details on controls for government auditors, covering change requests and controls for routine and emergency software modifications. Additionally, FISCAM calls for organizations to implement procedures for control over the distribution of new or revised software. The standard does not provide guidance on a universal change management system.

NIST Special Publications

NIST 800-53 combines change management controls with configuration management. It requires procedures for the proposal, justification, testing, review and disposition of changes. NIST also requires that organizations monitor and assess the impact of proposed changes to the information system. Additionally, it requires that emergency change control procedures be included in the configuration change management process.

The IT Infrastructure Library

ITIL Best Practice for Security Management 2.2.3 tells us that change management is a necessary part of security management. Potential processes that change management handles include handling the changes in the importance of tasks, physical and environmental alterations, changes in the way IT is assessed, changes in business and legal demands, changes in hardware and software, changes in threats to the organization and the introduction of new technology. 3.3.4 describes the goal of change management, which is to control and manage all changes concerned with an organization. The section also briefly mentions that part of changing something is documenting the change in the form of plans to implement it through to the final selected solution.

International Standards Organization

ISO 17799 covers the change management procedures as well as specific operational change controls. It does not address emergency changes, maintenance, release management, or patch management.

General Guidance

CobiT 4 AI6.1 calls for setting up formal change management procedures so that there is a standard format for handling change requests. AI6.2 requires organizations to ensure that all change requests are assessed using the defined procedures in a way that determines impacts on operational systems and functionality. AI6.3 indicates that organizations should create processes for defining, raising, assessing and authorizing emergency changes that may fall outside the established change processes. AI6.4 asks that organizations log and track all changes and report on them to stakeholders. AI6.5 says that when a change is implemented, the associated system and user documentation and procedures should be updated as well. AI3.3 calls for maintaining infrastructure by creating a strategy and a plan for this type of maintenance.

The **ISF Standard of Good Practices for Information Security** includes change management controls for its critical business applications, computer installations, and networks sections, primarily addressing change management procedures (including emergency changes), but not maintenance or release management.

United Kingdom and Canadian Guidance

BS 15000-2 covers most aspects of the change management process, although BS 15000-2 makes a distinction between change management and release management.

Change management controls the process by which changes are made to the IT configuration. This is not to be confused with configuration management, which governs the current IT configuration. You should establish a change management process to ensure that all changes are assessed, approved, implemented and reviewed in a controlled manner.

There are two main areas of change management: the people and the procedure. First, decide what people will be involved in change management and what their role, responsibilities, and access rights will be. Then, create the procedures your staff and maintenance personnel will follow.

The People

Depending on the size of your organization, and the role of IT, you may want to create a separate change management function or committee. All change requests and approvals would then have to go through this committee before they are approved. Just like with preventative maintenance, all system and software maintenance personnel must be specifically assigned and authorized by management. Personnel must follow appropriate security procedures and will be subject to access controls.

The Procedures

Once you have decided what kind of personnel you will be using to institute your change management program, you can move on to the procedures. Change management always begins with a request for change, system or supplier maintenance. This requires that you establish standards for the creation of a change request. One approach is to make use of an automated system for users to generate change requests, governed by pre-established standards. There are three other important controls relating to change requests:

- Prioritize change requests by importance and urgency

- Assess proposed changes based on overall business risk, cost and benefits, and impact on the IT operational environment

- Implement procedures to keep requestors informed about the status of their requests

Once you have established the procedures for change management requests, there are more procedures to follow for when a change has been approved:

- Schedule change for implementation based on risk, urgency and complexity

- Nominated owners of the asset and their user departments are responsible for implementation of the change

- Test, verify and approve changes

- Link changes to their associated configuration items, record them in the system and document them

- If changing large, complex information systems, implement an automatic system that monitors, records and tracks all changes

There are also specific procedures for software modifications:

- Ensure formal procedures are in place governing the release and distribution of software throughout the organization

- Include provisions in procedures that ensure software changes and releases are signed off, documented and distributed to the right places in a timely fashion

- Create a process to identify available software patched to improve performance and security and to correct problems

- Install software patches only if they have been tested

- Install software patches only if they are the latest version

- Ensure patches to software are appropriate

Although emergency changes can be sporadic, they still need to be handled with the same level of control as other changes. Here is the list of controls we suggest:

- Implement an abbreviated change request, evaluation and approval procedure

- Test emergency changes prior to implementation, if possible

- If testing is not possible, ensure that appropriate back-up systems and back-up files are in place, including detailed documentation of the changes

- Document all emergency changes as soon as possible after the change is implemented

Finally, institute a review process to take place after a change has been fully implemented. The review process should provide management with feedback about the change, information about any discovered vulnerabilities, and any problems encountered during the change.

How do you use and monitor system utilities?

An important question to ask yourself is: do you monitor systems utilities? If the answer is no, then you need to make an adjustment. If the answer is yes, keep reading, we may still have some insight for you.

> *The organization will monitor system utilities. Good system utility monitoring is about constant logging and review of the events that occur on them.*

In this section we will take a look at monitoring system utilities.

Guidance from the regulations and standards

Public Companies

The **AICPA Suitable Trust Services Criteria** address change request procedures for change management, as detailed above. The criteria also require that emergency changes be logged daily by IT management and reported to appropriate business line management.

Banking/Finance

The **FFIEC Handbooks** call for organizations to develop and implement change management standards and procedures. Most of the information on change control is discussed in the Development and Acquisitions handbook, though Information Security and Operations both briefly address the process. As previously pointed out, FFIEC merges configuration and change management into a single process, which does nothing more than to further reinforce their relationship. FFIEC details procedures for patch management in the Development and Acquisitions handbook, but also briefly addresses patch management in the Information Security and Operations handbooks. FFIEC does not address change procedures for software releases and distribution or maintenance (although the section on preventive maintenance certainly implies such procedures).

Credit Card

The **VISA CISP** and **MasterCard SDP** programs both require the installation of patches. VISA offers more detailed controls, calling for merchants to keep up with vendor changes to security patches, install them within one month of release, and to test all patches before they are deployed. The

MasterCard SDP requires that both system software and network software patches be installed, but does not offer any procedures other than requiring merchants to keep them up-to-date. While neither program provides change management procedures, VISA requires that organizations follow change control procedures for system and software configuration.

US Federal Security

FISCAM provides details on controls for government auditors, covering change requests and controls for routine and emergency software modifications. Additionally, FISCAM calls for organizations to implement procedures for control over the distribution of new or revised software. The standard does not provide guidance on a universal change management system.

NIST Special Publications

NIST 800-53 combines change management controls with configuration management. It requires procedures for the proposal, justification, testing, review and disposition of changes. NIST also requires that organizations monitor and assess the impact of proposed changes to the information system. Additionally, it requires that emergency change control procedures be included in the configuration change management process.

International Standards Organization

ISO 17799 covers the change management procedures as well as specific operational change controls. It does not address emergency changes, maintenance, release management, or patch management.

General Guidance

CobiT 4 DS13.3 says procedures should be implemented for monitoring IT infrastructure and related events. Operations logs should be maintained.

United Kingdom and Canadian Guidance

BS 15000-2 covers most aspects of the change management process, although BS 15000-2 makes a distinction between change management and release management. Neither standard addresses the installation of system or software patches, although CobiT does provide a general control objective on system software change controls. The ISF Standard includes change management controls for its critical business applications, computer installations, and networks sections, primarily addressing change management procedures (including emergency changes), but not maintenance or release management.

From regulation to reality – sure signs you are complying

Utility programs provide users with a variety of functions for configuring and maintaining systems. They often exist as part of an operating system, and provide tools for program debugging, file maintenance and corrupt data correction. Many system utilities allow users to create, modify, move, rename, copy or delete code and data from program libraries and data files.

System utilities can have a great impact on operating systems, access controls, and data. For this reason, you need to implement policies and standards for controlling, monitoring, and evaluating their use. These policies include:

- Strictly define responsibilities for use of system utilities.

- Log and monitor any use of system utilities.

- Remove utility programs from software libraries, placing them under dual control, and only load them into systems when absolutely necessary.

- Review logs of utility program usage periodically to confirm compliance.

What are conversions?

A conversion is a major change in an application or a system. Conversions can span multiple platforms and often introduce new systems or data as a result of a merger of acquisition. The control objective for this section is:

> In order to preserve integrity, systems continuity and continued operations, the organization will provide for detailed and systematic controls for conversions.

In this section we'll discuss what responsibilities staff members need to be assigned for this work as well as how to approach creating appropriate controls and procedures.

Guidance from the regulations and standards

Banking/Finance

The **FFIEC Development and Acquisitions and Operations handbooks** are the only standards that address conversion controls. Conversions should be treated as a separate project, utilizing a methodology like the SDLC. Management should be held responsible for implementing strategic planning, project management, requirements definitions, testing, implementation, contingency planning, vendor management, and post-implementation reviews.

Senior management's specific role should be to determine feasibility of a conversion and then work with IT to assess the risk and impact of proposed conversions on operational activities. Management should assess current and projected transaction, data storage, communication and processing requirements. They should also assess increased demands on balancing, reconcilement, error handling, problem management, user support, network connectivity and system administration.

Conversions also require close communication within an organization and between and organization and its vendors and service providers. Communication within the organization should call for communication procedures, lines of authority, and reporting requirements.

Management should also institute training procedures for all personnel involved in conversions or major hardware/software upgrades. The type, amount and timing of training should be defined for each affected business unit or user department.

Major conversions require detailed file mapping, especially following a merger or acquisition. Management should ensure that all appropriate technical, operational and business personnel are involved in the mapping process and that they have sufficient knowledge of all products and services involved to map and transfer data and accounts correctly.

Lastly, management should ensure that conversions are adequately tested and reviewed following implementation. Conversions should be documented using project plans.

From regulation to reality – sure signs you are complying

A conversion is a project in and of itself, and you can apply the SDLC methodology to the project to keep it organized and help ensure its success. The conversion process should use the following techniques:

- Strategic planning
- Project management
- Requirements definition
- Testing
- Implementation
- Contingency planning
- Vendor management
- Post-implementation reviews

The first step in the conversion process is to determine if the conversion is feasible and whether it supports organizational objectives. This is a job for senior management. Then senior management and IT management need to get together and assess the risk and impact of the proposed conversion on operational activities. The assessment should consider:

- Current and projected transactions
- Data storage
- Communication requirements
- Processing requirements
- Increasing demands on balancing
- Reconcilement
- Error handling

- Problem management
- User support
- Network connectivity
- System administration

The next step is to ensure that you communicate regularly with vendors and service providers. Additionally, you have to have close communication within the organization. Institute communication procedures, lines of authority, and reporting requirements.

Next, management should design training procedures for all personnel involved in conversions or major hardware/software upgrades. Training should be scheduled appropriately, as to not interfere with any operational functions. Define the type, amount, and timing of the training for each affected business unit or user department.

Any major conversion will require detailed file mapping, especially following a merger or acquisition. All appropriate technical, operational, and business personnel must be involved in the mapping process to incorporate all the necessary skills and knowledge. Before the mapping process begins, these personnel should have appropriate knowledge of all products and services to map and transfer data and accounts correctly.

Finally, remember to test! Conversions must be adequately tested and reviewed following the implementation process. Document the conversion using project plans.

How do you dispose of a system?

Well, you can't just throw a system in the trash can, now can you? First of all, the vultures would be there to pick at it and if you left any important data on any hardware, you could be facing serious liability. Just as we discussed in records disposal, systems must be disposed of completely, to ensure that you do not incur any liability for losing sensitive information.

> *In order to protect outdated and discarded systems and ensure no data is lost or stolen, the organization will properly dispose of systems. This includes destroying or archiving data to ensure that systems are clean when disposed of.*

To keep vultures out of your disposed systems, there are five disposal controls you should be aware of, all of which we will discuss in this section.

Guidance from the regulations and standards

Public Companies

The **Sarbanes-Oxley Act** and **PCAOB Auditing Standard No. 2** call for substantial penalties for organizations that destroy or alter any "tangible object" with the intent to impede investigations. This can include systems and any data stored on them. The **AICPA Privacy Framework** requires that organizations dispose of or destroy records containing personal information in accordance with retention policies.

Banking/Finance

The **FFIEC Development and Acquisitions** and **Information Security handbooks** address the disposal phase of systems maintenance. The requirements of these standards reflect those summarized above.

Credit Card

The **VISA CISP** and **MasterCard SDP** programs both call for destruction of cardholder information and associated media. Both programs also cite the need for degaussing media that could allow for the reconstruction of data.

US Federal Security

NIST 800-53 and **DoD 5015.2 Criteria** call for the destruction of media and records, respectively. Both address the issue of removing residual data. While NIST provides controls for organizations to implement, DoD, as always, includes these procedures as automated controls performed by records management systems.

Records Management

ISO 15489-1 and 15489-2 detail the disposition process extensively as summarized above, although only with respect to records.

NIST Special Publications

NIST 800-53 calls for the destruction of media and records, respectively. Both address the issue of removing residual data.

General Guidance

The **ISF Standard of Good Practices for Information Security** calls for disposition and destruction procedures.

CobiT does not specifically detail the disposition process as the others do, but does include a control objective addressing access rights to deleted or transferred records. None of the general standards include a systems disposal phase or disposition requirements for systems.

From regulation to reality – sure signs you are complying

When disposing of a system, keep the following list of controls in mind:

- System software and data should be archived or destroyed, based on your organizations retention policy

- When transferring data from production systems, subject it to appropriate back-up and testing procedures

- Store system documentation in case you have to reinstall a system into production

- If any data files or records require destruction, degauss or overwrite media or hardware in a manner that prevents the data from being reconstructed

- If media or hardware cannot be completely wiped clean of magnetic residue, physically destroy it to prevent tampering

For more information about disposal, take another look at the records management section and apply those controls to software and systems.

Physical Security

The Main Thing

What's the need for physical security?

The importance of physical security becomes very obvious when you try to run a bank without any. You'll find that within a very short period of time your most frequent customers are robbers. Even if your organization isn't a bank, physical security will be of the utmost importance. Therefore, we recommend you follow this control objective:

> *In order to ensure the integrity, availability and confidentiality of information resources, the organization will establish physical security controls.*

Your controls, encryptions, authentication methods, all of it means absolutely nothing if someone can walk in, pick up a server and leave with it. They're even less useful if you can't be bothered with environmental controls – something like a leaky roof can destroy your equipment in an instant. Ensure high quality physical security by checking to see if you've covered every issue we mention in this section.

Guidance from the regulations and standards

Public Companies

The **AICPA Privacy Framework and Suitable Trust Services Criteria** address the need for physical security by requiring physical security controls governing privacy, availability, integrity and confidentiality of information.

Banking/Finance

The **Gramm-Leach-Bliley Act** and accompanying Safeguards rule require financial organizations to implement appropriate safeguards to protect all information assets. This is further reflected in the **FFIEC Information Security** and **Operations handbooks**, detailing specific physical and environmental security controls.

Credit Card

The **VISA CISP** and **MasterCard SDP** programs both address the need for physical security.

NIST Special Publications

NIST 800-53 addresses the need for government agencies to employ physical and environmental controls. NIST is the only standard that calls for physical and environmental protection policies and procedures.

General Guidance

CobiT 4 DS12.2 calls for developing and implementing physical security measures in line with business requirements. These measures should include, layout of the security perimeter, security zones, location of critical equipment, and shipping and receiving areas.

From regulation to reality — sure signs you are complying

It's not enough to get a sturdy building and start locking things up in your organization left and right. Physical security, to be effective, needs to be implemented based on a strong understanding of what is required for it. You discover the requirements of your organization by conducting thorough risk assessments, analyzing the results and ascertaining what you need to protect based on these results. Items to protect include:

- all aspects of IT facilities

- equipment

- staff

- environmental controls

To ensure adequate protection, management should develop and implement physical and environmental policies and procedures for daily work activities. These procedures may form their own set of documents, or be included as part of the overall information security policy. They should be regularly reviewed and updated as needed.

Do you have adequate facilities management?

Top-notch physical security is dynamic. It involves more than placing extra walls around important equipment – it requires active management. Good facilities management is about constant vigilance. Maintain your physical security equipment, and train your staff to use and keep watch over it effectively. The control objective for this section is:

> *In order to protect the confidentiality, availability, accountability and integrity of information systems, customer data and business functions, the organization will have adequate facilities management.*

If your equipment is keeping track of who comes in and out of your buildings, and your staff is keeping track of what condition your equipment is in, your facilities management is adequate or better.

Guidance from the regulations and standards

Public Companies

The **AICPA Privacy Framework** calls for card access, sign-in logs and other techniques to control access to offices, data centers and other locations in which personal information is processed and stored. The **AICPA Suitable Trust Services Criteria** calls for procedures to restrict physical access to facilities, including the use of card systems and video surveillance. The criteria also call for appropriate management authorization for access. **SAS 94** also address physical security, calling for auditors to ensure that appropriate controls are in place.

Banking/Finance

The **FFIEC Information Security** and **Operations handbooks** call for detailed procedures concerning the physical security of the facilities and data centers of financial institutions. Neither document covers the institution of health and safety practices, but they are nevertheless more detailed than any other standard on physical security.

Healthcare and Life Sciences

HIPAA calls for organizations to implement policies and procedures to limit physical access to facilities housing systems containing electronic protected health information. It also specifically requires that organizations implement controls to authorize and validate access to facilities, including visitor control.

NIST 800-66 § 4.10 addresses § 164.310(a)(1) of the HIPAA Standard. This section talks about facility access controls and how to implement policies and procedures that limit physical access to electronic information systems and the facilities housing them, while still allowing authorized access. The chart describing the tasks to complete in order to achieve good facility access controls is very detailed and worth reading directly.

Credit Card

The **VISA CISP** and **MasterCard SDP** programs call for physical access controls to restrict individuals from accessing cardholder information. VISA directly requires visitors to be given a "physical token" (a badge or access device) and requires organizations to retain a visitor log containing a physical audit trail of activity for a minimum of three months. MasterCard does not specifically address visitor activity. Both programs require that some procedure be established for all individuals to identify them and control their access to cardholder information.

NIST Special Publications

NIST 800-53 requires agencies to authorize and control access to all facilities containing information systems through the use of defined physical controls. It addresses the use of keys, locks, badges, and security guards. It also calls for monitoring of physical entry through surveillance equipment and intrusion detection systems.

International Standards Organization

ISO 17799 also provides detailed physical security controls for facilities. CobiT and ISO 17799 require organizations to implement health and safety practices for all personnel. The ISF Standard suggests that staff be protected from intimidation by malicious third parties by providing duress alarms in susceptible public areas. The standard also calls for organizations to institute a process for responding to emergencies.

General Guidance

CobiT calls for organizations to establish physical security and access controls for facilities but do not provide many details. CobiT combines requirements for equipment security with physical security – the former will be addressed in a later summary.

CobiT 4 DS12.1 calls for selecting physical sites for IT equipment taking into account potential risks associated with natural and man-made disasters as well as relevant laws and regulations.

EU Guidance

The **OECD Risk Checklist** covers physical security pretty thoroughly, though all requirements are, as always, in the form of questions. The ISF Standard provides detailed controls for physically securing facilities, dividing them between sections on security management, computer installations and networks.

From regulation to reality – sure signs you are complying

There are multiple facilities maintenance issues. You must consider all of them if you want to provide high quality physical security. These include:

- physical barriers
- control access to buildings
- maintenance procedures
- access logs
- health and safety practices

Physical barriers

Physical barriers such as gates and fences may be placed around the perimeter of IT facilities to ensure their security. Additionally, you may add appropriate surveillance equipment to monitor activities within the area. Due to the potentially sensitive nature of IT facilities, management should work to keep a low profile on IT facilities. The easiest way to do this is to keep identifying signs to a minimum so that people outside your organization cannot locate it without a little bit of work.

Control access to buildings

Buildings other than just those housing IT facilities should also be rendered physically secure with controlled access. Doors and windows should be locked or secured by some other means as necessary. Wiring and cabling throughout the building should be adequately protected. Magnetic badge readers or similar devices should be installed and access should be restricted to individuals who are authorized to do so. Security guards should be assigned to different sections of the facility as needed. You may also need surveillance equipment within the facility, including closed-circuit television. Consider this equipment alongside other intruder detection devices, such as:

- switches
- light and laser beams
- ultraviolet beams
- sound and vibration detectors that are invisible to the intruder
- ultrasonic/radar devices that detect movement

Whichever of these systems you select should be connected to alarm systems as necessary.

Maintenance procedures

In addition to setting up surveillance equipment, badge readers, security guards and alarms, you need to implement a maintenance procedure. Each physical security device should be regularly examined to assure proper functionality. Each guard should also be examined to make sure she is performing her job correctly and has appropriate training for the work.

Access logs

Employees accessing highly secure areas in your organization should be required to sign in and identify themselves with a company issued ID badge. Any visitors to these areas should be escorted by employees and wear identification that clearly marks them as a visitor. Workers should be encouraged to point out people on the premise who do not have appropriate identification so they may be questioned to find out why they are there.

Health and safety practices

Management should develop and make available health and safety practices to all individuals using the facilities, including the posting of emergency exit signs and emergency procedures. All selected health and safety practices should conform to international, national, regional, state and local laws and regulations. Orientation and continuing education programs should address and endorse these practices and any emergency procedures should be included as part of business continuity training.

Have you secured your cabinets and vaults?

Throughout the organization, anywhere you have a safe, cabinet vault or physical container that holds information assets, they need to be appropriately secured and locked, or made resistant to burglary attempts by other means. If you leave your containers unattended and unsecured, you open all the information assets they contain to sabotage, compromise and misuse. Therefore, the control objective for this section is:

> *In order to promote security of information systems, the organization will secure cabinets and vaults. Additionally, an organization should secure all containers to improve its overall security.*

There's more to a secure container than locking it up, so check out this section for some other tips on what features your containers should possess.

Guidance from the regulations and standards

Public Companies

The **AICPA Privacy Framework** requires an entity's privacy policy to cover the physical protection of personal information stored in hard copy form, implying the use of locked cabinets or other physical containers.

Banking/Finance

The Safeguards requires that access to physical locations containing customer information be restricted only to authorized individuals. The **FFIEC Information Security Handbook** specifically addresses cabinet and vault security as summarized above.

NIST Special Publications

While **NIST 800-53** does not directly address cabinet and vault security, it suggests that backup information be stored in a "fire-rated container."

International Standards Organization

ISO 17799 also suggests the use of fire-resistance safes or cabinets for storing sensitive or critical information.

General Guidance

Although the **ISF Standard of Good Practice for Information Security** does not mention a specific control for establishing cabinet and vault security standards, it mentions the use of fireproof safes for holding sensitive media and back-ups in several sections.

CobiT 4 DS13.4 calls for establishing physical safeguards necessary for protecting sensitive IT assets such as special forms, negotiable instruments, special-purpose printers or security tokens.

From regulation to reality – sure signs you are complying

To protect the materials in the event of a disaster, all containers should be appropriately fire-resistant and display a label describing tolerance levels. All tolerance levels should be determined by your organization based on the sensitivity and importance of the information being protected. That way when it comes time to store something, you have an idea of what type of container it requires. It also makes it easier to recover items later – if you know the tolerance you can weed out anything outside that tolerance.

In certain cases, you may wish to extend security for cabinets, vaults and containers by designating the area in which they are stored a high-level security area. In this situation access is restricted to authorized individuals. It is especially key for super sensitive information such as cardholder data.

Do you have physical security for distributed IT assets?

It would be nice if all your assets could be locked away safely. However in today's day and age, it isn't possible. IT assets may be spread over a wide base, from highly secure data centers to public reception areas. User departments and offices contain desktop computers, information resources and laptops. Workers can carry laptops home and use wireless connections, or even connect from cell phones if they wish. The control objective for this section is:

> *To secure all distributed IT assets, many of which could be transmitting highly sensitive data, the organization will take special measures to see to it that they are physically controlled in such a way that they are safe from unauthorized access, theft, misuse or accidents.*

When determining physical security for mobile devices, take into account first of all, what type of information you will allow to be on a laptop that may be in a wireless environment and therefore more vulnerable to attack. Transmitting data across a wireless network, especially somewhere where it is offered for free like a coffee shop etc. is akin to standing up and shouting the details of what you're sending at the top of your lungs to passersby. If you have Tourettes, this might be normal, otherwise think long and hard about what you're comfortable shouting about your organization for everyone around you to hear.

Guidance from the regulations and standards

Public Companies

As previously stated, the **AICPA Privacy Framework** requires that an organization's privacy policy provide for the physical protection of systems contained personal information. The AICPA Trust Services Criteria requires that physical controls restrict access to file servers and other sensitive systems (such as LANs) to authorized individuals.

Banking/Finance

The **FFIEC Information Security Handbook** addresses the physical security of IT assets in "distributed IS environments." The standard covers the protection of PCs and notebook computers, networks and physical LAN access. It does not provide controls for the removal of property from an organization's premises.

Healthcare and Life Sciences

HIPAA requires that organizations implement policies and procedures to control the receipt and removal of devices or media containing electronic protected health information into and out of or within the facility.

Credit Card

The **VISA CISP** and **MasterCard SDP** programs both concentrate on physical controls to restrict access to systems storing sensitive cardholder data. MasterCard is a bit more specific and requires that sensitive cardholder data be physically separated from other data stored in the e-commerce environment.

Government

FIPS Publication 191 2.1.5 lists inadequate physical protection of LAN devices as a potential vulnerability to an organization's network.

NIST Special Publications

NIST 800-14 requires that all portable systems should be secured when not in use and the information stored on them, when cost-effective, should be encrypted.

NIST 800-41 § 4.6 describes the physical security of a firewall. If they can be easily accessed by intruders or accidentally damaged, no matter what kind of defense they might provide, they're highly vulnerable. It is recommended that they be stored behind locked doors, or kept with guards and physical security alarms.

NIST 800-53 calls for agencies to implement physical access controls over systems and devices that allow for the display or transmission of unencrypted information. The standard also calls for agencies to limit access to laptop computers or other portable information systems to authorized individuals. Additionally, the standard requires that agencies control the delivery and removal of information systems and generate records of such activity.

NIST 800-66 § 4.11-4.12 address § 164.310(b) and § 164.310(c) of the HIPAA Standard. Both sections cover workstations and how to implement policies and procedures for proper use and security of each employee workstation. Detailed lists of tasks to carry out in order to achieve proper use and security are provided. These lists contain so much information that it is best to read from the document directly.

4.13 matches up with § 164.310(d)(1) of the HIPAA Standard. The goal of this section is to provide detailed steps for implementing policies and procedures for the safe receipt and removal of hardware and electronic media containing electronic protected health information into and out of a facility. This goal is accomplished through the use of an elaborate activities chart describing the process by which an organization may implement appropriate policies and procedures. Due to the high volume of information, it is best to read this section directly.

International Standards Organization

ISO 17799 calls for a "clear desk and screen policy."

General Guidance

CobiT primarily addresses all physical security controls through a single control objective that was previously summarized, but does require that IT resources located in public areas should be physically protected.

CobiT 4 DS12.4 requires organizations to design and implement measures to defend against environmental factors.

The ISF Standard of Good Practices for Information Security specifically requires that critical equipment be physically separated and kept confidential.

From regulation to reality – sure signs you are complying

Physical security, much like any other kind of security is about restricting and monitoring access. Creating good physical security is a process much like a tightrope act. If you lean too far to one side, you fail by offering users too much access. If you lean too far to the other side, you fail by restricting too much. If you get it just right, the show goes on. There are many ways to have good physical security, including:

- restricting where sensitive information may be kept

- restricting access to hardware and workstations

- separating IT systems with sensitive information from other systems

- restricting physical access to LAN devices

- corporate culture choices
- proper removal of IT assets

Restricting where sensitive information may be kept

If necessary, restrict highly sensitive information to cables and devices that can be locked down and therefore more easily secured against theft. All computers, laptops that are not in use and other hardware located in a publicly accessible area of your organization should be locked in place or the disk drives should be removed and stored. If sensitive information is stored on a laptop, which is not recommended if it's avoidable, then the information should be encrypted so it is unreadable if stolen or lost.

Restricting access to hardware and workstations

Networks and methods for accessing your organization's systems can lie outside the reach of physical security, but you can still provide some defense for these systems by taking care to prevent unauthorized access to important equipment where possible. For example, you can ensure that only authorized individuals have access to network hardware, devices or applications and you can monitor workstation activity. Physical security practices for networks may also include power protection, physical locks and secured work areas complete with guards or by limiting access to a work area to those with magnetic badge readers.

Separating IT systems with sensitive information from other systems

Ideally, you should physically separate IT systems that contain sensitive information from other systems. That way key systems can receive high security, and time and money does not need to be expended maintaining the same level of security for less important systems that don't need it.

Restricting physical access to LAN devices

Other measures you can take to protect systems include restricting physical access to LAN devices to those whose jobs require such access. Network cabling should be protected through the use of conduits. Wiring should not be routed through publicly accessible areas whenever possible and network cables should be physically separated from power cables at all times.

Corporate culture choices

You can also improve physical security with corporate culture choices such as a clear desk policy. Insisting upon clear desks means employees must place all sensitive materials out of sight. If need be, your policy can include properly securing those materials and extend to other devices in the office. You may have a policy for example, stating that any sensitive materials printed out, or faxed in must be cleared from the device immediately.

Proper removal of IT assets

The last element of physical security to plan for is removal of IT assets. Management should develop procedures for authorizing the removal of property. Any removal should be approved by security to ensure that devices are only being removed when appropriate. All removals should be logged out and logged back in if the material is returned. Inventories of such practices should be reviewed regularly by management to ascertain whether all removals are authorized or not.

Have you developed appropriate environmental controls?

Environmental disasters will happen. Just recently, there was a monsoon in Arizona. Arizona gets 7 inches of rain a year, 4 of which came in one day. This caused massive flooding and massive IT problems. No one was expecting such heavy flooding and consequently, not everyone was prepared. But, if they would have thought about the potential environmental disasters and instituted appropriate controls, they could have saved themselves a lot of hassles. That is why we recommend you institute the following control objectives.

> *To protect business and IT facilities, the organization will identify and neutralize the environmental hazards that could potentially affect your organization. General potential problems include: fire, dust, smoke, floods, and power failures. The organization will implement defenses for each one. In doing so, the organization is a safer place for maintaining important records as well as the health and safety of your co-workers.*

Suggestions for what types of defenses you might use for each problem are discussed in detail in this section.

Guidance from the regulations and standards

Public Companies

The **AICPA Suitable Trust Services Criteria** requires management to implement measures to protect against environmental hazards. It calls for smoke detectors, fire suppression systems and water detectors, as well as UPSes and emergency power. The criteria indicates that emergency power equipment should be tested semi-annually.

Banking/Finance

The **FFIEC Operations handbook** covers all environmental controls as summarized above, providing numerous examples and scenarios. The Safeguards rule requires that measures be taken to protect equipment housing customer information from environmental hazards and technological failures, but does not provide specifics.

Government

FISCAM calls for agencies to implement adequate environmental controls and lists them briefly.

NIST Special Publications

NIST 800-14 addresses the need for environmental controls by listing the hazards and their accompanying dangers, but does not detail specific measures for mitigating them. The ISF Standard does not address emergency power or water detection, but does require environmental controls for fires, HVAC, and alternate telecommunications lines.

NIST 800-53 calls for agencies to employ and maintain emergency power solutions, fire suppression and detection systems, temperature and humidity controls, and water detection systems. The standard also calls for personnel to be trained in environmental controls and that controls should be tested and test records retained. NIST also calls for organizations to employ and maintain a master power or emergency cut-off switch at critical locations such as data centers, server rooms, and mainframe rooms.

International Standards Organization

ISO 17799 briefly addresses the need for controls to protect against environmental hazards, but only details the use of UPSes, multiple power feeds, back-up generators, and alternate telecommunication lines. ISO 17799 also encourages organizations to restrict eating, drinking and smoking near equipment and within facilities.

General Guidance

CobiT calls for IT management to implement sufficient measures to protect facilities from environmental hazards, but is not very detailed. CobiT 4 DS12.5 states that organizations should manage facilities including power and communications equipment in ways that keep them compliant with appropriate laws and regulations, and the organization's business and technical needs.

From regulation to reality – sure signs you are complying

Appropriate environmental controls are about understanding your organization's potential environmental problems and implementing solutions for each situation. It's more than that though. Appropriate controls need to be viewed as a package. You aren't offering proper controls if you leave something out – for example having great defense against floods and no fire extinguishers. To avoid this problem, all you need to do is be sure and cover potential problems with power, water, fire, dust and smoke.

Power is key to business continuity, so management should implement protection for those power sources responsible for maintaining computing equipment. In addition, to ensure that power is continuous, you should provide alternative power sources that do not rely on the local power grid. Such sources may include uninterruptible power supplies (UPSes), multiple power feeds and back-up generators. If you opt for a UPS, it should be configured to provide sufficient power supply in the event of a failure until an orderly transition to back-up generators can be completed. The back-up generators should provide enough power to accommodate all critical information system resources and processing demands. UPSes and back-up generators should be periodically checked and maintained to ensure that they meet requirements and are suitably re-configured and replenished following power emergencies. In addition, you should test UPSes and back-up generators to be certain they can maintain all critical systems in the event of an emergency.

As with power, when it comes to telecom feeds, you want to have multiple options available. IT operations management should ensure that facilities are connected to duplicate or multiple telecom feeds. Within your organization, feeds should be provided by a variety of vendors, and line checks should be made to eliminate the possibility of a single point of failure or redundancy path. Wiring configurations should support rapid switching from one vendor to another without the need for rerouting or rewiring.

Beyond power and telecom feeds, which ensure your equipment is running smoothly, you need to think about temperature. You should have appropriate HVAC (heating, ventilation and air conditioning) systems installed. Such systems make it pleasant for your employees to work by maintaining acceptable temperatures. This in turn results in higher productivity. These systems are also necessary for ensuring that equipment does not overheat or become too cold depending on the circumstances. You will also need back-up power sources for your HVAC system. Failure to maintain HVACs could result in system failure since many systems must be maintained at the correct temperature to function properly.

To protect employees from dangerous disasters within their work areas, you must install heat and smoke detection systems. This is important for your equipment as well. Good locations to place these devices include the ceiling, exhaust ducts and under raised flooring. Choose the location of each detector carefully, as placing a detector in a spot like an air conditioning vent or an intake duct that disburses smoke may cause alarms to trigger when there is no actual fire.

Other useful devices for detecting fire include systems such as a very early smoke detection alert system (VESDA). These systems are hypersensitive and sample air on a regular basis. They are useful for detecting smoldering wires before a fire starts, saving you money that might otherwise need to be spent replacing equipment that went up in flames.

In the event that a fire cannot be prevented, you need devices available for extinguishing them. A variety of devices are available, each employing a different strategy. Some available methods include depriving a fire of oxygen, as with Inergen, FM-200 or carbon dioxide. Water-based suppression systems are more common and include wet-pipe and dry-pipe configurations. Decide what's best for your organization's needs. It may be you prefer oxygen suppression systems in an area full of expensive equipment that could be badly damaged by water, but possibly salvaged if a fire was put out quickly by some other means. Some areas, water may be easier, since the only real problem would be workers who don't like being hosed down while you're dealing with a fire.

While we're on the subject of water, your organization also needs to defend against leaks. Water damage can affect the structural integrity of your buildings, spills from leaky roofs can create hazards for employees, and water can certainly damage valuable equipment. Consider installing water detectors under raised flooring to alert management to leaks that may be normally undetectable. In some situations, a floor drain may be useful. Before making any choices, study the structure of your plumbing systems and the location of shut-off valves.

Technical Security

The Main Thing

Why Do You Need Technical Security?

Information system stability depends upon technical security. And your staff depends upon your information systems. Technical security acts as a base in this chain of dependencies. Screw it up, and it's like yanking a table cloth from under the plates during a dinner, it destroys the flow of everything. The control objective for this section is:

> *The organization will establish the need for technical security to protect information systems and the daily work processes they support for all your staff.*

Good technical security keeps your information systems safe, your data safe, and allows your staff to work more efficiently because their system use won't be interrupted.

Guidance from the regulations and standards

Let's see what the regulations and standards have to say about the importance of technical security.

Public Companies

SAS 94, the **AICPA/CIC Privacy Framework**, and **AICPA Suitable Trust Services Criteria** all contain a significant amount of information on technical security.

Banking/Finance

The **FFIEC Information Security Handbook** contains the most information on technical security out of all the banking/finance regulations. The handbook explains that the goal of logical and administrative access control is to restrict access to system resources. Access should be provided only to authorized individuals whose identity is established, and their activities should be limited to the minimum required for business purposes.

The **FFIEC Audit**, **Business Continuity Planning**, and **Operations** Handbooks all touch on technical security. However, they point to FFIEC Information Security for elaborated guidance.

The **Appendix of 12 CFR 30** has technical security controls in access control, encryption, intrusion detection, and incident handling.

Healthcare and Life Sciences

HIPAA uses technical security to protect confidential and sensitive health information. **21 CFR 11** also touches on some elements of technical security.

Credit Card

The **VISA** and **MasterCard** regulations both are detailed when it comes to technical security. Protecting cardholder information through electronic information systems is a top priority in both of these regulations, and they address every topic in technical security.

US Federal Security

Almost all of the government regulations contain something about technical security. **FISMA, Clinger-Cohen Act, GAO**, and the **National Cyberspace Strategy** all touch on different elements of technical security. **FISCAM** has more in depth analysis of a wide range of technical security controls.

Records Management

The records management standards generally do not address technical security. However, **ISO-1549-2** and **DIRKS** both provide coverage of security and access classification schemes and steps.

NIST Special Publications

NIST 600-18 § 2.5-2.5.3 recommends viewing FIPS 200 for information about security controls for federal information systems. 2.5 offers a list of very general considerations regarding security controls. The key point is choosing controls that are appropriate for an organization's environment and needs. 2.5.2 discusses compensating security controls. These are management, operational and technical controls that are used in place of prescribed controls in the low, moderate, or high security control baselines. This section says compensating controls may be used but only when they are selected from the security control catalog provided in NIST 80053 and the organization can justify the use of this replacement control. The organization must also formally accept all risks associated with use of a compensating control. 2.5.3 suggests central management for development, implementation and assessment of common security controls designated by an organization. Each control should be documented once and then imported whenever it is referenced in a system security plan. Good use of security controls comes from an organization documenting and communicating each control, assigning responsibility for coordinating security control identification and review, having participation of higher management such as a CIO and consulting experts in common control areas identified. This section also recommends partitioning security controls into common security controls and system-specific security controls as this allows for assessment of common controls at the organizational level. Assessment results may then be reused and shared throughout the organization.

NIST 800-53 touches on different elements of technical security but does not directly handle the question 'why do you need technical security?'

General Guidance

Many of the General Guidance require technical security controls. **CobiT** is the leading standard in several subjects, including transaction security and intrusion response. The **ISF Standard of Good Practice for Information Security** addresses technical security on a variety of levels and with a variety of controls.

EU Guidance

The **OECD Risk Checklist** addresses each subject, providing a plethora of questions designed to extract a companies technical security controls.

From regulation to reality – sure signs you are complying

Networks, operating systems, and applications are delicate and expensive. They're open to attack from every possible angle. The hardware running your systems can be tampered with, either through maliciousness or stupidity. Hackers, internal saboteurs and viruses can also destroy your systems. Technical security works to prevent these problems by doing two things: limiting access and providing accountability for actions.

Limiting access is accomplished in a wide variety of ways. There's the very basic method of locking up important hardware so no one can tamper with it. Then there are fancier methods, such as using an anti-virus program to block viruses from accessing your system. What makes limiting access difficult is you can't simply lock all the doors and windows of your organization and allow no one in or out. Instead you create policies and methods for determining who can access what files within your organization, and who can't.

Providing accountability in technical security is about logging access, often through requiring authentication whenever someone accesses your systems.

If your system is well set up, and it's not easy to spoof authentication, or crack someone's password and login as them, you'll be able to see problems, and hold someone accountable for them. Hackers and saboteurs will still be able to sneak in around these in various ways. However, if you're logging system activities, you'll likely be able to detect suspicious activities that indicate an intruder is in your system.

If you don't want your confidential files to be exposed to hackers or viruses, you need technical security. Poor technical security enables anyone out there to browse through your organization's most personal files, whether you like it or not. Worse, it makes it hard for you to catch whoever's doing it, meaning the person can come back and look through your files again if he feels like it.

Each organization needs a different level of technical security depending on the size and structure of the organization. The security requirements for an organization's information system are directly related to the components of the system, the data contained therein, and the business needs of the organization. Whether your organization is large or small, simple or complex, you will have to take a look at the individual needs of your organization, to ensure that you have policies and procedures in place to fit those needs.

Have you established a Security and Access Classification Scheme?

A security and access classification scheme identifies legally required and/or legally enforceable rights, restrictions and access to records. It is a policy outlining staff access to records, as well as a way to classify the records themselves by varying levels of sensitivity. The following control objective applies to this section:

> *The organization will establish a security and access classification scheme that will describe what types of information can and can't be accessed by employees with certain job functions. It will cover how much security is required for data with different levels of sensitivity, as well as how such data should be handled.*

Good security and access classification schemes help improve security by letting your employees know exactly what they need to do with different types of data.

Guidance from the regulations and standards

Public Companies

While several public companies' regulations address the need to have user rights and regulations, only the **AICPA Suitable Trust Services Criteria** specifically addresses a company's responsibility to define and document the policies for the security of the information contained within the system as well as the activities of the users of the system.

Banking/Finance

The **FFIEC Audit** handbook calls for a written and adequate data security policy to be placed in effect covering all operating systems, databases, and applications.

Healthcare and Life Sciences

HIPAA requires implementation of technical policies and procedures for electronic information systems that maintain electronic protected health information and allow access only to those persons or software programs that have been granted access rights.

NIST 800-66 § 4.4 is intended up to match up with § 164.308(a)(4) from the HIPAA Standard. This section discusses how to implement policies and procedures for authorizing access to electronic protected health information. It provides a detailed list of activities to carry out in order to achieve this goal. The list should be viewed directly since it is very detailed. 4.14 is intended to address § 164.312(a)(1) and provides more details about access control. This section uses an activities chart to explain a good method for limiting access to different system resources as necessary.

US Federal Security

FISMA, the **Clinger-Cohen Act**, **FISCAM**, and **GAO** all address a security access classification scheme in one form or another. **FISMA** requires that both generally and within each agency program, an information security program be instituted defining access and unauthorized use procedures commensurate with the potential risk and magnitude of possible harm. The Clinger-Cohen Act requires a system security plan for all information collected, processed, and stored in the agency system. FISCAM requires that the sensitivity and criticality or various data and operations be determined and prioritized based on an overall risk assessment. Finally, GAO calls for an access control program limiting access to computer resources.

Records Management

Both **ISO 15489-1 & 2**, and **DIRKS** all address a security access classification scheme. However, **ISO 15489-2** provides the greatest detail and is a model to be followed. ISO 15489-2 explains the need for a security access classification scheme, stating the reasons why some information needs special protection, explaining the system of legal rights regarding access to information, and outlining the levels of restriction as reflecting organizational usage. Further, it breaks down access classification as applying to both the records and to the people using and managing the records.

NIST Special Publications

NIST 800-14 requires organizations to implement logical access control based on policy made by a management official responsible for a particular system, application, subsystem, or group of systems. The policy should balance the often-competing interests of security, operational requirements, and user-friendliness. In general, organizations should base access control policy on the principle of least privilege, which states that users should be granted access only to the resources they need to perform their official functions.

NIST 800-53 requires that a determination be made as to appropriate priorities for organizational information systems, addressing the sensitivity of information and categorizing according to the potential risk to this information.

General Guidance

The subject of a security and access classification scheme is well addresses by the General Guidance. **CobiT** discusses mainly data classification, explaining that all data should be classified by a formal and explicit decision by the data owner according to the data classification scheme. CobiT goes on to say that even data requiring "no protection" should require a formal decision to be so designated.

The **ISF Standard of Good Practice for Information Security** calls for a security and access classification scheme in critical business applications, computer installations, and networks. Lastly, **ISO 17799** requires controlling access to information according to policies for information dissemination and authorization.

From regulation to reality – sure signs you are complying

Granting access rights to people is not as simple as saying "yes" or "no". Instead, there are varying levels of access for the different job functions of personnel. The security and access classification scheme should take into consideration both those managing the access-classified records, and those who have access to some or all of the records. Policies need to be created for managers, staff, and temporary users alike. According to the FFIEC Information Security Handbook, organizations should keep the following four things in mind when developing an access scheme for users:

- Only grant access to system resources needed by users to perform their official job functions

- Update access rights regularly, especially after personnel or system changes

- Review access rights periodically based on risk to the information system

- Design acceptable use policies and require users to sign them

Classifying records is not simple either. Records can be confidential, or have certain confidential parts. They can contain a lot of sensitive information, or just one number that needs to be concealed. Having a system by which records and data are classified will allow for consistent application of organizational policy. All records should be classified in terms of sensitivity by a formal decision of the data owner according to the classification scheme.

What Do Users Need To Do Before Accessing Their Accounts?

When you give your neighbor a key to your house so that he can feed the cat, do you tell him not to give it to anyone else? This may seem to be implied in the nature of the task. However, when dealing with sensitive customer information and expensive information systems, you don't want to assume anything is implied when it comes to security. Use the following control objective:

> *The organization will document acceptable usage procedures, make sure everyone has a copy, and if necessary, train users on complex access procedures.*

Good account security isn't just about fancy passwords or good systems – it's also about the people that access these systems. If users aren't using proper procedures, they can compromise your entire system. By making sure they're aware of this, you improve the overall security of your organization.

Guidance from the regulations and standards

Public Companies

The **AICPA/CICA Privacy Framework** and the **AICPA Suitable Trust Services Criteria** both address user identification, authentication and access. Both standards discuss the need to identify and authenticate users, grant system access and privileges, and update user profiles. The AICPA Suitable Trust Services Criteria specifically discusses the need for individual user ID and passwords.

Banking/Finance

The **FFIEC Information Security** and **Operations** Handbooks both discuss this area in detail. FFIEC Information Security explains that Access should be provided only to authorized individuals whose identity is established, and their activities should be limited to the minimum required for business purposes. An effective control mechanism includes numerous controls to safeguard and limit access to key information system assets.

The controls include passwords, limiting privileges on unique user IDs, and regular monitoring of user activity. FFIEC Operations explains that management should employ the principle of least privilege throughout IT operations. The principle provides that individuals should only have minimum privileges on systems and access to functions that are required to perform their job function and assigned tasks.

The **Appendix of 12 CFR 30** calls for access controls of customer information systems, including controls to authenticate and permit access only to authorized individuals, and controls to prevent employees from providing customer information to unauthorized individuals.

Healthcare and Life Sciences

HIPAA requires that a unique name and user number be assigned for identifying or tracking user identity. HIPAA further addresses log-in monitoring and password management. **21 CFR 11.10** calls for limiting system access to authorized individuals and for the use of authority checks to ensure that only authorized individuals can use the system, electronically sign a record, access the operation or computer system input or output device, alter a record or perform the operation at hand.

Credit Card

Visa and **MasterCard** standards both address identification, authorization, and access thoroughly. The Visa standard is the most specific. It requires a unique user ID be assigned to each person with computer access, that all users be authenticated by one of the prescribed methods, and that adequate password management procedures take place. Password management and authentication include but are not limited to: revoking access of terminated users, removing inactive user accounts after 90 days, distributing password procedures and policies to all users, not permitting group passwords, controlling the addition, deletion, and modification of user IDs, changing user passwords every 90 days, requiring a minimum of 7 characters for the length of a password, and using passwords with both numeric and alphabetic characters. MasterCard requires a password policy for user name and identification, passwords that change on a yearly basis, and passwords that are adequately complex.

US Federal Security

The **Clinger-Cohen Act** calls for the distribution of password policies and procedures to all users. **FISCAM** calls for user identification procedures and explains that passwords are the most common form. However, FISCAM cautions the use of passwords and uses the following controls to ensure their safety: Passwords should be changed every 30-90 days; passwords should not be displayed when entered; passwords should be a minimum of 6 characters in length; individual users should be uniquely identified instead of having group passwords.

General Guidance

CobiT calls for management to establish procedures to ensure timely action related to requesting, establishing, issuing, suspending and closing of user accounts. A formal approval procedure outlining the data or system owner granting the access privileges should be included. Additionally, CobiT calls for management to have a control process in place to review and confirm access rights periodically. Periodic comparison of resources with recorded accountability should be made to help reduce the risk of errors, fraud, misuse or unauthorized alteration. Finally, CobiT explains that users should systematically control the activity of their proper account(s). Information mechanisms should be in place to allow them to oversee normal activity as well as to be alerted to unusual activity in a timely manner.

NIST Special Publications

NIST 800-14 calls for identification and authentication to prevent unauthorized people from entering the IT system. Access control allows the system to differentiate between users. NIST 800-14 addresses unique identification, maintenance of user ID and creating procedures to handle with inactive user ID. Finally, passwords can be used for authentication, however, users should be trained and passwords changed frequently.

NIST 800-53 calls for user identification and authorization procedures, unique user identification, and archiving user identification, but is not specific about the kind of user identification to be employed.

NIST 800-66 § 4.17 addresses § 164.312(d) of the HIPAA Standard. The goal of this section is to describe how to implement procedures that "verify that a person or entity seeking access to electronic protected health information is the one claimed. A list of activities are presented, and should be read directly from the source due to the level of detail.

International Standards Organization

The ISO 17799 Standard also is quite informative. It calls for all users to have unique user ID for their sole use so that activities can be traced to the responsible individual. User ID should not indicate the users privilege level. The ISO 17799 standards does allow for limited use of group ID, which is contrary to the majority of other standards that address this subject. The standard recognizes passwords as the most common method of authentication, but it does address other methods of authentication. Passwords should be controlled through a formal management process. Passwords should be changed frequently, kept confidential, and not shared with other users.

General Guidance

CobiT calls for management to establish procedures to ensure timely action related to requesting, establishing, issuing, suspending and closing of user accounts. A formal approval procedure outlining the data or system owner granting the access privileges should be included. Additionally, CobiT calls for management to have a control process in place to review and confirm access rights periodically. Periodic comparison of resources with recorded accountability should be made to help reduce the risk of errors, fraud, misuse or unauthorized alteration. Finally, CobiT explains that users should systematically control the activity of their proper account(s). Information mechanisms should be in place to allow them to oversee normal activity as well as to be alerted to unusual activity in a timely manner.

The **ISF Standards of Good Practice for Information Security** calls for user identification and authentication by password, and for user identification information to be unique to the user. Additionally, ISF calls for a procedure to terminate expired users.

EU Guidance

The **OECD Risk Checklist** calls for robust user passwords, termination of inactive user accounts, distribution of password policies, and passwords that are unique to individual users.

From regulation to reality – sure signs you are complying

Creating a security and access classification scheme lays the groundwork for access. It is the policy that establishes *what* users can access. The next step is to create procedures designating *how* a user accesses the information system. This is identification and authentication. Users need to identify themselves and make it clear that they are who they say they are before they can access their accounts. Generally, this authentication takes the form of a password, but there are other ways of authenticating. New technologies are developed every day, so make sure that the needs of your organization are met by the methods you choose to employ.

When managing user accounts, there are a whole host of considerations and techniques that help ensure that the appropriate people with necessary training and understanding are the ones actually accessing the information systems. The following are a few suggestions that will help you define your identification and authentication procedures.

- Control the addition, deletion, and modification of user ID's, credentials, and other identifier objects

- Immediately revoke access privileges of terminated users

- Remove inactive user accounts at least every 90 days

- Distribute password policies and procedures to all users who have access to sensitive information

- Do not permit group passwords

- Require a minimum length of at least seven characters

- Use passwords containing both numeric and alphabetic characters

- Set a minimum password age

- Do not allow an individual to submit a new password that is the same as any of the last four passwords he or she has used

The above procedures can of course be modified to suit your organization's needs. The best practice for minimum passwords is to set the minimum password age from one to seven days less than the maximum. As an example, if a user must change their password every 90 days (maximum), then the minimum password age would be 83 days. This will ensure that a user doesn't repeatedly change their password in order to re-use their favorite [DW]. The main thing is that you have procedures in place that stop unauthorized users from gaining access to the sensitive stuff, and authorized users to keep out of places they don't belong.

It is especially important to review user accounts for unusual activity. You want to ensure that users are not abusing access rights as well as determine if authentication controls have been violated. Equally important is that users have control over their own accounts. This means that controls are in place that allows users to oversee normal activity and alerts them in a timely manner when something unusual is going on in their account. In this way, there are multiple checks on the same account so that suspicious activity is identified quickly and acted on promptly.

Why Do You Need Security Surveillance?

It's nice to know when something bad happens to your systems so you can fix it. It's even nicer when you can catch the person who did it so they can't do anything to your systems again. That's where security surveillance comes in handy. The following control objective applies to this section:

> The organization will create and maintain a "proper usage" monitoring program through the use of both physical and logical monitoring tools.

This section covers the four basic steps for quality security surveillance.

Guidance from the regulations and standards

Check out what the regulations and standards have to tell you about security surveillance requirements.

Public Companies

The public companies standards generally do not have much to say concerning IT security surveillance. However, the **AICPA/CICA Privacy Framework** standard explains that an organization must assign responsibility for security administration.

Banking/Finance

The **FFIEC Information Security Handbook** calls for the logging and auditing of privileged access to IT systems. The **FFIEC Operations Handbook** calls for the creation of reports to management and audit on the use of monitoring tools. The **FFIEC Audit Handbook** calls for the recording, monitoring and response to all unauthorized attempts to gain access to the operating and applications systems.

Healthcare and Life Sciences

HIPAA calls for the implementation of security incident procedures and requires response and reporting of known security incidents as well as documentation of the incident and outcome. In addition, mitigation of harmful effects is required.

Credit Card

Visa CISP requires that security alerts are monitored and analyzed.

US Federal Security

FISMA requires the periodic testing and evaluation of information security controls and techniques to ensure they are effectively implemented. **FISCAM** calls for the use of access control software to monitor and protect against security violations. The **GAO** calls for properly functioning security access software and access limiting security controls.

International Standards Organization

ISO 17799 requires the logging of all system activities and the review of these logs for threats to the system.

General Guidance

CobiT 3 requires that IT security administration ensure that security activity is logged, and any indication of imminent security violation is reported immediately to all who may be concerned, internally and externally, and is acted upon in a timely manner. The **ISF Standard of Good Practice for Information Security** calls for the logging of all access. Access logs are to be set to include all security related events, reviewed periodically, and protected against unauthorized change.

US State Laws

CA 1386 calls for the monitoring of employee activity through security procedures.

From regulation to reality — sure signs you are complying

Security surveillance is a key element in a comprehensive access control program. It lets you know if the access system you created is working properly or if something unusual is going on. There are four basic steps to follow to ensure good surveillance:

1. Have your IT security staff log all security activity. This includes logging all access attempts, successful and unsuccessful.

2. Establish a notification plan – and follow it. Different types of violations call for different types of notification plans.

3. Act on all security violations in a timely manner for prompt investigation into the cause of the violation.

4. Test and evaluate security controls frequently and regularly to ensure they are effectively implemented.

The use of access control software can aid your organization in maintaining consistent security monitoring and surveillance. Remember, the four steps listed above are recommended, but not set in stone. How you decide to implement access security controls is not as important as the final result-- a quality security surveillance system.

Do You Manage Access Rights?

An implemented access and classification scheme combined with user access procedures is good, but a managed implementation is better.

> The organization will ensure that all access rights to the facilities, systems, applications, and documents are managed in accordance with organizational confidentiality rules.

Management of access rights is a great way to solve simple potential security issues, such as terminated employees still being able to access your system.

Guidance from the regulations and standards

Banking/Finance

The **FFIEC Information Security Handbook** calls for the periodic review of users' access rights at an appropriate frequency based on the risk to the application system. The **FFIEC Operations Handbook** calls for management to document data ownership.

US Federal Security

FISCAM calls for the entity to identify and control all access paths and manage all users.

International Standards Organization

ISO 17799 states that the allocation and use of privileges and access should be monitored and controlled.

General Guidance

CobiT calls for controls to be put in place to ensure that identification and access rights of users as well as the identity of system and data ownership are established and managed in a unique and central manner to obtain consistency and efficiency of global access control.

The **ISF Standard of Good Practices for Information Security** requires user access rights to be restricted according to defined policy, restricted according to the users' individual roles, authorized by the application owner, revoked promptly when an individual no longer needs access, and enforced to ensure individual accountability.

EU Guidance

The **OECD Risk Checklist** calls for access to be restricted to the minimum amount necessary to complete a certain job. Further, access controls should be monitored.

From regulation to reality – sure signs you are complying

Establish controls to monitor your access and classification scheme and your user access procedures. Effective management consistently and efficiently ensures that up-to-date, effective procedures and rights remain in place. Such management is accomplished by determining how frequently you review rights. This determination is based on the sensitivity levels of each aspect of your scheme and access procedures. Risk to the organization is also a factor to consider. In general, high risk, highly sensitive levels of your scheme and procedures should be reviewed most often, and less important levels can be reviewed as infrequently as once per year in certain cases.

During the course of a review, if it becomes apparent that updates are necessary, make all appropriate changes. This keeps your scheme and procedures current and useful.

Why Is Network Configuration So Important?

When building a house, you first create a diagram or blueprint. In doing this, you decide where you want the doors and windows to be, what kind of security system to install and so on. Think of network configuration like building a house. Start with the blueprint; then add all the specific amenities and protections that best suit your organization's needs. As you go, keep the following control objective in mind:

> *The organization will ensure that all network access and security configurations are properly created and maintained, with network diagrams, access points, and access requirements properly documented.*

A poorly created network is difficult to extend, may crash frequently or allow attacks, and as a result lose your organization time, money and credibility. There are five basic steps to go through if you want good network configuration. Read on to find out more.

Guidance from the regulations and standards

Public Companies

SAS 94 calls for general controls over data center and network operations.

Banking/Finance

The **FFIEC Information Security Handbook** provides in depth analysis of network access and configuration. It maintains that financial institutions should secure access to their networks through multiple layers of access controls to protect against unauthorized access. Institutions should: group network servers, applications, data, and users into security domains; establish appropriate access requirements within and between each security domain; and, implement appropriate technological controls to meet those access requirements consistently. Other requirements include the creation of a network diagram, identification of all access points, and establishment of minimum access requirements for network services. The institution should determine the most appropriate network configuration to ensure adequate security and performance. Finally, DMZs or demilitarized zones can be used to restrict access.

The **FFIEC Audit Handbook** calls for the full documentation of the network, with adequate network updating and testing procedures in place for configuration. The **FFIEC Operations Handbook** also calls for the full documentation of network configuration as well as the creation and documentation of the network topology- a technical blueprint of network structure.

Credit Card

VISA CISP calls for the establishment of a formal process for approving all network connections. Connections between publicly accessible servers and any component storing cardholder data, including any connections from wireless networks, are restricted. External network direct public access to any system component that is storing cardholder information is prohibited.

MasterCard SDP calls for all network changes to be planned for and approved. In addition, all network changes are to be tracked and logged. Servers should be restricted in their own domain and protected behind a firewall. Scanning for unknown work stations and the use of a DMZ are also required.

US Federal Security

FISCAM calls for the identification and control of all network access paths. Careful analysis is needed to identify all of the systems entry points and paths to sensitive files. **FISCAM** calls for the creation of an access path diagram identifying: the users of the system; the type of device from which they can access the system; the software used in the system; the resources they may access; the system on which these resources reside; and the modes of operation and telecommunication. The access path diagram should be reviewed and updated to include network changes.

The **National Cyberspace Strategy** calls for federal agencies to consider installing systems that continuously check for unauthorized connections to their networks.

FIPS Publication 191 calls for strong network configuration to defend against unauthorized LAN access. It describes in 2.1.1 a variety of vulnerabilities to which a LAN may fall prey. These include inappropriate identification schemes, poor password management, unprotected modems, poor physical control of network devices, lack of disconnect for multiple login failures, no logging of activities or time outs when an account is left inactive for an extended period of time. 2.1.3 talks about problems that may be encountered when a LAN needs to protect sensitive data. Potential vulnerabilities mentioned include improper access control settings, data or application source code stored in unencrypted form, viewable monitors in high traffic areas, printer stations in high traffic areas and data and software backup copies stored in open areas. 2.1.7 describes ways in which LAN functions may be disrupted. Disruptions may come from inability to detect unusual traffic patterns, inability to reroute traffic, single point failure configurations, unauthorized changes to hardware components, improper maintenance and poor physical security. It is implied that good network configuration will defend against or avoid most if not all of these problems.

NIST Special Publications

NIST 800-41 § 3.2 describes what a DeMilitarized Zone (DMZ) network is. The section also recommends a service leg configuration for a DMZ network. This is set up with three network interfaces. One attaches to a boundary router, another network interface attaches to an internal connection point such as a network switch and the third network interface forms the DMZ network. A drawback of this configuration is that it puts the firewall at an increased risk of service degradation during a denial-of-service attack aimed at servers on the DMZ. The firewall must examine all network traffic before the traffic reaches a DMZ-attached source. This can slow organizational traffic.

NIST 800-61 § 4.2.2 mentions that when working to prevent denial of service attacks, network perimeters should be configured to deny all incoming and outgoing traffic that is not expressly permitted.

International Standards Organization

ISO 17799 calls for a policy to be formulated concerning the use of networks and network services.

General Guidance

The **ISF Standard of Good Practice for Information Security** provides that a network design should incorporate a coherent, integrated set of technical standards. An organization should aim to minimize single points of failure, and restrict the number of entry points into a system. ISF calls for the creation of network configuration diagrams, showing nodes and connections. Network performance is to be monitored by reviewing logs of network activity regularly.

EU Guidance

The **OECD Risk Checklist** calls an inventory of each access point to the network to identify potential points of vulnerability. Proper system configuration suggested as well as a frequently reviewed network topology diagram. Organizations should scan for unknown system users and unidentified access attempts.

From regulation to reality – sure signs you are complying

The following five steps comprise our approach to network configuration:

- Create a network diagram
- Segregate security restricted servers into their own security domain
- Define DMZ areas
- Plan for and have approved all network changes
- Scan for unknown workstations and default deny access

The first thing you want to do is to create a network diagram. A network diagram is an illustration of how your information system is connected together. This is the blueprint of your network structure. Once a general diagram has been created, the network should be mapped and configured to control all access points. Access points should be identified and careful consideration should be taken concerning access paths to sensitive files.

It may be helpful to create an access path diagram, more specific than the network diagram. An access path diagram has the following parts:

- The users of the system
- The type of device from which they can access the system
- The software used in the system
- The resources they may access
- The system on which these resources reside
- The modes of operation and telecommunication

You don't have to redo the network diagram or the access path diagram every time something changes. Instead, just update it to reflect the changes in the organization.

The next step is to segregate security restricted servers into their own domain. This includes grouping network servers, applications, data, and users into security domains. Establish appropriate access requirements within each domain and implement appropriate technological controls to meet those access requirements consistently.

When configuring a network, the next consideration is the DMZs or demilitarized zones. DMZs are used to restrict access. They prevents outside users from getting direct access to a server that holds company data. Once you have determined your access paths, you can use the DMZs to ensure that only internal users gain access to the information.

In order for this system to work, you must plan for and have approved all network changes. It may be helpful to create a policy, detailing the approval process for changes. This includes tracking and logging all network changes so that appropriate modifications can be made to the network diagram and the access path diagram. Appropriate testing of the network configuration is also an important part of this process! Testing will help you to identify what is working, and what is not.

Finally, your IT department must scan for any unknown workstations. You need to seek out any computers attached to the system that should not be there. On the other end of an unknown workstation is someone who could do the organization harm, and identifying them and stopping them before they do permanent damage to the information system will save you a lot of time and money.

It is important for organizational policy to spell out the meaning of unauthorized use of the network and related components, and the penalty for such a violation. This may be critical to seeking damages or prosecution of those suspected of an unauthorized access to your network [DW].

This may all seem to be a bit overwhelming, or maybe it is old hat. But going through the steps one at a time, documenting everything as you go, will inevitably save you time in the long run. If you configure the network right the first time, then all the additional changes will just be added to the foundation that already exists.

Are you defending your protocols and ports?

When a potential intruder scans your ports, it's the equivalent of a guy going around a neighborhood checking doors and windows to see if anything's been left open. If he finds something unlocked, that's the place he robs.

> *The organization will maintain a current list of all active ports and protocols for all key servers. This list will form the foundation of our "pinhole" strategy for firewall access. Any ports and protocols not on this list will be denied through the firewall "deny all but explicit ports and protocols" policy.*

If you're not monitoring your ports and providing defenses for them, you are liable to end up getting attacked. The worst part is, you may not even realize it until one day something important is missing, or compromised.

Understand – guidance from the standards and regulations

Banking/Finance

The **FFIEC Information Security Handbook** covers protocols and ports in detail. The handbook explains that different networks use different types of protocols. The internet and most intranets and extranets are based on the TCP/IP layered model of protocols. Each layer contains vulnerabilities and corresponding attack strategies, which is a necessary consideration in evaluating the necessary controls. Hardware and software can use the protocols to restrict network access, and attackers can use weaknesses in the protocols to attack networks.

TCP/IP is a packet based communication system. IP is used to route messages between devices on a network, and operates at the Internet layer. TCP operates at the host-to-host layer, and provides a connection oriented, full-duplex, virtual circuit between hosts. Different protocols support different services for the network. The different services often introduce additional vulnerabilities.

Credit Card

VISA CISP requires a formal process for approving all network connections, including protocols and ports.

US Federal Security

The government regulations are fairly limited as to protocols and ports. The following two regulations address this subject, however brief. **FISCAM** Calls for a communications port protection device. The **National Cyberspace strategy** calls for the reliability and security of key protocols.

NIST Special Publications

NIST 800-14 calls for the consideration of port protection devices that authorize access to the port itself.

EU Guidance

The **OECD Risk Checklist** calls for prevention of entry or exit through any network port that is not required by the organization. Additionally, OECD requires prevention of any network protocol not in use by the organization.

From regulation to reality – sure signs you are complying

Network communications rely on software protocols to ensure the proper flow of information. A protocol is a set of rules defining how communication is to occur between two points in a telecommunications connection. Different types of networks use different protocols. The Internet and most extranets are based in the TCP/IP layered model of protocols. Each layer contains vulnerabilities and corresponding attack strategies. Hardware and software can use the protocols to restrict network access. Attackers can use weaknesses in the protocols to attack networks.

The primary TCP/IP protocols are the Internet Protocol and the Transmission Control Protocol. IP is used to route messages between devices on a network, and operates at the Internet layer. TCP operates at the host-to-host layer, and provides a connection-oriented, full-duplex, virtual circuit between hosts. Different protocols support different services for the network.

TCP/IP is a packet-based communication system. A packet consists of a header and a data payload. A header is analogous to a mail envelope, containing the information necessary for delivery of the envelope. Therefore, the IP packet header contains the address of the sender and the intended recipient. The data payload is the contents of the envelope. If the IP packet indicates the protocol is TCP, then the TCP header will immediately follow the IP header. The TCP header contains source and destination ports, the sequence number, and other information.

There are many ways attackers can exploit TCP/IP weakness. Some of the most common attacks include using TCP information packet headers to present misleading information such as a false IP address. An IP session may also be hijacked. If x and y are transferring information, a hacker can pretend to be x, push the real x out of his session, and y will never be the wiser. Then the hacker can do what he wants with the session he's stolen. Similarly, the protocol field can indicate a different protocol than actually carried. The attacker can craft an attack to pass through a firewall (see below) and attack with an otherwise unacceptable protocol.

Other attacks on your system may include overloading your servers with requests until they can't handle it, altering data, destroying data, stealing data or accessing your systems without authorization. You can avoid attacks on your system in several ways. First and foremost, if you have any ports that aren't being used, shut them down. An attacker can get into your system through any entry you have. It could be as simple as physically leaving a door unlocked. In our case, it could be as simple as leaving a port unattended.

Beyond this, you need a policy for ports and protocols. Collect your general management, IT managers and network administrators and get them to create a protocol policy. In this policy you should include:

- Detailed procedures for taking action on an attack
- Reporting procedures for any security incidents
- Security standards for ports and protocols

Of these three, security standards will be the most vital. These will help your employees decide whether to shut down certain ports, how to configure appropriate firewalls and how to improve any weaknesses you encounter. For best results, you should regularly update and strengthen your policy.

Have you secured routers and the DNS System?

Picture someone wandering around your company rifling through files, kicking a couple of computers over, swapping your data around and swiping a few things. If this sounds appealing, prepare to go out of business soon! Otherwise, consider the following control objective:

> *The organization will extend security practices to **all** routers and **all** DNS, LDAP, and Active Directory servers.*

Knowing what to think about and what types of problems are likely to plague your system lets you determine the best approach to securing them.

Guidance from the regulations and standards

Banking/Finance

The **FFIEC Information Security Handbook** is the leading source for information concerning routing and the DNS system. Organizations should put in place security policies defining the filtering required by the router, including the type of access permitted between sensitive source and destination IP addresses. Network administrators implement these policies configuring an access configuration table, which creates a filtering router or a basic firewall. Organizations should periodically audit network equipment to ensure that only authorized and maintained equipment resides on the network.

The **FFIEC Audit Handbook** states only that logical controls should be in place to limit access to authorized persons only to network software, including routers.

Credit Card

MasterCard SDP calls for securing a router configuration against unauthorized changes. Each router contains a configuration that is specific to the environment in which it is used. Router configuration must include ingress and egress filters. A secure protocol must be used for router configuration.

US Federal Security

The **National Cyberspace Strategy** calls for securing of the DNS system. Increased use of address verification and out-of-band management is also recommended.

International Standards Organization

ISO 17799 calls for shared networks to incorporate routing controls to ensure that computer connections and information flows do not breach the access control policy of the business applications. Routing controls should be based on positive source and destination address checking mechanisms. Network address translation can be used for isolating networks and preventing routes to propagate from the network of one organization into the network of another.

General Guidance

The **ISF Standard of Good Practice for Information Security** calls for the configuration of routers to prevent unauthorized or incorrect updates by: verifying the source of routing updates, verifying the destination of routing updates, protecting the exchange of routing information, and encrypting the routing information being exchanged.

EU Guidance

The **OECD Risk Checklist** calls for proper configuration of routers to meet an organization's system requirements. Further, access to the management of interfaces of routers must be secured.

From regulation to reality – sure signs you are complying

Router configuration and security determine the quality of the flow of information throughout your organization. A router directs data packets by telling them where to go based on the IP addresses of the destination machine and the next machine to receive the packets. The packets go from router to router until they reach their destination. The router will either refuse to forward or quarantine any "undesirable" or "unapproved" packets.

How your router decides to refuse or pass on information depends upon the provisions you make for router configuration in your security policy and the implementation of those provisions.

In general, the security policy should define filtering requirements for the router. Types of access should be classified as appropriate or inappropriate. What to do with each type of access should also be discussed. This makes it easier to implement suitable filters later.

Be clear and specific-- your network administrators will have to implement and configure routers according to the policy provided.

Prior to implementation, network administrators construct an access configuration table, which creates the filters for the routers. Upon completion the configuration is tested to ensure it functions appropriately. Periodically, all network equipment should be audited to ensure that only authorized equipment resides on the network.

In addition to securing your routers through appropriate configuration, you will want to secure your DNS system. DNS service translates user-friendly domain names like www.ilovedoughnuts.com into the cold hard numerical IP addresses they really are, like 260.105.231.2. Lack of DNS security will leave this service exposed and ripe for attack by hackers. The details of the attacks themselves will not be discussed here. However, you should prepare yourself to face four basic types of attack on your DNS system:

1. Footprinting

2. Denial-of-service attack

3. Data modification

4. Redirection

Defending against these attack methods comes in three basic varieties: low, medium and high security. Now would be a good time to get out your security policy to figure out where the DNS needs to have high security, and where you can have low security. If you don't care about a particular activity or type of data, consider low-level security, or in simpler terms, no security. This is where you leave your DNS system fully exposed to the Internet. Full exposure is about the most horrible idea around if you're hoping to prevent attacks on it. On the other hand, it's perfectly ok if you're not passing around anything important. *Nothing* of importance, we mean it.

Medium-level security improves upon low-level security instantaneously by offering at least a few options. It includes limiting exposure to the Internet by forbidding certain activities. For example unsecured dynamic update may be disallowed. Or internal DNS servers may be configured to communicate with external DNS servers through a firewall that only allows a limited list of source and destination addresses. There are many other elements you can include at medium-level. The general difference between medium and low security is that you don't completely expose your systems.

High-level security differs from medium-level security by providing *no* internet communication by means of internal DNS servers. More limits are included than with medium and low-level security. Chances are, you'll put your organization's DNS security somewhere between medium and high level security.

Both DNS and router security are dictated by the provisions of your security policy. Be sure to include a detailed explanation of how DNS security is to be implemented for various situations in your organization, just as you did for the routers. Later, network administrators will implement the security laid out in the policy.

Are your firewalls configured properly?

Firewalls help defend your systems from unauthorized access, by providing a wall of fire, if you will, between you and potential attackers. Of course we're not actually talking about real walls of fire, but that's how these bad boys act. Appropriate traffic enters your system through a firewall, cool as a cucumber. Malicious traffic gets sizzled to a crisp. Check out our control objective on this topic:

> *The organization will maintain a firewall with "deny all by default" access rules. All further access rules will be coordinated with the organizational port and protocol policies. Where possible, Network Address Translation (NAT) will be enabled on all secure zones for further security.*

It's not always easy to decide what to crisp and what to keep, but our discussion of what's important in a firewall policy should help you determine what counts as appropriate and inappropriate traffic.

Guidance from the regulations and standards

Public Companies

The **AICPA Suitable Trust Services Criteria** and the **AICPA/CICA Privacy Framework** both call for firewalls to be used to prevent unauthorized access. The former further provides that firewalls should be logged and reviewed daily by the security administrator.

Banking/Finance

The **FFIEC Information Security Handbook** has a wealth of information concerning firewalls. First, the FFIEC lays out the four primary types of firewalls from which to choose: packet filters, proxy servers, stateful inspection, and application level-firewalls. Firewalls may provide some additional services such as Network Address Translation (NAT), which readdresses outbound packets to mask the internal IP address of the network.

The FFIEC also calls for a firewall policy, stating the management's expectations for how the firewall should function, and is a component of the overall security policy. Management needs to update the firewall policy as the organizations security needs and the risks change.

The **FFIEC Audit Handbook** also touches on firewalls, stating that firewalls should be used to limit logical access to authorized individuals.

Credit Card

The **Visa CISP** calls for firewalls to be used as a key protection mechanism. A firewall should be built that will deny all "untrusted" networks/hosts. Additionally, VISA calls for implementation of Internet Protocol (IP) masquerading to prevent internal addresses from being revealed, and the use of technologies that implement RFC 1918 address space, such as Port Address Translation (PAT) or Network Address Translation (NAT).

MasterCard SDP calls for a formal procedure modifying firewall configuration. Configure the firewall to deny all traffic, and then reconfigure the firewall to allow only necessary traffic. Access to the firewall should be limited both logically and physically. When a packet is dropped off at the firewall, an entry must be created in the log file and this log file must be reviewed regularly. Finally, the firewall configuration must hide the internal network topology, but use NAT.

US Federal Security

FISCAM calls for the use of firewalls to limit network access.

NIST Special Publications

NIST 800-14 calls for secure firewalls to block or filter access between two networks, often between a private network and a larger, more public network such as the internet. Secure gateways allow internal users to connect to external networks while protecting internal systems from compromise.

NIST 800-41 offers a lot of general information on firewall design. 2.2 and 2.4-2.6 discuss different firewalls, how they work and their strengths and weaknesses, making it easier for an organization to choose what is right for their environment. 2.2 describes packet filter firewalls, concluding they are best for high-speed environments where user authentication is not important. 2.4 presents application-proxy firewalls. The final judgment on these is that they are good for creating user authentication, but are very slow and must have their vulnerability to address spoofing attacks defended against. 2.5 describes a non-firewall option, dedicated proxy servers. It explains how to pair one with a firewall as well as their usefulness in defending against internally based attacks and malicious behavior. 2.6 covers hybrid firewall technologies. Because there are many different varieties, organizations must take the time and care to evaluate a firewall project before purchasing anything.

3.1 provides four guidelines for building an ideal firewall environment. These include keeping a project as simple as possible, using any devices as they are meant to be used, creating defenses that include multiple layers and being sure to focus on external *and* internal threats to an organization's network.

5.3 offers additional strategies for handling firewalls. This section recommends having a failover strategy. That way, if one firewall fails, all traffic shifts over to a backup firewall and defenses are still in place.

5.7 talks about firewalls that are created to protect specific, special-purpose systems. These can be used with a network firewall to limit user access to resources inside an organization.

2.7 recommends using PAT for network address translation as it is often the most secure method for hiding the structure of a network behind a firewall.

NIST 800-41 also discusses appropriate firewall policies for an organization. 4.1 describes the steps to creating a firewall policy. First, determine what network applications are necessary for successful operations. Then determine the vulnerabilities for those applications. Next, conduct a cost-benefits analysis of methods for securing each application. The next step is to create an applications traffic matrix showing protection method and finally, create a firewall ruleset based on the matrix. 4.2 describes how to implement the ruleset discussed in 4.1 It presents a recommendation for what type of traffic should be blocked. 4.3 talks about testing firewall policy. This involves comparing the firewall's actual configuration to a written description of the configuration to ensure they match up. Another way to test is to mimic attacks on the system and see if the firewall does the job it is intended to do.

2.9 suggests that as an added security feature, each laptop in an organization should be equipped with a firewall.

NIST 800-61 § A.2.1 offers firewall configuration advice for preventing denial of service incidents. It is recommended that firewall rulesets be configured to prevent reflector attacks by rejecting all suspicious combinations of source and destination ports.

General Guidance

CobiT requires the following when a connection to the Internet or other public network exists: adequate firewalls to be operative to protect against denial of services and any unauthorized access to the internal resources; control of any application and infrastructure management flows in both directions; and protection against denial of service attacks.

The **ISF Standard of Good Practice for Information Security** calls for use of a firewall for any network that is linked to other networks or sub-networks. There should be documented standards/procedures for managing firewalls covering filtering of traffic, blocking or restricting particular sources of traffic, protecting firewalls against attack or failure, and limiting divulgence of information about the network. Finally, all laptops should be equipped with a firewall.

EU Guidance

The **OECD Risk Checklist** calls for certified firewalls or use of specific criteria when deciding on a specific firewall. Additionally, it calls for a comprehensive list of what should be allowed through the firewall, and strategic placement of firewalls. A network should be explicitly configured to restrict access for everything that does not need to enter the firewall. Finally, firewall logs must be monitored to be sure they are correctly capturing data.

From regulation to reality – sure signs you are complying

Before writing your firewall policy, choose the type or types of firewalls your organization is going to employ. There are four primary types of firewalls your organization can choose from: packet filters, proxy servers, stateful inspection, and application level-firewalls. Although we won't go into detail about each of these here, you should use the firewalls that will best meet your organizations needs. Firewalls may also provide some additional services such as Port Address Translation (PAT) or Network Address Translation (NAT), which readdresses the outbound packets to mask the internal IP addresses of the network.

When you've determined the firewall type that is most appropriate for your organization, you're ready to create a firewall policy. This policy lays out the guidelines detailing how the firewall should function. The following is a suggested list of procedures and techniques to include in your firewall policy:

- Procedures for changing firewall configuration

- Details on logging and firewall log files

- Access policies, including logical and physical access restrictions

- A comprehensive list of what should be allowed through a firewall

- Details on strategic placement of firewalls

- Procedures concerning the protection of firewalls from attack or failure

- Policies on firewalls for laptops

Do you need remote access, and if so, is it secured?

Remote access into your organization's information systems can be a serious security problem. It's hard to figure out how to let the good guys in and keep the bad guys out. Particularly if you're dealing with wireless or internet access, information your employees are sending is highly susceptible to password hijacking, compromise of data and host spoofing. And there's modem access to be concerned about too. Using a modem might offer better defense against session hijacks or interception by hostile parties, but frequently people set up their modems incorrectly. You have no good way of knowing how Joe Schlabotnik plans to connect to your organization's information, how he plans to send the organization his work and whether he knows how to protect his connection. The point of all this isn't to scare you (BOO! just kidding), but to get you thinking about some of the security issues you'll encounter if you opt to allow remote access. The following control objective should help you deal with remote access security:

> *All remote access to the organizational network will be directed to clearly defined and highly secured remote access points. All other possible remote access points will be disabled.*

If you're an organization that doesn't need remote access, the solution to your problem is simple. Otherwise, check out the details in this section for guidance on what you need to ensure secure remote access.

Guidance from the regulations and standards

Banking/Finance

The **FFIEC Information Security handbook** calls for financial institutions to secure remote access to and from their systems by: disabling remote communication at the operating system level if no business need exists, tightly controlling access through management approvals and subsequent audits, implementing robust controls over configuration to disallow potential malicious use, logging and monitoring remote access, securing remote access devices, and using strong authentication and encryption to secure communications.

The FFIEC Information Security handbook requires management to institute policies restricting remote access and they should be aware of all remote access devices attached to their system. Management approval should be required for remote access. Two-factor authentication should be implemented for all remote access.

Credit Card

Visa CISP calls for a formal process for remote access connections. Additionally, a two-factor authentication for remote access to the network should be implemented.

MasterCard SDP does not allow incoming connections on modems, because the router and the firewall protections may be bypassed. A two factor authentication system should be adopted. Remote access accounts should be protected from eavesdropping. Remote access accounts should be closely monitored to prevent access by unauthorized users.

US Federal Security

The **National Cyberspace Strategy** calls for federal agencies to consider installing systems that continuously check for unauthorized connections to networks. Agency policy and procedures should reflect careful consideration of additional risk reduction methods such as bi-directional authentication, shielding standards and other technical security considerations.

FISCAM calls for all access points to be identified to prevent unauthorized remote access to the network.

FIPS Publication 191 § 1.5.2 calls for controlling remote computing so that only authorized users may access remote components and applications. An authentication mechanism for remote users must be provided.

NIST Special Publications

NIST 800-53 calls for the organization to document, monitor, and control all methods of remote access to the information systems including remote access for privileged functions. Appropriate organization officials should authorize each remote access method for the information system and authorize only the necessary users for each access method. Dial-up based remote access should be limited and unauthorized connections must be protected against.

General Guidance

The **ISF Standard of Good Practice for Information Security** requires computers used by staff working in remote locations to operate as intended, remain available and do not compromise the security of any facilities to which they can be connected. Remote working should be documented by standards or procedures.

EU Guidance

The **OECD Risk Checklist** calls for monitoring of unusual instances of remote users, logs to be regularly reviewed, and the utilization of two-factor identification. Each user should only be allowed one remote access computer.

From regulation to reality – sure signs you are complying

Starting from a high-level overview, your mission should you choose to accept it, is to take appropriate security measures to defend against attacks on remote access. Begin by identifying risks to your organization from remote access. There are a few basic categories; your people can do something stupid to compromise security, a third party can launch a hostile attack and intercept data, or remote access devices can be inadequately defended against compromise.

The best line of defense for remote access issues is to limit and tightly control access. The FFIEC suggests that you do this by:

- requiring management approval and audits of any remote access

- implementing controls over configuration to prevent malicious use

- logging and monitoring remote access

- securing remote access devices

- using strong authentication and encryption to secure communications

These issues, at a minimum, should be included in a remote access policy for your organization. The policy should strike the appropriate balance between effective operation of the business and placing the business in jeopardy [JMM].

It is important to remember in constructing your policy, what types of regulations you wish to comply with. They will influence the policy significantly. If you choose to follow the security measures outlined by MasterCard SDP for example, you will not be able to allow incoming connections on modems.

In general, to help you get a feel for what kinds of controls you might add to your organization and provide for in your policy, here are a few examples:

- Use two-factor authentication where possible

- Continuously check for unauthorized connections to networks

- Identify all possible legitimate access points to make it easier to pinpoint unauthorized access

- When looking for unauthorized access points, don't overlook those multi-function fax/printers and PBXes. Network security controls have been successfully bypassed through dialing in to management software on various fax devices or managed copiers and PBXes connected to corporate networks [JMM].

- Make staff with remote access privileges aware of security issues, any protective precautions they need to take with the devices they use to access the network, etc.

How Do You Secure Operating System Access?

As the manager, you want a trusted operating system. One you know can withstand attacks from outside your organization, stupidity from employees within your organization, and even sabotage. In order to obtain such a trusted operating system, we recommend you follow this control objective:

> *With regard to operating system access, the organization will secure access to system utilities, restrict and monitor privileged access, log and monitor user program access to sensitive resources, update the operating system with security patches, and secure the devices that can that can access the operating system through physical or logical means.*

Operating systems don't come trustworthy; you have to install the trust by adding certain monitoring and security measures to the system. But, you are in luck. The system, unlike most human beings, will follow directions, won't talk back, and can generally make your life a whole lot easier.

Guidance from the regulations and standards

Public Companies

SAS 94 does not specifically call for operating system access security and control. However, the standard discusses the benefits of an IT system, including the implementation of security controls in applications, databases, and operating systems.

The **AICPA/CICA Suitable Trust Services Criteria** calls for login sessions to be terminated after three unsuccessful attempts. Terminated login sessions should be logged for follow up by a security administrator.

Banking/Finance

The **FFIEC Information Security Handbook** contains extensive information on operating system access. It calls for institutions to secure access to the operating systems of all system components by securing access to system utilities, restricting and monitoring privileged access, logging and monitoring user or program access to sensitive resources and alerting on security events, updating the operating system with security patches and securing the devices that can access the operating system through physical and logical means. The administrator must have the proper capabilities to achieve these goals, including the ability to restrict access to sensitive or critical system resources, log and monitor user or program access, and filter logs for security events. Other controls include ensuring that authentication methods are suited to restrict system access to both users and applications, and segregating the operating system access, where possible, to limit full or root-level access to the system.

Healthcare and Life Sciences

HIPAA requires proper authentication of operating system users, by implementing procedures to verify that a person or entity seeking access to electronic protected health information is the one claimed. HIPAA addresses logging access attempts, and automatic logging out of an idle computer.

Credit Card

Both the **Visa CISP** and **MasterCard SDP** address operating system access. Visa CISP calls for establishing a mechanism for systems with multiple users that restricts access based on a user's need to know. Additionally, VISA CISP requires authentication of users, monitoring of system access attempts, limiting repeat access attempts to six, setting the lockout duration at 30 minutes or until an administrator enables the user ID, and logging out a session if it has been idle for 15 minutes.

MasterCard SDP calls for restricting access to systems on a need-to-know basis, establishing thresholds that lock out an account after multiple unsuccessful attempts, and providing for systems that automatically lock when not in use.

US Federal Security

FIPS Publication 191 § 2.1.2 calls for robust controls for operating system access. This is done through a privilege mechanism which limits users to system resources that are necessary for their jobs. Care should be taken when thinking through operating system access, to ensure that privilege mechanisms are granular enough to avoid granting more privileges than a person needs for work.

NIST Special Publications

NIST 800-14 requires user to authenticate as well as restricting access to authenticated data. Log-on attempts should be limited after a failed number of attempts. ISF calls for a sign in process before users should be allowed to access the system and sign-on attempts should be limited.

NIST 800-53 calls for identification of users and disabling the user's login to the system after a period of inactivity. FISCAM calls for authorization access to be appropriately limited and segregated. FISCAM further requires that inactive terminals are logged off and the number of unsuccessful login attempts is limited.

International Standards Organization

ISO 17799 provides detail about operating system access and calls for security facilities at the operating system level to computer resources. System facilities should be capable of identifying and verifying the identity, and if necessary, the terminal and location of each authorized user; recording successful and failed system access; providing appropriate means for authentication; and where appropriate, restricting the connection times of users. Additionally, the number of unsuccessful log-on attempts should be limited (three is recommended), keeping a record of unsuccessful attempts should be considered, and forcing a time delay before further log-on attempts is allowed.

From regulation to reality – sure signs you are complying

Operating systems make it possible to restrict access to certain parts of your organization's information system, as well as separate different kinds of data and provide different levels of information security. But, it is not enough for these controls to be a mere possibility – these controls must be a reality.

A good way to turn your operating system into one you can trust, is to keep an eye on who accesses it. You can secure access by identifying the identity and terminal location of each authorized user. By requiring authentication such as a password (and accompanying password management system) for logins, you will be able to deter unauthorized access. Many operating systems provide security by limiting the number of unsuccessful login attempts a user is allowed in succession, and automatic locking if a computer is left unused for a short period of time such as fifteen minutes.

It is not enough to directly secure access to the operating system. Go further by assigning specific user privileges. We have said this many times, but it is always worth repeating – not everybody needs access to everything all the time. Develop policies for ascertaining whether an employee gets certain access privileges or not. Compare employees' assigned roles in the company to what kind of information they need to do their jobs properly. Any place you find access rights that aren't critical for their work, remove them. The best way to secure your operating system is to give employees information on a need-to-know basis. It makes it harder for them to mess something up by accident or on purpose.

If certain workers are granted special access privileges, take extra security measures. Extra access privileges imply more sensitive or critical data. Thus you should take extra care to monitor their use of those privileges. Periodically, review any special privileges that have been granted to determine whether they are still necessary for daily work.

An important aspect of your operating system access security will be the system administrator. This person or group will have the role of updating security patches, ensuring devices are secure, examining monitoring and logging to make sure it is running properly, viewing access attempt information to make sure it is normal and implementing the restriction of access to different portions of the system. Choose a system administrator(s) wisely. Take the time to do background checks to make sure they are trustworthy and offer the appropriate job skills. Finally, be sure the administrator has the proper tools and privileges at her disposal to make decisions and implement appropriate security solutions.

Crunchy Outsides and Gooey Centers: Is Your Organization a Tootsie Pop Because of Poor Application Access Security?

Tootsie pops are tasty treats, but you don't want your organization's defense measures to mimic one, otherwise every hacker out there will be tempted to go after you. That's why you not only need to monitor operating system access and network access, but application access. If you don't have a method for determining who is accessing data contained in your applications, you have no way of knowing if they're doing what they're supposed to be doing, or compromising the integrity of your information. Avoid this problem with the following control objective:

> To promote the technical integrity of applications and information, the organizations will restrict logical access to system software and applications for authorized users only. Furthermore, the organization will ensure that application systems control user access to information and application system functions in accordance with the defined business access control policy.

By securing your organization's applications, you make yourself less vulnerable to internal damage should an attacker get past your outer line of defense – which is particularly possible if someone inside the organization decides to launch an attack.

Guidance from the regulations and standards

Banking/Finance

The **FFIEC Information Security Handbook** calls for financial institutions to control access to applications by: using authentication and authorization controls appropriately robust for the risk of the application; monitoring access rights to ensure they are the minimum required for the user's current business needs; using time of day limitations on access as appropriate; and using software that enables rapid analysis of user activities. Other issues to consider are maintaining consistent processes for assigning new user access or changing existing user access, logging access and events, and utilizing software that supports group profiles.

US Federal Security

The **Clinger-Cohen Act** calls for an application security plan, planning for the adequate security of each major application that is operating within the system. Access rules should be as stringent as possible to provide adequate security for the application and the information in it.

International Standards Organization

ISO 17799 has a wealth of information on application access. It calls for a defined business access control policy to define and monitor user access to applications. Operating system software should provide protection from unauthorized use. The security of other systems with which resources are shared should not be compromised by the application system. Finally, the sensitivity of an application system should be explicitly identified and documented by the application owner.

General Guidance

The **ISF Standard of Good Practice for Information Security** explains that access to applications and associated information should be restricted to authorized individuals and enforced accordingly. Users of the application should be identified, authenticated, and authorized. Subject system administrators to strong authentication. Create a method of ensuring that users do not share identification or authentication details. Log access to applications and provide enough information to provide a satisfactory audit.

From regulation to reality – sure signs you are complying

Many of the techniques for dealing with operating system access apply to applications access. That is to say, you'll want to use authentication methods such as passwords, log all uses of critical applications and ensure that employees have access rights on a need-to-know basis. Basic security training must also be included, such as logging off, or enforcing an automatic log off if a computer is left unattended for 15 minutes or more.

Application specific techniques include ensuring that applications are not compromising operating system security as well as checking to be sure that the operating system does not have inappropriate override abilities. Application security won't mean much if someone can override the need for those security controls from the operating system.

Ideally, you will want to construct an application security plan. Outline what methods you will use to protect applications, how employees fit into this security and how you will make them aware of their role in maintaining application security. Simple training might be telling workers why they should not trade identification or password information with other users or outside parties.

How do you secure your transactions and transmissions?

It seems that more and more, computers are ordering supplies from other computers, giving the thumbs-up to the orders, and processing the shipments of the orders – without the need for intervention by humans. One of the methods for ensuring that these transactions have good integrity is to protect the orders while in transmit between the computers. You can narrow down transaction security problems to shoulder surfing and third parties forwarding messages around by protecting messages and transactions during transmission of information made by your organization. Consider the following control objective for this topic:

> *In order to protect the confidentiality and integrity of data, the organization will protect transmissions of secure information by protecting sensitive information during transmission and transport from unauthorized access, modification, and misaddressing. If data is transmitted over the Internet or any public network, management will implement policies and procedures to ensure integrity, confidentiality, and non-repudiation of sensitive messages.*

Securing transactions and transmissions can be a difficult task, but well worth it. The better defenses you have, the more reliable your organization is, and in turn, that allows customers to trust you with their accounts far more than an organization with poor security.

Guidance from the regulations and standards

Public Companies

The issue of transaction security is generally addressed or implied in several of the public companies standards. The issue is strongly recognized in **SAS 94**, however, no specific guidelines are addressed.

17 CFR 240.15d-15 calls for reasonable assurance that transactions are recorded as necessary to permit preparation of financial statements in accordance with generally accepted accounting principles, and that all receipts and expenditures of the issuer are made in accordance with authorization of management and directors of the issuer.

Banking/Finance

The **FFIEC Information Security Handbook** explains that as customers and merchants originate an increasing number of transactions, authentication and encryption become increasingly important to ensure non-repudiation of transactions.

Healthcare and Life Sciences

HIPAA calls for the implementation of technical security measures to guard against unauthorized access to electronic information that is being transmitted over an electronic communications network. Additionally, protection against improper modification of electronically transmitted health information is addressed.

NIST 800-66 § 4.18 addresses § 164.312(e)(1) of the HIPAA Standard. The section discusses how to implement technical security measures to protect against unauthorized access to protected health information transmitted over electronic communications networks. A chart provides a list of activities to carry out to achieve a defense. It merits a direct read through since it is too detailed to write up here.

Credit Card

VISA CISP calls for the use of strong cryptography and encryption techniques to safeguard sensitive cardholder data during transmission over public networks. Use of a trusted path is also required.

MasterCard SDP requires the transmission of sensitive cardholder information between the merchant or MSP server and the consumer's browser to be encrypted using SSL communication. It also recommends the use of a trusted path.

US Federal Security

FIPS Publication 191 § 1.5.4 describes that messaging services add additional risk to information stored on a server or in transit. If email is not protected adequately, it can be easily captured, altered and retransmitted. 1.5.5 mentions inadequate protection during transmission as a LAN security concern. 2.1.5 discusses the way confidentiality of information may be breached when that information is in transit. It lists several potential vulnerabilities including inadequate physical protection of LAN devices as well as transmitting unencrypted data cross the LAN and beyond. 2.1.6 describes the way LAN traffic may be spoofed by exploiting several vulnerabilities. These include transmitting unencrypted data, lack of authentication mechanisms and lack of audit trails and logs of activity. 2.2.5 elaborates on this by calling for non-repudiation for communications. It recommends using public key digital signatures to accomplish this. 1.5.3 suggests passive and active wiretapping to help ensure that data gets where it needs to go without being altered or intercepted. 2.2.4 discusses data and message integrity service to help create trusted paths for data. Mechanisms that provide this integrity include message authentication codes for software and files, secret keys based on an electronic signature, use of a public key digital signature, granular privilege mechanisms, appropriate access control settings, virus detection software and workstations with no local storage or disk drives.

NIST Special Publications

NIST 800-14 calls for the protection of data transmitted over public or shared data networks. The ISF Standard requires the protection and integrity of sensitive information. It explains that the transfer of sensitive information should be protected from unauthorized disclosure by

encrypting the information, applying dual controls over the encryption mechanisms, sending portions of the information by different routes/media, and by using fiber optic cable or exceptionally critical or sensitive information.

NIST 800-53 contains much information on non-repudiation, as well as transaction security in general. NIST 800-53 requires the information system to provide the capability to determine whether a given individual took a particular action. Non-repudiation protects against later false claims by an individual for not haven taken a particular action. Non-repudiation services can be used to determine if information originated from an individual, or if an individual took specific actions (e.g., sending an email, signing a contract, approving a procurement request) or received specific information. Non-repudiation services are obtained by employing digital signatures, digital message receipts, and time stamps.

Additionally, NIST 800-53 calls for the information system to protect the integrity of transmitted information. Transmitted information should be confidential and the use of a trusted communications path is required.

International Standards Organization

ISO 17799 calls for the use of non-repudiation service.

General Guidance

CobiT has an abundance of information on transaction security. "Management should ensure that adequate protection of sensitive information is provided during transmission and transport against unauthorized access, modification, and misaddressing. Management should develop policies and protocols regarding data transmitted over the Internet or public networks, to ensure integrity, confidentiality and non-repudiation of sensitive messages."

Regarding non-repudiation, "organizational policy should ensure that, where appropriate, transactions cannot be denied by either party, and controls are implemented to provide non-repudiation of origin or receipt of transactions. Organizational policy should also ensure that sensitive transaction data is only exchanged over a trusted path. Trusted channels may need to be established using encryption between users, between users and systems, and between systems. Finally, all security related hardware and software should at all times be protected against tampering to maintain the integrity and against disclosure of security keys."

From regulation to reality — sure signs you are complying

The most important thing for you to remember is that data can be encrypted when sent, and that you should be using sound business judgment and information technology governance rules for deciding when that should take place. Encryption is the key to protecting your sensitive transmissions from outsiders trying to catch a glimpse of what you're sending. If you are protecting particularly sensitive data such as cardholder data, employ strong cryptography along with other encryption techniques. When you send information, be sure to employ trusted communication paths to do so. Use non-repudiation services to be absolutely sure that a message leaves from and arrives at its intended location.

Encrypting your sensitive transmissions will help ensure confidentiality. But, that is not the end of it. We mentioned above that another way sensitive transmissions are intercepted is when employees or third-parties make stupid (or intentional) errors, such as forwarding sensitive messages, or leaving an email on their screen when they go for a cup of coffee. Avoid these problems by training your staff not to do this. Perhaps you can use fear-- "If certain documents get lost, it could affect the reputation of the organization, in turn affecting our revenue, which would affect our ability to pay you..." or something like that. Maybe this approach is not for you, but at the very least, your staff must understand there are consequences to exposing confidential information.

Because transaction security is based off other areas such as network, applications and operating system security, part of a good transaction security method involves robust security in all the other areas mentioned. This is an interconnected system, and it requires strength in all parts to make a strong whole. Which means that you can't forget physical media encryption either. Because the amount of data on backup media is so large and the possible loss of backup media (especially in off-site transit and storage) would be so catastrophic, it is imperative that all backup media be encrypted [JMM].

What kind of encryption are you going to use?

Now that you know encryption is important to protect sensitive transmissions of information, you can address what exactly encryption is and what kind of encryption best suits the needs of your organization. Think of encryption like the lock on a safe. The more money you have in that safe, the more secure you want that safe to be. Similarly, the more sensitive the data you wish to protect, the stronger the encryption should be. For any encryption, security is based on both the strength of the encryption and the management of the keys. If you don't manage the keys correctly, it can be as dangerous as handing the pass code to your safe to a stranger and telling him where it is and what's inside. It does not take a genius to figure out that's a bad idea. Therefore, the control objective for this section is twofold:

> In order to promote technical integrity and confidentiality, the organization will employ the use of encryption to mitigate the risk of disclosure or alteration of sensitive information is storage or transit. Equally as important as the encryption itself, the organizations will create adequate key management policies and procedures.

Encryption itself can be a little confusing. Take a look at the regulations and standards for some background information. Only after you understand encryption should you move on to developing policies surrounding it.

Guidance from the regulations and standards

Public Companies

The **AICPA Suitable Trust Services Criteria** requires that encryption or other equivalent security techniques be used to protect user authentication information and the corresponding session transmitted over the Internet or other public network.

Banking/Finance

The **FFIEC Information Security Handbook** explains that financial institutions should employ encryption to mitigate the risk of disclosure or alteration of sensitive information in storage and in transit. *"Encryption implementations should include: encryption strength sufficient to protect the information from disclosure until such time as disclosure poses no material risk; effective key management practices; robust reliability; and appropriate protection of the encrypted communication's endpoints."*

The FFIEC Information Security Handbook has a wealth of information concerning how encryption works. For instance, encryption functions by taking data and a variable, called a "key," and processing those items through a fixed algorithm to create the encrypted text. Additionally, the handbook suggests that an institution set key management policies and procedures because security is primarily based on encryption keys.

The **Appendix of 12 CFR 30** calls for the encryption of customer information including while in transit or while being stored in the network.

Healthcare and Life Sciences

HIPAA addresses encryption by suggesting the implementation of a mechanism to encrypt and decrypt electronic protected health information. **21 CFR Part 11 §11.30** calls for the use of encryption to ensure the authenticity, integrity, and confidentiality of records.

Credit Card

VISA CISP requires the implementation of a cryptographic solution that is isolated so that secret data cannot be disclosed. Encryption keys should be protected against disclosure and misuse, access to keys should be restricted and stored securely in the fewest possible places and forms. Finally, the full documentation of key management processes and procedures is required.

MasterCard SDP establishes the importance of encrypting all communication with systems containing or processing sensitive information. Keys should be stored safely to reduce the risk of key exposure or theft. MasterCard calls for the use of dual control, requiring two people for the most critical tasks involving key manipulation used for encrypting and decrypting sensitive account information.

US Federal Security

The **National Cyberspace Strategy** encourages the use of strong encryption. Finally, **FISCAM** provides a generous amount of general information on the use of encryption to protect sensitive information from unauthorized access.

FIPS Publication 191 § 2.2.3 calls for use of cryptography to protect important data and email messages. Two encryption methods are suggested, secret key cryptography and public key cryptography. Secret key cryptography involves the use of a single key between two parties. It is used to encrypt and decrypt data. Public key cryptography makes use of two keys, public and private. Each party has its own public and private key pairing. The private key is always kept secret.

NIST Special Publications

NIST 800-14 explains that while encryption can provide strong access control, it is accompanied by the need for strong key management. All keys need to be managed against modification, and secret keys and private keys need protection against unauthorized disclosure. Key management involves the procedures and protocols, both manual and automated, used throughout the entire life cycle of the keys. This includes, generation, distribution, storage, entry, use, destruction, and archiving of cryptographic keys.

NIST 800-53 calls for the information system to employ automated mechanisms with supporting procedures or manual procedures for cryptographic key establishment and key management.

General Guidance

CobiT explains that management should define and implement procedures and protocols to be used for generation, change, revocation, destruction, distribution, certification, storage, use, entry and archiving of cryptographic keys to ensure the protection of keys against modification and unauthorized disclosure.

The **OECD Risk Checklist** calls for an established policy regarding key management, requires storage of keys in a secure location, and proper management of keys when they are in need of retirement/replacement.

The **ISF Standard of Good Practice for Information Security**'s objective when dealing with cryptography is to ensure that cryptographic services are managed effectively, thereby protecting the confidentiality of sensitive information, preserving the integrity of critical information, and confirming the identity of the originator of information. Encryption should be used to protect the confidentiality of sensitive information and to determine if critical information has been altered. There should be documented standards/procedures for the use of cryptography which define when cryptography should be used, cover the selection of key algorithms and key lengths, address the management of cryptographic keys and cover the restrictions of the use of cryptographic keys.

ISO 17799 calls for the use of encryption, a cryptographic key management policy with consideration given to regulations and national restrictions, and the protection of cryptographic keys from modification and destruction.

CA 1386 calls for the use of encryption, where feasible, to protect higher-risk personal information.

From regulation to reality – sure signs you are complying

Encryption converts data into a secret code. There are two components to encryption, the key and the algorithm. The algorithm is the series of steps that mathematically transforms the plain-text into unintelligible cipher text. The key is the code to break the algorithm.

Data is scrambled and only the computer who has the key (the code) can unscramble the data. Many of the regulations suggest that you use "128-bit" encryption. "128-bit" encryption refers to the length of the key. The longer the key, the harder it is for someone to break the code. "128-bit" encryption technology is so strong that it is often called "domestic" encryption because there are laws against the export of this technology to other countries.

Let's take a step back for a moment. There are a lot of choices for encrypting both communications and data storage. Sturdy encryption is especially important for authentication credentials and transmission of sensitive information. That's why you want to do a thorough investigation of what kinds of encryption are available to you and what best suits your needs. Here are some basics to get you going.

There are two categories of encryption:

- Symmetric-key encryption
- Public key encryption

Symmetric-key encryption involves computers having secret codes (the key), which it uses to encrypt packets of information before it sends it. You must know which computers will be communicating with each other, so that each computer can have the key installed to facilitate the decoding. These computers can then send messages in code and the other can decode the message using the installed key.

With symmetric-key encryption, the encryption process is simple. Each computer can use the same publicly known encryption algorithm. Here, security is dependant on the length of the key. So if you use "40-bit" encryption, you are getting car alarm security. If you use "128-bit" encryption, you are getting Fort Knox. The downside to using symmetric-key encryption is that both parties involved must agree on a key for their respective computers. Each party you plan on sharing information with requires a secret key be maintained for just that relationship. So, if you have 100 parties to share information with, you need 100 keys. Management of keys can be problematic with this system and authenticity issues often arise.

Public-key encryption uses two keys, a public and a private one. The private key is known only by the computer, and the public key is given to your computer by any computer wishing to communicate with it. The computer then uses both keys in combination to decode the message.

Public-key encryption can take a lot of computing. Therefore many systems use a combination of public key and symmetry. With this method, one computer creates a symmetric key and sends it to the other computer using public-key encryption. The two computers communicate using the symmetric-key encryption and when the session is over, they throw away the symmetric key used for that session.

What does this all mean for you? Well, it means that unless you have a large organization with a lot of computing power, you would benefit from using the combination of encryption technology described above. Whatever you do, make sure you do your homework on encryption, it could mean the difference between secure transmissions and unfortunate disasters.

Once you have determined the type of encryption you wish to employ, then you can move on to the organizational policies surrounding it. Develop a key management policy and implement appropriate procedures alongside it. It cannot be stressed enough just how important key management really is. You don't want to spend time and energy encrypting information just to throw it all away with lousy key management. Consider how you will secure and isolate encryption keys, how you will monitor access to keys, how you will store keys, and what employees will be able to work with the keys. For safety it is recommended that a small number of people have access to keys. Two is best, with each person knowing a different piece of information about the encryption keys so no one person can sabotage the system.

Fleshing out your key management policy involves determining how you will generate keys, remove them, change them, destroy, distribute, certify, store, use and archive your keys. If you cover all these points thoroughly, you will have an excellent encryption system available.

How do you defend your organization against malicious code?

If you catch termites in your house right away, they can be exterminated before they cause a problem. But, if those little suckers bury themselves deep in the fabric of the house, you are looking forward to life in a tent until you can fix your home or buy a new one. Malicious code is similar to termites. The problem it causes can be small and solved if caught quickly. Or, if it goes unnoticed, malicious code can destroy an information system. Because malicious code can be such a problem, we recommend you follow this control objective:

> *In order to protect the availability of information systems, the organization will protect itself against malicious code by using prevention and detection mechanisms such as anti-virus and other detection products at gateways, mail servers, and workstations. For best results, the organization will use a variety of techniques at a variety of locations within the system, monitoring and logging all malicious code to protect against repetition.*

Avoid the nightmare of malicious code by regularly testing and examining your organization's defenses.

Guidance from the regulations and standards

Public Companies

The **AICPA/CICA Privacy Framework** and the **AICPA Suitable Trust Services Criteria** both require procedures to protect against infection by computer viruses, malicious codes, and unauthorized software.

Banking/Finance

The **FFIEC Information Security Handbook** provides a generous amount of information concerning malicious code, what it is, what protections are available and so forth. Financial institutions should protect against the risk of malicious code by: using anti-virus products on clients and servers; using an appropriate blocking strategy on the network perimeter; filtering input into applications; and creating, implementing, and training staff in appropriate computing policies and strategies.

The handbook recommends installing anti-virus software and other detection programs to scan for known signatures of a variety of malicious code.

Additionally, since new malicious code is created daily, signatures need to be updated continually. Anti-virus tools and code blocking, however, are not comprehensive solutions. Protection against new malicious code usually comes from creation of policies and procedures, and awareness training.

Healthcare and Life Sciences

HIPAA addresses protection from malicious software, recommending a company institute procedures for guarding against, detecting, and reporting malicious software.

Credit Card

VISA CISP requires the use and regular update of anti-virus software. It points out that many vulnerabilities and malicious viruses enter the network through employee's email activities. Anti-virus software should be used on all email systems and desktops to protect all systems from such malicious software. Additionally, it calls for the deployment of anti-virus mechanisms on all Windows-based systems, keeping them current and actively running. Finally, anti-virus software must be capable of creating audit logs.

MasterCard SDP calls for the installation of a state-of-the-art virus scanner. The virus scanning software must automatically update the signature file.

US Federal Security

FIPS Publication 191 § 2.1.4 describes vulnerabilities that may be exploited to insert malicious code into data and applications. The vulnerabilities include allowing write permissions to users who only need read access, not detecting changes to software, lack of cryptographic checksum on sensitive data and lack of virus protection and detection tools.

NIST Special Publications

NIST 800-53 calls for malicious code protection that includes the capability for automatic updates. The organization should employ anti-viral mechanisms at critical entry points, and at each workstation, server, or mobile computing device. The anti-viral mechanisms should be used to secure email accounts, and the anti-viral mechanisms should be updated as frequently as possible.

NIST 800-61 A.2.2 discusses different methods for preventing malicious code issues from occurring. Different concepts that are described include making users aware of malicious code issues, reading all anti-virus bulletins, deploying host-based intrusion detection systems including file integrity checkers to critical hosts, using antivirus software and keeping it updated, configuring software to block suspicious files and eliminating open windows shares. 5.2.1-5.2.2 repeats these, but includes discussions about limiting the use of nonessential programs with file transfer capabilities, educating users on the safe handling of email attachments, using web browser security to limit mobile code and configuring email clients to act more securely. All of these are useful ways to prevent malicious code from infiltrating an organization's systems and are worth reading through for specifics.

International Standards Organization

ISO 17799 requires protection against malicious software. Precautions are required to prevent and detect the introduction of malicious software. Users should be made aware of the dangers of malicious software and trained in accordance with the dangers. Controls should be used and a formal policy concerning malicious software should be maintained. Some of the listed controls include maintaining the anti-virus software regularly, conducting regular reviews of the software and malicious code attacks, and ensuring that anti-virus software works on email.

General Guidance

CobiT calls for controls regarding malicious software prevention, detection and correction. Regarding malicious software, management should establish a framework of adequate preventative, detective and corrective control measures, and occurrence response and reporting. Business and IT management should ensure that procedures are established across the organization to protect information systems and technology from computer viruses. Procedures should incorporate virus protection, detection, occurrence response and reporting.

The **ISF Standard of Good Practice for Information Security** requires protection from virus attack and the ability to respond to virus infection within critical timescales. There is a wealth of information in the ISF Standards, including the following requirements. There should be documented standards/procedures providing protection against viruses, anti-virus software should be installed, and all incoming and outgoing traffic should be scanned.

EU Guidance

The **OECD Risk Checklist** requires signatures to be updated on a daily basis, actions to be taken to discover viruses, and the procedures used to discover viruses to be documented.

Every organization has to deal with the possibility that they will be attacked by malicious code. The big problem with malicious code is that it can replicate itself, transmit itself between computers and change, insert or delete data. Without even directly targeting your organization, incoming malicious code can easily harm or destroy your systems. Fortunately, there is a cure for this malaise.

The best defense is an anti-virus system that regularly updates its signatures to stay current with the latest viruses. You can have someone manually update the system, or employ automatic updates. Out of the two, automatic updates are best since they consistently fetch any new signatures whereas a person may be inclined to put it off at times to handle other job functions. If you do choose an automatic update system, it still needs to be monitored regularly.

Your anti-virus software and other detection programs should be placed at the system and individual worker computer levels. Particular care should be taken to scan email since it is easy for incoming messages to carry viruses with them, then replicate and spread from an unwitting employee's computer.

To complete your defense against malicious code, you need more than anti-virus and protective software. You will need a policy that states a procedure for reporting and responding to malicious code issues. For best results, your policy should include:

- A description of a training program to be administered to all employees

- Awareness of viruses and how they spread (especially through email)

- How to tell if a computer may be infected

- A list of procedures to use when a virus is detected

A malicious code policy including these items will vastly improve your defense against malicious code attacks.

Can you detect intruders?

A good intrusion detection system is like an alarm on a house. Once it goes off, you have 30 seconds to punch in a code before the police are called. If you don't know the code, then expect a visit straight from the local donut shop. For an information system, when the alarm goes off, the intrusion detection system responds. And you won't have to wait for it to finish a coffee. The following control objective is recommended for intrusion detection:

> The organizations will ensure the capability to detect and respond to an information system intrusion commensurate with defined levels of risk. Preparation for intrusion detection will involve identifying data flows to monitor for clues to an intrusion, deciding on the scope and nature of monitoring, implementing that monitoring, and establishing a process to analyze and maintain custody over the resulting information.

Different intrusion detection systems do different things, which is why it is so important to do your research and figure out what will work best for your organization's information system. To do this, take a look at the standards and regulations to get a general idea about intrusion detection systems, then, look to the battle plan. Finally, you will have to create your own plan with the tools we provide.

Guidance from the regulations and standards

Public Companies

The **AICPA Suitable Trust Services Criteria** calls for intrusion detection systems to be used to provide continuous monitoring of the entity's network and early identification of potential security breaches.

Banking/Finance

The **FFIEC Information Security Handbook** contains several pages of information on intrusion detection. After establishing the general need for intrusion detection, the handbook discusses automatic intrusion detection in detail.

Automatic intrusion detection systems use one of two methodologies;` signature and heuristics. Each has their advantages and disadvantages. For instance, a weakness of signature-based detection is that a signature must exist for an alert to be generated. Another general weakness of the signature based IDS is the capacity to read traffic. If the IDS falls behind, traffic may be allowed to bypass the IDS. On the other hand, weaknesses in the heuristic, or behavior, method involve the ability of the system to adequately model activity, the relationship between the valid activity in the period being modeled and valid activity in future periods, and the potential for malicious activity to take place while the modeling is performed. Both systems result in false positives and false negatives.

The handbook also discusses honeypots, which are network devices that an institution uses to attract attackers to a harmless and monitored area of the network. Honeypots have three key advantages over IDS systems. Since the only function of the honeypot is to be attacked, any network traffic to or from the honeypot potentially signals an intrusion. Monitoring that traffic is also simpler than monitoring all traffic passing a network IDS. Finally, all of the data a honeypot collects is highly relevant.

Lastly, the handbook discusses pre-establishing which system processing data streams will be monitored for anomalies, defining which anomalies constitute an indicator of intrusion, and the frequency of the monitoring.

The **Appendix of 12 CFR 30** calls for the monitoring of systems and procedures to detect actual attacks on or intrusions into customer information systems.

Credit Card

VISA CISP calls for the use of intrusion detection systems to monitor all network traffic and alert personnel to suspected compromises. Additionally, file integrity monitoring should be deployed to alert personnel to unauthorized modification of critical system or content files.

MasterCard SDP calls for the installation of intrusion detection systems where appropriate.

US Federal Security

The **National Cyberspace Strategy** encourages consideration of intrusion detection programs.

NIST Special Publications

NIST 800-41 § 3.7 describes the two basic types of intrusion detection system, host-based IDS and network-based IDS. The section discusses the flaws in each system. It offers general advice, such as ensuring someone in an organization has a thorough understanding of the flow of data across networks and systems so they can properly implement an intrusion detection system solution. The section also recommends placement of intrusion detection tools anywhere network traffic from external entities is allowed to enter. 5.5 talks about what constitutes a security incident. Ultimately, it depends on an organization's security policy definition of a security incident. This section also covers responsibilities of line administrators in the event that an intruder is detected. Line administrators are ideally expected to restore production access in a way that won't impact the forensic evidence necessary to prosecute the supposed intruder.

NIST 800-53 calls for the organization to employ automated mechanisms to make security alert and advisory information available throughout the organization as needed.

NIST 800-61 A.3 lists different controls that aid an organization in intrusion detection. The information is very detailed and generally covers: identifying indications of incidents through alerts generated by several types of security software, establishing mechanisms for outside parties to report incidents, requiring a baseline level of logging and auditing on all systems, profiling networks and systems, understanding normal behaviors of networks, systems, and applications, using centralized logging and creating a retention policy, performing event correlations, keeping all host clocks synchronized, maintaining and using a knowledge base of information, creating a diagnosis matrix for less experienced staff, documenting of incidents right when they are suspected onwards, safeguarding incident data, prioritizing incidents by business impact and including provisions regarding incident reporting.

NIST 800-61 covers specifics of intrusion detection by discussing different types of incidents an organization should monitor for. The information is too detailed to describe here, so what follows is a summary of information that may be found on intrusion detection in each pertinent area of NIST 800-61. In 6.2-6.3 activities for preventing unauthorized access incidents as well as how to detect them effectively are covered. A.2.3 offers a summary of things that must be done to defend against unauthorized access incidents.

In 7.2-7.3 how to prepare for and prevent inappropriate usage incidents is discussed. A.2.4 offers a summary of things that must be done to defend against inappropriate usage incidents.

4.2-4.3 discusses how to prepare for and prevent denial of service attacks. A.2.1 covers steps an organization may take to defend against denial of service attacks.

5.2-5.3 discusses how to prepare for and prevent malicious code incidents. A.2.2 covers steps an organization may take to defend against malicious code attacks.

Finally, 8.2 discusses how to prepare to handle and detect multiple component attacks. A.2.5 recommends using centralized logging and event correlation software to identify an incident as having multiple components more quickly.

General Guidance

The **ISF Standard of Good Practice for Information Security** calls for intrusion detection methods to be employed for critical systems and networks. Intrusion detection methods should be supported by documented standards/procedures. Intrusion detection systems should be supported by the appropriate software. Suspected intrusions should be analyzed.

US State Laws

CA 1386 requires use of intrusion detection technology and procedures to ensure rapid detection of unauthorized access to higher-risk personal information.

EU Guidance

The **OECD Risk Checklist** calls for IDS use or host-based intrusion detection systems. IDS systems should be appropriately configured for system anomalies. System monitoring of all intrusions should be kept up to date. Honeypots may be used.

From regulation to reality – sure signs you are complying

Intrusion detection is key to preventing compromise of your data and system integrity. Good intrusion detection setups cover all critical systems and networks. They are supported by documented standards and procedures and are supported by appropriate software such as logging or auditing programs. Any suspected intrusions should be analyzed immediately to determine if there is a legitimate security problem or not.

An automatic intrusion detection system is a helpful tool since employees cannot monitor every aspect of your organization's systems manually at all times. There are two possible types of system for you to consider, signature and heuristic. A signature-based system detects signatures and determines whether they are appropriate or not. If they are found to be inappropriate, an alert is generated. A weakness of this system is that an improper signature must be present to trigger an alert. Otherwise, the intrusion goes undetected.

A heuristic method is based on the ability of the system to adequately model activity, the relationship between valid activity in the period being modeled and valid activity in future periods, and the potential for malicious activity to take place while the modeling is performed. This process has the weakness of sometimes modeling inaccurately and causing a false positive or a false negative. Decide what weaknesses are easiest to cope with, and whether to employ both types of systems.

Another intrusion detection tool you can use are honeypots. Do *not* make the mistake of just using a honeypot for intrusion detection. A honeypot is used to attract attackers to a harmless, monitored area of your organization's network. The advantage of a honeypot is that its sole purpose is to attract attackers. That means if anything is in the honeypot, you know you have an intrusion. It's also easier to monitor traffic in the pot, and any data collected there is assuredly about an incoming attacker and useful for analysis purposes.

Problems with honeypots include the fact that they do not attract all attackers and they can be used to launch an attack on other parts of your system. Because honeypots can be bypassed, they should never be your only intrusion detection device [JMM]. If an attacker breaks through a honeypot, you also need other devices that make it clear this has happened.

Are you prepared to deal with breach notifications?

You have your intrusion detection system in place. So, what do you do when a breach occurs? Follow this control objective:

> In order to promote the integrity and availability of information systems, the organization will monitor intrusion detection systems for errors and inconsistencies. To ensure the continued effectiveness of the internal system, management will report on these findings to the affected parties. Periodic assessment will be necessary to ensure that security controls are operating according to stated requirements.

If you report regularly on the success of your intrusion detection systems, you will discover breaches more swiftly and be able to take more immediate action to remedy a breach. If you stay unprepared, with reports coming few and far between, your organization is liable to end up like an unattended candy store full of kids – attackers will be able to take whatever they want whenever they want.

Guidance from the regulations and standards

Public Companies

The **AICPA Suitable Trust Services Criteria** calls for a process for informing the entity about breaches of the system security and for submitting complaints, and that this process is communicated to the authorized users.

Banking/Finance

The **FFIEC Information Security Handbook** explains that preparation determines the success of any intrusion response. Preparation involves defining the policies and procedures that guide the response, assigning responsibilities to individuals and providing appropriate training, formalizing information flows, and selecting, installing, and understanding the tools used in the response effort.

Credit Card

VISA CISP calls for personnel to be on call on a 24/7 basis to respond to compromise alerts. **MasterCard SDP** calls for the constant review of intrusion detection logs for penetration.

NIST 800-61 3.1- 3.1.1 provide a general overview of how to prepare to handle security incidents. A list of tools and resources for incident handlers is provided, and definitely worth reviewing. 3.1.2 discusses the importance of keeping the number of incidents as low as possible. It gives an overview of recommended security practices to prepare against attacks, such as patch management, host security, network security, malicious code prevention and user/staff awareness and training. 3.2.2-3.2.4 reviews how to accurately detect and assess potential incidents. It describes the challenge presented by three factors, incidents may be detected many different ways, there is a great volume of potential signs of incidents and deep specialized technical knowledge and extensive experience are necessary for proper analysis of incident-related data. These sections provide a list of potential sources and what they might display that indicates an incident is happening. 3.2.4 discusses how to analyze findings as well as tasks to carry out that make incident analysis easier. Due to the level of detail, it is recommended that readers go directly to the NIST 800-61 document and read.

Another important aspect of being prepared for breaches includes having a well defined team structure and a clear idea of the services they offer. 2.4-2.4.3 describes different types of teams and the different staffing models they can use. Because there are multiple selections, how to choose what is best based on an organization's specific needs is also discussed. Finally, how to choose a team leader, maintain motivation in being part of the team and keeping everyone current with the latest technology through training is discussed. 2.5 lists potential services an incident response team may want to consider offering. A.1.2 offers tips for creating an ideal team.

2.3.1 talks about the elements of incident response policies and procedures. It is recommended that policies include a statement of management commitment, purpose and objectives of the policy, the scope of the policy, the definition of computer security incidents and their consequences, organizational structure and delineation of roles, responsibilities and levels of authority, prioritization or severity ratings of incidents, performance measures and reporting and contact forms.

2.6 offers detailed recommendations for organizing a computer security incident handling capability. It includes such measures as creating an incident response policy, establishing procedures, keeping people updated on incidents, choosing incident response team members with appropriate skills, deciding what services the team should offer and coordinating participation with other key groups in the event of an incident.

A.1-A.1.1 summarizes information presented in 2.6.

Part of being prepared for incident response is knowing who to share information with. 2.4.4 covers all the different groups that may need to help with a security incident when it occurs. These groups, depending upon the situation, may include selected management, members of the information security team, telecommunications staff (if an incident involves unauthorized access to telephone lines), IT support, legal departments, public affairs and media relations, human resources, business continuity planning and physical security and facilities management.

More information on interacting with other groups and determining what information to share and what services they can offer is found in 2.3.2.1-3. These sections cover sharing information with the media, law enforcement, incident reporting organizations and other outside parties. 3.2.7 includes more authorities to contact in the event of a security incident. The list includes the CIO, head of information security, local information security officer, other incident response teams within the organization, system owner, human resources, public affairs and the legal department.

3.5 talks about incident response from the perspective of how to handle one at the start. It provides a checklist of tasks to step through to handle the incident.

3.2.5 explains that organizations should immediately begin recording facts regarding an incident once one is occurring, or has been discovered to have occurred. Thorough documentation will summarize the incident, include the status of the incident, actions taken to resolve it, contact information for all involved parties, a list of evidence gathered during incident investigation, comments from incident handlers and the next steps to be taken.

General Guidance

The **CobiT** Control Objectives have the most information and are the standards to follow when discussing preparation for breach notification. When dealing with internal control monitoring, management should monitor the effectiveness of internal controls in the normal course of operations through management and supervisory activities, comparisons, reconciliations and other routine actions. Deviations should evoke analysis and corrective action. In addition, deviations should be communicated to the individual responsible for the function and also at least one level of management above that individual. Serious deviations should be reported to senior management.

Reliance on internal controls requires that controls operate promptly to highlight errors and inconsistencies, and that these are corrected before they impact production and delivery. Information regarding errors, inconsistencies, and exceptions should be kept and systematically reported to management.

Management should report information on internal control levels and exceptions to the affected parties to ensure the continued effectiveness of the internal control system. Actions should be taken to identify what information is needed at a particular level of decision making.

Operational security and internal control assurance should be established and periodically repeated, with self-assessment or independent audit to examine whether or not the security and internal controls are operating according to the stated or implied security and internal control requirements. Ongoing monitoring activities by management should look for vulnerabilities and security problems.

US State Laws

CA 1386 explains that one individual must be responsible for coordinating the internal notification procedures. Additionally, written procedures should be adopted for internal notification of security incidents that may involve unauthorized access to higher-risk personal information.

From regulation to reality – sure signs you are complying

It's one thing to have intrusion detection in place, and another thing to know what to do when your system catches something. The effectiveness of your organization's ability to deal with such a notification depends on how fast you respond to the event. How fast you respond to the event depends upon how well you've defined the policies and procedures surrounding response, assigned clear responsibilities to employees and provided appropriate training.

Create policies and procedures that will guide your response to incidents. Have a step by step plan of what to do when an incident occurs. Develop specific procedures that identify what to do when unauthorized access to high-risk or confidential information has occurred. Different incidents will require different responses. For example, if sensitive customer information has been stolen, you may have to notify the customer or data owner of the breach.

Once you have created policies and procedures, you will need to assign roles and responsibilities of staff and management. Some things you can do to make the process as successful as possible are:

- Assign someone to do routine checks of intrusion detection logs for anything suspicious.

- Have employees on call around the clock to respond to any intrusion alerts that occur.

- Have one specific individual in charge of coordinating internal notification procedures. This person can be the go to person when breach occurs, because they will have the best grasp of all the procedures and which ones to follow for particular breach.

Management will have specific roles and responsibilities as well. It is management who monitors the internal controls for effectiveness, looking for deviations from normal operating functions. When a deviation occurs, management should act with analysis and corrective actions. The aim of the section is what to do when there has been a breach. It is managements job to notify the individuals responsible for the function in which the deviation has occurred of the deviation, as well as notify their immediate superior. Notifying their superior provides insurance that something will get done. A good rule of thumb is, the more serious the deviation, the higher up the ladder the notification should go, to ensure proper measures are taken.

We have said it before and will say it again: train your staff on their roles and responsibilities. It is never enough to just assign the roles and responsibilities and expect that your staff will miraculously understand what they should do in every situations. If you want an effective team, you have to train them, and the better the training, the better your breach notification procedures will be.

A response effort will not be based entirely on people. There are tools and devices that will be used, such as software. These tools should be selected and installed with an understanding of the breach procedures. Train staff on how to use these tools, as well as management, so that when the time comes, procedures are executed smoothly.

Once a breach has occurred and the procedures have been executed, the incident should be documented and disseminated internally to senior management. Take a full accounting of the incident and the breach notification process. If anything did not go as intended, record this and adjust procedures accordingly.

Big picture, management should take the time to review intrusion detection and response procedures. This helps locate any inefficiencies in the process, any recurring system weaknesses and also lets you know what your staff is doing right.

How do you respond to an intrusion?

Intrusion detection by itself does not mitigate the risk of an intrusion. Mitigation only occurs through effective and timely response. The goal of the response is to minimize damage to the institution and its customers through containment of the intrusion, and restoration of systems. The quality of intrusion response is a function of the organization's culture, procedures, and training. The following control objective will lead your quest to efficient intrusion response:

> *In order to promote the integrity, availability and accountability of information systems, the organization will create an intrusion response procedure. A security incident response plan will be created along with procedures to execute the plan. Immediate actions along with restoration strategies will be included.*

The more clearly defined and understood these procedures are, the better your staff's response to intrusion will be. It is a good idea to take the time to document everything in precise, easy to comprehend terms.

Guidance from the regulations and standards

Public Companies

The **AICPA Suitable Trust Services Criteria** calls for procedures to identify, report, and act on system security breaches and other incidents.

Banking/Finance

The **FFIEC Information Security Handbook** explains that response typically involves people, not technologies. A response policy and procedure should be in place and requires the assignment of responsibilities and training. Some organizations formalize the response with a security incident response team. Other organizations may outsource some of their intrusion response functions.

Institutions can assess best the adequacy of their preparations through testing. This can include isolating the compromised systems, searching for additional compromised systems, collecting and preserving evidence and communicating with affected parties. Restoration strategies may include elimination of an intruder's means of access; restoration of systems, programs and data to known good state; filing of a suspicious activity report; and again, communicating with affected parties.

The **Appendix of 12 CFR 30** calls for response programs that specify actions to be taken when the bank suspects or detects that unauthorized individuals have gained access to customer information systems.

Healthcare and Life Sciences

HIPAA requires the identification and response to suspected or known security incidents; mitigation, to the extent practicable, of harmful effects of security incidents that are known to the covered entity; and documentation of security incidents and outcomes.

Credit Card

VISA CISP calls for preparation to respond immediately to a system breach. A system response plan should be created to be used in the event of a system compromise. The plan should address at a minimum: system response procedures; business recovery and continuity procedures; roles and responsibilities; and communication and contact strategies. **MasterCard SDP** requires that each merchant should develop a plan for handling security incidents.

US Federal Security

FISCAM calls for an entity to have documented security procedures in place for responding to security incidents. The **National Cyberspace Strategy** agrees with FISCAM, encouraging procedures to be created that deal with intrusion response.

12 CFR Part 748 pg. 85-86 calls for the creation of an incident response program. Procedures to be contained by the program include assessing the nature and scope of an incident, notifying the appropriate NCUA Regional Director of the incident (if you are a credit union), notifying appropriate law enforcement and taking corrective measures to fix the problem and prevent it from recurring.

NIST Special Publications

NIST 800-53 calls for the organization to implement an incident handling capability for security incidents that includes preparation, detection and analysis, containment, eradication, and recovery. The organization should track and document information system security incidents on an ongoing basis. The organization should promptly report any incident to the appropriate authorities.

NIST 800-61 § 2.1 provides a general definition of a security incident and general definitions for different types of security incidents an organization may experience. 4.1-4.1.4 defines different types of denial of service attacks that may be experienced. These include reflector attacks, amplifier attacks, distributed denial of service attacks and synfloods. 5.1.1-5.1.5 defines different types of malicious code attacks. These include different varieties of viruses, Trojan horses, worms, mobile code and blended attacks. 6.1 gives a definition of unauthorized access incidents and provides examples of different kinds that may be encountered. 7.1 defines what an inappropriate usage incident is.

Containing, eradicating and recovering from an incident is another important part of intrusion and incident response. NIST 800-61 has a lot to say on the topic. In 3.3-3.3.4 walks readers through key steps in taking care of an incident. It describes how to choose an appropriate containment strategy, gather and handle evidence, identify the attacker, eradicate components of the incident if necessary – such as malicious code, and finally recover from the incident by securing systems against attack in that method in the future.

4.4-4.5 focuses specifically on containing, and recovering from denial of service incidents. A checklist of tasks to step through is provided. A.2.1 provides a summary of the methods used to prevent denial of service attacks.

5.4-5.5 covers containing, eradicating and recovering from malicious code attacks. Recommendations on how to defend against them as well as a checklist of steps to take during an incident to handle them is included. A.2.2 summarizes some of the defense methods described in 5.4-5.5.

6.4-6.5 provides the same kind of information as discussed for 4.4-4.5 and 5.4-5.5, but focuses on the topic of handling unauthorized users. A.2.3 provides a summary of the methods for dealing with unauthorized users.

7.4-7.5 describes how to contain an inappropriate usage incident and recover from it. A.2.4 summarizes some of the techniques used to handle an incident like this.

8.3-8.4 calls for separately prioritizing handling a multiple component attack, with the worst component of the attack being handled first. A checklist describing how to prioritize incidents is provided. A.2.5 recommends using centralized logging and event correlation software when handling a multiple component incident.

After containing an incident, the next step is to report the incident to appropriate authorities. 2.3.2.3 indicates that every federal organization must have a primary and secondary point of contact with FedCIRC. These contacts will receive reports about all incidents. Organizations will internally document corrective actions for each incident. If an organization is not federal, it does not need to report to FedCIRC, unless the incident affects Federal agencies. The incident still needs to be reported somewhere, and a choice of potential reporting centers is offered in this section.

After wrapping up a security incident, recommendations for better handling as well as prevention of further attacks of that type should be written up in a report. 4.6 offers general recommendations for denial of service incidents, 5.6 offers recommendations for handling malicious code incidents, 6.6 covers recommendations for handling unauthorized access incidents, 7.6 discusses recommendations for handling inappropriate usage incidents. 8.5 offers recommendations for handling multiple component incidents. Because each section is very detailed, it is best to read the section of the document directly.

In addition to recommendations, taking time to learn what could be done better is important. 3.4.1 talks about how to effectively take away information from an incident that can help in the future. It calls for meetings to discuss and analyze the incident, and documenting what everyone has learned.

3.4.2 discusses collecting incident data together to make the lessons learned phase easier. Recommended materials to collect include the number of incidents handled, the amount of time it took to handle each incident, an objective assessment of each incident and a subjective assessment of each incident.

3.4.3 covers retention issues for evidence collected from an incident. Retention time is different for each set of evidence for each incident, so three factors should be considered when determining how long to keep information. The first factor is prosecution, is it likely an attacker will be prosecuted? The second factor is data retention, what policies does an organization have? Finally the third factor, cost – how much does it cost to store evidence? Each item should be considered in order to reach a conclusion about retention.

General Guidance

The **CobiT** Control Objectives call for management to establish a computer security incident handling capability to address security incidents by providing a centralized platform with sufficient expertise and equipped with rapid and secure communications facilities. Incident management responsibilities and procedures should be established to ensure appropriate, effective and timely response to security incidents.

IT security administration should ensure that violation and security activity is logged, reported, reviewed and appropriately escalated on a regular basis to identify and resolve incidents involving unauthorized activity. The logical access to the security and other logs should be granted upon the principle of the least privilege, or need-to-know. Management should ensure that reaccredidation of security is periodically performed to keep up-to-date the formally approved security level and the acceptance of residual risk.

US State Laws

CA 1386 calls for an incident response plan. Written procedures for notification of affected individuals should be adopted, as well as response actions documented.

EU Guidance

The **OECD Risk Checklist** calls for an incident response plan, outlining when you report and incident and to whom. Finally, the ISF Standard calls for a response plan, defining how to deal with attacks, and who is on the response team.

From regulation to reality – sure signs you are complying

The goal of an intrusion response is first and foremost, to minimize damage to the institution and its customers through containment of the intrusion and restoration of systems. What makes intrusion response more difficult than other processes, is it is typically a staff heavy operation. Workers must be on hand when a problem occurs to deal with it in the most swift, efficient way possible.

A good way to coordinate responses is to form a security incident response team. This is a group of individuals in your organization who are trained and ready to respond to any conceivable incident. If you are a small operation, or you prefer to have a third party handle your incident response, this is totally acceptable as well. Outsourcing some or all of the work to an incident response organization will free up your employees to focus on other things.

Whether you outsource or keep your security response team in-house, or employ some other method of dealing with security breaches, write an incident response plan. This is the map to effective incident response. The plan will include all the necessary response procedures, roles and responsibilities of staff or third parties, communication strategies and contact lists, business recovery strategies, restoration strategies, and continuity procedures. Additionally, include in the plan procedures for incident tracking and reporting. Identify reporting procedures, who needs to receive reports, and how the reports should be put together. Reports will be important during audits, where they may be used to help identify security weaknesses in your organization's systems.

Once the plan is written, test the plan, test the procedures, and train your staff. By now you know just how important testing and training are to effective business functions, and nowhere is this more true than in incident response. Have assigned teams or workers read and understand the plan so they know what to do when a security problem arises.

Your plan will provide for restorations and recovery strategies. This is the most important part of the incident repose process. Restoring systems to normal functions is the goal. Restoration strategies will include:

- Identifying an intruders means of access and eliminating this access.

- Restoring systems, software, and information to a pre-incident state

- Creating reports outlining suspicious activity, and

- Communicating with affected parties

Incident response will get easier and more efficient as time goes on and procedures have been modified according to what worked, and what didn't. It's a learning process. Each time an incident occurs, you will get one step closer to the ideal plan for your organization.

Do you log and collect data?

Collecting and logging data will advance your organization. These steps provide the tools to understand what is working, what is not. Collecting and logging data will point out what is going wrong. You want to have a trail of actions, like bread crumbs leading you home after a long battle with a crazy witch. The control objective you should keep in mind is:

> *In order to promote the accountability of business functions, the organization will take reasonable steps to ensure that sufficient data is collected from secure log files to identify and respond to security incidents and to monitor and enforce policy compliance. When determining whether and what data to log, organizations should consider the importance of the related systems information, the importance of monitoring the access controls, the value of the logged data, and the means to effectively analyze the data. Finally, an effective means of tracing a security event through the system should be employed.*

If you cover every aspect of the control objective, you'll have many golden opportunities to find out what is going right with your organization, and what is going wrong.

Guidance from the regulations and standards

Banking/Finance

The **FFIEC Information Security Handbook** has a wealth of information of logging and data collection. Financial institutions should identify the system components that warrant logging, determine the level of data logged for each component, and establish policies securely handling and analyzing log files. The following data are typically logged: inbound and outbound internet traffic, internal network traffic, firewall events, intrusion detection system events, network and host performance, operating system access, application access, and remote access. Logs should generally capture source identification information, session ID, terminal ID, and the date, time and nature of the access attempt. A financial institution should have adequate means of tracing a security event through the system.

Healthcare and Life Sciences

HIPAA requires audit controls. Implementation of hardware, software, and/or procedural mechanisms that record and examine activity in information systems that contain or use electronic protected health information.

Credit Card

MasterCard SDP calls for control and logging of access to secure administrator accounts, power user accounts, and power-tools. Further audit logs must contain a time stamp, which tracks user activity. Audit logs should be reviewed on a regular basis and protected against alteration, deletion, and access. It must be impossible to disable an audit log.

US Federal Security

FISCAM calls for audit trails to be maintained. Audit trails may include user ID, resources accessed, date, time, terminal location, and specific data modified. Procedures for maintaining audit trails should be based on the value or sensitivity of data and other resources affected, as well as the processing environment, technical feasibility, and legal and regulatory requirements.

FIPS Publication 191 § 2.2.6 says logging and monitoring are useful because they provide the ability to detect the occurrence of threats, which may then be traced through the system. Logging and monitoring also makes it easy to provide system and network managers with statistics that indicate all systems are functioning properly. Important areas to consider logging include I&A information, changes to access control information, use of sensitive files, modification made to critical software, use of LAN traffic management tools and use of auditing tools.

NIST Special Publications

NIST 800-53 calls for audit logs to be time stamped and reviewed regularly.

NIST 800-14 calls for the use of audit trails to: support accountability by providing a trace of user actions, for reconstruction of events after they have occurred, to assist in intrusion detection, and to help identify problems other than intrusions as they occur. Additionally, audit logs should include the type of event, the time the event occurred, the user ID associated with the event, and the program or command used to initiate the event. Organizations should protect the audit trail from unauthorized access. Finally, audit trails should be reviewed periodically.

International Standards Organization

ISO 17799 has an abundance of information on logging and data collection. Logging and reviewing events is required, although notice is taken as to the volume of information and the need to copy appropriate security messages to a second log. The audit logs should record the user ID, dates and times, and successful and rejected system access and resource access attempts. Computers should be clock synchronized, so that the audit log can reflect the accurate time.

General Guidance

The **ISF Standard of Good Practice for Information Security** calls for the keeping of audit logs and reviewing of the logs regularly.

From regulation to reality – sure signs you are complying

To respond properly to security incidents and maintain organization policy compliance, you need as much valid data on these topics as you can get. Such data should be available in secure system log files. Because it's not feasible to log and monitor every aspect of every system, an important goal should be determining what to log and what to skip. Be careful with this, as system security relies on your ability to review and analyze the right logs for security weaknesses. Another important consideration when collecting log data is to ensure that you are capturing all RAW data from each device, in its original format. Once captured and stored, log data can be parsed based upon specific rules or pre-defined policies. Data should not be normalized in any way before it is stored [DW].

Typically, an organization should log data such as inbound and outbound internet traffic, internal network traffic, firewall events, intrusion detection system events, network and host performance, operating system access, application access and remote access. For each of these things, a log should capture source identification information, session ID, terminal ID, the date and the time and nature of the access attempt.

These logs or trails are useful so long as you ensure they are secure and kept in such a way that they cannot be compromised or disabled. You can review such trails to find system trends to improve efficiency, improve security and track user actions. In the case of a problem involving an employee, well kept trails may be used as evidence of some behavior. Poorly kept trails will be inadmissible in a court of law. Additionally as John Mayes has pointed out, auditing may be inadmissible if the audit activity is suddenly increased beyond your normal auditing profile (as you might be inclined to do if you want to capture additional information about an attack). The issues raised in this instance include questioning the reliability of new information-gathering processes, or whether the IT staff was suddenly acting as an agent of law enforcement in gathering evidence at their request. The best practice is, if you anticipate ever needing to log at that level as part of your reporting process, that you do it at all times, not just when an event triggers the extra auditing [JMM] To avoid this type of problem, be aware of compliance requirements for auditing and logging system and user actions.

Records Management

The Main Thing

How do you determine the scope of your record preservation obligations?

Every day, your employees are creating and receiving documents, emails, instant messages, text files and faxes. Each of these things is a record with its own preservation obligations. Think of them as plants in a garden-- some of them are flowers that should be babied and preserved carefully and some of them are weeds that need to be eliminated. So how do you tell the weeds from the roses? Heck what if you don't have weeds and roses, what if you're into Zen gardens and it's more about what twigs and rocks count as tranquil garden display versus harmony destroying debris? Simple -- You develop a method for determining what records are important to your organization, as well as how important each type is. That way you know what the good stuff is, and what you need to weed out. Start by following this control objective:

> In order to preserve the integrity and availability of records, the organization will determine the scope of its records preservation obligations. The scope is determined by the regulations an organization must comply with, as well as looking at issues of business obligations, discovery hurdles, ease of access and business continuity.

There are three basic steps for creating a viable method that we'll review in this section. Step one, you examine your organization's goals for record preservation, prioritize them and write them on paper. Step two, you observe daily business activities to see what kinds of records you have in your organization and how they integrate with your preservation goals. Step three, you choose storage methods based on these goals.

Guidance from the regulations and standards

Let's turn to the regulations and standards for guidance on creating how to determine your record preservation obligations.

Public Companies

The **Sarbanes-Oxley** Act and associated SEC rules and regulations require that records relating to a financial audit or review must be captured and retained for no less than seven years.

NASD/NYSE

SEC Rule 17a-3 defines the various books and records that must be created and retained by securities exchange members, brokers and dealers. Rule 17a-1 specifies that all such records must be retained for no less than five years. Rule 17ad-7 requires various periods of retention, depending on the nature of the records. Rule 240.17a-4 requires the above persons to retain indexes and make them available for examination by staffs of the commission and auditors. They are also charged with preserving indexes for as long as the records require retention.

SEC Rule 240.17 Ad-6 in its entirety contains a variety of procedures for recordkeeping. It is best to read the documentation for the rule directly.

Healthcare and Life Science

21 CFR 11.10 requires that organizations prepare for discovery by having records available for inspection and review by the FDA but does not explicitly mention indexing capability.

Credit Card

VISA CISP requires minimal retention of cardholder information as applicable to business, legal and regulatory requirements. The program also prohibits the capture of sensitive authentication data subsequent to a transaction authorization, such as PINs or passwords.

US Federal Security

OMB Circular A-130 covers records preservation obligations by stating "record, preserve and make accessible sufficient information to ensure the management and accountability of agency programs, and to protect the legal and financial rights of the Federal Government." It also calls on agencies to receive approval from the Archivist of the United States for approval of retention schedules.

US Internal Revenue Service

IRS Revenue Procedure 98-25 requires that any machine-sensible records containing financial taxpayer information must be retained so long as the contents may become material in the administration of any internal revenue law. For the purposes of discovery, procedure 97-22 requires that any hardcopy books and records stored electronically must be made available to the service upon request. The same is true for machine-sensible records outlined in 98-25. Furthermore, 97-22 requires that indexes of electronic records be available for retrieval of such information.

Records Management

ISO 15489-1 and 15489-2 call for the determination of records to be captured. ISO 15489-2 goes into more detail on determining how long records must be retained and assesses all requirements above. Neither standard directly addresses preparation for discovery. The Sedona Principles, on the other hand, addresses preservation obligations and emphasizes the need for preparing all captured documents and data in terms of discovery. None of these standards address the availability and preservation of indexes with respect to discovery.

ISO 15489-2 § 4.2.4 states that there are several basic steps for creating an ideal records management system. The first five steps have to do with scoping to some extent. They include:

- Conduct a preliminary investigation to find out what you need

- Analyze business activity to see how needs and activities can be combined

- Identify requirements for records of various identified business activities

- Assess existing systems for recording business activities

- Identify strategies for dealing with recording identified business activities after determining existing system flaws.

With this information you could then design the system, because you've sufficiently scoped and planned.

The **Sedona Principles** discuss preservation of records when an organization is dealing with litigation. Principle 5 (a) specifically discusses that is it's alright to continue routine destruction of records so long as those records do not include materials necessary for evidence in the litigation. Routine recycling of materials such as magnetic tapes may also be permitted. The Sedona Principles suggest striking a balance between an organization's duty to preserve relevant data and an organization's need to continue operations.

General Guidance

CobiT addresses the need for "source documents" of any data be collected and accounted for. It also requires that retention periods should be defined for documents, data, reports and messages and the data used to encrypt them. The standard does not address preparation for discovery.

You must define the goals of record preservation in your organization. Common goals to think about include compliance with appropriate regulations, business continuity, discovery and ease of access. Once you've established your goals it quickly becomes apparent what matters most to your organization and what matters least. Based on this information you can then prioritize what records to keep and what to throw away. Write out your priorities, which act as your record preservation obligations.

With your goals in mind, observe daily business activities within your organization. If you have a large organization, assign an overall manager the task of coordinating the observation. Develop procedures for teams to observe and report on their findings to this manager. If you have a small organization, it might be as simple as assigning one person to go around, collect information about daily activities and write it up in a report. Whichever method you choose, be thorough. Note all the different kinds of records you see coming in and out of the office, and how they are handled.

Now take your inventory of record types and integrate them with your list of record preservation obligations. For example to be in compliance with Sarbanes-Oxley you are required to maintain records relating to financial audit or review for at least seven years.

Look through the inventory and determine what types of records relate to financial audit. Repeat this process for each record preservation obligation and write down everything. When you finish, you will have a list of the records that satisfy the different obligations.

The final step is to choose methods and strategies for storing the data. Because you've prioritized your obligations and matched up records with each one, you can instantly see what items require the most attention. Examine your existing record keeping systems to ascertain whether they adequately meet your needs. Test each system to ensure it is still usable and accurately maintains information. If a system does not meet the needs of your record preservation obligations, or there is no system, make a note of it, along with any recommendations you have for acquiring new systems or the help of a consultant. The emphasis here is on *note*; don't write yourself a memo. Make it a full report that can be reviewed later if need be. When that's done, congratulations, you've just scoped your record preservation obligations.

How do you capture and classify your records?

In ancient Babylonia record capture and classification was a breeze. Anything important went on a clay tablet, everything not important didn't. Because writing on clay was annoying, very few things were deemed important, making it easy to secure these items – they all went in a stack in a locked up room. Today, record keeping involves a little more effort. Good systems include a way to classify records for different levels of security, register each record for tracking and use purposes and easily retrieve information. Therefore, the control objective for this section is:

> *In order to preserve the availability of records, the organization will create a records classification scheme that determines a record's sensitivity level as well as the length of time a record must be preserved.*

In this section we will take a look at records capture and classification, starting with a look at the regulations and standards.

Guidance from the regulations and standards

NASD/NYSE

SEC Rule 240.17a-4 requires that records and indexes can be downloaded from electronic storage media.

Banking/Finance

FFIEC Operations handbook addresses usage by requiring controls over the production and distribution of system output reports, both hardcopy and electronic.

Healthcare and Life Science

21 CFR 11 calls for validation and proper access authorization of systems to control the accuracy and reliability of information processing with regards to electronic records. The regulation also calls for time-stamped audit trails to record the creation, modification and disposal of electronic records.

Credit Card

The **VISA CISP** and **MasterCard SDP** both require strict authorization protocols for user access to cardholder information. These protocols are throughout each document and it is best to search them if you need information on specific protocols for some purpose.

US Federal Security

DOD Design Criteria are primarily concerned with the performance of an organization's records management system. The document requires that systems provide the capability to capture, register and index electronic records.

US Internal Revenue Service

IRS Revenue Procedure 97-22 requires the creation of an indexing system when taxpayers transfer hardcopy books and records into electronic storage. The indexing system should be sufficiently functional that a separate description database is not required for reference.

Records Management

ISO 15489-1 and **15489-2** define the above records processes in detail, from capture to usage and tracking. However, since this standard considers records to be static, rather than alterable, it does not include controls surrounding input, processing and output.

NIST Special Publications

NIST 800-53 calls for strict access controls to information in printed form or on digital media.

International Standards Organization

ISO 17799 addresses classification of information through categorization based on value and sensitivity. ISO 17799 require strict controls over input, processing and output validation, handling and authorization.

General Guidance

CobiT calls for capture of records through "source document data collection." **CobiT** also requires strict controls over input, processing and output validation, handling and authorization.

A good classification system is intuitive where possible and integrates tightly with your organization's record preservation obligations. It should include definitions for what constitutes a record that requires high security, low security and what the storage differences for these entails. For example one difference might be that high security items must be stored in a separate area from low security items so that access to them is more easily restricted.

The usability of your classification system must also be considered. A super anal retentive system ensures that records are properly classified and filed. It also ensures that employees spend a smaller percentage of their time working and a higher percentage of their time classifying. A super lax system means more productive employees, but it also means a higher chance of records being compromised, corrupted or inappropriately filed. Your job is to strike a balance between these extremes. If possible, test your classification system on a sample group before documenting and disseminating it across the organization.

Registration of records for use and tracking relies heavily upon your classification system. You will have different registration procedures for items classified at different security levels. Low level items will likely use easily accessible registration and tracking systems. For instance in some companies, the receptionist logs incoming packages using a notebook that anyone can view. This is fine for packages. However, it probably wouldn't do for registering something like a financial statement for your organization. This type of record would be considered high security, and need a tamperproof registration mechanism. That way later, if you need to track changes to the statement, or where it travels, you could open the log and find an accurate account of what happened. Tamperproof logs require a good deal of vigilance and security to be made possible, so choose carefully when it comes to deciding what records are to be logged this way.

After classifying and registering records, you need a system for locating them.

Imagine for a second, that you check a bag at the airport. They register this information, log where it's going, then lose the bag. That airline wouldn't be in business very long if the answer to your question "where's my stuff?" was "well we have that information on file…somewhere." Granted it's not much better when you're in LA and they tell you "your bag is in Tahiti", but it's slightly better. That's because once you know where information is located; you can do something with it, such as retrieve it. In the case of our example, you could insist the airline send your bag to you in LA. This example illustrates why it's important for you to create an index for all your records. Most regulations require a well-kept, regularly updated index that allows for easy information retrieval. Even without input from a regulation, you want easy retrieval to make daily work more efficient. The more quickly employees can get the information they need, the more quickly they can get their work done.

How do you make good records storage decisions?

Good record storage decisions spring from an in-depth understanding of your organization's security, capacity for storage and record tracking ability. Security of records involves following your organization's classification rules. Storage capacity for records depends upon what your organization has available. Finally, record tracking relies on the systems you implement to determine where each record travels as well as who is responsible for them. The control objective for this section is:

> *In order to promote the availability of records, the organization will create records storage procedures. This includes determining the level of security necessary to protect records from harm.*

In this section we examine how to harmonize these three areas with one another to create the ultimate record storage system.

Guidance from the regulations and standards

Banking/Finance

FFIEC Operations calls for organizations to consider their data storage requirements. The standard requires consideration of institution growth, cost-benefit analyses, configuration and vendor options and risk assessment. The handbook also briefly discusses performance monitoring and reporting as well as capacity planning, which could initially define or modify records storage requirements.

Healthcare and Life Science

21 CFR 11 calls for time-stamped audit trails whenever records are created, modified or deleted. This functions as an element of reporting that can change requirements for records storage.

Credit Card

VISA CISP calls for an automated solution to compare critical files. This would essentially be considered a component of monitoring. If certain critical records or data change, storage requirements (in terms of security or accessibility) may need to change, as well.

US Federal Security

DoD 5015.2 calls for records management systems to monitor and report storage statistics to continuously provide information regarding current capacity.

FIPS Publication 191 1.4.1 suggests the use of distributed file storing, which provides users direct access to mass storage on a remote server. It also provides capabilities such as remote filing and remote printing.

Records Management

ISO 15489-2 discusses records storage decisions as detailed above, and implies but does not directly address capacity planning or performance monitoring.

NIST Special Publications

NIST 800-53 calls for storage capacity and monitoring and reporting with respect to audit records.

International Standards Organization

ISO 17799 calls for capacity and availability management. CobiT covers performance monitoring and reporting, as well. These control objectives come from an overall IT perspective, however, and do not specifically mention records storage decisions.

From regulation to reality — sure signs you are complying

Deciding how much security is necessary to store a given record is as easy as examining how it's been classified. What isn't quite so easy is deciding what a classification means. For example, if you're trying to store cardholder data, you know it's high security, but what does high security storage look like in your organization? Does it vary for different media? What if material of varying levels of sensitivity is stored on the same type of media? Decide what measures you want to take for each of these questions.

Tracking is discussed at greater length further on, but in general, you need to develop a system you can confidently say will keep track of where records travel to and from. Think about ways to make this system efficient. One way is to integrate storage and registration. Each record needs to be registered on creation, so one possibility is including useful storage information during registration. Then when it comes time to index it, less work needs to be done.

Finally, you need to consider the capacity for storage you have available. It may be necessary to tweak some of your record management goals if you don't have as much capacity as you'd like. Another concern is performance, does storing information have a negative effect on any of your other systems? Can you counteract this effect? If you can answer these questions as well as those questions surrounding security and tracking, your records management is in good shape.

How do you deal with online digital storage?

Because online digital storage requires more surveillance than other types of storage, your organization must adequately protect data from being compromised or accessed by unauthorized personnel. In order to do this, the following control objective should be adhered to:

> In order to preserve the integrity and availability of records that are stored on digital media, an organization must ensure formats are suitable and that proper controls are built into the media.

In this section, we will investigate online digital storage and what an organization must do to protect digital media.

Guidance from the regulations and standards

Public Companies

17 CFR 15d-15 calls for internal controls over financial reporting, including controls that ensure the availability and integrity of transaction records through proper maintenance (in this case, controls over digital storage).

NASD/NYSE

17 CFR 240.17a-4 and 17ad-7 both require the above formats and controls for electronic storage media, but do not directly call for encryption.

Banking/Finance

FFIEC Information Security calls for sensitive media to possess automated controls to guard against alteration.

Healthcare and Life Science

21 CFR 11.70 requires that electronic and hand-written signatures be linked to their respective electronic records to ensure that records do not contain false signatures.

HIPAA requires that mechanisms be activated to encrypt all electronically stored health information.

Credit Card

VISA CISP requires that sensitive cardholder data be rendered unreadable through encryption anywhere it is stored.

US Internal Revenue Service

IRS Revenue Procedure 97-22 calls for the implementation of availability and integrity controls for any books and records residing in an electronic storage system (including digital media).

Records Management

Though ISO 15489-2 discusses prevention of physical damage to media through copying, it is more of a back-up control and should be addressed in that line-item.

US Federal Security

Federal Information Processing Standards Publications 191 1.5.1 states that an issue with high availability, digital storage is that personal computers belonging to users often do not offer adequate protection mechanisms. Meaning that when a user copies a file onto their machine, it becomes vulnerable to attacks such as theft or undesired modifications.

International Standards Organization

ISO 17799 covers controls over encryption, but does note that it should be used to protect sensitive or critical information.

General Guidance

CobiT mentions that procedures should be developed for data storage, but it is not very specific.

US State Laws

Though it does not specifically mention digital media, CA 1386 advises organizations to use encryption whenever possible to protect high-risk personal information.

Ah, the digital age. Today people have everything from digital TV to cameras. And, you can even store your records as online digital media. The problem is, this can be as tricky as getting that digital camera to work right. For some, that may be a cinch; but if you are like most people, it doesn't come as second nature. To make this easier, it is recommended that you take the time to decide what you will do with records you choose to store as online digital media while you make your records storage decisions.

To preserve the availability and integrity of this kind of data, you will need to ensure formats are suitable and that proper controls are built into the media. You will also need a system that verifies the quality and authenticity of this type of data when written to, serializes and time dates each record for retention, and has the capacity to hold indexes of the material along with the material itself. The system should also have manual and automated controls for confirming integrity and validity, detect alteration, removal or deterioration of records and recover modified, damaged or lost records as necessary.

In terms of physical storage, records should be encrypted prior to storage if they are high security information such as cardholder data, and otherwise they should be stored in non-rewriteable, non-erasable formats.

Do your stored materials have high availability?

There is little point in storing media that you need to use, if it is not available when you need to use it. Therefore, it is imperative that you design your records storage systems with availability in mind. To start, take a look at this control objective:

> *In order to promote ease of access, availability, and integrity in business functions, an organization must ensure that all stored materials are highly available for retrieval by authorized employees.*

Although the guidance from the regulations and standards is slim for this section, keep reading because we have a battle plan for you.

Guidance from the regulations and standards

NASD/NYSE

17 CFR 240.17a-4 requires that members, brokers and dealers have available at all times, facilities for immediate and easily readable records stored on electronic media.

Healthcare and Life Science

Though 21 CFR 11.10 calls for the ability to generate accurate and complete copies of records, it does not place an emphasis on quick accessibility.

From regulation to reality – sure signs you are complying

If you're storing digital media, it must be made immediately accessible and available for retrieval by authorized employees. If your storage facility is located too far away, the materials stored there may not be easy to access. However, if it is located too close, you run the risk of exposing the stored materials to any threat the primary facility may face. Storage facilities are discussed in detail in the systems continuity chapter.

The materials themselves must also be easily accessible. Having a well organized storage system will help with this, so that what you need is easy to find and wont take a long time to retrieve, especially if there is an emergency. Make sure everything is labeled and its location is recorded in a master list. Several copies of this list should be kept, one by management, one by the staff in charge of records, and one at an offsite location.

Availability of stored materials is key for effective business continuity as well as convenience. You must also ensure data integrity, so that retrievals of information yield accurate records. Accurate retrieval falls under storage security, which is discussed earlier in this chapter.

Do you create back-up or duplicate copies of records?

Back-ups and duplicates of important work are must-haves to secure business continuity. However, the key word is important. You don't need to save every last thing, and in fact, you probably don't have the capacity to do so. In this section, the focus is on the following control objective:

> *In order to promote efficiency and availability in records management, the organization will create a back-up system for records. This includes creating a procedure for duplicating records, prioritizing records in order of importance and sensitivity, and periodically reviewing back-up records and procedures for necessary updates.*

In this section we will determine what needs to be backed-up, how to prioritize records, and how to create updating procedures.

Guidance from the regulations and standards

Public Companies

AICPA Suitable Trust Services criteria calls for back-up procedures to follow an entity's documented back-up strategy and requires back-up data to be stored at an off-site facility.

NASD/NYSE

17 CFR 240.17a-4 and **17ad-7** both require that members, brokers, dealers and transfer agents create and store duplicate copies of media containing both records and indexes. **NASD** and **NYSE Rules 3510**(c) and **446**(c), respectively, call for back-up and recovery of books and records (as documented in business continuity plans).

Banking/Finance

The **FFIEC Operations handbook** advises that organizations should keep "secondary on-site copies of data" and also provides guidance on creating back-up copies. The **FFIEC Business Continuity handbook** details strategies and procedures for storing back-up media.

FFIEC Business Continuity Pgs. E 4-7 states that choosing software and data file back up should be dependent upon the criticality of the software and data files regarding the financial institution's operations. Institution management should consider the potential impact of the loss of software or data files to determine priority. Page E 5 points out consideration points such as:

- *"Loss of these files would significantly impair the institution's operations*

- *The files are being used to manage corporate assets or to make decisions regarding their use*

- *The files contain updated security and operating system configurations that would be necessary to resume operations in a secure manner*

- *The loss of files would result in loss of revenue*

- *Any inaccuracy or data loss would result in significant impact on the institution (including reputation) or its customers.*

- *Critical data that is identified should be backed up regularly using the multiple generation method, and rotated off site at least daily. Backup techniques may include mirroring, electronic vaulting at a separate processing facility or good old back-up tape storage. If you use tapes do NOT leave backup tapes at the primary site overnight, they need to be rotated out immediately. Tapes should also be tested periodically to ensure they are still readable.*

- *For operating system software, it must be backed up whenever there is a change or update to the system."*

Healthcare and Life Science

HIPAA calls for procedures to create and maintain exact copies of electronic protected health information. This is within the context of creating a "data back-up plan."

Credit Card

VISA CISP calls for nightly back-ups and storage of media in an off-site facility.

MasterCard SDP requires that all cardholder information stored on back-up media must be encrypted.

US Federal Security

DoD 5015.2 Design Criteria calls for records management systems to automatically create back-up or duplicate copies of records and their metadata.

Records Management

ISO 15489 calls for a backup process that requires the creation of multiple copies of electronic records on various digital media as well as a regular back-up schedule.

International Standards Organization

ISO 17799 calls for proper procedures for the back-up of media, storage of back-ups, and the capability for restoration of data from back-ups following a disaster.

General Guidance

CobiT, the ISF Standard of Good Practices for Information Security and calls for proper procedures for the back-up of media, storage of back-ups, and the capability for restoration of data from back-ups following a disaster.

From regulation to reality – sure signs you are complying

You need to create and store back-up records no matter how failsafe your system for storing original records may be. That's because all failsafe systems fail sometimes. If they didn't, they wouldn't constantly put out new failsafe systems every year-- they'd stick with the one that worked.

The way you back-up records depends upon your record preservation obligations. In general, you want to have your back-up record creation and storage procedures in line with business requirements and business continuity plans.

To avoid taking up a lot of space storing tons of back-up records, review the preservation obligations you initially wrote out. Examine the list to see if you've excluded important records or included trivial records. Some questions to consider when choosing items to back-up include:

- Would losing a particular set of files significantly impair your organization's operations?

- Do the files contain updated security and operating system configurations that would be necessary to resume operations in a secure manner?

- Would the loss of the files result in a loss of revenue?

- Would inaccuracy or data loss on the files result in a significant impact on your organization (including reputation) or other customers?

If you answer yes to all these questions for a certain kind of file, consider it to be critical information and back it up. If you answer no to most or all of these questions, it's at your discretion, but likely a back-up record is less important.

After creating back-up records and procedures for moving them to safe storage off-site, be sure to also implement a check-up for the records. Periodically, someone should take a sampling of files and determine whether they still function correctly.

What Are Digital Media Controls?

Digital media controls are used to protect information from compromise. Having an established set of rules relating to digital media is particularly important for records storage, because you will not be able to check in on every record to ascertain whether it maintains integrity. Instead, you will need to rely on the security features you choose to implement. Good controls provide you with stored records you can trust. Records management is about promoting accurate records in an organized system. We recommend that you institute the following control objective for digital media:

> *In order to promote the integrity, availability and confidentiality of records, the organization will define, create, and implement controls for all records stored on digital media. These controls must be properly maintained for both original and duplicate media.*

Keeping track of what is stored on digital media can be a challenge. Creating and enforcing adequate controls can make the task a little simpler.

Guidance from the regulations and standards

Public Companies

AICPA Suitable Trust Services Criteria requires that back-up copies of media be stored securely at an off-site facility.

NASD/NYSE

17 CFR 240.17a-4 and **17ad-7** requires members, brokers, dealers and transfer agents store duplicate copies of digital media separately from originals.

Banking/Finance

The **FFIEC Operations** and **Business Continuity handbooks** require that back-up copies of media be stored securely at an off-site facility.

Credit Card

VISA CISP requires a proper inventory of media containing cardholder information.

US Federal Security

FISCAM and the **GAO Financial Audit Guide** call for back-up media to be stored at an off-site facility. The **DoD 5015.2 Criteria** requires that the method used to back-up records databases create copies to be stored off-line or at a separate location or locations.

Records Management

ISO 15489-2 requires dispersed storage locations for back-up media. The **Sedona Principles** addresses back-up media as evidence, stating that typically back-up media should not be relied upon as evidence because it is over-written so regularly. The principle in question does not state that back-up media can not be used as evidence, but that it will prove more costly for organizations to use it in such a way as the media will have to be retained for a longer period of time. The principle instead suggests that archived copies of media might be used instead as evidence.

NIST Special Publications

NIST 800-53 calls for back-up media to be stored at an off-site facility.

International Standards Organization

ISO 17799 calls for back-up copies of digital media to be stored off-site (in addition to on-site) and also require inventory of media but do not distinguish between confidential and non-critical data for this purpose.

General Guidance

CobiT and the **ISF Standard of Good Practices for Information Security** call for back-up copies of digital media to be stored off-site (in addition to on-site). CobiT alsos require inventory of media but do not distinguish between confidential and non-critical data for this purpose.

From regulation to reality – sure signs you are complying

The first step in defining the right digital media controls for your organization is to sit down and do some brainstorming. You must think about what's necessary to keep digital records safe, secure, and available. Start with the following list of basic controls:

- Inventory media containing classified information

- Securely store back-up copies of digital media at an off-site facility
- Store duplicate copies of digital media separately from originals

Now, elaborate on these controls in a way that best suits the needs of your organization. Lets start with inventorying media containing classified information. What information is classified or confidential in your organization? Do you have customer information that must be kept confidential? What is the lifespan of this confidential information? Ask questions about your organization's classified information to prompt controls specific to your organization's needs.

Next, think about securing back-up media at an off site facility. We previously discussed storage facilities in the Systems Continuity chapter. Now that you have a storage facility, you have to decide what needs to be backed-up and stored at this facility. Think about the layout of the storage, and creating a organizational system for the storage. Is it best for your organization to categorize media by date? Alphabetically? Is the storage facility secure? Is the media protected from harm?

Follow the principal of separation when it comes to original and duplicate media. You want the two to be a good distance from the each other, so that the fate of one will not be the fate of the other. For instance, if a fire takes out the primary facility where the originals are stored, you don't want the same fire to take out the back-up copies too. Most likely, if you get some miles in between the two, they will be safe. Of course, this is not guaranteed. If there is an earthquake, it is possible that both sets of media may be destroyed. If you think reasonably about potential events, and plan accordingly, most disasters will be averted.

Finally, when you have brainstormed the above controls and created controls that are right for your organization, we have one more question for you to consider. Are you planning on using back-up media as evidence? If you are, think again. Query the use of back-up media as evidence because it is over-written regularly. This affects the quality of the records as evidence as well as brings up authentication problems. The use of back-up media as evidence may also prove to be costly, since it will have to be retained for a long time. Instead of using back-up media as evidence, we recommend using archived copies of media as evidence to avoid any legal problems or unnecessary costs.

How do you protect digital media in transit?

Even digital media must travel. It is not going to get in the car and drive itself away, but it will be moved around to various locations and change custody several times. Digital media will be distributed both internally and externally, transported to storage and to alternate processing facilities. It will even pass through different owners. But, if you follow the control objective below, and use the guidelines in this chapter, you can ensure that your digital media's traveling experience is much more pleasant that a cross-Atlantic flight in the last row of coach.

> In order to protect digital media in transit, the organization will establish procedures and controls concerning handling, distribution and transfer of ownership. This will ensure that at every stage of the transportation and custody exchange, procedures exists to guide staff and others through the process.

Now that you understand that digital media does travel, lets take a look at how to protect digital media while in transit.

Guidance from the regulations and standards

Banking/Finance

FFIEC Information Security requires that security be applied to any media in transit. It requires that media be properly packaged to protect it from harm and that only approved couriers be used for delivery.

Credit Card

VISA CISP is very detailed in its requirements for the transit of cardholder information. It requires all summarized controls above.

Records Management

ISO 15489-2 addresses the transfer of custody of records that includes internal distribution. It is not specific with regards to controls for physical transit.

ISO 15489-2 § 4.3.9.4 lists elements to consider when dealing with transfer of ownership of records . The most important thing is to figure out who is held accountable for the records, and this can be done by asking some of these questions:

a) *Have the operational and administrative needs for transfer of the records been authoritatively established?*

b) *Have the issues of authority and accountability for records been addressed?*

c) *Has the impact on the transferring institution's records been taken into account?*

d) *Have the ongoing legislative, policy and regulatory obligations been fulfilled?*

If electronic records are transferred, such issues as the following need to be considered:

a) *hardware and software compatibility;*

b) *metadata (control and contextual information);*

c) *data documentation (technical information on data processing and data structure);*

d) *licensing agreements;*

e) *standards.*

NIST Special Publications

NIST 800-53 calls for controls to restrict all transit activities pertaining to digital media to authorized individuals. The standard also calls for external labeling of digital media that includes handling and distribution information.

International Standards Organization

ISO 17799 requires physical labeling and physical protection through tamper-evident packaging of all media being transported.

General Guidance

The **ISF Standard of Good Practices for Information Security** also states that sensitive material should be labeled by its security classification.

The first step in assuring well-protected transit for media is requiring management approval before doing it. Once you've gained approval, label traveling media, especially if it is confidential. This will help alleviate any confusion about what is being transferred, where it is going, and how sensitive the media is.

Sometimes, digital media will not only be moved, but will change ownership entirely. When dealing with the transfer of ownership of digital media, it is imperative to identify the person accountable for the records. You don't want to give digital media to an organization and be done with it. Instead, you must know the exact person it is going to so that later, you can check with him to be sure he received it. The following are a few considerations to keep in mind when transferring ownership of digital media:

- Hardware and software compatibility
- Metadata
- Data documentation
- Licensing agreements
- Standards

Making sure that the above things are addressed will make the transfer of ownership much easier, and you won't find yourself arguing with the new owner about a lack of documentation or a missing license.

How do you continuously retain records on digital media?

Sometimes the life expectancy of storage media runs a good deal shorter than the amount of time for which you want to retain information. In situations like this, you need to transfer the information to new media. To be sure you aren't regularly losing important records, we recommend following the control objective below:

> In order to promote the integrity and availability of stored data and records, the organization will transfer expired media before data is corrupted. Organizations should develop procedures and create timetables identifying both the life span of storage media and the length of time needed to retain certain documents.

Now, let's take a look at how to best retain records on digital media.

Guidance from the regulations and standards

NASD/NYSE

Rule 240.17ad-7 calls for security controls to preserve the integrity of records. No SEC rules further address continued retention.

Healthcare and Life Science

HIPAA calls for security measures to ensure that electronic protected health information is not improperly modified without detection until disposed of.

US Internal Revenue Service

IRS Revenue Procedure 97-22 calls for reasonable controls to prevent modification (including deterioration) of electronically stored books and records.

Records Management

ISO 15489-2 addresses continuing retention as a method of disposition. If a record is to be retained for a longer period of time, the standard offers three methods: copying, conversion and migration.

NIST Special Publications

NIST 800-53 calls for organizations to protect stored media using appropriate techniques and procedures until it is properly disposed of.

General Guidance

CobiT calls for the continued integrity of stored data through periodic checks. Especially important to the control objective are value tokens, reference files, and privacy information.

From regulation to reality – sure signs you are complying

While you may want to preserve digital media forever, that is about as unlikely as a Golden retriever living to the ripe old age of fifty. Like all of us, digital media is durable to an extent, but it wears out after a while. It has a life span which is sometimes incompatible with record retention requirements. For example, say you have a record retention requirement of ten years and the expected life of the digital tape is three years. You are going to need to transfer those records before they are no longer available.

Technology provides new back-up solutions every day, so you may wish to convert already existing records to one of these new back-up solutions. If a new media technology will allow records to be stored for up to ten years, consider using it to retain records that must be kept that long. Whatever retention hurdles you face, your organization should have procedures in place for the continuing retention of documents and data stored on digital media, maintaining their integrity, and physically destroying obsolete or deteriorated media that is no longer being used.

How do you properly dispose of and destroy records?

Proper disposition and destruction techniques are essential to organizational safety and compliance. If you throw your credit card bill in the trash without shredding it, you run the risk of someone stealing the information on it. If you improperly dispose of a record, you expose yourself to many risks such as theft, exposure and sanctions. The control objective for this section is:

> *To promote the integrity and confidentiality of records, the organization will properly dispose of records. To avoid improper disposal, organizations must consider timeliness of disposal, the creation of a Disposition of Authority document, sanitizing of media for reuse and a disposition and destruction policy.*

Proper disposal and destruction can protect your organization from liability. Keep reading to find out what you can do to avoid this liability.

Guidance from the regulations and standards

Public Companies

Sarbanes-Oxley and associated rules and standards do not provide a process for disposition of records, but addresses the penalties for destruction of records as a malicious act. This stresses the obvious importance of correct disposition procedures and authorization.

NASD/NYSE

SEC Rules for securities members, brokers, dealers and transfer agents address retention specifically, but not disposition.

Banking/Finance

The **FFIEC Information Security** and **Operations handbooks** detail specific procedures for disposal of records and media. The standards encourage proper disposal procedures and authorization, and also mention special care should be taken with third-party disposal of records.

FFIEC Information Security Pg. 63 states that *"policies should prohibit employees from discarding sensitive media along with regular garbage to avoid accidental disclosure. Many institutions shred paper-based media on site or use a* *collection and disposal service to ensure the media is rendered unreadable and un-reconstructable before disposal." Choose vendors for disposition purposes carefully and conduct thorough background checks, employ proper controls and select vendors with the proper level of experience."*

Pages 63-64 continue by stating that *"for computer based media, because residual data often remains on media after erasure, it is important to employ additional disposal techniques where sensitive data is concerned. Physical destruction such as subjecting a compact disc to a microwave, can make the data unrecoverable. Additionally, data can be destroyed by overwriting, though not always. Overwriting is a preferred method when media is to be re-used. Base your disposal policy on the sensitivity of the information contained on the media and, through policies, procedures, and training, ensure that the actions taken to securely dispose of computer-based media adequately protect the data from risks of reconstruction. Where practical, management should log the disposal of sensitive media, especially computer-based media."*

FFIEC Operations Pg. 30 States that proper disposal is essential for compliance with **Gramm-Leach-Bliley Act** regarding safeguarding customer info, and also essential to protect against reputational exposure. Management should define procedures for the destruction and disposal of media containing sensitive information. The procedures should be risk-based relative to the sensitivity of the information and the type of media used to store the information. For example, prior to disposing electronic media w/ sensitive customer information, it should be degaussed as a matter of standard procedure. Obsolete optical media, such as "write once, read many times" (WORM), should be destroyed or defaced so that the data is unrecoverable. Printed sensitive material should be destroyed through shredding or burning. Additional disposal techniques may be necessary for tapes, electronic media, disk drives, etc.

Healthcare and Life Science

21 CFR 11.10 calls for written policies that hold personnel accountable for actions taken with regards to records, thus implying, but not explicitly stating, the need for a Disposition Authority document.

Credit Card

VISA CISP and **MasterCard SDP** both call for destruction of cardholder information and associated media. Both programs also cite the need for degaussing media that could allow for the reconstruction of data. Furthermore, VISA requires that disposal procedures be documented, indicating the need for something resembling a Disposition Authority document.

US Federal Security

The **DoD 5015.2 Criteria** calls for the destruction of media and records, respectively. Both address the issue of removing residual data. DoD, includes these procedures as automated controls performed by records management systems.

Records Management

ISO 15489-1 and 15489-2 detail the disposition process extensively as summarized above. For the purposes of discovery, the **Sedona Principles** state that "good faith destruction in compliance with a reasonable records management policy" should not be considered sanctionable conduct. In other words, provided an organization has records management policies and procedures in place that can anticipate litigation prior to disposition, they should not be subject to penalties for records already destroyed.

NIST Special Publications

NIST 800-53 calls for the destruction of media and records, respectively. Both address the issue of removing residual data.

International Standards Organization

ISO 17799 calls for disposition and destruction procedures.

General Guidance

The **ISF Standard of Good Practices for Information Security** calls for disposition and destruction procedures.

CobiT does not specifically detail the disposition process as the others do, but does include a control objective addressing access rights to deleted or transferred records.

From regulation to reality – sure signs you are complying

There are four steps in a records disposition program:

- Timely disposition of records
- Creation of a disposition authority document
- Degaussing sensitive information

- Creation of a disposition policy

Timely disposition of records will ensure that you keep only what is necessary for compliance and business functions, and free yourself of any unnecessary records. This will also free you of any unnecessary liability. You will be kicking yourself if you lose confidential information that you don't need to have in the first place. Therefore, dispose of records in a timely fashion, as dictated by records disposition status and any accompanying policies and procedures. Disposition status is generally determined during records capture and registration. Your organization's disposition authority, usually senior management or business unit leader, will make the status determination. Disposition status does not always denote destruction, as it can also determine continued retention after transfer of records. If the disposition status denotes destruction and disposal, get rid of the records immediately.

Next, create a Disposition Authority document, which clearly lays out the policies and procedures surrounding disposition. Proper disposal of records is crucial where sensitive data is concerned. When creating the Disposition Authority document, make sure that procedures are risk-based relative to the sensitivity of the information and the type of media used to store it.

When dealing with electronic media, you want to wipe the slate clean if you are to be using any of the media. Residual data can remain on the record after erasure, so it is suggested that electronic media with sensitive information is "degaussed." Degaussing will eliminate possible magnetic signals and erase media for reuse. Reuse is recommended where possible. Media that is "write once" or that cannot be reused should be completely destroyed to ensure that the data is unrecoverable.

Finally, in anticipation of litigation, you should have a disposition and destruction policy in place. This policy will serve to protect you from liability when you destroy records you are not longer required to keep. As long as any previous records destruction was in good faith under a pre-existing policy, you cannot get sanctioned for an inability to produce certain records during litigation.

Do you provide training for employees so they know how to use the record keeping system?

It is not enough to have a well-organized, robust records system within your company. That's because a records system is only as good as the people using it. If you want people using your system correctly, you must train them. Not only do you need to train them, but you need to clearly set out the roles and responsibilities for your employees regarding the use and creation of records. It follows that the control objective for this section is:

> *In order to protect the integrity, availability and confidentiality of records, the organization will train staff in records management, clearly defining their roles and responsibilities.*

Training staff doesn't have to be a painful process. Take a look below at some tips for making training a breeze.

Guidance from the regulations and standards

Public Companies

AICPA Suitable Trust Services Criteria calls for a system security, availability, processing and confidentiality training.

NASD/NYSE

NASD Rule 3010(d)(2) calls for training in a firm's procedures governing correspondence (incoming and outgoing).

Healthcare and Life Science

21 CFR 11.10 calls for personnel who create, use or maintain electronic records to receive appropriate training.

Credit Card

MasterCard SDP calls for an awareness training program for personnel associated with the merchant or MSP environment.

VISA CISP does not mention a program but does advise that all employees are aware of the importance of cardholder information security and receive appropriate training literature.

US Federal Security

The **OMB Circular A-130** requires "training and guidance as appropriate to all agency officials and employees and contractors regarding their Federal records management responsibilities."

Records Management

ISO 15489-1 and **15489-2** call for records management training programs. ISO 15489-2 describes a very detailed procedure and lists suggested methods.

Specifically, **ISO 15489-2** § 6.1 states that *"a training program should ensure that the functions and benefits of managing records are widely understood in an organization. It should explain the policies and procedures in place and processes in a context that gives staff an understanding of why they are required."* They should be tailored to the needs of particular groups of staff (ISO 15489-2 § 6.1). Roles and responsibilities for records management should be defined (ISO 15489-2 § 6.2).

NIST Special Publications

NIST 800-53 calls for an awareness training program for all employees.

General Guidance

CobiT and the **ISF Standard of Good Practice for Information Security** call for employee education and training. CobiT and ISF cover numerous areas of IT training.

From regulation to reality – sure signs you are complying

From an overview perspective, records management training should indicate to staff what makes managing records necessary and beneficial to the organization. The goals, organization philosophy, policies and procedures for record management must be described to employees in a way that makes it clear why they are requirements. Because not all employees will participate in records management in the same way, separate them into groups based on assigned roles and responsibilities. Then train each group.

In addition to describing the purpose of record management, a thorough training program will cover the following areas:

- confidentiality
- correspondence procedures
- information security awareness
- electronic records

Training for confidentiality should cover how employees can help protect records from being viewed by unwanted sources. Stress the importance of properly logging off your machine so no one can use your account to examine company records, not handing out your password to other workers since it makes it impossible to track usage correctly, and other similar topics. Instruct staff on what types of records are most important to protect. For example customer cardholder information is often prioritized as needing very high security. Explain why it is prioritized and what it means to the organization if confidentiality of this material is lost. Your staff needs to know the "why" as much as they need to know the "how."

Correspondence procedures are especially important to cover. In this day and age, sending an email is the equivalent of reading a postcard – anyone can read it and see what your employee is up to. You may feel safe because the email is carefully encrypted, but you don't know what happens to an email when it reaches its source. It takes seconds for someone to forward an email around an office, and it's easy for a fellow worker to read an email over another worker's shoulder. In addition, emails from employees in your organization are representative of your organization as a whole. One inappropriate email to the wrong person can cause all kinds of problems. Thus, it's important you take the time to make employees aware of what affect email can have, and how easy it is to pass around and store it.

Other correspondence procedures should also be addressed. If necessary, review with employees what kinds of phone messages are appropriate to leave and what kinds are not. For faxes, make it clear how these should be stored, and how they should be handled. Is it alright to leave a fax in the machine for half a day in your office? Or should a fax be cleared and stored immediately? Making rules of conduct for these processes evident to your employees enhances security, and the quality of record keeping. If employees are taught how to create appropriate records such as emails, faxes or phone messages, the likelihood that they will breach confidentiality measures will be greatly cut down.

In general for all records and all organization data, it is important to make your employees aware of the security measures you have in place. Go through different security classifications and priorities. Review any vulnerabilities that have to do with staff, such as not logging off properly. Talk about how to make information security better, and talk about what workers need to do to help maintain existing security. This in turn will improve the security of your records. Once people are aware of the security measures, they can interact with them more effectively.

The creation and preservation of electronic records is especially important to cover in training if your employees are working with customer data. Losing account information or order information can lose you a customer. Poor handling of electronic records by staff can lead to loss of confidentiality and integrity. Ultimately, this can lead to the loss of reputation – your organization may become one that customers don't feel they can trust. Take the time to go over proper procedures for dealing with high security electronic documents so you can avoid this.

The last thing to remember about a training program is that it's only as good as the information that employees retain from it. Offer written documents that describe important policies or procedures and require regular refresher training for best results.

What Are Discovery Parameters?

Before we get started on discovery parameters, what the heck is discovery anyway? Discovery is the identification, collection, and analysis of records relevant to an investigation or litigation. Discovery used to mean gathering boxes and boxes of records from the opposing side and arduously looking through them for the right documents relevant to the litigation. Today, discovery has taken on a whole new dynamic. With the birth of electronic documents came the birth of electronic discovery. Now, identification, collection and analysis are conducted on computer data as well.

We live in a litigious society, one where the parameters of business are defined by laws and regulations. Sometimes your organization will face litigation or investigation. This brings about the process of discovery. If you don't want to be caught without a procedure for discovery, use the following control objective:

> *In order to promote the integrity and availability of records for discovery, the organization will create a procedure for complying with discovery parameters. These procedures include complying with notice requirements and following the standard of production.*

Now that we understand what discovery is and how it affects your organization, let's take a look at some specifics for defining discovery parameters.

Guidance from the regulations and standards

The **Federal Rules of Civil Procedure** and the **Sedona Principles,** both documents on discovery, are the only standards that mention these elements of records discovery.

Federal Rules of Civil Procedure, Rule 34 addresses the litigant's request and the obligation of the organization to determine the scope of its discovery obligations. It also discusses the notice requirements.

The **Sedona Principles** are more detailed and provide real-life examples of fair and unencumbered expectations for initial discovery preparation. *See Principles 5.d, 5.g & 6.b for the full discussion.*

Although discovery can be a tedious process, often taking up time and resources, it does not have to be like searching the desert with a fine tooth comb either. Instead, you stick to the scope of the requested documents and survive the experience with at most, a minor inconvenience.

Once litigation or investigation is threatened or pending, organizations must issue a "notice to affected persons." The notice indicates the scope of the relevant records, both paper and electronic, to be preserved. It is distributed to all "affected persons," namely those individuals in your organization responsible for maintaining documents and data relevant to the litigation.

The standard for the production of data as evidence is to take steps reasonably necessary to produce the relevant data. This does not mean that you should freeze all records and shut down computer systems looking for every scrap of information that "just might be evidence." Instead, define the scope of electronic data collection needed to appropriately and fairly address the issues of the case, and *that is all!*

How Do You Prepare for Discovery?

Hopefully, you will never be engaged in litigation. But if that day comes, you want to be prepared. And you will be, if you use the following control objective as your guide:

> *To prepare for an event of legal discovery, the organization will define the search methodology you will use to produce documents and data. The party requesting the documents will often specify search terms or other selection criteria. The organization under investigation must then search for appropriate records containing those key terms.*

In this section we'll review the details of how to set up a good search methodology and how your organization can be prepared for records discovery.

Guidance from the regulations and standards

Once again, discovery search methodologies and the procedures that accompany them are only discussed in the **Federal Rules of Civil Procedure** and the **Sedona Principles.**

Federal Rule 34 allows discovering parties to "sample any tangible things which constitute or contain matters within the scope of [relevance]."

The **Sedona Principles** discuss searching and sampling, providing numerous examples (Prin. 11(a) and 11(b)). *There is a wealth of information on this topic in the Sedona Principles. See the Sedona Principles 11(a) and 11 (b) for a detailed discussion.*

From regulation to reality — sure signs you are complying

Sometimes large volumes of data are involved in discovery, and searching, even with good search terms can be a slow, painful process. In this situation, we recommend the use of sampling. Sampling provides the searcher with a portion of documents or data that, when viewed, will generally indicate whether or not the remaining bulk of the respective records fall under the scope of discovery. It is like tasting wine, then purchasing a bottle of what you tasted. Most likely, they will taste quite similar. Sampling can also aid in locating duplicate entries of information, thus narrowing the searches further. Pay close attention to the scope of search terms or sampling. If they provide an unreasonably myopic methodology, courts may order additional searches, which can substantially increase costs.

Finally, prepare an "auditors" view for all search samples provided. Unrelated confidential and sensitive information should be blacked out or hidden to preserve its integrity and security.

What is Retrieval of Records?

Retrieval of records is the process by which you collect and retrieve data for discovery purposes. The control objective for the retrieval of records is:

> *Once all pertinent records have been determined through search or sampling, the organization will retrieve the files and data for discovery. Collection procedures should be defined, validated and documented.*

In this section we review what tools and procedures you need in place to effectively retrieve records for the purposes of meeting discovery requests.

Guidance from the regulations and standards

Once again, the **Federal Rules of Civil Procedure** and the **Sedona Principles** are the only documents that address production procedures in detail. **IRS Revenue Procedure 97-22** calls for taxpayers to establish a retrieval system for any electronic storage of books and records that must be made available to the IRS during discovery. The Sedona Principles call for the validation and documentation of collection procedures and also recommend an agreed upon format for all produced records. According to Federal Rule 34, litigants can sometimes also indicate desired format upon initial request.

The **Sedona Principles** state, in detail, when developing data collection procedures, organizations should consider the scope of the collection, the cost, any burden and disruption of normal activities, and the defensibility of the process. All collection processes should be accompanied by documentation and validation appropriate to the needs of the particular case. Well-documented data collection and production procedures provide for a sort of checks and balances, because it ensures that the right (or necessary) data is collected, and not anything unnecessary. The documentation should outline the what is collected procedures and steps used to validate collection. The documentation should of course be revised or updated as the organization changes(Principle 6.e).

The **Sedona Principles** also state that the production of electronic documents should only be provided in one format. Produce electronic data in a form that preserves the substantive information of the data relative to the claims and defenses in an action. Ordinary parties are only required to produce documents in one format (Principle 12.c). See Sedona Principles, Principle 12.c for a further discussion.

The **Federal Rules of Civil Procedure**, Rule 34 embodies procedures for the retrieval of discovery materials. A request for discovery materials must set forth the items to be inspected, and describe each with "reasonable particularity." The request shall state a reasonable time, place, and manner of making the inspection and performing the related acts (FRCP 34).

From regulation to reality – sure signs you are complying

What does all of this mean? It means that you have to define and defend the process by which you collect discovery materials. This process is all about having a methodology and sticking to it. Detail everything about the data collection procedures, from the cost to any burden on business functions. These factors are all relevant. The process you use should be one that you can defend.

After defining the collection processes, they must be validated and documented. Validation will ensure that only relevant records are produced and that retrieval procedures are sound and justified. Documentation should outline both the collection procedures and the steps you took to validate the collection.

To promote consistency, documents and data should all be in the same format, such as PDF or TIF. Remember, the production of records needs to satisfy the timeframe that was outlined during the conference with the opposing party or based on an internal schedule.

Systems Continuity

The Main Thing

Why do we need business continuity planning?

Before you can start the business continuity planning process, you have to be convinced that you need it. Knowing why you need business continuity will help guide you in the creation of a top-notch program. Therefore, the control objective for this section is:

> *In order to ensure continued operations and prevent loss to business activities and assets, the organization will engage in the business continuity planning process. The business continuity planning process will provide preparation in the event of disaster, disruption, or emergency.*

What's to stop you from engaging in adequate preparation? Well, yourself for one. But after you have bridged that gap, there are thousands of threats out there just waiting to exploit your vulnerabilities. Before we get to the threats and action you need to take to counter these threats, let's take a look at what the regulations have to say about the need for business continuity planning.

Guidance from the regulations and standards

Banking/Finance

All financial standards recognize the need for business continuity. **Graham-Leach Bliley, FFIEC Business Continuity Planning handbook** and the **Sound Practices of Operational Risk** call for banks and financial institutions to develop business continuity plans.

Sound Practices of Operational Risk Pg. 7 States:

"Because a severe event may occur beyond a bank's control, preventing it from fulfilling some of its business obligations, it is important for a bank to have a disaster recovery plan. To create a good one the bank needs to take into account all the different types of plausible scenarios to which the bank may be vulnerable. Then the bank should identify critical business processes, including those where there is dependence on external vendors/other third parties for which rapid resumption of service would be most essential.

Periodically, the bank should review their disaster recovery and business continuity plans to make sure they're consistent with the bank's current operations and business strategies. The plans should also be tested frequently to ensure that they are executable and effective."

FFIEC Information Security Pg. 75 indicates:

"Business continuity plans should be created and regularly reviewed as an integral part of the security process. Any risk assessments conducted should consider the changing risks that appear in business continuity scenarios so an appropriate security approach can be established. Strategies should consider what risks affect the organization in the event that continuity plans need to be implemented. Staff should be appropriately trained for their security roles and all security plans surrounding the implementation of a business continuity plan should be tested along side the business continuity plan."

FFIEC Business Continuity Planning Pg. 1 defines business continuity planning as:

"[T]he process whereby financial institutions ensure the maintenance or recovery of operations, including services to customers, when confronted with adverse events such as natural disasters, technological failures, human error, or terrorism" (FFIEC Business Continuity Planning Pg. 1). If you change business processes you must change the BCP (business continuity plan).

The plan should be reviewed regularly against benchmarks for an effective plan. Particular care should be taken to ensure that the BCP takes into account the potential for wide-area disasters that impact an entire region."

FFIEC Operations Pg. 5 says:

"To ensure uninterrupted product and service delivery, operations management should develop a business continuity plan (BCP). At the basic level the plan should allow you to implement a system robust enough to deal with ordinary interruptions to operations and to facilitate prompt restoration without escalating to more drastic and costly disaster recovery procedures."

Healthcare and Life Sciences

HIPAA requires the establishment and implementation of a contingency plan for any organization storing electronically protected health information.

HIPAA Section .308(a)(7) requires that a compliant continuity plan include an applications and data criticality analysis, a data backup plan, a disaster recovery plan, an emergency mode operation plan, and testing and revision procedures. The plan is scalable depending on what different size organizations need.

Credit Card

VISA CISP calls for organizations to create an "incident response plan" in the event of a security breach.

VISA CISP § 10.7 requires that the disaster recovery plan include a crisis-management team to handle important decisions and training for staff so they know their emergency roles. The plan should be tested at least annually.

US Federal Security

The **National Strategy to Secure Cyberspace** calls for contingency planning in government agencies. Both standards require the development and implementation of contingency plans. **National Strategy to Secure Cyberspace** § I.A.4(a) tells us that: "America needs a national cyber disaster recovery plan" involving public institutions, private institutions and cyber centers. These centers will perform analysis, monitor use, enable information exchange and facilitate restoration efforts.

NIST Special Publications

NIST 800-14 § 3.6 indicates that:

"The organization's business plan should identify functions and set priorities for them, so that in the event of disaster, the organization can avoid performing least important functions. The prioritizations should be approved by senior management."

NIST 800-53 § CP instructs organizations to have a business continuity plan developed, distributed and regularly updated by the organization. The plan should be formally documented and address purpose, scope, roles, responsibilities and compliance. Any important procedures necessary to implement the business continuity plan should also be documented.

To ensure business continuity plan success, it should be integrated with other important plans such as the Disaster Recovery Plan, Continuity of Operations Plan, Incident Response Plan, Business Recovery Plan.

Staff should be trained in how to do their part in an emergency situation. Refresher training should also be provided so they stay on top of their work.

A completed continuity plan should be tested to ascertain whether it functions at all, and if it does function, whether it functions effectively. The plan should be regularly updated to reflect the current state of the business.

Some aspects of a continuity plan you may wish to consider including:

- A storage site that is geographically separate from the primary storage site, but close enough to facilitate timely recovery.

- An alternate processing site that is geographically separate from the primary processing site, fully configured to handle primary processing, has priority of service provisions and has a way to deal with accessibility problems in the event of an area-wide disruption.

- Alternate telecommunications services with agreements containing priority of service provisions in accordance with the organization's availability requirements, set ups that do not share a single point of failure with primary telecommunications services, service providers that are sufficiently separate from the primary service providers and overall, service providers with adequate continuity plans of their own.

- Information system backup with backup information being tested, with the backup information being used in the restoration of information system functions as part of contingency plan testing and with stores of backup copies of the operation system and other critical system information.

International Standards Organization

ISO 17799 § 11.1 calls for a managed process in place for developing a business continuity plan that brings together a variety of key elements:

- Understanding risks the organization faces in terms of their likelihood and impact, including an identification and prioritization of critical business processes

- Understanding the impact which interruptions are likely to have on the business

- Considering the purchase of suitable insurance which may form part of the business continuity process

- Formulating and documenting a business continuity strategy consistent with the agreed business objectives and priorities

- Formulating and documenting business continuity plans in line with the agreed strategy

- Regular testing and updating of the plans and processes put in place

- Ensuring that the management of business continuity is incorporated in the organization's processes and structure.

General Guidance

CobiT, COSO, and the ISF Standard call for business continuity planning. While CobiT refers to an overall business continuity plan, it primarily addresses IT continuity planning.

CobiT 3 Section DS4 suggests seven areas for ensuring continuous service:

IT Continuity Framework, IT Continuity Plan Strategy and Philosophy, IT Continuity Plan Contents, Minimizing IT Continuity Requirements, Maintaining the IT Continuity Plan and Testing the IT Continuity Plan.

The IT Continuity framework is where the roles, responsibilities and chosen approach to business continuity are laid out, along with the rules and structures for documenting the continuity plan.

The IT Continuity Plan strategy and philosophy involves management ensuring that the plan is in line with the overall business continuity plan for the sake of consistency.

The actual IT continuity plan itself should contain the following:

- Guidelines on how to use the continuity plan
- Response procedures meant to bring the business back to the state it was in before the incident or disaster
- Recovery procedures meant to bring the business back to the state it was in before the incident or disaster
- Procedures to safeguard and reconstruct the home site
- Co-ordination procedures with public authorities
- Communication procedures with stakeholders, employees, key customers, critical suppliers, stockholders and management
- Critical information on continuity teams, affected staff, customers, suppliers, public authorities and media

Other important aspects of the continuity plan will be discussed at length in other summaries and are left off here.

EU Guidance

OECD Risk Checklist § Q 42(f) requires that policies, procedures and standards that govern security requirements address:

- Due diligence requirements

- Security service level and operational readiness requirements

- The general security scope and timing of third-party assurance reviews (e.g., SAS70 Level II, SysTrust, WebTrust certifications)

- Existence and adequacy of insurance to protect against financial losses due to third-party negligence and/or unauthorized access to service provider systems

- Privacy policy

- Disaster recovery and business continuity plan

- Process of change management

From regulation to reality – sure signs you are complying

If the people who were in charge of the Titanic would have spent more time planning for the possibility of disaster, and less time thinking about fame and fortune, do you think the ship still would have gone down? Without speculating about what could have happened, it is clear that the people in charge of the Titanic thought the ship was unsinkable. So, instead of spending money and time making sure the ship had enough life boats, they spent time making sure the ship was pleasing to the eye. However, had those in charge planned for the possibility of disaster and trained the crew on evacuation procedures, ensured that the ship was stocked with safety devices and just plain prepared for the worst, then one of the biggest disasters of the century could have been avoided. Think of your organization like a huge ship. It may seem to be unsinkable, but that is an illusion. There are many disasters that can sink your ship if you're unprepared to deal with them.

Systems continuity is preparation. There is no doubt that your organization will face some kind of disruption, disaster or emergency that has the potential to do great damage to your ability to operate. The question is not if, but when. You can't know when a disaster will strike, but you can know how to meet problems head on and keep your organization running. You can have procedures in place to ensure safety and to preserve the most critical assets and business functions. Critical personnel will be trained and ready to go. You'll have anticipated potential problems and planned accordingly. Business continuity planning will ensure that your organization is as prepared as it can be, with everyone knowing their roles and responsibilities, and everything in place so that your organization can survive even the biggest disaster.

The survival skills of your organization are only as great as the plan you create. If you walk out into the desert armed only with the clothes on your back, more likely than not, the hot sun will catch up with you before you find a source of water. If you walk out into the desert with an emergency plan, a well stocked backpack, and a destination, it is more likely that you'll survive the experience. You may even learn something in the process.

Your organization needs guidance. And, there is no greater need for it than when disaster strikes. Guidance comes in many forms, all of which we will discuss in this chapter. Before we get into that, the first thing you need to do is resolve to plan for emergencies, and determine what kind of planning will best suit your organization. We will give you suggestions along the way, but there is no better person to determine what works best for your organization than you!

Now that you have decided you need business continuity planning, you are ready to start the process. Create an organizational policy that supports business continuity. In this way, it is a documented responsibility of the organization. Then, take a look at the risk assessments and the business impact analysis (BIA) that you learned about last chapter. These documents will serve as guidance tools for you throughout the continuity planning process.

The time has come to plan, write, test and update the business continuity plan (BCP). Each of the following sections describes one essential piece of business continuity planning. Together, they form a process to keep you afloat when all signs indicate you will sink.

What is the business continuity framework?

Business Continuity planning and implementation is like an onion. It has many layers, each building off of each other to form a whole. The first layer is the all-encompassing business continuity framework. The framework dictates the roles and responsibilities of personnel and procedures for developing business continuity plans. Within this framework are the complex internal layers of your business continuity plan. The control objective for this section is:

> *In order to promote the integrity, availability and accountability of systems and business functions in case of disruption, the organization will construct a business continuity framework. The business continuity framework should contain essential procedures and identifies the roles and responsibilities of personnel.*

In this chapter, we will discuss how to plan for these layers, which contain your organization's strategic goals and business objectives.

Guidance from the regulations and standards

Public Companies

AICPA Suitable Trust Services Criteria calls for management to develop a business continuity strategy, and approve and review disaster recovery plans. Furthermore, a BCP coordinator is called upon to review and update the business impact analysis annually.

NASD/NYSE

NASD/NYSE Rules 3510 and **446** require that every member develop a business continuity plan and disclose a summary of that plan to its customers. Members and member organizations must also designate and notify the Exchange of a senior officer whose assumes the responsibility of approving and annually reviewing all plans.

Banking/Finance

FFIEC Business Continuity Planning institutes a business continuity planning process that includes a BIA and risk assessment. Though these are essential tasks that must be completed before a plan is conceived, they should already be covered under the organization's risk management process. The **FFIEC Business Continuity Planning handbook** also clearly emphasizes the need to consider business continuity from an enterprise-wide perspective.

FFIEC assigns responsibilities for business continuity planning to board members and senior management. The board is responsible for allocating necessary resources to fund the development of the BCP. It is also responsible for prioritizing critical business functions based on the business impact analysis. Furthermore, the board must approve the BCP and review business continuity test results. Both the board and senior management are responsible for determining which personnel participate in BCP development. It is also their responsibility to ensure that employees are aware of their role in business continuity and receive proper training.

NIST Special Publications

NIST 800-53 calls for a contingency planning policy to oversee the creation and implementation of plans. It also requires "designated officials within the organization" to review and approve contingency plans and their test results. They are charged with distributing multiple copies of plans to key contingency personnel.

NIST 800-14 § 3.6.4 and 3.6.1 states that contingency planning strategies should be developed based on practical considerations, including feasibility and cost. Strategies should include: emergency response, recovery, and resumption with guidelines to effective implementation.

Emergency response: The initial actions to be taken that will protect lives and limit damage should be documented.

Recovery: Plan steps for continued support of critical functions.

Resumption: Determine what is required in order to return to normal operations. The relationship between recovery and resumption is important. The longer it takes to resume normal operations, the longer the organization will have to operate in recovery mode.

Implementation: Includes documenting of procedures, training employees, and make general preparations. Many procedures are ongoing.

International Standards Organization

ISO 17799 calls for allocation of information security responsibilities by a management forum that designates owners. Business continuity planning responsibilities would then be subject to these designations.

ISO 17799 § 11.1.1 addresses the allocation of information security responsibilities, by stating that:

The security policy should include in it allocation of roles and responsibilities. Specifically, local responsibilities for individual physical and information assets and security processes, such as business continuity planning, should be clearly defined.

ISO also calls for the formulation and documentation of the business continuity plan in line with an agreed upon strategy.

General Guidance

Where **CobiT 3** calls for a framework, the ISF Standard calls for a formal planning process. Both standards require that the business continuity strategy adhere to the overall business objectives of the company and be based on the results of a risk analysis.

For nearly every aspect of business continuity planning, CobiT calls for management and business process owner involvement. The ISF Standard implies, but does not specifically state that management is responsible for the development and implementation of business continuity. It does require, however, a custodial authority to see to the security and storage of the plan.

CobiT 3 DS4.1 calls on IT management, in cooperation with business process owners, to establish a continuity framework which defines the roles, responsibilities and the risk based approach/ methodology to be adopted, and the rules and structures to document the continuity plan as well as the approval procedures. CobiT also discusses the IT continuity plan strategy and philosophy, stating that it is managements responsibility to ensure that the IT continuity plan is consistent with the overall business continuity plan. The IT continuity plan should also be consistent with the IT long and short range plans.

CobiT 4 DS4.1 indicates that a framework for IT continuity should be developed. This framework should address the creation of an organizational structure for continuity management, covering the roles, tasks and responsibilities of internal and external service providers, the rules and structures to document, test and execute disaster recovery and IT contingency plans. DS4.2 requires organizations to take their IT continuity framework and use it to develop IT continuity plans. These plans should be designed to reduce the impact of a major disruption on key business functions and processes.

ISF Standard of Good Practice for Information Security Section SM4.5.2 describes a strategy or philosophy towards BCP's involves documented procedures for the development of business continuity plans. These procedures should provide that:

1. all critical parts of the organization are provided for in the plan

2. the plan is base on the results of a documented risk analysis

3. the plan is distributed to all staff requiring them in case of an emergency

4. the plan is kept up to date and subject to standard change management practices

5. the plan is backed up by a copy held at an offsite location.

ISF also addresses roles and responsibilities, by requiring that custody of the plan should be the responsibility of a specific individual or a working group. Additionally, the plan itself should address the responsibilities for carrying out tasks an activities, including deputies, and procedures to be followed by business users.

From regulation to reality – sure signs you are complying

The time has come to establish your business continuity framework. This process is broken down into two sections:

• Roles and responsibilities of personnel

• Strategies for developing business continuity plans

Roles and Responsibilities of Personnel

Roles and responsibilities of personnel determine who does what in business continuity planning. From the top down, the board of directors and senior management have the most responsibility. The board is in charge of allocating the necessary resources to adequately fund the development of the BCP and prioritizing critical business functions based on the business impact analysis. The board also approves the final BCP and any updates or changes made to the plan.

Under board supervision, senior management determines which personnel participate in the development of the BCP. Senior management ensures that all staff members are aware of their role in business continuity. Senior management will handle training, guaranteeing that all staff members have been appropriately trained in their business continuity responsibilities.

There are just a few other responsibilities for you to be aware of:

- Who should have custody of the plan, as specific individual or a group?
- Does the plan address procedures for business users?
- Are all the roles and responsibilities documented in the plan?

Strategies for Developing Business Continuity Plans

After establishing who is responsible for what, you will develop an overall strategy or philosophy to guide your organization in the creation of the BCP. This will take into account the risk assessment and BIA completed by your organization, as well as the overall business strategies your organization has adopted over time.

The strategy acts as a tool to lead you through the process. If you can see the path your planning process will take, you've done your half of the job. The other half is marking out all the places where something needs to be done. For example, when participating in a scavenger hunt you know the goal is to find everything on the list. But, you are not going to get very far if you don't know what's on the list. In business continuity planning, you probably know that the planning path will lead you to a written document. But you also need to strategize how you will get to that written document, and what you need to collect on the way. Each process discussed in the following sections is a pit stop on the path. You stop, accomplish something, then you bring it with you to the next stop along the way. By the time you get to the pit stop marked "writing the plan" you will have done most of the work.

When developing the strategy, remember these four concepts: emergency planning, recovery, resumption and implementation. These are the four phases you will move through in order to successfully survive a disaster. This chapter is mainly about emergency planning. As we move through the layers of business continuity, notice how each layer draws on one or more of these concepts.

Have you identified critical business functions?

Learning to tell the difference between what's critical and what's not can mean life or death for your organization. In order to ensure you keep the critical functions operational and protected during disruption or disaster, you must plan ahead. Planning ahead starts with understanding what functions are critical. It follows that the control objective for this section is:

> Based on the business impact analysis (BIA) and risk assessment, the organization will define and prioritize critical business functions to be documented in the business continuity plan. These include vital business processes, crucial records such as financial information, and critical operations that the company requires to keep business running without interruption.

In this section we will guide you in the identification of critical business functions. Let's start with guidance from the regulations.

Guidance from the regulations and standards

NASD/NYSE

While **NASD/NYSE Rules 3500** and **446** call for the consideration of "critical constituent, bank and counter-party impact", this is more of a BIA than an assessment of critical business functions.

Banking/Finance

Critical business functions are addressed in **FFIEC Business Continuity Planning handbook's** BIA and risk assessment procedures included in the business continuity planning process. They are not, however, specifically addressed as a strategy. The **Sound Practices of Operational Risk** requires banks to identify critical business processes that are essential to business resumption.

Healthcare and Life Sciences

HIPAA calls for an "emergency mode operation plan" that defines procedures for continuation of critical business processes.

In HIPAA .308(a)(7)(ii)(C) it states that an emergency mode operation plan establishes procedures to enable the continuation of critical business processes for the protection of the security of electronic protected health information (sensitive data) while operating in emergency mode.

US Federal Security

FISCAM requires that critical operations be defined and prioritized for security purposes and inclusion in the business continuity plan.

Specifically, FISCAM § SC-1.1 also states that critical data and operations are to be prioritized. A list should be created that prioritizes data and operations, is approved by senior management and reflects current conditions.

Records Management

Though records management standards do not regularly address business continuity, ISO 15489-2 states that vital records must be identified as part of risk analysis. As such, critical records must be defined in the business continuity plan.

NIST Special Publications

NIST 800-14, on the other hand, states explicitly that business function priorities must be set following their identification.

NIST 800-14 § 3.6.4 and §3.6.1 requires organizations to identify mission or business critical functions. The identification of critical functions is referred to as a business plan. The business plan should identify functions and set priorities for them. In the event of a disaster, certain functions will not be performed. If appropriate priorities have been set, it could mean the difference in the organization's ability to survive a disaster.

General Guidance

CobiT and the ISF standard address critical business and operational processes but do not specifically require their prioritization in the business continuity plan.

CobiT 4 DS4.3 discusses prioritization of IT assets according to how important they are to business operations. The IT continuity plan for an organization should be set up so these items are recovered first. DS4.9 talks about storage priorities. All critical back up media and other resources necessary for IT recovery should be kept offsite with appropriate security. These materials should regularly be tested to ensure they may be used in recovery procedures.

When you're under pressure, it becomes increasingly difficult to discern what functions in your organization are critical and need immediate attention and what functions are not. It's much easier if you make necessary determinations such as these ahead of time.

The first thing you'll do is identify and prioritize critical business functions. For help with this, turn to the risk assessment and BIA that we keep speaking about. Critical business functions include:

- Vital business purposes

- Crucial records

- Crucial operations required to keep the company running

Draw up a list or "business plan" that documents the identified and prioritized critical business functions. Management will approve this documentation as an accurate account of the most important assets and functions of your organization.

The point of the list is this: In the event of disaster, don't perform unnecessary functions and protect critical functions. During recovery, you only want to spend time and energy on those functions critical to the survival of the business.

Have you identified critical personnel?

Just as we mentioned in the last section, defining what's critical means a great deal to an organization's survival. Here, the critical asset we are identifying is people. Some people need to be around to help with recovery. Other people would just be in the way. It is your job to distinguish these groups of people, as well as adhere to this control objective:

> To ensure that all necessary personnel are available for recovery, the organization will define critical personnel to be included in the business continuity plan. These personnel form the foundation for recovery from a disaster or significant business disruption. Every critical person, whether organizational staff or not, must be provided for in the process.

In this section, you will learn how to identify critical personnel as well as other tips relating to communication in a disaster.

Guidance from the regulations and standards

Public Companies

AICPA Suitable Trust Services Criteria calls for the business continuity plan to define roles and responsibilities for critical personnel.

NASD/NYSE

Rules 3520 (NASD) and **446(g) (NYSE)** require that the business continuity plan define emergency contact personnel roles in the event of a significant business disruption. These personnel must be a registered principal and member of senior management. Rule 3520 calls for a minimum of two such personnel.

Banking/Finance

FFIEC Business Continuity Planning handbook requires that the business continuity plan define roles and assign responsibilities for critical personnel involved in the response and recovery process. It calls for the formation of BCP teams to cover all areas of business restoration, as well as primary contact personnel for vendors, suppliers and third-party service providers. Personnel should also be assigned to oversee information and physical security. In addition, the standard requires the plan to include contingencies in the event that critical personnel are unavailable.

US Federal Security

FISCAM requires that personnel be defined that are associated with previously determined critical operations.

NIST Special Publications

NIST 800-53 requires that contingency plans address roles and responsibilities and assign individuals as emergency contacts.

NIST 800-14 calls for critical personnel to be identified and included in the business continuity plan. The standards are not specific regarding roles and responsibilities.

General Guidance

CobiT and the ISF Standard of Good Practice for Information Security call for critical personnel to be identified and included in the business continuity plan. The standards are not specific regarding roles and responsibilities.

From regulation to reality – sure signs you are complying

In the event of an emergency, you can't have people running around like chickens with their heads cut off. Everything needs to be organized and efficient to run smoothly. This is accomplished by distinguishing the critical folks from those who aren't, so that only those who are needed stick around.

Identify who needs to be present to bring the organization back from disaster. This is your hardworking recovery team, those who are trained and ready to ensure that the organization suffers as little disruption as possible. Group these critical personnel into teams, assigning them various response and recovery responsibilities.

Create a list of emergency contact personnel and include it in the BCP. Establish contingencies for crucial management and other personnel should they be unavailable. Define critical vendors, suppliers and other third-party service providers in the plan as well, including their primary contacts. Finally, include any personnel that are associated with previously determined critical business functions in the list of critical personnel.

Have you identified critical IT resources?

The third set of critical assets to identify are critical resources. This comes after personnel and business functions because the list of critical resources is based, in part, on the other critical assets. You probably won't know which resources are most important until you establish which business functions and personnel (human resources) are critical. This all starts with the following control objective:

> *The organization will define critical IT resources to be included in the business continuity plan. These components include software applications, hardware, operational data and processing equipment, telecommunications and networking equipment, time frames, office equipment and supplies and critical third-party services.*

Now that you have identified critical business functions and personnel, you are ready to dive into critical resources. In this section, we will give you advice to keep you from hitting your head on the bottom of the pool.

Guidance from the regulations and standards

Public Companies

AICPA Suitable Trust Services Criteria calls for the business continuity plan to define critical IT application programs, operating systems, data files and time frames required for recovery.

NASD/NYSE

Rules 3510 and **446(g)** call for the business continuity plan to define all "mission critical systems" necessary for complete processing of securities transactions, including customer account maintenance and delivery of funds.

Banking/Finance

FFIEC Business Continuity Planning calls for the business continuity plan to define and prioritize all the above technological components. Furthermore, it specifies that financial institutions must consider telephone, internet banking and ATM systems as critical components to be included in the recovery process.

Healthcare and Life Sciences

HIPAA requires the business continuity plan to include an assessment of the "criticality of specific applications and data" that contain or process health information.

US Federal Security

FISCAM requires that data criticality is defined for security purposes and for inclusion in the business continuity plan. It further requires that any other resources be defined that support previously determined vital business operations and data. Specifically, resources supporting critical data include:

- hardware
- software
- computer supplies
- system documentation
- telecommunications
- office facilities and supplies
- human resources

General Guidance

CobiT calls for the business continuity plan to define critical IT resources as described above. CobiT emphasizes that operational data should be prioritized and documented.

CobiT Section DS4.10 specifically calls for the following critical IT resources to be identified in the continuity plan:

- applications
- third-party services
- operating systems
- data files
- personnel and supplies
- time frames needed for recover post disaster

United Kingdom and Canadian Guidance

BS 15000-2 requires that SLAs include consideration of continuity in order to re-initiate critical IT services in the event of business disruption or disaster.

From regulation to reality – sure signs you are complying

Resources are the last critical assets to identify. Using the previously defined critical business functions and personnel documents, create the prioritized list of critical IT resources. In doing so, consider the:

- Hardware
- Software
- Computer supplies
- System documentation
- Telecommunications and network equipment
- Office facilities and supplies
- Operational data and processing equipment

Next, define critical third-party services. When forming contracts or service level agreements (SLAs), remember to include continuity clauses consistent with your BCP. Finally, include with the list any timeframes needed for recovery post disaster.

When determining what is critical, remember this-- You never know when disaster will strike, or what form it will take. Identifying and prioritizing the most essential components of your organization will allow you to effectively handle any situation.

Do you have alternative site strategies?

Strategizing may seem like something a lawyer does before court or an organization does in the marketing department. But, developing strategies for your alternative site(s) will ensure that you get is right. For instance, you wouldn't want to buy a vacation home without careful research and planning. You need to determine the best location, how much money you have to spend, and what assets you desire the house to come with. The same is true for an alternative site. Therefore, the control objective for this section is:

> *In order to ensure that processing capability can be resurrected and recovered as soon as possible, the organizations will develop strategies for alternate data center sites. Before the alternate processing facility is chosen and prepared, the organization will determine the nature and capabilities of the site.*

So, let's get down to business developing your alternate site strategy. First, we will start with the regulations and standards.

Guidance from the regulations and standards

Banking/Finance

FFIEC Business Continuity Planning is really the only standard that mentions alternate site strategies. From FFIEC we see that there are three generally accepted alternatives for data centers an entity can consider.

First, the organization could set up a hot site, which is essentially a mirror site of the primary facility that contains identical equipment and composes duplicate operations. In this way, each facility can back up the other and provide for immediate resumption of activities provided the primary site fails. This tends to be a costly alternative and can also provide issues if an organization wants data centers to be more geographically separated.

The next alternative for an organization would be a warm site, whereby the alternate processing facility is fully configured much like the hot site but is not always active. The warm site can typically be made operational within a few hours. Back-up media must be procured from the primary facility on a daily basis to maintain the warm site's capabilities.

Finally, an organization can choose to go with a cold site, which is essentially a physical location with facilities and power but no equipment. The strategy for the alternate data center should be included in an organization's business continuity plan.

NASD/NYSE

These rules do not directly address alternate site strategies. The standard also suggests that organizations might utilize "tertiary locations", which are basically alternative sites for alternative sites. It provides a secondary backup to the backup site in the event of another disruption to business continuity.

General Guidance

CobiT mentions that the continuity methodology should provide alternatives for back-up sites (in this case it means data centers) but does not explicitly define possibilities.

From regulation to reality – sure signs you are complying

For maximum efficiency, develop strategies for recovering through the use of alternate data center sites. Before you choose and prepare the site, determine the nature and capability of the site. There are three generally accepted alternatives for data centers an entity can consider.

- A Hot Site

- A Warm Site

- A Cold Site

This isn't Goldie Locks and the Three Bears, but it's much like choosing the right temperature of porridge for your organization's needs. The type of recovery site you choose will depend very much on the criticality of the processes being recovered and recovery time objectives.

A "hot site" is a mirror of the primary facility. It contains identical equipment and composes duplicate operations. This allows each facility to back up the other and provides for immediate resumption of activities if the primary site fails. Establishing a hot site requires relocating employees to the site in the case of disruption, as well as transferring back-up media off-site on a daily basis. A hot site is geographically closer to the primary site than some prefer. And, as you may have guessed, this is a costly alternative. So, if you are a smaller organization with limited resources, you could opt for a mobile hot site, like a trailer equipped with necessary hardware.

The next alternative is a "warm site." A warm site whereby is configured much like the hot site, but is not always active. It can generally be operational within a couple of hours. Again, you will transfer back-up media off-site on a daily basis.

The "cold site" is part of a long-term recovery strategy. The site provides a back-up location with power and all the appropriate wiring and controls, but with no equipment. Cold sites can take up to several weeks to activate, and are often used in addition to a hot or warm site.

You also want to consider other points when determining what temperature of porridge or in your case site, is right for your organization. Some questions to ask are:

- Does your organization need a tertiary location?

- Should you to hire a third-party service provider for installation?

- Have you subjected the secondary sites to a threat scenario analysis when trying to determine the location of the alternate site?

Whatever site temperature your organization chooses to be the right one, it is important to document the choice and the strategy behind the choice in the BCP.

Do you have network recovery strategies?

Like we mentioned before, strategies are key to acquiring assets and implementing solid policies and procedures. Creating strategies for network recovery will empower you with the knowledge of what works and what doesn't, so when it comes time to actually implement the strategies, recovery is a breeze. To help with recovery, we have identified the following control objective for this section:

> Faced with the possibility of network or telecommunications disruptions or failures, the organization will define network recovery strategies and include them in business continuity plans.

It may seem like common sense to plan for the possibility of disaster. But, there are plenty of us in San Francisco who don't carry renters insurance, even though we live in earthquake country. While that is an individual choice, creating network recovery strategies for your organization is a choice you make for the survival of your organization. In this section, we will help you create your network recovery strategies.

Guidance from the regulations and standards

Public Companies

The **AICPA Suitable Trust Services Criteria** does not directly address network recovery strategies but does mention server redundancy as a back-up requirement.

NASD/NYSE

Rules 3510(c) and 446(c) indicate that the business continuity plan must include arrangements for alternate communications between a firm and its customers and employees but does not specify a network recovery strategy.

Banking/Finance

FFIEC Business Continuity Planning handbook discusses at length the necessity for documenting a network recovery strategy in business continuity plans. The standard addresses all forms of voice and data communication and calls for the above-mentioned strategies.

Viable business continuity arrangements should exist for voice and data services.

"At a minimum, telecommunications plans should address skilled human resources, internal and external connectivity, communications media, network equipment and telecommunication management systems. The BCP should establish priorities and identify critical network components. Original plan components such as reliability, flexibility, and compatibility must also be considered in formulating the back-up plan. . . The BCP should also address the practicality of each component. Selected alternatives should be able to accommodate the anticipated volumes or capacities at necessary speeds to meet the established priorities" (FFIEC Business Continuity Plan Pg. D-2)

NIST Special Publications

NIST 800-53 calls for alternate telecommunications services but does not address network redundancy or resilience.

General Guidance

The **ISF Standard for Good Practices of Information Security** calls for network resilience and communications strategies that provide security, back-up and recovery in the event of disruption or failure. According to the ISF Standard § NW1.3:

"The network should be run on robust, reliable hardware and software, supported by alternative or duplicate facilities. Single points of failure should be minimized, risk of malfunction of critical communication equipment, software, links, and services should be reduced, and the availability of external network services should be protected."

From regulation to reality – sure signs you are complying

The time has come to define network recovery strategies and put these strategies in the BCP. The following are a sampling of effective network recovery strategies.

- Build a high level of resiliency and redundancy into networking systems.

- Consider alternative telecommunications carriers and equipment for use in recovery operations.

- Run your network on robust, reliable hardware and software that is supported by alternative or duplicate facilities.

- Minimize single points of failure by considering primary and duplicate network infrastructures and alternative points of communication with telecommunication providers.

Keep in mind that the BCP should define back-up strategies for networks and telecommunications services both for an organization's primary and alternative processing facilities.

Have you made adequate preparations for alternate facilities?

It is not enough just to have alternate processing facilities. You must prepare them. Processing facilities need to be equipped and procedures created that govern the use of the alternate facilities. Additionally, there are guidelines concerning distance from the primary facility that you should adhere to. Therefore, the control objective for this section is:

> *In order to ensure continued business functions in the event of disaster or disruption, the organization will make adequate preparations for alternate processing facilities. This includes site identification and initiation, distance requirements and security.*

In this section we will address the points made in this control objective and many more, so keep reading!

Guidance from the regulations and standards

NASD/NYSE

Rules 3510(c) and 446(c) require business continuity plans to include alternate physical locations for employees, implying the selection of an alternate processing site. The rules do not go into any further detail.

Banking/Finance

FFIEC Business Continuity Planning handbook calls for the selection and preparation of alternate data center sites. The alternate site should receive a greater level of security protection, both physically and electronically, than the primary site. The Sound Practices of Operational Risk also notes that banks should ensure the alternate processing facility is an adequate distance from the primary site so that it is not susceptible to the same hazards.

US Federal Security

The GAO Financial Audit Manual indicates an organization implements stand-by arrangements to use a second processing facility in the event that the primary data center is destroyed.

NIST Special Publications

NIST 800-53 calls for an identification of the alternate processing site and the initiation of agreements to resume critical business operations (contingency arrangements). It also specifies that the alternate site must be geographically separated from the main site so that it is not susceptible to the same hazards. In its brief mention of business continuity,

General Guidance

CobiT requires the selection of an alternative processing facility, but does not go into detail concerning the site or contingency arrangements. On the other hand, the **ISF Standard of Good Practice for Information Security** calls for an alternative processing site and contingency arrangements to facilitate the recovery and resumption of business processes. The standards indicates these arrangements should cover all business users and offices that are involved in recovery activities.

From regulation to reality – sure signs you are complying

You may or may not already have an alternate processing facility. If you don't, it is highly recommended that you get one to ensure you don't lose any business during the recovery of the primary site. If you have an alternate processing facility, the business continuity planning process will help you determine if the site you have is adequate to suit your organization's needs.

Adequate preparations start with selecting and preparing the alternate processing facility. Consider the size, location, capacity and required amenities to facilitate recovery and resumption of critical business functions. Determine contingency arrangements and other recovery procedures for all affected user departments and offices. Consider vital resources, such as files, records and documentation required for processing, including those that must be acquired from an off-site storage facility. All logistical procedures for re-locating personnel must be thoroughly thought out.

Location and security are crucial to having an adequate alternate processing facility. When determining the appropriate geographical distance for the alternate site, consider the possible exposure of the alternate site to any physical dangers the primary facility is exposed to. You want it to be far enough away so that if a fire takes out the primary site, the alternate site does not go up in smoke. On the other hand, you want the site to be close enough that any critical back-up media can be produced easily and critical personnel can be relocated. Secure the alternate site is physically and electronically secure. And as usual, provide for this in this in the plan.

What should be considered when determining the location and policies surrounding off-site media storage?

Storing media on site would be like storing your home owners insurance policy inside your home. If that policy is critical to your financial survival should your home go up in flames, you should store it in a location removed from your home, such as a safety deposit box. Similarly, records and other files can be critical to an organization's survival after a disaster strikes. Protecting these records can mean the financial survival of an organization. Therefore, we recommend you follow this control objective:

> In order to protect critical data, records, software and documentation and provide the capability to recover from a significant business disruption or disaster, the organization will secure an off-site media storage location and institute procedures for backing up such information.

In this section we will guide you in the quest to understand off-site media storage policies and requirements.

Guidance from the regulations and standards

Public Companies

The **AICPA Suitable Trust Services Criteria** calls for back-up and recovery procedures to follow an entity's established system policies. The Criteria requires that daily and weekly back-ups be stored off-site and calls for annual verifications of stored contents.

Banking/Finance

FFIEC Business Continuity planning addresses securing an offsite location and addressing procedures surrounding such storage. The off-site location should be provided by a third-party or commercial service and contracts should reflect any security and continuity issues. The site must also be appropriately protected and secured and adequately distant from the company's primary processing facility in the event of a physical disaster. However, the location of the storage facility must also be close to an organization's alternate data center to aid in prompt recovery and resumption of business.

All media must be stored in accordance with the organization's back-up and recovery strategies and policies. Particularly critical data should be backed up daily, either incrementally or as a whole. Operating system, application and utility software should be backed up whenever it its modified, updated or changed. Regardless of the type of media being stored, all information must be subject to an entity's information labeling, handling and access security policies. Furthermore, the capability of backed up media to contribute to a business' recovery from disaster or disruption should be periodically tested. Annual verifications of stored media and off-site premises must also be performed to ensure content, availability and security.

Finally, a copy of the business continuity plan and any associated plans, including particularly sensitive or crucial procedures and escrowed documentation should also be stored at the off-site facility.

Healthcare and Life Sciences

HIPAA calls for organizations to establish procedures for archiving and retrieving electronic health information, but does not address specific procedures or the selection of off-site media storage facilities.

Credit Card

VISA CISP calls for media to be backed up nightly and requires back-ups to be stored in an off-site third-party or commercial storage facility.

US Federal Security

FISCAM and The GAO Financial Audit Manual all call for storage of back-up media in an off-site location. NIST is the most detailed and also suggests geographical separation of the off-site storage facility from primary operations. FISCAM also requires that organizations develop back-up procedures in accordance with appropriate policies.

FISCAM § SC-2.1 explains:

Backup should files to be created on a prescribed basis and rotated offsite often enough to avoid disruption if current files are lost or damaged. System application documentation should be maintained at the offsite location. The backup storage site should be geographically removed from the primary site and protected by environmental controls and physical access controls.

The GAO Financial Audit Manual, § 395 C ¶ 5 states that:

Records to be protected against physical harm, and procedures to be established ensuring that current files can be recovered in the event of a computer failure.

Records Management

ISO 15489-1 calls for critical records to be "protected and recovered as needed" but does not require the use of an off-site media storage location.

NIST Special Publications

NIST 800-53, § CP-6 specifically states that:

- *The alternate storage site should be geographically separated from the primary storage site so as not to be susceptible to the same hazards.*

- *The alternate storage site should be sufficiently close to the alternate processing site to facilitate timely and effective recovery operations.*

- *The organization should identify potential accessibility problems to the alternate storage site on the event of an area-wide disruption or disaster and outline explicit mitigations actions.*

NIST 800-53 § CP-9 calls for information systems backup including:

- *testing backup information to ensure media reliability and information integrity*

- *Using selective backup information in the restoration of information system functions as part of contingency planning testing.*

- *Backup copies of the operation system and other critical system software should be stores in a fire-rated container that is not collocated with the operational software.*

From regulation to reality – sure signs you are complying

You have arrived at a place in your business continuity planning where you have the tools to decide where to store your back-up media. Securing an off-site media storage location and instituting procedures for backing up such information are necessary functions of protecting critical data, records, software and documentation.

First, you will choose the location. This is dependent on the location of the alternate processing facility. Choose a location that is far enough from the primary processing facility to protect the storage site in case disaster strikes the primary facility. Balance this with a location that is close enough to the alternate processing facility to aid prompt recovery in case of a disaster. Adequately secure and protect the off-site location to ensure the safety of its contents. Since a third-party or commercial service will be providing the off-site storage, contracts should reflect any security or continuity issues.

Once the location details have been worked out, address the media storage policies and procedures. Store media in accordance with your organization's back-up and recovery strategies and policies. It is up to you to determine what will work best for your organization. But, as usual, we have some suggestions:

- Back-up critical data daily, either incrementally or as a whole

- Rotate back-up data off-site often enough to avoid disruption in case of disaster

- Back-up operating system, application and utility software whenever it is modified, updated or changed

- Store back-up copies of the operating system and other critical system software in a fire-rated container that is not co-located with the operational software

- Subject all information to the organization's information handling, labeling and access security policies, regardless of the type of media being stored

- Periodically, test the capability of back-up media to contribute to the organization's recovery

- Verify the content, availability and security of stored media and off-site premises annually

- Store a copy of the business plan and any associated plans, including particularly sensitive or crucial procedures and escrowed documentation at the off-site storage facility.

Have you planned for emergency communications?

When disaster strikes, communication is a key part of survival. You'll use it to account for employees, salvage materials if need be, and in most cases, fix the disaster so you can resume normal business processes. If you don't want to be caught in an emergency situation with nothing but smoke signals and semaphore at your disposal, you must plan your emergency communication methods. To start, take a look at the following control objective:

> *In order to protect critical business functions and assets during a disaster, the organization will plan for emergency communications. This includes identifying communication channels as well as solidifying contact information and meeting procedures.*

In this section, we will take a look at emergency communications to ensure you can reach the people you need to reach in an emergency.

Guidance from the regulations and standards

NASD/NYSE

Rules 3510(c) and **446(c)** do not provide procedures for emergency communications planning, but do note that the business continuity plan should provide for alternate communications between the firm, employees and customers.

Banking/Finance

FFIEC Business Continuity Planning provides the most detailed guidance on emergency communications planning and also suggests contacting a designated media spokesperson for the company if required.

"Communication planning should identify alternate communication channels to utilize during a disaster, such as pagers, cell phones, e-mail, or two-way radios. An emergency telephone number, e-mail address, and physical address list should be provided to employees to assist in communication efforts during a disaster. The list should provide all alternate numbers since one or more telecommunications systems could be unavailable. Additionally, the phone list should provide numbers for vendors, emergency services, transportation, and regulatory agencies. Wallet cards, Internet postings, and calling trees are possible ways to distribute information to employees. Further, institutions should establish reporting or calling locations to assist them in accounting for all personnel following a disaster.

Financial institutions should consider developing an awareness program to let customers, service providers, and regulators know how to contact the institution if normal communication channels are not in operation. The plan should also designate personnel who will communicate with the media, government, vendors, and other companies and provide for the type of information to be communicated" (FFIEC Business Continuity Planning Pg. 14, E8).

General Guidance

CobiT mentions emergency communications as being part of the business continuity plan contents but does not provide details for procedures or alternate modes of communication. **COSO** provides the same information but does not put it in terms of business continuity.

From regulation to reality – sure signs you are complying

In the event of a disaster, you will need to communicate. Unfortunately, you are not Princess Lea, and you don't have R2D2 to run around the galaxy looking for Obi-wan Kenobi when disaster strikes. There are no droids to do your dirty work. Instead, you will have to use much more primitive forms of communication.

The first step is to define alternate communications channels that are to be used in case of disruption. Some alternate solutions are:

- Pagers
- Cell phones
- Email
- Two-way radios

Provide employees with a list of emergency phone numbers, physical and email addresses, and other aids to assist in emergency communications. Include plenty of alternate numbers, because you never know what communications will be disrupted in the disaster. The list is not complete without numbers for vendors, emergency services and transportation. Require staff to report to a calling center so that each person can be accounted for and can await instruction.

How do you write a business continuity plan?

We have reached the all important step of planning and writing your business continuity plan. This is the document that will lead you to recovery in the event of a disaster. This is your guide to success in an emergency. You have spent the preceding steps gathering information and creating certain components of the plan. Now, it is time to apply this knowledge and create the document itself. The following control objective is step number one in writing the plan:

> *The organization will prepare and document a business continuity plan. Plan contents must include all continuity planning strategies and procedures previously summarized. Any additional response, recovery, resumption procedures, or controls specific to the entity's business functions must also be documented. The plan should specifically address any scenarios that might trigger its implementation, and be written in a manner that makes it easy to execute.*

Writing a plan is not as hard as it may seem. You will use all the information you have gathered and arrange it by priority. We are here to help you, so read on for tips to writing a business continuity plan.

Guidance from the regulations and standards

Public Companies

The **AICPA Suitable Trust Services Criteria** specifies that disaster recovery and contingency plans must be documented.

NASD/NYSE

Rules 3510 and **446** call for the creation of a business continuity plan. The contents of the plan are consistent with the strategies mentioned by the rules. In addition, the rules require each member to communicate to customers how prompt access to funds and securities will be arranged in the event the member can no longer conduct business.

Banking/Finance

FFIEC Business Continuity Planning Pg. 10 calls for the BCP to be:

1. *Written and disseminated so that various groups of personnel can implement it in a timely manner;*

2. *Specific regarding what conditions should prompt implementation of the plan;*

3. *Specific regarding what immediate steps should be taken during a disruption;*

4. *Flexible to respond to unanticipated threat scenarios and changing internal conditions;*

5. *Focused on how to get the business up and running in the event that a specific facility or function is disrupted, rather than the precise nature of the disruption; and*

6. *Effective in minimizing the service disruptions and financial loss.*

Healthcare and Life Sciences

HIPAA calls for a data backup, disaster recovery, and emergency mode operation plan all with respect to ensuring the continuity of protected health information.

Credit Card

VISA CISP calls for an "incident response plan" to be used in the event of a system breach.

US Federal Security

NIST 800-53 and the National Strategy to Secure Cyberspace both call for written contingency plans. NIST is more specific about contents than the National Strategy is, and lists many of the continuity strategies as additional control objectives. NIST 800-53 § CP-2 explains:

The organization is to implement a contingency plan for the information system addressing contingency roles, responsibilities, assigned individuals with contact information and activities associated with restoring the system after a disruption or failure. The plan should be reviewed and approved by designated individuals and copies distributed to key personnel.

NIST Special Publications

As discussed in Business Continuity plan strategies, **NIST 800-14** calls for the following to be in the written plan:

Emergency response: The initial actions to be taken that will protect lives and limit damage should be documented.

Recovery: Plan steps for continued support of critical functions.

Resumption: Determine what is required in order to return to normal operations. The relationship between recovery and resumption is important. The longer it takes to resume normal operations, the longer the organization will have to operate in recovery mode.

Implementation: Includes documenting of procedures, training employees, and make general preparations. Many procedures are ongoing.

International Standards Organization

ISO 17799 § 11.1.3 & 11.1.4 explain:

Plans should be developed to maintain or restore business operations in the required time scales following interruption to, or failure of, critical business processes. The business continuity planning process should consider the following:

a) *identification and agreement of all responsibilities and emergency procedures;*

b) *implementation of emergency procedures to allow recovery and restoration in required time-scales. Particular attention needs to be given to the assessment of external business dependencies and the contracts in place;*

c) *documentation of agreed procedures and processes;*

d) *appropriate education of staff in the agreed emergency procedures and processes including crisis management;*

e) *testing and updating of the plans.*

The planning process should focus on the required business objectives, e.g. restoring of specific services to customers in an acceptable amount of time. The services and resources that will enable this to occur should be considered, including staffing, non-information processing resources, as well as fallback arrangements for information processing facilities.

General Guidance

CobiT, and the **ISF Standard for Good Practices of Information Security**, call for a written business continuity plan. CobiT is more narrowly focused on an "IT continuity plan" but does mention that it is part of a larger business continuity plan. Much in the same way, the ISF Standard breaks its business continuity plan down into contingency plans depending on the service affected.

CobiT 3 § DS 4.3 calls for the IT continuity plan to contain the following items:

1. *Guidelines on how to use the plan*

2. *Emergency procedures to ensure staff safety*

3. *Response procedures to ensure the business returns to the state it was in before disaster*

4. *Recovery procedures to ensure the business returns to the state it was in before disaster*

5. *procedures to safeguard and reconstruct the home site*

6. *Co-ordination procedures with authorities*

7. *Communication procedures with stakeholders, employees, key customers, critical suppliers, stockholders and management*

8. *Critical information on continuity teams, affected staff, customers, suppliers, public authorities and media.*

The **ISF Standard for Good Practices of Information Security** § CI6.1.1 & CI6.1.4 calls for the plan to specify:

- *conditions for its invocation,*
- *the critical timescales associated with the business application supported by the installation,*
- *a schedule of key tasks to be carried out,*
- *procedures in sufficient detail so that they can be followed by individuals who do not normally carry them out,*
- *information security controls applied during the recovery process.*

All the layers of the onion have been exposed; all the components of the BCP have been addressed. So, what do you do with all the information now that you've collected it? You turn it into the business continuity plan.

Remember what we said at the very beginning of this chapter. Systems continuity is preparation. You have waded through ten steps to prepare for writing the BCP. Now it's time for the easy part-- the writing.

Remember the four basic components of the BCP: emergency planning, recovery, resumption, and implementation. These are the root of all components of your plan. We have created a list of things we think should be in your plan, based on the previous ten steps and on these four concepts. The plan should include:

- A documentation of the specific conditions prompting implementation.

- A documentation of the specific steps to be taken during a disruption.

- A documentation of emergency communication procedures,

- Alternate site procedures,

- Staff training procedures

- Critical function and asset procedures.

- Recovery procedures ensuring the organization returns to a functional and productive state.

- Procedures to safeguard and reconstruct the home site.

- Specific plan testing procedures.

- Emergency procedures that ensure the safety of personnel.

- Any additional response, resumption, and recovery procedures, or controls specific to the organization's critical business functions.

- Any other critical information concerning recovery teams, staff, customers, suppliers and media.

Write the plan in a manner that makes it easy to execute. Ensure that the plan focuses on how to get the business up and running in the event that a specific facility or function is disrupted, rather than the precise nature of the disruption. The plan should be effective in minimizing service disruptions and financial loss. Tailoring the plan to each potential problem instead of generalizing makes it easier to use in the event of emergency.

How do you minimize continuity requirements?

When you hike out into the wilderness with everything you need for survival on your back, you learn how to distinguish what you need from what you don't. Every pound you carry slows your progress, so minimizing your gear to the bare minimum will help you succeed in your trek. Similarly, continuity requirements are also burdensome. They can cause a slowing of the recovery process, which is not beneficial to an organization that needs to recovery to continue operating. Therefore, the organization will follow this control objective to minimize continuity requirements:

> *The organization will attempt to minimize its business continuity requirements through specific guidelines and procedures. In so doing, the organizations will consider personnel, software, hardware, facilities, equipment, forms and furniture.*

Take a look at this section for help with minimizing continuity requirements.

Guidance from the regulations and standards

Banking/Finance

While the **FFIEC Business Continuity Planning handbook** does not call for procedures to minimize business continuity requirements, it urges organizations to create a business continuity plan containing specifics. This is effectively a way of minimizing requirements.

General Guidance

CobiT is the only general standard that calls for a minimization of business continuity requirements.

CobiT § DS 4.4 calls on IT management to establish procedures and guidelines for minimizing the continuity requirements with regard to personnel, facilities, hardware, software, equipment, forms, supplies, and furniture.

From regulation to reality – sure signs you are complying

So what does it mean to minimize continuity requirements? Minimizing continuity requirements is focusing your business continuity policies so that there is nothing unnecessary in your continuity plan. You will focus your energy on what is important and needed, and not on insignificant steps, policies, or procedures. Think of it like the toolbox you keep in the back of you car for emergencies. The flashlight, flares, spare cell phone battery and jumper cables are all very helpful in case you experience problems.

Minimizing continuity requirements can be implemented in two ways. First, be specific about procedures, policies, assets, personnel, and facilities when you create your plan. Don't generalize or make unfounded groupings or classifications. Second, minimize your requirements to those that are directly necessary and imperative to recovery. If you do this, the implementation of the business continuity plan will be smoother, and will aid in better communication, and faster, more efficient recovery.

Are you maintaining your business continuity plan?

Maintaining your business continuity plan is as important as maintaining your '79 Stingray. It is detrimental to the life of the car, or the plan, to ignore the pressing need to do maintenance. Therefore, the control objective for this section is:

> The organization's business continuity plan grows and changes with each new or modified business requirement. To keep up with these changes, the organization will establish plan maintenance procedures for the plan itself in order to maintain pace with overall organizational changes.

Let's take a look at the regulations for guidance with this section.

Guidance from the regulations and standards

Public Companies

The **AICPA Suitable Trust Services Criteria** calls for annual testing, review and updating of the disaster recovery and contingency plans. It also requires that any testing results and changes be reported to a management committee. The criteria further requires that all critical personnel hold current versions of the plan, both onsite and off-site.

NASD/NYSE

Rules 3510(b) and **446(b)** require that the business continuity plan be reviewed on an annual basis and updated to reflect any changes in the member's operations, structure, business or location.

Banking/Finance

The **FFIEC Business Continuity Planning handbook** covers all aspects of business continuity plan maintenance. The standard also requires a test plan for each business continuity testing method and provides examples of methods to employ.

Healthcare and Life Sciences

HIPAA requires periodic testing and revision of contingency plans, but does not specifically call for annual testing.

Credit Card

The **VISA CISP** requires that the incident response plan is tested annually and appropriate training is given to personnel with responsibilities concerning security breaches.

US Federal Security

FISCAM calls for business continuity training of critical personnel.

The **National Strategy to Secure Cyberspace** requires that government agencies' contingency plans be tested.

NIST Special Publications

NIST 800-53 requires that government agencies' contingency plans be tested. NIST is the most specific standard, calling for annual testing and updates, as well as simulations of recovery and resumption as part of the testing process.

International Standards Organization

ISO 17799 calls for change management procedures to govern the maintenance of business continuity plans.

General Guidance

The **ISF Standard for Good Practices of Information Security** is the only document that requires annual testing and simulations, although CobiT implies this. Most of the standards also call for business continuity plan training and distribution to all authorized and critical personnel.

CobiT 4 DS4.4 recommends encouraging IT management to define and execute change control procedures to ensure that the IT continuity plan is kept up to date and continually reflects actual business requirements. DS4.5 requires organizations to regularly test their IT continuity plan to ensure it is effective and all systems can be recovered in appropriate amounts of time. DS4.6 asks that organizations train their staff in carrying out the IT continuity plan so they are prepared in the event it must be used. DS4.7 suggests that an organization distribute its IT continuity plan so everyone in the organization is aware of it.

United Kingdom

BS 15000-2 calls for service continuity testing, training and distribution.

From regulation to reality – sure signs you are complying

The plan you create will not update itself whenever organizational changes occur. That means you need to institute change management procedures to ensure the plan remains in accordance with any new or modified business requirements. Test the plan annually, including simulations of business disruptions or disasters and participation by all critical personnel and affected parties. Train personnel and management in awareness, response, recovery and resumption prior to any testing or simulations.

Whenever there is significant modification to the organization, or introduction of new personnel, business functions, requirements or locations, update the plan. Management is responsible for reviewing test results and recommended updates before they are enacted. Each time the plan is updated, the new modified plan should be distributed to all personnel. Periodically test the plan, to ensure it is functional, and that each employee not only knows their role, but is familiar with performing that role.

What Do You Do After a Disaster or Disruption?

There are steps to take after a disaster is over and recovery is complete, besides enjoying cocktails and sighs of relief. The organization will learn from each incident, because the lessons are the most valuable. Therefore, the control objective for this section is:

> *Upon successful recovery and resumption following a disaster or disruption of business, management and appropriate personnel will assess the adequacy of the BCP and update it accordingly.*

Take a look at the regulations and standards for help with this section.

Guidance from the regulations and standards

Public Companies

Although the **AICPA Suitable Trust Services Criteria** calls for annual updates of the plan, it does not specifically address assessment and revision following an actual business disruption or disaster.

Banking/Finance

FFIEC Business Continuity Planning calls for updates to the business continuity plan but does not address wrap-up procedures following a successful recovery.

General Guidance

CobiT specifically calls for wrap-up procedures upon successful resumption of business functions following a disaster.

CobiT 4 DS4.10 says that once an organization resumes IT functionality after a disaster, continuity plans should be updated to include any modifications that may be necessary as a result of handling the disaster.

From regulation to reality — sure signs you are complying

You always have a lesson to learn. Life presents us with lessons in the most difficult times. Some would say, the harder a fall, the more valuable the lesson. It's clear that surviving a disruption or disaster will teach you many things about your organization, your business continuity program, and how to improve both. It is because of this that we recommend that whenever there is an event where you have instituted even a portion of your business continuity principles, you take the time to reflect.

Management will set some time aside to collect all the information surrounding the event. How did the organization handle the event? Were the emergency communications working? Were the right personnel on hand? Were the critical business functions and resources protected? Go through each part of your continuity plan and assess its value in the situation. Update the portions of the plan that did not seem to work so well. Highlight those that did to ensure that they are repeated in the future. This process will not only help you become more familiar with the workings or your organization, but will teach you how to handle delicate situations with ease and confidence. Knowing what works and what doesn't before the next incident will improve your skills as a leader and help the cohesion of your organization under pressure.

Should You Obtain Insurance?

Insurance is a necessity for any organization. Your job is to decide what kind of insurance meets your needs. The control objective for this section is:

> *In order to protect organizational assets in the case of disaster, the organization will purchase insurance for any loss that cannot be prevented.*

In this section we take a look at methods you can use to choose insurance that's right for you.

Guidance from the regulations and standards

Banking/Finance

FFIEC Business Continuity Planning bases the decision for insurance coverage on the BIA and emphasizes that insurance is "by no means a substitute for the BCP" and suggests that a company assess needs for both. The **Sound Practices of Operational Risk** primarily discusses insurance with respect to risk assessment, but does mention its applicability to natural disasters.

The following is what the **FFIEC Information Security handbook**, Pgs. 75-77 has to say on insurance:

"Insurance is commonly used to recoup losses from risks that cannot be completely prevented. Generally, insurance coverage is obtained for risks that cannot be entirely controlled, yet could represent a significant potential for financial loss or other disastrous consequences. The decision to obtain insurance should be based on the probability and degree of loss identified during the BIA. Financial institutions should determine potential exposure for various types of disasters and review the insurance options available to ensure appropriate insurance coverage is provided. Management should know the limits and coverage detailed in insurance policies to make sure coverage is appropriate given the risk profile of the institution. Institutions should perform an annual insurance review to ensure the level and types of coverage are commercially reasonable, and consistent with any legal, management, and board requirements. Also, institutions should create and retain a comprehensive hardware and software inventory list in a secure off-site location in order to facilitate the claims process.

Financial institutions should be aware of the limitations of insurance. Insurance can reimburse an institution for some or all of the financial losses incurred as the result of a disaster or other significant event. However, insurance is by no means a substitute for an effective BCP, since its primary objective is not the recovery of the business. For example, insurance cannot reimburse an institution for damage to its reputation."

International Standards Organization

ISO 17799 includes insurance selection in the business continuity process.

General Guidance

CobiT address insurance selection as part of risk assessment.

From regulation to reality – sure signs you are complying

Whether or not to obtain insurance is a silly question, and no doubt the majority of organizations will want to procure insurance. The more important question is: what kind of insurance should you obtain? Insurance is necessary to recoup for losses that cannot be entirely controlled, or risks that cannot be prevented. These risks could present serious losses, and insurance can help provide the organization with means to recover from those losses.

The BIA and risk assessment provide the basis for deciding if your organization needs insurance, how much and what kind. Insurance selection and coverage should take into account what strategies of the BCP may compensate for the need for insurance, but should not override any elements of the business continuity process. Reviews of insurance coverage should take place periodically, to ensure that if the business continuity plan has been updated, the insurance is still consistent with the needs of the organization. Finally, hardware and software inventories should be maintained at off-site facilities, in anticipation of any claims.

Your organization should be aware of the limits of insurance. Insurance can reimburse an organization for some or all of the financial losses incurred as the result of a disaster or other significant event. But, insurance does not take the place of a well-planned BCP. The BCP plans for recovery of the business, not just financial repair, and insurance is no substitute for total preparation.

Systems Design and Development

The Main Thing

Have you defined roles and responsibilities for your project management?

Project management is vital to the success of any project. Well thought-out roles and responsibilities for workers as well as goals and deadlines make it easy to figure out where your project is at, where it needs to be, and how easy it will be to reach the finished product. It also makes it easier to figure out who to blame if something goes wrong. Just kidding! The control objective for this section is:

> *To ensure strong project management, the organization will endeavor to define and clearly document job roles and their corresponding responsibilities.*

Clear role and responsibility definitions help avoid confusion among workers regarding their daily tasks and unnecessary overlapping or duplication of work.

Guidance from the regulations and standards

Banking/Finance

The **FFIEC Development and Acquisition** handbook defines general project management roles and responsibilities, from senior management to IT and audit personnel – roles are clearly delineated and defined.

FFIEC Development and Acquisition Pgs. 5-6 lists primary roles and responsibilities including:

- *"Corporate Management – Corporate managers are responsible for approving major projects and ensuring projects support, not drive, business objectives.*

- *Senior Management – Senior managers are responsible for*

- *approving and promoting projects within their authority and ensuring adequate resources are available to complete projects.*

- *Technology Steering Committee – Technology steering committees are responsible for establishing and approving major project deliverables and coordinating interdepartmental activities. The committees often include the project manager, a board member, and executives from all organizational departments. Large organizations often establish project management offices to coordinate multiple projects.*

- *Project Manager – Project managers are responsible for ensuring projects support business objectives, project goals and expectations are clearly defined, and project tasks are identified, scheduled, and completed. Project managers are also responsible for monitoring and reporting a project's status to senior management.*

- *Project Sponsor – Project sponsors are responsible for developing support within user departments, defining deliverables, and providing end users for testing purposes. Project sponsors often provide financial resources to a project.*

- *Technology Department – The technology department is responsible for maintaining the technology resources used by project teams and assisting in the testing and implementation phases. Department members should assist in defining the scope of a project by identifying database and network resources and constraints.*

- *Quality Assurance – Quality assurance personnel are responsible for validating project assumptions and ensuring the quality of phase deliverables. Quality assurance personnel should be independent of the development process and use predefined standards and procedures to assess deliverables throughout project life cycles.*

- *User Departments – User departments assist project managers,*

- *designers, and programmers in defining and testing functional*

- *requirements (system features). End-user involvement throughout a project is critical to ensuring accurate definitions and adequate tests. Large projects may include a subject matter expert or data analyst responsible for communicating user information and functional requirements to project teams.*

- *Auditors – Auditors assist user departments, project managers, and system designers in identifying system control requirements and testing the controls during development and after implementation.*

- *Security Managers – Security managers assist user departments, project managers, and system designers in identifying security requirements and testing the features during development and after implementation."*

US Federal Security

Though a few government regulations address project management (**FISMA, Clinger-Cohen Act, FISCAM**), they do not directly address project management roles and responsibilities.

Records Management

Records management standards, most notably **DIRKS**, define roles and responsibilities with respect to managing a recordkeeping project.

General Guidelines

CobiT and the ISF standard call for definition of roles and responsibilities within an organization's project management framework. CobiT defines specific responsibilities throughout its project management standards control objectives rather than as one control objective.

CobiT 4 PO10.3 says that roles, responsibilities and accountabilities for all employees involved in an IT project should be set out clearly.

From regulation to reality – sure signs you are complying

At a high level, it is best to develop methods for constructing project management roles and responsibilities. An ideal method is to write up a document containing the expectations you have of employees. This will act as a useful framework for your employees when they need to assign tasks. Think about how detailed roles and responsibilities need to be as well as the scope of assignments. Questions you might consider asking yourself are 'how detailed do assigned roles and responsibilities need to be for a project?' 'what is the scope of assignments, does everybody get an individual task, or do you just assign a set of tasks to a group leader and allow her to divide the work among her workers?'

Depending upon the size of your organization and the level of detail required for various projects, the answers may vary. You may even find that there are different sets of rules for different size projects. Perhaps a small team can be assigned tasks individually, while a large team will be broken into groups that receive roles and responsibilities that way.

What are your standards for project management?

Every building is different, but they all have a few things in common, such as bathrooms, empty rectangular spaces for work or furniture, etc. Unless we're talking about a shack, in which case all bets are off. Barring the shack, the idea of repeating rooms in buildings is one we can use for project management, along with the following control objective:

> *Every project the organization undertakes will be governed by a generalized set of project management standards. These standards indicate the structure projects will take, how to assign roles and responsibilities and seek funding and approval for your work.*

By creating generalized standards you ensure that even if special changes need to be made, all your projects follow the same basic outline. This makes for greater efficiency and ease of understanding when management looks over work schedules.

Guidance from the regulations and standards

Banking/Finance

FFIEC Development and Acquisitions calls for developing project management standards, most specifically for defining a project management methodology, testing and documentation standards.

Records Management

DIRKS calls for creation a project plans and accompanied training but does not explicitly state the need for project management standards.

General Guidelines

CobiT calls for project management standards, beginning with a project management methodology – CobiT is the only general standard that outlines each standard specifically.

CobiT 4 PO10.1 calls for creation of a program management framework. The framework should have provisions making it possible to identify, define, evaluate, prioritize select, initiate, manage and control projects. PO10.2 calls for a project management framework. This framework should make it possible to define the scope and boundaries of each project as well as how to approach each project. Topics to cover are initiating, planning, executing, controlling and closing project stages. PO10.8 says organizations should define responsibilities, relationships, authorities and performance criteria as part of project standards. PO10.5 requests that organizations determine what a project will cover and then document this. The documentation should be provided to stakeholders to help them understand the scope of the project. PO10.6 says that before initiating any phase of a project, it should be formally approved and communicated to all stakeholders. Approval should be based on review of the deliverables for the prior phase. PO10.12 requires organizations to identify project planning assurance tasks that provide assurance that internal controls and security features are up to appropriate standards. Care should be taken to ensure all tasks are completed. PO10.9 tells us that organizations should conduct risk management for each project. Work should include eliminating and minimizing risks associated with the project. AI7.2 suggests developing test plans. These cover test preparation, training requirements, installation or update of a defined test environment, planning/performing/documenting/retaining test cases, error handling and correction, and formal approval. AI7.1 says organizations should train staff in accordance with defined training and implementation plans for the organization.

From regulation to reality – sure signs you are complying

A repeatable project management structure makes it easier for employees to plan since they will be familiar with what is expected in the outline for each project. The following should be required for all projects:

- Project management framework and methodology

- User department participation in project initiation

- Project team membership and responsibilities

- Project definition

- Project and project phase approval

- Project master plan

- Planning of assurance methods

- Formal project risk management

- Test plans

- Training plans

- Post-implementation review plans

Decide what order these requirements need to be completed in and who needs to be involved with each part of the process. If possible, write it out. It is always best to have a document to refer to so confusion may be avoided.

Do you have quality assurance standards for project management?

All the project planning in the world won't mean anything if you don't have clear cut quality assurance standards. What is high quality work and what isn't might seem obvious to you, but rest assured, someone else has a different interpretation. A great example of how easy it is to have a miscommunication can be found with colors. Say a manager tells his employees to make sure they bring back their documents written up on blue paper. Everyone nods, and one person returns with primary blue documents, someone else comes back with turquoise, they all did what was requested, but they didn't get it right, because it turns out the manager was thinking of periwinkle blue. This example pertains to all kinds of group work, but it's never more important than when it comes to quality assurance. Huge problems can occur especially with third parties, where they are under contract. If the contract doesn't specify what you mean by high quality, then it's open to interpretation, fights and possibly a lawsuit if they turn in something you're extremely unhappy with. Use the following control objective when determining how to deal with quality assurance standards:

> The organization will assemble a thorough set of standards stating what the organization expects from workers and what it won't stand for in terms of quality assurance. These should be documented and clearly communicated to all staff involved in a project. If possible each worker should receive a copy of the standards to refer to.

There are many ways to select standards, and if you are working to be compliant with a particular regulation, be sure to check what kinds of quality assurance rules it offers. The quality assurance standards we'll discuss here are the most comprehensive set of standards around.

Guidance from the regulations and standards

Banking/Finance

FFIEC Development and Acquisitions calls for quality assurance standards, but does not define all listed measures specifically. FFIEC calls for a system development life cycle methodology separately from QA standards and offers alternative methodologies as well.

FFIEC Development and Acquisition Pgs. 9-10 state that management should address quality assurance standards such as:

- *"Commitment – Successful projects require commitment from all involved parties. Senior managers should adequately support and promote projects throughout an organization to enhance organizational acceptance of a project. End users should assist in defining and testing functional requirements and project teams should efficiently complete tasks. All parties should clearly define their expectations and effectively communicate throughout a project.*

- *Management's failure to implement or support quality assurance programs decreases an organization's ability to detect project weaknesses and programming errors quickly. The later weaknesses and errors are detected, the more difficult and costly they are to correct.*

- *Completeness – Each phase within a project life cycle includes procedures to follow and items to deliver. Therefore, quality assurance programs should parallel all phases of the life cycle. For example, the project initiation phase includes the presentation of a business case, the request for desired functional requirements, and the identification of interconnected system components. Quality assurance personnel should verify the justification for a project, the necessity of requested functional features, and the accuracy of system connections before projects move into the project planning phase. Audit and compliance employees should assist quality assurance personnel verify compliance with internal and external project requirements.*

- *Scalability – Projects vary in size and complexity. Quality assurance standards should match project characteristics and risks.*

- *Measurability – Organizations cannot evaluate a project's success accurately unless they assess results against defined expectations.*

- *Therefore, quality assurance personnel should assess the quality of products and processes against measurable standards, metrics, and expectations.*

- *Tracking – Project personnel should properly record, report, and monitor problems to ensure effective problem resolution.*

- *Independence – Audit and quality assurance personnel should be independent of the project they are reviewing."*

Records Management

DIRKS calls for the development of a SDLC and program documentation standards with respect to developing recordkeeping systems, but does not otherwise directly address quality assurance standards for project management.

NIST Special Publications

NIST 800-53 calls for the development of a SDLC but does not otherwise directly address quality assurance standards for project management.

General Guidelines

CobiT details all the above measures of quality assurance standards, including the development of a SDLC as a commitment to quality. The ISF standard calls for general quality assurance standards in addition to a SDLC but does not lists more specific measures.

CobiT 4 PO10.10 says organizations should prepare a quality management plan describing the quality project system and how it will be implemented. PO8.6 requires an organization to define, plan and implement measurements necessary for monitoring compliance with the implemented quality management system.

From regulation to reality – sure signs you are complying

There are eighteen different areas you want to consider and document for top-notch quality assurance:

- General quality plan
- Quality assurance approach
- Quality assurance planning
- Quality assurance review of adherence to IT standards
- System quality assurance plan
- Systems development life cycle (SDLC) methodology
- Coordination and communication
- Acquisition and maintenance framework for the technology infrastructure
- Third-party implementer relationships
- Program documentation standards
- Program testing standards
- System testing standards
- Parallel/Pilot testing
- System testing documentation

- Quality assurance evaluation of adherence to development standards
- Quality assurance review of the achievement of IT objectives
- Quality metrics
- Reports of quality assurance reviews

General Quality Plan

Area number one is a general plan for how quality assurance is going to work throughout your organization. Management should create a quality plan that takes into account the long-range plans for IT and the organization. The plan should be regularly reviewed and updated as necessary.

Quality Assurance Approach

The next item is a quality assurance approach. Develop a standard set of activities to conduct to determine whether the quality of a project is appropriate. This set should be documented, with each activity and outcome expectations described. The standards should tie back into the general quality plan constructed by method. Each activity should do something to help achieve the goals and maintain the philosophy of quality assurance in the general quality plan.

Quality Assurance Planning

Quality assurance planning is where you figure out when to do quality assurance work. How will it fit into project schedules? How much time do you need for it, what kind of resources are necessary? Answering these questions and coming up with a procedure for estimating the answers in a way that is consistently accurate is what quality assurance planning is all about.

Quality Assurance Review of Adherence to IT Standards and Procedures

Part of good quality assurance is ensuring that work going on is compatible with existing systems and compliance requirements. Hence the quality assurance review of adherence to IT standards and procedures. This process should be done by quality assurance personnel. They will go through different groups of people and ascertain whether work is being carried out in methods compliant with the organization's IT standards.

System Development Life Cycle Methodology

To maintain quality for developing, acquiring, implementing and maintaining computerized information systems and related technology, management should define and implement IT standards. Because these processes can be complex, a complete system development life cycle (SDLC) methodology should be created detailing how to go about each of these activities to guarantee the highest quality results. The methodology should include defining an approach to dealing with major changes to existing technology. Provisions for periodically reviewing and updating the SDLC should also be present to ensure it remains current and useful.

Coordination and Communication

To prevent the possibility of a high number of irate customers, management should implement a process that allows customers and IT system implementers to communicate and coordinate their actions with one another. The final process for this should be based on the SDLC methodology and the general quality plan so that it is effective.

Acquisition and Maintenance Framework for the Technology Infrastructure

To assure you have a high-quality technology infrastructure, create a general framework that describes how new aspects of the infrastructure will be acquired and how existing infrastructure will be maintained. The documentation for the framework should include steps to be followed for programming, documenting, testing, parameter setting, maintaining and applying fixes.

Third-Party Implementer Relationships

Good working relationships with third parties are important to your organization. The best way to have a good relationship is to be clear and up front about your goals and expectations. This is why management should implement a process that provides acceptance criteria, handling of changes, problems during development, user roles, facilities, tools, software, standards and procedures for work to be done by the third party.

Program Documentation Standards

Standards must be set so that for each program, the documentation follows the same format. This will make it easier to review and add to the programs later as well as organize and store the information. Program documentation standards should be included in the SDLC.

Program Testing Standards

To ensure consistency of quality, testing standards should be set for programs. Your organization's SDLC should include standards that cover test requirements, verification, documentation and retention for each software unit as well as aggregated programs created as part of every information system development or modification project.

System Testing Standards

Along with program testing standards, system testing standards should be created and maintained to ensure quality. These standards should cover test requirements, verification, documentation and retention for the testing of the total system. All this information should be put into the SDLC.

Parallel/Pilot Testing

If parallel and/or pilot testing of new and existing systems is to be conducted, the reasons for conducting such tests should be set out in the SDLC.

System Testing Documentation

Any testing of any system needs to be documented. This is key for audits, which will involve an auditor reviewing the documentation to look for any weaknesses in the system, or problems with the way a test was conducted that may need to be fixed.

Quality Assurance Evaluation of Adherence to Development Standards

Once your organization's quality assurance team has completed a review of work, their approach to the task should be reviewed along with their findings to be sure the team adheres to the goals and policies set out for such work in the SDLC.

Quality Assurance Review of the Achievement of IT Objectives

When the quality assurance team is reviewing work, they should also review the extent to which other employees maintained IT objectives while carrying out activities involving systems and application development.

Quality Metrics

A quantitative system should be employed in measuring quality of activities within your organization. This type of system makes it easier to figure out if quality goals have been achieved or not.

Reports of Quality Assurance Reviews

Once quality assurance reviews are complete, they should be written up as formal reports and submitted to the managers of user departments and the IT function.

These eighteen areas are all elements you need to consider when creating processes, documentation of processes and a system development lifecycle methodology. Each of these items will improve your ability to guarantee high quality finished products. Since much of the quality process calls for documenting work, it will also enable you to figure out how to do the work better the next time around.

Have you conducted a preliminary investigation for your project?

Before you undertake the implementation of a project, investigate it. You don't have to go all out and do it Dragnet style, but something along the lines of our control objective is definitely in order:

> *The organization will conduct preliminary investigations for projects in order to determine if they are feasible and useful.*

Investigating a project before undertaking it saves you time and money. With a little bit of research, you can spot the next big success for your organization as well as the next big flop. Read on to see what investigative measures you can take for your projects.

Guidance from the regulations and standards

Banking/Finance

FFIEC Development and Acquisitions calls for an "initiation phase" that includes consideration of functional requirements and cost/benefit analyses in addition to the preliminary investigation.

FFIEC Development and Acquisitions Pgs. 17-18 calls for the initiation phase to begin when an opportunity to add, improve, or correct a system is identified and formally requested through the presentation of a business case. The case should describe a proposal's purpose, identify expected benefits, and explain how the proposed system supports one of the organization's business strategies. It should also identify alternative solutions and detail as many informational, functional, and network requirements as possible.

The case is useful to management because they can then reject a proposal if need be before allocating resources for a feasibility study. Part of reviewing the case should involve determining a proposal's validity and whether the equipment recommended for the project is all mandatory. Once approval for a proposal is obtained, the next phase is to conduct a feasibility study.

Records Management

ISO 15489 and **DIRKS** both call for an extensive preliminary investigation before any initiation of a recordkeeping project within an organization.

NIST Special Publications

NIST 800-14 also calls for a definition of scope with respect to the security aspects of the project.

General Guidelines

Though **CobiT** does not specifically call for a preliminary investigation, elements of its project management standards (see appropriate summary) call for the same requirements. Project definition defines scope, while approval considers the feasibility of the project.

From regulation to reality – sure signs you are complying

You conduct preliminary investigations for projects to get a handle on what needs to be done and what kind of equipment you need to do it. Whoever is in charge of managing a project should be responsible for the investigation. The basic goals of the job are to collect enough information from document sources pertinent to the project (such as strategic plans, business process re-engineering, risk assessments, policies, reports) and use them to define the scope of the project.

Alongside scoping, a cost/benefit analysis may also be conducted. This analysis enables you to find out whether the project is worth doing in the first place.

Have you conducted an analysis of business activities?

Business activities if left unattended, have a special way of becoming more and more inefficient and cumbersome over time until finally they resemble dinosaurs, lumbering along, doing little else except using up resources and waiting for something catastrophic to knock them out of existence. However, business activities that are regularly analyzed for efficiency and usefulness versus how much they cost to do are likely to stay lively. If they don't, you'll weed them out, possibly along with the person responsible for doing those activities. For best analysis results, we recommend the following control objective:

> *The organization will regularly analyze their business activities to determine whether they are necessary for business operations and whether they are carried out as smoothly as possible.*

Analyzing your organization's business activities lets you pinpoint what you do effectively, and what needs some patching up. In this section we'll take a look at what makes business activity analysis so important.

Guidance from the regulations and standards

Public Companies

Public standards do not directly address the analysis of business activities as part of project management but do mention the auditor's role in understanding a business activities, functions and transactions with respect to financial activities.

Banking/Finance

FFIEC Development and Acquisitions requires a consideration of business goals and objectives but does not explicitly require an analysis of business activity – this is covered in the creation of a high-level IT strategic plan as part of defining objectives and leadership (see appropriate summary).

Records Management

The **DIRKS** methodology (part B) calls for an analysis of business activity and everything it entails, going into further detail for each control objective, and is also reflected (though less detailed) in **ISO 15489**.

In **ISO 15489-1**, analysis of business activity is defined as collecting information from documentary sources and interviews, identifying and documenting each business function, activity and transaction and establishing a hierarchy of them – a business classification system that identifies and documents the flow of business processes and the transactions which comprise them.

ISO 15489-2 §3.2.3 calls for organizations to develop a conceptual model of what an organization does and how it does it. This includes how records relate to both the organization's business and business processes. It contributes decisions in subsequent steps about creation, capture, control, storage and disposition of records, and about access to them.

"An analysis of business activity and processes will provide an understanding of the relationship between the organization's business and its records.

The products coming from this step may include

a) *documentation describing the organization's business and business processes,*

b) *a business classification scheme that shows the organization's functions, activities and transactions in a hierarchical relationship, and*

c) *a map of the organization's business processes that shows the points at which records are produced or received as products of business activity.*

The analysis provides the basis for developing records management tools, which may include

a) *a thesaurus of terms to control the language for titling and indexing records in a specific business context, and*

b) *a disposition authority that defines the retention periods and consequent disposition actions for records.*

The analysis will also help in identifying and implementing appropriate metadata strategies and in formally assigning responsibilities for keeping records."

General Guidelines

Though general standards do not directly address analysis of business activity as part of project management, **CobiT**, and the **ISF Standard of Good Practices for Information Security** call for an analysis of business activity as part of the initial establishment of need and definition of objectives and should be incorporated here.

CobiT 4 PO10.4 says organizations should obtain commitment and participation from stakeholders in the definition and execution of IT projects.

From regulation to reality — sure signs you are complying

Part of initial project planning includes defining goals and objectives. This is never more important than when you're thinking and planning for your organization as a whole. What kinds of activities does your business conduct? Are all of them useful? What is the ultimate purpose of each activity or groups of certain activities? If you know these things, you know whether your business and your projects are headed in the right direction.

It's also important to look outside your organization. Don't just figure out where your business needs to go, figure out where your customers need to go as well. What relationship do your customers and stakeholders have with the projects within your organization? What projects are most and least important? Answering these questions improves efficiency by allowing you to accurately prioritize the most crucial work above other activities to achieve the biggest payoffs first.

Did you identify all the requirements for your project?

Every good project defines all of its requirements up front. You might find out you need something extra later, but the fewer the number of surprises that crop up during a project, the better. You can help yourself avoid surprises by keeping in mind the following control objective for project requirements:

> There are four basic categories of requirements that the organization will plan for before working on a project. They are: Functional requirements, Recordkeeping requirements, Relevant sources of information pertinent to requirements, Regulatory requirements

You should cover each of these four categories in-depth to create a comprehensive requirements list for your project.

Guidance from the regulations and standards

Public Companies

Sarbanes Oxley, and the **PCAOB Audit Standard No. 2** require security, privacy and retention with respect to financial records – these standards should be considered for any project involving the creation of records.

NASD/NYSE

NASD/NYSE and **17 CFR SEC** identify specific requirements for the retention of financial records, another consideration for projects involving the creation of records.

Banking/Finance

FFIEC Development and Acquisitions includes the identification and consideration of functional requirements, which includes security requirements, but does not address specific regulatory requirements.

Healthcare and Life Sciences

HIPAA requires security with respect to private health information and thus any organization utilizing such information as part of a project must consider these requirements.

Credit Card

VISA CISP, **MasterCard SDP**, and **Amex** all address security with respect to customer data.

US Internal Revenue Service

IRS regulations provide standards for financial records security, file-format, and documentation with respect to tax-related requirements.

E-Signatures

ESIGN and **UETA** both call for records retention requirements, and should be considered for any projects requiring the creation of electronic records.

Records Management

DIRKS calls for identification of recordkeeping requirements through consultation of sources relevant to project requirements, and the identification of any regulatory requirements regarding the development or management of recordkeeping systems. **The Federal Rules of Civil Procedure** and other discovery standards call for strict recordkeeping retention requirements that should also be considered for any projects requiring the creation of records.

NIST Special Publications

The **NIST 800** series calls for the identification of functional requirements but do not specifically address the identification of regulatory requirements as part of the project management control objective.

General Guidelines

CobiT and the **ISF Standard of Good Practice for Information Security** call for identification of requirements and address the need for considering regulatory requirements as well, but are not as specific as DIRKS.

US State Laws

CA 1386 protects personal information and should be considered a privacy policy requirement. If applicable, these regulatory requirements should be considered as part of this control objective.

Each project has functional, recordkeeping, information source and regulatory requirements. Identifying these would be easy, if it wasn't also easy to confuse these categories or mix around what goes where. Fortunately, we can clear this up by defining the work you'll do for each area.

Functional Requirements

For functional requirements, decide what equipment is necessary to the project and how it may affect other projects. Special scheduling may be needed if your work interferes with the work of other employees.

Recordkeeping Requirements

Most projects will generate some kind of record, and hence you need to think about classification and storage. Do you have the capacity to store the resulting records from a project? The appropriate security if the records are highly sensitive?

Information Source Requirements

In addition to recordkeeping and functional requirements there may be sources of information within your organization that you will draw upon for your work. Some information may be classified or require special permission to use. If this is the case make arrangements to collect this information for your work.

Regulatory Requirements

Finally, you'll have to deal with regulatory requirements. There may be rules for how records generated by your project are to be kept, there may be general privacy of information requirements or a host of other possibilities. Decide what regulation you need to comply with, and read through it to be sure you are maintaining compliance.

Did you conduct an assessment of your existing systems?

Prior to the start of any project involving the development of systems or software, your organization must assess its existing systems. This process helps prevent workers from re-inventing the wheel when a solution is already available. Use this control objective when thinking about assessments:

> *Existing systems within the organization will be regularly assessed to determine whether they are efficient, useful and readily able to accommodate new additions and different types of work.*

All assessments should be documented so you can compare one assessment to another. This enables you to see what you've done well at over time, and what you still need to work on.

Guidance from the regulations and standards

Banking/Finance

FFIEC Development and Acquisitions does not explicitly call for assessment of existing systems in the initial planning of a project but does require consideration of the "benefits measured against the value of current technology" which implies that an assessment of current IT resources and systems would be analyzed.

Records Management

DIRKS and **ISO 15489** call for an assessment of existing information and recordkeeping systems as a measure against requirements for development of a new system. DIRKS further requires a formal gap analysis report to determine any weaknesses and needed improvements in recordkeeping systems.

The IT Infrastructure Library

ITIL Best Practice for Security Management § 4.2.1.2 requires that an organization have an overview of all key information sources and systems.

General Guidelines

General standards do not explicitly call for assessment of existing system as part of the initial planning of a project but include this control objective as a requirement when developing a high-level strategic IT plan when defining objectives for the organization – the assessment would most likely be incorporated here.

From regulation to reality – sure signs you are complying

To assess systems, begin by identifying all current systems infrastructure and any controls. Then analyze the functionality and basic requirements for each of these to determine any gaps or weaknesses. Finally, compare the gaps and weaknesses to the project you want to do, to see if it fills in gaps or meets requirements that haven't been met or improves upon the current solution.

Have you identified strategies for systems requirements?

You can work to meet system, business, security and functional requirements specified for new projects individually, but there's no doubt that the whole thing would be easier if you had a repeatable strategy.

> To choose the best system requirements for the organization, the organization will create strategies that describe what you expect out of your system and how to approach achieving your expectations.

Strategies for systems requirements save you time and money in the long run. That's because before you start dealing with requirements, you'll know how you want to approach attaining them, and what the requirements together are supposed to achieve for your organization.

Guidance from the regulations and standards

Banking/Finance

FFIEC Development and Acquisitions calls for an assessment of current technology investment and funding, consideration of potential addition or reduction of IT personnel and corporate culture as strategies to meet requirements during initial planning.

Records Management

ISO 15489 and **DIRKS** call for the identification of strategies to satisfy recordkeeping requirements and encourage the adoption of an overall strategy for meeting those requirements prior to design or redesign of recordkeeping systems.

General Guidelines

CobiT is the only general standard that addresses the identification of strategies for satisfying systems requirements – the standard covers the assessment of current technology investment and funding, the information architecture model, IT staffing needs and the adoption and communication of an overall systems development strategy at various points in the standard rather than specifically as part of product management. Regardless of this, the product management methodology covers most of the requirements strategies.

From regulation to reality – sure signs you are complying

Identifying an appropriate strategy depends upon a number of factors such as:

- existing policies
- design tactics
- implementation tactics
- standards compliance
- corporate culture
- current technology investment and funding
- current ability to meet existing requirements
- existing information architecture model
- IT staffing needs and their relationship to the systems they work with

The culture of your organization will determine the flavor of the strategy you will use for system development, software, or other types of projects. If your organization does not care much for change, but is a stickler for keeping track of what is going on, it will be easy to implement strategies to meet recordkeeping requirements. However, if you need new software because it offers better security options, you may need a special strategy to convince your organization to adopt it, particularly if the old method seems to be working just fine.

Existing policies, design tactics and implementation tactics need to be examined before undertaking a new project so that you can develop an effective strategy either based on using the existing work tactics and policies, or by altering those tactics and policies to suit a strategy. The former is generally preferred to the latter.

Compliance and ability to meet requirements should also be considered in creating a strategy. If you're doing a good job meeting requirements, perhaps your strategy for dealing with projects involving changes to systems should include more maintenance than implementation aspects.

Overall, you need to step through what you have, decide what you want to keep, what you want to change, and how easy it will be to do either of those things. Then adopt a strategy that suits your findings and your organization's culture.

How do you develop your project plan?

When starting to develop a project plan, the old saying 'there are many ways to skin a cat' comes to mind. So many ways in fact, that you might want to develop a project plan for that too. How do you get started creating a decent project plan? A good place to begin is with this control objective:

> *Each project plan the organization creates will address thirteen key points. These points are: Project Overview, Roles and Responsibilities, Communication, Defined Deliverables, Control Requirements, Risk Management, Change Management, Standards, Documentation, Scheduling, Budget, Testing and Staff Development.*

If your project plan covers each of these thirteen points you've created a plan. If you're not sure what each of these points is exactly, don't worry, we'll go over each one in this section.

Guidance from the regulations and standards

Banking/Finance

FFIEC Development and Acquisitions calls for development of project plans commensurate with all project characteristics and risks.

Records Management

Though more heavily concentrated on the initial planning stage of project management, **DIRKS** and **ISO 15489** call for the development of a project plan for development of recordkeeping systems.

General Guidelines

CobiT calls for the development of a project master plan for each approved project which contains all elements of CobiT's project management standards. The ISF standard does not directly call for a project plan but implies that one should be developed as part of its systems development methodology.

CobiT 3 PO 10.7 states that there should be a project master plan for each approved project which is adequate for maintaining control over the project throughout its life. It should include a method for monitoring the time and costs incurred throughout the life of the project. The content of the project plan should include statements of scope, objectives, required resources and responsibilities and should provide information to permit management to measure progress.

CobiT 4 PO10.7 says organizations should have a formal project plan approved ahead of time. This plan should be used to guide execution and project control throughout the life of the project. If there are multiple products depending upon one another their dependencies should be documented.

From regulation to reality – sure signs you are complying

When you've formulated an overall plan for how you will conduct project management and quality assurance, it's time to construct a specific plan for a specific project. The project plan you write should include all the information you've gathered during the preliminary scoping phase such as references to standards, pertinent documentation, roles and responsibilities, budget and costs and risks associated with the project.

The written plan should include thirteen basic areas:

1. Project Overview – an outline of the overall project, its goals, and development strategies

2. Roles and Responsibilities – describe the key roles of all the people involved in the project, including sponsors, managers, team members and any necessary third parties or vendors

3. Communication – explain how the different people involved in the project will communicate, as defined communication methods improve project efficiency

4. Defined Deliverables – clearly indicate what the finished product will be, and what is expected of this final product in terms of quality and functionality

5. Control Requirements – describe how automated control and security features will be designed and built for your project to the best of your ability at this phase

6. Risk Management – ensure that you have a process for assessing, monitoring and dealing with internal and external risks

7. Change Management – write out a procedure for dealing with modifications and additions to the project you've planned, including cut-off dates for such changes and standards for each change

8. Standards – reference any standards that relate to project oversight activities, system controls, and quality assurance

9. Documentation – outline what type and level of documentation must be produced by team members for each phase of the project

10. Scheduling – a complete schedule for the project should be included with the plan along with schedule flexibility since estimates are never perfect

11. Budget – provide a budget estimate with the project plan so it can easily be determined whether the project is feasible or not

12. Testing – describe how your project's product is going to be tested and who will be included in the testing procedures

13. Staff Development – if training is necessary for the completion of your project, outline how it will be done and who will receive it

If your project plan covers each of these thirteen points, you have the foundation for a solid plan that will help ensure efficiency and attainable goals.

Have you established design methodologies that meet industry standards?

The first element of designing systems is establishing design methodologies that meet industry standards. Just as you would not like to find out the car you are driving is not on par with industry standards, your customers and other interested parties would not like to find out that your information systems design does not meet industry standards. To ensure you're meeting proper standards, keep this control objective in mind:

> *The organization will develop design methodologies to comply with the organization's security policy, legal and regulatory requirements, and specific business security requirements.*

With a design methodology in place, it will be a snap to see if your products are as good as they need to be, better than they need to be, or if you need to get back to work on them.

Guidance from the regulations and standards

Banking/Finance

FFIEC Development and Acquisition Pg. 15 states that organizations *"should establish systems and application development methodologies. The methodologies should match a project's characteristics and risks require appropriate:*

- *Project Plans;*

- *Definitions of project expectations;*

- *Project standards and procedures;*

- *Definitions of project phase deliverables, including assurance that deliverables will meet any applicable legal and regulatory requirements;*

- *Development of security, audit, and automated control features;*

- *Quality assurance, risk management, and testing standards and procedures;*

- *Involvement by all affected parties; and,*

- *Project communication techniques. "*

On page 15, the FFIEC Development and Acquisition handbook calls for a systems development lifecycle methodology (SDLC) that incorporates a design methodology as part of systems development – it calls for the creation and approval of design specifications as part of the design phase. *"The SDLC is a project management technique that divides complex projects into smaller, more easily managed segments or phase. Segmenting projects allows managers to verify the successful completion of project phases before allocating resources to subsequent phases."*

Credit Card

The **VISA CISP** and **MasterCard SDP** programs call for a software development process that incorporates industry standards and best practices in the context of information security and data protection, but do not call specifically for design specifications.

US Federal Security

FISCAM calls for an organization to adopt an SDLC for the purposes of integrating information security within the scope of an audit process.

Records Management

DIRKS Step F is in itself a design methodology for recordkeeping systems. It calls for design documentation as part of recordkeeping system design but does not explicitly call for approval of design documentation.

NIST Special Publications

NIST 800-53 calls for an organization to adopt a SDLC for the purposes of integrating information security.

General Guidelines

CobiT calls for a design methodology that draws on "appropriate procedures and techniques" to develop and receive approval for a design specification. The ISF standard calls for a design methodology in its initial requirement of a SDLC but does specify requirement of design specifications development and approval.

CobiT AI 2.1 lays out three steps that are of relevance here. First is design methods. *"The organizations SDLC methodology should provide that appropriate procedures and techniques . . . are applied to create design specifications for each new information system development project and verify design specifications against user requirements."* Second, in the event of major changes to existing systems, management should ensure a development process similar to new system development is observed (CobiT AI 2.2). Third, the organization's

SDLC methodology should ensure design specifications for all development and modification projects are reviewed and approved by management (Co-biT AI 2.3).

The **ISF Standard of Good Practice for Information Security** § SD 1.2.1 also states that *"systems should be developed to comply with enterprise-wide security policy, legal and regulatory requirements and particular business requirements for security."*

From regulation to reality – sure signs you are complying

To begin creating a good design methodology, review your organization's systems development lifecycle methodology (SDLC). Is it brilliant? Chances are if it is, your design methodology will be just as good, because we're going to recommend you base it on your SDLC.

The two are not identical, so any thought of doing a search and replace for SDLC with design methodology isn't quite going to cut it. You'll need to read the SDLC methodology carefully, and then transform the methods written there for developing a system into designing a system. Some information listed in the SDLC methodology will carry over directly – for example hopefully your methodology requires that you finish a phase of a project before moving to the next. This is a good practice that can be incorporated into a development lifecycle methodology.

If you're not totally sold on the idea of tweaking your existing methodology, just think of how lame it is 99% of the time whenever someone reinvents the wheel. In a certain way, system design is a lot like system development. You use system development methodologies to address major changes to existing systems. A brand new system could be seen as a very major change. So major that you need something a bit specialized – like a design methodology.

While creating the design methodology, be sure to get lots of input during the process. Run the final version past management for review and approval before instituting it.

Have you assigned systems design roles and responsibilities?

Starting the systems design process can be as easy and efficient as starting your day after three hours sleep and no coffee if you don't have things in order. Once the process gets going, it can be a little bit like telling a group of construction workers to build a house without individually assigning people tasks. To avoid these problems consider the following control objective:

> *The organization will define and document roles and responsibilities for all personnel involved in the design and development of systems. For best results, use the delegation techniques discussed in this portion of the chapter.*

By giving everyone a job you increase efficiency by being certain that each staff member has something to do. You also avoid accidental overlaps in tasks and are more readily able to organize and assign appropriate work to people.

Guidance from the regulations and standards

Public Companies

Sarbanes Oxley and accompanying standards specify the need for senior management and business unit leaders to be aware of their role in the systems development process.

Banking/Finance

FFIEC Development and Acquisitions defines roles and responsibilities for systems development as a whole and includes responsibilities for the design phase – it does not specify separation of the development and production environments. *For a complete description of individual roles and responsibilities, see FFIEC Development and Acquisition pg. 5-6.*

Credit Card

MasterCard SDP does not specify design roles and responsibilities but does require design personnel work in a separate development environment and be restricted from accessing production environments.

Records Management

ISO 15489 calls for general responsibilities to be assigned with respect to the design of a recordkeeping system. **DIRKS** calls for the assignment of roles and responsibilities for recordkeeping functions and tasks within the context of designing or redesigning a recordkeeping system. DIRKS § F.4.2 advises that roles and responsibilities be clearly documented, to help ensure accountability for recordkeeping action or inaction. Neither standard calls for segregation of work environments.

International Standards Organization

ISO 17799 addresses the need for separate development and operation environments (§ 8.1.5).

General Guidelines

CobiT and the **ISF Standard of Good Practices for Information Security** define roles and responsibilities for systems development as a whole and incorporate design responsibilities into the design process. The ISF Standard calls for the appropriate awareness of personnel and the segregation of work environments (separate system development environments should be established.) ISF states: *"Overall responsibility for development activity should be clearly assigned to an individual, such as the head of systems development. Business 'owners' should be appointed to be responsible for particular development activities. Responsibility for key tasks (such as compliance with development standards, definition of requirements, risk analysis, design/build, testing and implementation) should be assigned to individuals who are capable of performing them."* (ISF Standard SD 1.1.1-2).

From regulation to reality – sure signs you are complying

There are three items to use as a general outline when preparing to delegate roles and responsibilities for a project:

- Assign overall responsibility for the development activity to one individual, such as the head of systems development.

- Appoint business owners for particular development activities.

- Assign key tasks (such as compliance with development standards, definition of requirements, risks analysis, design/build, testing and implementation) to individuals who are capable of performing these tasks.

The size and complexity of a project determines the number and qualifications of the needed personnel. For lower-risk projects or in small organizations, duties may overlap. However, it is generally good practice to appropriately segregate duties. Production environments should be segregated to reinforce accountability and control design.

In addition to defining and assigning roles and responsibilities, ensure that the IT staff and managers are aware of their specified roles in the design process. By clearly documenting roles, staff can be held accountable for action or inaction regarding specific tasks.

Do you redesign work processes?

Redesigning work processes is a great way to determine ideal systems development workflow and design processes for each system under development. Because it can be hard to figure out what this process entails, we've boiled it down to the following control objective:

> *To ensure quality redesign work, the organization will ensure that its processes include these six features: File requirements definition and documentation, Program specifications, Source data collection design, Input requirements definition and documentation, Determining business activity requirements, and the role of metadata in discovery*

Your process should be clearly documented and communicated to the staff affected by the redesign.

Guidance from the regulations and standards

Banking/Finance

The **FFIEC handbooks** do not explicitly call for a design or redesign of work processes or the development of detailed program specifications but does call for the design of input controls. The business activity classification of design is also not referenced but is rather assumed to have been addressed during the initial planning process.

Records Management

DIRKS calls for a design or redesign of work processes in order to incorporate the design of recordkeeping functionality. **ISO 15489-2** calls for consideration of business activity with respect to designing recordkeeping systems. DIRKS does not call for detailed program specifications at this point (but does in the following section, F.4.4). ISO 15489-2 and the **Sedona Principles** also require the consideration of metadata in systems design for discovery purposes.

General Guidelines

CobiT calls for the design of work processes to define and document file format and input requirements, design source data collection, and develop detailed program specifications for each system under development. The business activity classification of design is considered as part of the overall project management framework and is addressed primarily in the creation of a high-level strategic IT plan.

From regulation to reality – sure signs you are complying

There are six elements required for successfully redesigning work processes. Hit each of the items we discuss here, and you'll be in good shape.

File Requirements Definition and Documentation

You need to define and document the file format for each information system development or modification project. A procedure for accomplishing this should be laid out in the design methodology. This procedure should ensure that the data dictionary rules are respected.

Program Specification

Detailed, written program specifications need to be prepared for each information system development or modification project. Again, this should be provided for in the design methodology. Program specifications should agree with system design specifications.

Source Data Collection Design

The design methodology should call for source data collection design. Specify adequate mechanisms for the collection and entry of data for each information system development or modification project.

Input Requirements Definition and Documentation

Define and document the input requirements for each information system development or modification project. Input requirements act as a guide to ensure that employees accurately input information, systems accurately record input, and systems either reject, or accept and record, input errors for later review and correction.

Determining Business Activity Requirements

When developing or modifying information systems, business activities, business functions, and transactions should all be considered. These considerations are helpful in providing a systematic framework for development and modification.

The Role of Metadata in Discovery

Consider metadata in systems design for discovery purposes.

It is quite possible that redesigning work processes will cause major disruption to staff and to organizational business. Any redesign of work processes should be handled sensitively and within a change management framework.

Have you designed system procedures?

System design procedures are the functions and processes built into each system while it is under development. Taking time and care to develop these leads to more intuitive, easy to use systems. There are a number of procedure types you need to take into account to achieve quality usability, which is why we recommend the following control objective:

> *The organization will design system procedures, including the design and documentation of all internal, external and user-machine interfaces, processing, output, and database management systems.*

We'll discuss each type of procedure in greater detail within this section. By the end you'll have an idea of what you need to design.

Guidance from the regulations and standards

Banking/Finance

FFIEC Development and Acquisitions calls for design of systems procedures, covering user-machine interfaces, processing, output, and database management systems. *For detailed discussion of these procedures, see FFIEC Design & Acquisition page 23-24, & 38.*

Credit Card

VISA CISP and **MasterCard SDP** and **AMEX** regulations do not directly address the design of system procedures but require the incorporation of security controls into design (see security control line item summary).

Records Management

DIRKS calls for the design of all above system procedures into a system for the purposes of records creation, capture and control.

General Guidelines

CobiT calls for the design of system procedures, but does not directly address the need to design a database management system.

CobiT states that the SDLC methodology *"should provide that all external and internal interfaces are properly specified, designed and documented"* (CobiT AI 2.8). Additionally, the SDLC should provide for the *"development of an interface between the user and the machine which is easy to use and self-documenting"* (CobiT AI 2.9). The SDLC *"should require that adequate mechanisms exist for defining and documenting the processing requirements for each information system development or modification project"*(CobiT AI 2.10). Finally, *"adequate mechanisms should exist for defining and documenting the output requirements for each information system development or modification project"* (CobiT AI 2.11)

From regulation to reality – sure signs you are complying

System procedures are the "functions" or "processes" built into information systems. Your organization has to design these procedures, and there are five components to this design process:

- Definition of interfaces
- User-machine interface
- Processing requirements definition and documentation
- Output requirements definition and documentation
- Database management systems

We start with the proper specification, design and documentation of all internal and external interfaces. User interfaces, such as menus and dialog boxes, enable users to interact with a system. Develop an interface between the user and the machine that is easy and self-documenting.

Processing requirements ensure systems accurately process and record information and either reject, or process and record, errors for later review and correction. Processing includes merging files, modifying data, updating master files, and performing file maintenance. You should have adequate methods in place for defining and documenting the processing requirements for every development or modification project.

Automated output requirements help ensure systems securely maintain and properly distribute processed information. Once again, create methods for defining and documenting output requirements for development and modification projects.

Database management systems are software programs that control a database user's access and modification rights. The systems also facilitate referential integrity, support data import and export functions, and provide backup and recovery services. Database management systems may also provide access to data dictionaries. When reviewing the design and configuration of database management systems, make sure you include access controls and auditing features. Restrict direct access to a database to authorized personnel. Additionally, if available, employ automatic auditing tools that identify who accessed or attempted to access a database, and what, if any, data was changed.

Have you designed security controls?

Well designed security controls prevent attackers from ruining your systems, save you time and money and do not act as a hindrance to every-day operations within your organization. Everyone wants a good security system, but whether you can create one depends on whether or not you can hit every requirement we recommend in the following control objective:

> The organization will consider security requirements and industry internal control standards for each system during the design phase and incorporate security controls into the design of application software and systems (such as input and output validation, processing controls, and data encryption), provide for development and support (design change control), and ensure that all source code for use in development has been independently reviewed and tested.

A top-notch security system will not only do a better job defending you from attacks in the first place, it will let you know when someone makes a successful attack more quickly so you can neutralize the problem.

Guidance from the regulations and standards

Public Companies

Public standards do not directly address the incorporation of security controls into systems design but, as with **SAS 94**, state that an audit of financial information will be directly affected by the internal security controls built into applications.

Banking/Finance

FFIEC Information Security and **Development and Acquisitions** call for the development of security requirements for any new or modified systems and further call for the incorporation of security controls in application software, including the encryption of stored data in database management systems. FFIEC Information Security addresses the need for development and support security controls to ensure proper change control procedures and the review and testing of source code prior to development in order to detect any covert channels or other code weaknesses.

Credit Card

Visa CISP, MasterCard SDP and **AMEX** programs call for security requirements to be a part of an organization's entire system development life cycle, and require the incorporation of security controls into systems design, most notably application software controls and database encryption. MasterCard and Amex specify at least 128-bit triple DES encryption.

US Federal Security

The **Clinger-Cohen Act** and **The National Strategy to Secure Cyberspace** all require the incorporation of security controls into initial systems design.

NIST Special Publications

NIST 800-53 requires the incorporation of security controls into initial systems design.

International Standards Organization

ISO 17799 § 10.1 & 2 specifically call for *"security to be built into information systems. This includes infrastructure, business applications and user development applications, the design and implementation of the business process supporting the application or service can be crucial for security. Security requirements should be identified and agreed on prior to the development of information systems. All security requirements, including the need for fallback arrangements, should be identified at the requirements phase of a project and justified, agreed and documented as part of the overall business case for an information system.*

Statements of business requirements for new systems, or enhancements to existing systems should specify the requirements for controls. Such specifications should consider the automated controls to be incorporated in the system, and the need for supporting manual controls. Similar considerations should be applied when evaluating software packages for business applications. If considered appropriate, management may wish to make use of independently evaluated and certified products.

Security requirements and controls should reflect the business value of the information assets involved, and the potential business damage, which might result from a failure or absence of security. The framework for analyzing security requirements and identifying controls to fulfill them is risk assessment and risk management.

Controls introduced at the design state are significantly cheaper to implement and maintain than those included during or after implementation.

Finally, to prevent loss, modification or misuse of user data in application systems, appropriate controls and audit trails or activity logs should be designed into application systems, including user written applications. These should include the validation of input data, internal processing, and output data."

General Guidelines

CobiT and the **ISF Standard of Good Practice for Information Security** call for the development of security requirements and the incorporation of security controls into application software during design. The ISF Standard (*SD 4.1-3*) includes requirements for encrypting databases and together with ISO 17799 requires change control procedures for development and support. ISO 17799 also calls for source code review and testing prior to development of applications software.

From regulation to reality – sure signs you are complying

When you design a system, security is a main concern. Security should be built into information systems from the get go. It should not be an after thought. There are four steps to consider when designing security controls.

- Security Requirements and Standards
- Security Controls in Application Software
- Development and Support
- Source Code Review and Testing

You know that complying with standards is important. After all, you are reading this book, aren't you? Security standards for system design are no exception. Whichever standards you are required to comply with, take a look at the sections on security, especially system design security before you design your system. For instance, if you have to comply with ISO 17799, you want to know that it specifically calls for security requirements to be identified and agreed on prior to the development of information systems. These security requirements, including the need for fallback arrangements, must be identified at the requirements phase of a project and justified, agreed on and documented as part of the overall business case for an information system. The main point is to define security requirements before developing or modifying systems and incorporate widely recognized security standards into the development process.

Once you have defined security requirements and addressed standards, you can take a closer look at security. This closer look begins with security controls in application software. When developing applications, you are simultaneously developing the security controls for these applications, including audit trails and activity logs. These application security controls will help ensure the accuracy, completeness, timeliness, and authorization of inputs, processing and outputs. Application security controls also include validation controls for data entry and data processing. Again, the goal of these security controls is to record changes to data, suspicious activity, error checks, and require authorization for transmission of sensitive data. These security controls will balance the access controls and staff training. The two work together to ensure the highest level of security and integrity.

A couple of specifics are in order when it comes to application security controls. First, store sensitive information in encrypted form. Encrypt databases with customer information or anything that is confidential. This will help ensure integrity and minimize repudiation of transactions. Second, according to a variety of standards, including MasterCard, Amex, and FFIEC, encryption should be at least 128-bit triple DES. For more information on encryption, take a look at the chapter on Technical Security.

Next, we take a look at security in the development and support process. ISO 17799 is a leading source of information on this topic. As ISO explains, you want to have strict controls over implementing changes. Develop formal change control procedures and enforce them. Change control procedures help to ensure that:

- Security and control procedures are not compromised,

- Programmers are given only the access necessary to complete their job function, and

- Approval for change is required

  ISO 17799 also explains that wherever practicable, application and operational change control procedures should be integrated. This process should include:

- Maintaining a record of agreed authorization levels;

- Ensuring changes are submitted to authorized users;

- Reviewing controls ad integrity procedures to ensure that they will not be compromised by the changes;

- Identifying all computer software, information, database entries and hardware that require amendment;

- Obtaining formal approval for detailed proposals before work commences;

- Ensuring that the authorized user accepts changes prior to implementation;

- Ensuring that implementation is carried out to minimize business disruption;

- Ensuring that the system documentation set is updated on the completion of each change and that old documentation is achieved or disposed of;

- Maintaining a version control for all software updates;

- Maintaining an audit trail of all change requests;

- Ensuring that operation documentation and user procedures are changes as necessary to be appropriate;

- Ensuring that the implementation of changes takes place at the right time and is not disturbing the business process involved.

We suggest keeping the software testing environment separate from the development and production environments.

Finally, we reach the topic of source code review and testing. By now you should know how important it is to test for vulnerabilities. Systems design is no exception. Application system source code can have numerous vulnerabilities from programming errors or misconfiguration. Whenever possible, use software that has been subjected to independent security reviews. According to the FFIEC guide on information security, "software can contain erroneous or intentional code that introduces covert channels, backdoors, and other security risks into systems and applications." Watch out. Hidden access points can provide unauthorized access to systems or data! Repeat source code reviews after any significant changes.

Security is an ongoing process. It takes testing and retesting, approval and authorization for changes, and constant attention to audit trails and logs. When you integrate security into the design process, from the very beginning, you will have a more effective security program in place.

Have you created a design review process?

A design review process is a key part of putting out a good final product. It's a time to figure out if a design is going to work, and discuss any problems that might arise. We recommend the following control objective for this process:

> *In order to ensure functionality of the system, less disparity between requirements and design, and a smooth transition to development, the organization will create a design review process to analyze and review each new system or software design before it is developed and implemented.*

Your clients will appreciate a well thought out design process whether they know about it or not. That's because a good design process leads to a quality final product.

Guidance from the regulations and standards

Banking/Finance

FFIEC Development and Acquisitions does not call for a formal design review process but does suggest end users of systems under development should approve designs to ensure they possess the required functionality. The standard also mentions reviews of prototyping tools as a design method (mock-ups, and so on) and suggests that they should be reviewed and refined in an iterative process by appropriate personnel. *For more detailed discussion on this topic, see FFIEC Development and Acquisition Pg. 21.*

Records Management

DIRKS calls for iterative design review: a formal review process following the design of each major component of a system.

General Guidelines

CobiT does not explicitly call for a formal design review process but does require reassessment of system design following any technical or logical discrepancies discovered during development or testing phases. The ISF Standard does not call for a formal design review process either, but does mention the need for review before approval of the final design. *For more* *detailed discussion of this topic, see the CobiT AI 2.17 and the ISF Standard SD 4.1.1.*

From regulation to reality – sure signs you are complying

If you were designing a building, the blueprints and plans would be thoroughly reviewed by a group pf architects and land-use planners before the building begins. The same is true with systems design. Once a system or an application has been designed, it must be reviewed and approved by IT managers, the head of systems development, and business owners. To make sure this happens, institute a design review process.

Creation of a design review process ensures functionality of the system, less disparity between requirements and design, and a smooth transition to development. It is key to have designs reviewed before approval of a final design. At a minimum, your organization should:

- Approve all designs before they go to the development phase

- Reassess system design following discrepancies discovered during development or testing

- Require end users to approve designs to ensure they posses the required functionality

Approving systems design at every stage in the process will provide you with the checks you need to create a top-notch end product. You will spend less money and less manpower building your system because you went through the process one step at a time and approved it at each juncture.

Have you developed a training plan?

Training plans help you figure out what you definitely need to teach your staff, what you should probably teach your staff, and what you could get away with not showing them. They do this by providing estimates of time and cost for each type of training. To develop a good training plan, employ the following control objective:

> *Prior to development, management of the organization will develop an initial high-level training plan for all IT personnel that includes training program requirements, identification of personnel to be trained, high-level training, and security awareness training.*

A good training plan balances all the important training requirements. In this section we'll discuss what your plan should include.

Guidance from the regulations and standards

Public Companies

The **AICPA Suitable Trust Services Criteria** calls for a security awareness program but does not specify the development of initial training plans.

Banking/Finance

FFIEC Development and Acquisitions calls for the development of an initial training plan during the planning phase of a project that identifies training requirements and schedules personnel to be trained. **FFIEC Information Security** also requires security awareness training as part of the training program.

Healthcare and Life Sciences

HIPAA requires security awareness training as part of compliance with the standard, but does not address an initial training plan or any training in software development.

Credit Card

MasterCard SDP calls for a security awareness training program that should be repeated annually, while Visa specifies that personnel responsible for responding to security breaches be appropriately trained.

US Federal Security

All government standards and regulations require a need for some amount of security awareness training. **FISCAM** calls for general training program requirements but only as a control measure for auditors to consider.

The IT Infrastructure Library

ITIL Best Practice for Security Management 4.2.2.2 recommends offering all personnel in an organization security awareness training. For personnel that handle security incidents directly, more specialized training may be required.

Records Management

DIRKS *(F.4.8)* calls for development of an initial training plan on good recordkeeping practices and provides possible content for training and training methods. **ISO 15489** (especially Part 2) elaborates on employee training, calling for definition of training program requirements, selection of personnel to be trained, and training of records management personnel. Neither standard addresses the need for security awareness training, though it seems to be implied as DIRKS works security into its recordkeeping practices.

ISO 15489 § 7-4 specifically states that *"it is important to assign responsibility for implementing and managing is records management training program to a manager at a suitable level and to resource the program adequately. An organization may choose to use a third party supplier to provide some or all of its records management training. A formal training program will only be effective if staff can see that management is committed to implementing the policies and procedures covered in the program.*

It is important that appropriate training be provided for all personnel with any kind of responsibility for records. This includes:

- *Managers*
- *Senior managers*
- *Employees*
- *Contractors*
- *Volunteers*
- *Any other personnel with access to records*

Higher level training requires that the mangers have knowledge of the organization's business, objectives and processes. Relevant technical skills may also be required."

International Standards Organization

ISO 17799 § 6.2.1 specifically states that *"all employees of the organization and, where relevant, third party users, should receive appropriate training and regular updates in organizational policies and procedures. This includes security requirements, legal responsibilities and business controls, as well as training in the correct use of information processing facilities e.g. log-on procedure, use of software packages, before access to information or services is granted."*

General Guidelines

CobiT, and the **ISF Standard of Good Practices for Information Security** call for the development of initial training plans and procedures as part of initial planning and design. CobiT specifies that training program requirements should be in line with the IT long-range plan and that a training curriculum should be developed for each group of employees. CobiT objectives include identification of training needs, training organization, and security principles and awareness training (CobiT DS 7.1-3).

CobiT 4 AI4.2 tells us that business management should receive enough knowledge from IT to understand and own the systems and the data they work with. This enables them to exercise responsibility for service delivery and quality, internal control, and application administration processes. AI4.3 extends knowledge transfer to end users. All users should be given the skills necessary to efficiently use applications that support business processes. AI4.4 continues with knowledge transfer, but this time for operations and support staff. These people should be given the information required to properly support and maintain application systems and associated infrastructure. AI7.1 indicates that employees across the organization are to be trained in accordance with the organization's defined training and implementation plan.

US State Laws

CA OPPA guidelines calls for security awareness training with respect to privacy laws.

EU Guidance

The **OECD Risk Checklist** calls for high-level training of management.

A seeing eye dog goes through a ton of training before becoming certified to actually lead the blind. Before development of information systems and applications, staff and managers need to be adequately prepared for the task. There are four elements included in a training plan:

- Training program requirements

- The personnel to be trained

- High level training

- Security awareness training

The first step in developing a training plan is to establish training program requirements. This includes identifying training requirements, documenting these requirements and establishing training methods. Design the structure of your training program with organizational and system design functions in mind.

When choosing a delivery method, employ a variety of ideas. There are different training methods you can use, including:

- Face-to-face training, with hands on practice on a live system

- Online training

- Training documentation with tips and hints, regularly updated with responses to recently encountered problems

- User guides and manuals, in hard copy form and/or available on your organizations intranet

- User help-desk facilities

It is advised, at least for initial training, to have face-to-face sessions, where trainees can ask questions and get hands on experience. Chose alternate methods of training in case face-to-face training is not available, or if you need to provide follow-up guidance.

Training should be provided for all personnel with any kind of systems design responsibility. This includes:

- Senior managers and managers

- Employees

- Contractors

- Volunteers

When training personnel, the training should be done in groups, relative to the tasks they will be performing. You don't want to train folks on tasks they will not be engaging in. Once you have created logical training groups, then you have to think about the content of the training sessions. Train individuals only on what they need to know, but make sure they get all the information they need to be successful.

Not only do you want to train those employees actually doing the hands on work, but you also must train the managers and higher-level employees supervising the work. Higher-level employees must have knowledge of the organization's business, objectives and process. They must be fully versed on the systems design process and have knowledge of the roles and responsibilities of staff. You want your managers and higher-level employees to have the appropriate amount of technical skills to suit their position. They should be as comfortable with the systems design process as any other employee involved in the project.

As we have already stressed, security is key to successful information systems design. It should come as no surprise that security is as much a part of training as it is systems design. Security awareness training is the last step in a successful training program. All trainees must receive regular updates in security requirements and legal responsibilities.

A well-trained staff will provide a smooth systems design process. A staff that is encouraged to ask questions, and one that has access to a wide range of training resources and guides will operate with ease and ability. When it comes time to approve projects at each step in the process, you will find that there are less problems and more advancement when you have a comfortable, confident, well-trained staff.

Do you develop your systems in accordance with documented standards and procedures?

After you design systems, you have to develop them. Systems development includes both developing systems in accordance with standards and procedures and addressing user reference and support materials. We begin with the former and with the following control objective:

> *The organization will develop systems in accordance with documented standards and procedures, considering standards developed as part of their software development lifecycle methodology. All outsourced development, source code libraries and software versioning should be strictly managed and controlled.*

By developing your systems in accordance with your standards, you ensure they are all similar to one another and meet all the requirements of your organization. This saves time and money over haphazard systems which may employ multiple methodologies and approaches – making them difficult to improve or alter later on.

Guidance from the regulations and standards

Banking/Finance

FFIEC Development and Acquisitions addresses the development of systems and software. It specifies that development standards should be created determining the responsibilities of application and system programmers through library and version controls. FFIEC Information Security requires consideration of requirements and controls for outsourced developers.

Credit Card

VISA CISP and **MasterCard SDP** require the incorporation of security into the software development process, but do not explicitly mention library or version controls, or outsourced development.

US Federal Security

FISCAM requires control of software libraries during development.

NIST Special Publications

NIST 800-53 calls for general security controls over outsourced development.

International Standards Organization

ISO 17799 addresses the need for security through library and version controls.

General Guidelines

The **ISF Standard of Good Practice for Information Security** is the only general standard that specifically addresses the need for documented standards and procedures when developing systems or applications Though not explicitly stated, ISF calls for version controls over new or modified source code.

CobiT obviously assumes development and covers SDLC methodology as part of its overall project management standards.

From regulation to reality – sure signs you are complying

Before developing a system in a project, make sure your plans for development are in alignment with the documented standards and procedures set out by your organization's system development lifecycle methodology. There is no reason create and document standards and procedures if you are not going to develop systems in accordance with them. This is what they are there for, so use them in the development phase.

Any development, internal, or outsourced, along with source code libraries and software versioning should be strictly managed and controlled. If you plan to modify any code, be sure your procedures call for versioning the code as well as adequate security for code libraries. Source code libraries are like copyright jewelry boxes. To avoid any copyright violations and liability, you want to ensure that all software requiring a license to use is not freely distributed.

Do you offer user reference and support materials?

Sometimes people learn better when they're given a chance to figure things out themselves. For instance, if you do your child's first book report, the next one is going to be just as hard for her to figure out. On the other hand, the book report was probably not a task given to your child without any instructions. In fact, the teacher probably handed out written guidelines for the project that could be referenced along the way. Furthermore, a good teacher is always available for questions.

In much the same way, you do not want to do everything for your staff. They have to figure it out for themselves. But, users of newly developed software should not be let loose on that software without a little guidance, a reference manual, and someone available to answer any questions. Therefore the control objective for this section is:

> *The organization will prepare user documentation and in the form of reference and support manuals for every development project.*

High quality user documentation and support for new software improves worker efficiency as well as worker attitude toward changes in the workplace. A bad experience with a new product that has terrible support and documentation convinces workers that change is also bad. A good experience on the other hand, is likely to make them more receptive to changes that improve efficiency. Take the time to provide quality support and documentation to workers when you offer them new systems or software.

Guidance from the regulations and standards

Banking/Finance

FFIEC Development and Acquisitions specifies the need to create end-user documentation, including online help and system error messages built into applications and systems.

General Guidelines

CobiT calls for the preparation of user reference and support materials for every systems or applications development project and specifies electronic format as preferable.

Building furniture from a box is a pretty simple task for most people. You take the parts, lay them out, look at the instructions and bam, you have a desk. But, without those instructions, things get tricky. And, if you take away those little stickers with the letters on them telling you which parts go where, the chances of building that desk have gone down tremendously. Luckily, those do-it-yourself pieces of furniture do not come without instructions, and neither should your systems and software.

Whenever you develop a new product, you have to assume that users are not going to be able to figure out how to use it without a little help. You shouldn't give new software or a new system to users and tell them to have a ball. Instead, you need to show them how to use it, and give them a manual or other documentation that they can use for reference.

Newly developed systems and applications must be accompanied by user documentation in the form of reference and support manuals. Include these items in each and every development project. Build online help and system error messages into any applications and systems as needed. If you take the time to do these things, usability is greatly increased. Written documentation is useful to end users and new employees, who can quickly read up on how to use your organization's products without needing a lot of explanation by other workers. Of course, there should be someone there who can guide users when the questions just cannot be answered by a manual. But, reserve that kind of instruction for a minority of cases, those that require personal assistance. Most "training" can be done by user manuals and reference guides.

Have you developed testing strategies and plans?

Testing, as we have touted and stressed, is imperative to healthy systems. Testing ensures that systems run accurately and appropriately for the needs of your organization. Use of a variety of tests, coupled with the proper IT oversight will guarantee that systems and applications are designed appropriately.

Step one of testing is developing the test strategies and plans. For this step, we have developed the following control objective:

> *To ensure the integrity and accountability of systems and applications, the organization will develop testing strategies and plans. These testing strategies and plans must be finalized and approved by management prior to any system testing. A test plan should be created for each component of the new system.*

Testing plans allow you to be sure that you have covered every aspect of testing that is necessary before beginning the actual process. Without a plan, it's easy to forget to review something before it's too late.

Guidance from the regulations and standards

Banking/Finance

FFIEC Development and Acquisitions calls for the completion of test plans before the testing phase even begins (during the systems development phase), but requires that test plans be in place and be approved before system or applications testing.

US Federal Security

FISCAM details the development of test plans as part of the testing process of new or modified systems or software applications.

Records Management

DIRKS calls for the development of a recordkeeping system test plan at the end of the design phase (although for DIRKS this is also the end of the development stage) that includes the testing strategies prior to implementation of the recordkeeping system.

General Guidelines

CobiT and the ISF standard call for systems testing strategies and plans prior to system testing activities.

CobiT 4 AI7.6 says changes must be tested in accordance with the defined acceptance plan and based on an impact and resource assessment that includes performance sizing in a separate test environment by an independent test group before use in the regular operational environment begins. AI7.7 indicates that a final acceptance test should be conducted before fully introducing something to the organization's systems. The tests should make sure the new additions integrate appropriately with existing systems and meet organizational compliance standards.

From regulation to reality — sure signs you are complying

In life there are two kinds of people, the planners and the perceivers. This applies to many facets of life and is applicable here as well. Most of the time, a planner will prepare before undertaking a project or vacation. A perceiver will just sense things will work out a certain way and dive in. For many aspects of life, such as going on a spontaneous trip, perceiving may work fine. For testing of systems design, you better have a plan.

Before you finish the design and development phase, you want to develop testing strategies and plans. Test plans must be approved *before* the testing phase. Create a testing plan for each component of a new system or application. Different standards list different things that test plans should cover. For example, according to ISF, test plans should have the following components:

- The types of hardware, software and services to be tested
- The use of test plans, including user involvement
- Key components of the testing process
- Documentation, review and sign off of the testing process

The use of test plans increases the likelihood that weaknesses will be identified before systems or applications go on to the implementation phase. Testers should anticipate the possible results and document the results you are looking for. The goal of testing is to achieve those results, but if you don't, testing gives you the tools to go back and fix anything that didn't work out. The test plan must provide procedures for ensuring that staff repair any weaknesses identified in the testing phase. Any corrections made should be documented.

What do you need to test anyway?

Before you use any system or employ any new processes and procedures you need to test them. Chances are, they don't work the first time you try them out. Maybe they don't work the second time either. But don't despair – that's what the testing is for. Each time you test and find out something isn't working, you have the chance to make it better. The best thing you can do when it comes to testing, is to test everything early and often, as indicated by the following control objective:

> *The organization will perform various tests in stages, in accordance with test plans and strategies. The testing process must ensure that tests do not utilize production data in order to preserve confidentiality of information. Formal procedures should be developed to evaluate, accredit and accept test results, and accept residual risk remaining after all tests have been performed. The designated user or custodian of the system or application must run an operational test in an isolated environment to validate its operation as a complete product.*

Testing in stages allows you to avoid the scenario of investing a lot of time and money in something that, once completed, doesn't work the way you expected! Instead, you can see each step of the way what does and doesn't work, and adjust a project accordingly.

Guidance from the regulations and standards

Public Companies

The **AICPA Suitable Trust Service Criteria** refers to system testing from an organization security perspective.

Banking/Finance

FFIEC Development and Acquisitions calls for testing of a system or application software and provides for all the testing criteria above – however it does not include security testing and accreditation or operational tests. It should be noted that FFIEC also does not include parallel or pilot testing in the testing phase, but rather, like **DIRKS**, as part of the implementation phase before final promotion to the production environment.

Credit Card

MasterCard SDP requires a thorough testing of software prior to implementation and specifies the need for keeping production data from entering testing for confidentiality purposes.

VISA CISP specifies the need to test application code for any vulnerabilities prior to implementation.

US Federal Security

FISMA calls for testing of security controls in applications prior to implementation, while **FISCAM** calls for testing of new systems and applications, including acceptance testing, and requires testing not use production data to preserve confidentiality.

Records Management

DIRKS calls for testing but is not very specific about procedures. The standard integrates the testing of recordkeeping systems with implementation. It does mention parallel and pilot testing but only as a part of recordkeeping system conversion, which is a part of implementation, not testing.

The IT Infrastructure Library

ITIL Best Practice for Security Management 3.3.5 requires that software be introduced into a new system in a controlled manner. The software should be tested before being added, introduction should be authorized, the software should be legal, it should be virus free, it should be registered, and the way it is introduced to the system should be planned out and tested in advance.

NIST Special Publications

NIST 800-14 is not to detailed but does address the need to test systems security controls and accept results and risks through accreditation.

General Guidelines

CobiT calls for testing systems and applications software, including the acceptance of test results and residual risk and an operational test prior to implementation. The ISF standard details similar testing procedures and the testing of security controls.

For a more detailed discussion of this topic, see the CobiT AI 2.15 & 5.7-11. Additionally, the **ISF Standard of Good Practices for Information Security** sections SD 5.1.5, 5.2 & 5.2.2 all have a great deal to say on this topic.

From regulation to reality – sure signs you are complying

You need to test everything. You want to make sure that all vulnerabilities have been identified and all major problems have been adjusted before implementing a system or application. When testing new systems and applications, there are eight elements to keep in mind:

- Ensure that testing does not use production data
- Application software testing
- Testing of security objectives
- Testing of changes
- Parallel/pilot testing criteria and performance
- Final acceptance test
- Security testing and accreditation
- Operational test

Ensure Testing Does Not Use Production Data

When testing new systems or applications, it is key to keep the same level of security that you would in ordinary business functions. This means that testing shouldn't use production data, especially if the data contains sensitive information. You want to ensure that confidentiality is maintained throughout the testing process.

Application Software Testing

Unit testing, application testing, integration testing, system testing, and load and stress testing all need to be performed as part of the application software testing process. Perform these tests according to specifications in the test plan and established testing standards before the application is approved.

Testing Security Objectives

Test security controls and objectives in systems and applications. Complete this step prior to implementation. It is not enough to build these controls into systems and applications, you have to make sure they work and are effective.

Testing of Changes

Changes to systems or applications also need to be tested. Management must ensure that changes are tested in accordance with the impact and resource assessment, in a separate test environment by an independent test group. This includes developing back-out plans.

Parallel/Pilot Testing Criteria and Performance

Institute procedures that provide for parallel or pilot testing. This will ensure that new applications provide output as good as similar, already established applications. Perform these tests in accordance with a pre-established plan that specifies criteria for terminating the testing process in advance.

Final Acceptance Test

Perform acceptance tests for all new systems and applications, in an environment that is isolated from the live environment and performed independently of the development staff. According to ISF, acceptance tests should:

- Involve business users;

- Simulate the live environment;

- Involve running the full suite of system components, including application functionality, database management utilities and the underlying operating system;

- Feature full integration testing, to ensure there will be no adverse effects on existing systems;

- Involve independent security assessments of the critical code to detect vulnerabilities and insecure use of programming features; and,

- Include attempts to breach the security of the system, for example by performing penetration tests.

Provide for the final acceptance test in the testing procedures and cover all components of the information system.

Security Testing and Accreditation

Define and implement procedures to ensure that operations and user management formally accept the test results, system security, and any remaining residual risks. According to CobiT, these procedures should reflect the agreed upon roles and responsibilities of end users, system development, network management and system operations personnel, taking into account segregation, supervision and control issues.

Operational Test

Before the system is moved into operation, it must be validated as a complete product. The operational test is to be conducted under conditions similar to the application environment and in the same manner as the systems will be run in the production environment.

Testing procedures need to be developed for each and every one of these steps. These procedures are used to evaluate, accredit and accept test results, and to accept the residual risk remaining after all tests have been performed.

Have you prepared an implementation plan?

As the name suggests the final stage in the design and implementation process is implementation of the systems and applications you've designed. The implementation process includes preparing the implementation plan, managing the plan, and developing a maintenance plan. We start the implementation process with preparing the plan, and with the following control objective:

> Following testing of a system or application software, the organization will plan the process for implementation of the system, take into account implementation strategies, procedures (such as conversion, installation, and so on), and personnel training and formulate them into a documented implementation plan. The plan should be reviewed and approved by appropriate project management personnel.

Preparing and approving an implementation plan helps ensure that your plan is feasible in terms of labor and equipment requirements. It also gives you a strong road map indicating where your project needs to go to be a success.

Guidance from the regulations and standards

Banking/Finance

FFIEC Development and Acquisitions does not call directly for an implementation plan but plans the process through implementation schedules and allocation of responsibilities for implementation.

Records Management

ISO 15489-2 and **DIRKS** call for the development of an implementation plan for new recordkeeping systems. DIRKS specifies the need to select implementation strategies and plan the implementation process.

For a more detailed discussion of this topic, see **DIRKS** F.4.9 & G.4.1-2.

General Guidelines

CobiT calls for a development of a detailed implementation plan that must be reviewed and approved prior to any implementation procedures. The **ISF Standard of Good Practices for Information Security** does not explicitly call for an implementation plan but does call for documented implementation processes. See CobiT AI 5.3 for more information.

CobiT 4 AI7.3 suggests establishing an implementation plan for a project. It should define release design, build of release packages, rollout procedures/installation, incident handling, distribution controls, storage of software, review of the release and documentation of changes.

From regulation to reality – sure signs you are complying

Planning is important, whether it is for testing, security, or implementation. Planning can mean the difference between success and failure. An implementation plan must integrate several considerations, including:

- Implementation strategies
- Site preparation
- Equipment acquisition and installation
- User training
- Installation of operating software changes
- Implementation of operating procedures
- Conversion

Once the plan is written, it needs to be reviewed by appropriate managers and IT staff for accuracy and then documented.

Do you manage your implementation?

Leaving implementation processes for new systems unattended is an open invitation to arguments, overlapping inefficient work and a cruddy final product. Avoid these problems by managing implementation work that is done in your organization. The following control objective sums up what must be done:

> To ensure the integrity and accountability of systems, the organization will manage the implementation of new or modified systems or application software. Organizations must conduct a post-implementation review that includes an assessment of whether user requirements are being met by the new system and whether benefits promised by the project have been realized.

Be sure to document the details of your management work as well as the review. These are useful later in the case that you are being audited, or if you want to compare a set of reviews to determine your progress, success and failure.

Guidance from the regulations and standards

Banking/Finance

FFIEC Development and Acquisitions calls for the implementation of newly developed systems and applications, specifying systems conversion, installation, and a post-implementation review.

Records Management

ISO 15489 and **DIRKS** call for an implementation process that requires installation, conversion and review of recordkeeping systems. It also addresses allocating recordkeeping responsibilities, training in the managing of records and the inception of a program for disposal of records.

NIST Special Publications

NIST 800-14 reiterates testing with respect to security and requires review of the system.

General Guidelines

CobiT, and the **ISF Standard of Good Practice for Information Security** call for a process for implementation new systems and software and differ slightly in what they include. CobiT calls for application software performance sizing (determination of resources and capacity for implementation), systems and data conversion, and a post-implementation review that assesses user requirements and expected benefits. The ISF Standard calls for a similar process but does not specifically call for conversion of old systems. Each standard does include the need for training personnel on the new system or software.

Both CobiT and the **ISF Standard of Good Practices for Information Security** have a lot of information on this topic. See the CobiT AI 5.2, 4-5 & 12-14, and ISF Standard's SD 6.1.2 & 6.2-3 for more information.

From regulation to reality – sure signs you are complying

Based on the strategies and process defined in the implementation plan, you must manage the implementation of new or modified systems or application software. You wouldn't spend all this time and money on developing, designing and testing the new product without keeping a watchful eye on how it is implemented and whether it is working as anticipated. At this point, consider and approve any final resources or performance capability required for implementation. Convert systems and data from the old systems and applications to new systems. Of course, the new systems should then be promoted to production.

Schedule the promotion of new systems in advance, to avoid disrupting information processing activities and enable installation in a timely manner. Make sure that promotion to production is approved by the appropriate managers and owners before the old system is disconnected and discontinued. Once the system or application has been promoted, evaluate it to ensure it is meeting user requirements and needs. Finally, conduct a post-implementation review, to study whether the new system or application has met the desired benefits envisioned by your organization, and whether this was done in a cost effective manner.

Have you developed a maintenance plan?

You have done it! You have created the perfect system or software for your organization. It fits your organizations needs just right, and you are proud of all the preparation and effort that has gone into developing this new IT solution. We hate to break it to you, but you are not done yet. Not unless you have developed, documented and implemented a maintenance plan. That is why we recommend you follow this control objective:

> *In order to promote the integrity and accountability of new IT solutions, organizational management will develop a plan to maintain the system, including the policies and procedures, tools and documentation associated with it.*

Maintenance of your new system or software is key to keeping it working in prime condition. If you keep it finely tuned, it will turn around and give back to your organization for years to come.

Guidance from the regulations and standards

Banking/Finance

FFIEC Development and Acquisitions calls for a maintenance phase but does not explicitly require the development of a maintenance plan. The standard specifies that the maintenance process involves change management procedures, but these procedures are part of operational management, not project management.

Records Management

DIRKS calls for the development of a maintenance plan that incorporates provisions for the ongoing maintenance of a recordkeeping system.

General Guidelines

General standards do not call for a maintenance plan, but primarily cover maintenance of systems with respect to operational management.

You have just spent a great deal of tie planning, developing, testing and implementing your system. You have invested resources, manpower and energy into this project. What a waste it would be to let it all fall by the wayside. Instead of letting it all fall apart, try developing a maintenance plan and sticking to it, so that you can preserve and appreciate that which you spent so long creating.

Management must develop a plan to maintain the new information system or application, including the policies and procedures, tools, and documentation associated with it. This will guide the maintenance phase and provide for a consistent process of review. You will be on top of any changes that need to be made to the system, in turn keeping the system working for your organization. Regularly update the plan and include any repairs or modifications that have been made, to identify any patterns or persistent problems.

Maintenance only works if it is constant. This means developing a schedule that lets you know when checks must be made. It also includes creating a system of documentation, indicating what is working well, what isn't and how each incident was handled. Once the maintenance plan is developed and instituted, a little fine-tuning will keep the maintenance current. Finally, when it comes time to overhaul a system or software, you can use this plan to develop a new plan for the new system or software. The experience will make the next go around even more productive.

Systems Acquisition

The Main Thing

Have you thought of everything for your IT acquisition plan?

Acquiring a new system is like preparing to bring a new pet into your home. You have to check for anything that could be dangerous, make sure you have food and toys, and block off any rooms you don't want messed. For systems, you need to do the same kind of preparation. Whether you are buying off the shelf, or from a trusted vendor, you need to consider security, safety, assets and procedure. In order to remember all the steps your organization will need to take during the systems acquisition process, there is nothing that'll benefit you more than making a list, checking it twice, and turning it into your IT acquisition plan. We have written the following control objective for this step in IT acquisitions:

> *The organization will create an IT acquisition plan to define the strategy, processes and procedures for acquiring information technology software, hardware, systems and services. Much like the systems development lifecycle methodology (SDLC), the organization will create a methodology that exists in the plan, document it, and create a process of acquisition.*

It can be difficult to remember everything you'll need when creating the plan, so be sure to check and double check it before putting it to use. Once it's done, it will serve as the checklist for what you'll need to acquire for your organization.

Guidance from the regulations and standards

Banking/Finance

FFIEC Development and Acquisitions calls for an acquisition project plan for acquisition projects, but assumes the acquisition strategy to be restricted to off-the-shelf or third party vendors. It compares the IT acquisition methodology to the SDLC but calls for distinct project plans and processes between the two.

US Federal Security

The **Clinger-Cohen Act** does not define a documented plan for general governmental acquisition of IT, but does require a similar, albeit more narrowly focused acquisition plan for use in its "Solutions-based Contracting" pilot program (§ 5312(c)(1)).

Records Management

Like FFIEC, **DIRKS** does not directly call for an IT acquisition plan, but works IT acquisition methodology into the initially planning phase for recordkeeping projects. Thus, the initial project plan for development of a recordkeeping system would distinguish and define the IT acquisition process.

NIST Special Publications

NIST 800-14 makes a brief mention of creating a plan for acquiring IT resources within the context of security purposes, while the ISF standard defines a plan much like FFIEC Development and Acquisitions, wherein the acquisition plan and procedures are entirely separate from the SDLC (yet still inherently linked).

General Guidance

CobiT calls for an acquisition plan as a document entirely focused on determining an IT acquisition strategy – however it does address all considerations and procedures for IT acquisition (as listed above), which is what should be considered when developing the IT acquisition plan.

From regulation to reality – sure signs you are complying

If you want to acquire information technology software, hardware, systems or services, your organization will need an IT acquisition plan. An acquisition plan, in brief, shows what services and products your organization needs and how these things will be obtained. A bad acquisition plan or no plan at all will very likely lead to your organization losing money and possibly being ripped off or acquiring deficient services. Avoiding each problem by documenting how it will be dealt with in an acquisition might end up being complicated, but fortunately, if you already have a system development lifecycle (SDLC), it's easier than you think. There is a good deal of overlap between the SDLC and an acquisition plan with the chief difference being your acquisition plan contains a bidding process rather than a design and development phase.

Generally, there are a number of things you want to consider when acquiring IT resources:

- Have you defined your information and security requirements?
- Did you consider alternative courses of action?

- Do you have an acquisition strategy (i.e. a preference for off-the-shelf solutions vs. internally developed solutions vs. third-party solutions or a combination)?

- How will you conduct technological and economic feasibility studies?

- Have you analyzed the risk of acquisition of the product or service?

- What process do you use to select system software?

- What are your procurement control standards and procedures?

- Have you considered how you will acquire software and deal with escrow and software licensing issues?

- How do you handle third-party software maintenance?

- What arrangements are in place for dealing with contract application programming?

- Have you dealt with acceptance of facilities and technology?

We will address these questions in detail later in this chapter, but they're good to keep in mind at the start so you have an idea of what you need to include in an IT acquisition plan. Failure to adequately answer any of these questions in an IT acquisition plan can lead to big problems down the road, most often through miscommunication or contractual issues, but also budget, and probability of success.

What are your information and security requirements?

Having well defined information and security requirements will help your organization move through the systems acquisition process with ease and comfort. You have to know what your requirements are before you try and fit those requirements. Otherwise, it would be like sending someone to the grocery store to get stuff for dinner but not giving them a list of ingredients. Therefore, keep the following control objective in mind for this phase of systems acquisition:

> In order to have an effective IT acquisition plan and process, the organization will define the business, functional and security requirements of the system (software, infrastructure or services) to be procured.

Some standards equate this process as equivalent to defining design requirements, while others recognize it as isolated to systems acquisition. We think it is helpful for both. Design aside, defining information and security requirements is a necessary step in systems acquisition.

Guidance from the regulations and standards

Banking/Finance

FFIEC Development and Acquisitions calls for the development of "detailed functional, security and system requirements" for the system acquisition with the assumption that the acquisition strategy has already been determined to solicit third parties for IT solutions.

"Acquisition projects are similar to development projects. Organizations often employ structured acquisition methodologies similar to the SDLC when acquiring significant hardware and software products.

The difference is that instead of design and development phases, an acquisition project has a bid solicitation process involving developing detailed lists of functional, security, and system requirements and distributing them to third parties.

Key tools in managing acquisition projects include invitations-to-tender and request-for-proposals. Invitations-to-tender involve soliciting bids from vendors when acquiring hardware or integrated systems of hardware and software. Request-for-proposals involve soliciting bids when acquiring off-the-shelf or third-party developed software. These terms may sometimes be used interchangeably.

Have management establish acquisition standards for functional, security and operational requirements. Make sure these requirements are appropriately defined in RFPs and ITTs. Be sure they assess the risk of the acquisitions as well. Software for word processing is very low risk, but a financial application is likely a lot higher. You will need evaluation procedures for both, and these procedures may be less strict for the word processing vs. financial applications. Figure out how to determine what procedures are required under what circumstances" (FFIEC Development and Acquisition Pg. 39)

US Federal Security

While the **Clinger-Cohen Act** defines an IT acquisition process, it does not explicitly provide a procedure for defining acquisition requirements. It does, however, state that the decisions made with respect to acquisition will be based on requirements, thus implying their definition.

Records Management

DIRKS addresses the need for defining requirements as part of the overall design and development of a recordkeeping system, but does not call for a definition of requirements specific to systems acquisition as it assumes that these requirements will be one and the same.

General Guidance

Much in the same way as DIRKS, **CobiT** and the **ISF Standard of Good Practices for Information Security** do not explicitly call for a definition of requirements, as they incorporate consideration of systems to be acquired directly into the SDLC design phase. CobiT, however, does address the need for cost-effective security.

From regulation to reality – sure signs you are complying

You can't plan very well if you don't know what it is you're planning for. That's why the first step of creating an IT acquisition plan involves defining your goals. What sorts of information does your organization deal with? What security features do you need for the different kinds of information? Do you want to enhance existing security or get something brand new?

Once you've answered those questions you're halfway there. But, there are still a few more considerations. Namely, how much will your acquisitions cost the organization? Are they compatible with audit-trail requirements? And finally, are there any ergonomic issues for automated solutions?

Be thorough in defining all the requirements and answering all the questions we've put forth. Your answers will become the foundation for the IT acquisition plan. They'll also come in handy when you deal with third-parties. You can hand any third-party a list of your information and security requirements to see if they adequately meet your needs. In addition to the list, have management come up with acquisition standards for functional, security and operational requirements. That way, your workers as well as third-parties completely understand what kind of results you expect to see.

Part of defining information and security requirements includes creating the standard request-for-proposal and invitation-to-tender. A request-for-proposal is created to aid your organization when soliciting bids for off the shelf or third-party developed software. Invitations-to-tender are for soliciting bids from vendors when acquiring hardware or a combination of hardware and software. Amongst other things, these documents indicate what it is you are looking for in IT acquisitions. Whichever acquisition you are currently undergoing, you need to utilize the defined information and security requirements in the creation of these documents. Then, when it's time to purchase something, you'll have a template to work with instead of starting from scratch each time.

Finally, you want to conduct a risk assessment when defining your requirements. Some acquisitions are low-risk, such as word processing software. Conversely, a financial application is very high risk as glitches in this kind of software can mean accounting problems for you. Create evaluation procedures for the different levels of risk you will encounter during an acquisition so that workers know what is acceptable for an acquisition and what is not.

Have you considered alternative courses of action?

If you have identified an IT acquisition solution that just isn't feasible for your organization, what are you going to do? Well, you won't be asking that if during the planning process you come up with a back-up plan for when you can't get the IT solution you want most. Therefore, control objective for this section is:

> *Provided that an IT acquisition determined by the business and functional requirements of the organization cannot be satisfied, the organization will consider alternative courses of action to best meet requirements for information technology needs.*

Having alternative courses of action at your disposal will make your organization more flexible and as a result, better able to deal with situations that don't turn out ideally.

Guidance from the regulations and standards

General Guidance

CobiT calls for consideration of alternative courses of action provided the identified solution cannot meet current business requirements, while the **ISF Standard of Good Practices for Information Security** calls for the same with respect to meeting security requirements.

From regulation to reality – sure signs you are complying

Sometimes viable acquisition options that solve your requirements issues aren't available. IT may be that they don't exist, or that they just aren't feasible for an organization of your size or resources. Whatever the problem is, you need a backup plan. Your organization must meet its information and security needs, or you are bound to wind up with even more problems.

Create a procedure for how you will determine alternative courses of action when it is just not possible to get the most appropriate IT solutions. This will make the process of finding and implementing a solution much simpler than creating the process as you go along. Document appropriate procedures for creating and choosing alternative courses of action and make sure they are readily available for upper management should you run into this problem.

Determining alternate courses of action is a project best suited for your own staff and management. Solving this problem in-house will provide you with a reasonable solution that will fit the needs of your organization. Why? Because no one knows the needs of your organization like those of you who run it day to day.

The procedures should include sitting down with your IT staff and management and brainstorming how to take your resources and current IT systems and turn them into systems that will meet your information and security requirements. Only after you have an plan on how to meet those needs can you go back out to find the off the shelf or third party provided items you will need to make it all happen.

Have you conducted a feasibility study?

Whether or not IT solutions are feasible for your organization can determine whether or not you obtain them. Instead of waiting to the last minute and realizing you don't have the funds to cover the IT solution developed through this process, conduct a feasibility study for the proposed acquisition. This process will allow you to know what is and is not possible for your organization. We recommend you follow this control objective:

> *Once requirements have been defined for systems acquisition, the organization will conduct a feasibility study to determine the technological and economic feasibility of the proposed acquisition. Such a study involves examining all business objectives, IT objectives and requirements for projects using acquired systems.*

The results of this study can then help determine individual acquisition strategies and the requirements included in RFPs (request for proposals) for third party vendors.

Guidance from the regulations and standards

Banking/Finance

FFIEC Development and Acquisitions calls for a feasibility study following the definition of initial requirements and a business case detailing the systems acquisition request. FFIEC also suggests personnel who should be consulted during the feasibility study.

FFIEC Development and Acquisitions Pg. 42 suggests that you begin an acquisitions project by submitting a project request. Procedures should be in place to ensure the request process is easy and that management systematically reviews all requests. Each request should include a business case for acquiring product, identify desired system features, describe information requirements, network interfaces, hardware components, and software applications that will support and interact with a new product.

Have management conduct a feasibility study to determine if the project can be supported by its business case. All affected parties should document their approval of the project. During the feasibility study, management should take care to consider business objectives, technology objectives, functional requirements, security requirements, internal control requirements, documentation requirements, performance requirements, network requirements, system interface requirements, expandability requirements, reliability requirements, maintenance requirements, installation requirements, conversion requirements, personnel requirements, processing requirements, product development standards, product design standards, testing requirements, training requirements, vendor's financial strength, vendor's support levels and cost/benefit analysis.

Another aspect of the study should include management consulting various personnel who are deemed appropriate for the project depending on their role in relation to the system being acquired. Personnel may include audit personnel, business unit managers, database administrators, end users, legal counsel, network administrators, network technicians, quality assurance personnel, security administrators, systems analysts, technology department managers and vendor personnel.

Once a request appears feasible, the feasibility study may be used to flesh out the request by defining functional, system and organizational requirements included in the request-for-proposals and invitations-to-tender that management distributes to third parties in the bid solicitation process.

After a bid is received, the organization should analyze and compare the bids with one another and their requirements to see who is best. Good bids from vendors will address everything clearly that the organization requires and include software issues such as confidentiality standards, compatible operating systems, copyright standards, delivery dates, escrow criteria, liability limitations, licensing restrictions, maintenance procedures, next release date, regulatory requirements, software language, subcontractor details, testing standards, training provided and warranty specifications. The bid should also include hardware issues such as backup options, maintenance requirements, memory capacities, performance capabilities and servicing options.

Procedures should be in place to ensure bids are properly reviewed, that bids can be narrowed to potential vendors, and that management reviews the financial stability and service commitment of these vendors. Once a product and vendor is selected and the contract negotiated, have legal counsel review it prior to signing.

US Federal Security

Though the **Clinger-Cohen Act** does not specifically call for a feasibility study, its IT acquisition process clearly calls for a consideration of whether to acquire systems based on "minimum criteria", "shared benefits and costs", and "net benefits."

General Guidance

CobiT calls for both a technological and economic feasibility study for both the proposed acquisition and any alternative courses of action. CobiT requires that feasibility be considered within the domain of an organization's information

From regulation to reality — sure signs you are complying

When you're enthusiastic about a project, such as an IT acquisition, nothing sounds better than diving right in and getting things moving. However, sometimes diving right in means whacking your head on the bottom of the pool. That's why before undertaking any IT acquisition project, you should conduct a thorough feasibility study.

Feasibility studies begin with the submission of a project request. What the submission should include and how it should be examined are procedural issues that management needs to create and document so they are repeatable. In general, each submission should include the reasons for acquisition, the system features the acquisition offers, what the information requirements are, the network interfaces involved, the hardware components and the software applications that need to support and interact with the product.

Management then takes the project request and examines it for weaknesses. Potential problems include:

- incompatibility with key systems and applications
- cost vs. benefit
- alignment with business objectives
- alignment with technology objectives
- functional requirements
- performance requirements
- personnel requirements, processing requirements
- product development standards
- design standards
- testing requirements
- training requirements
- financial strength of vendors to be hired for the acquisition

- support offered by vendors

If the project request survives the scrutiny of management on enough fronts to be considered acceptable, management should then consult personnel that are appropriate for the project. Questions for personnel include whether they will have time to work on the project, if they have appropriate training, if the project meets their standards and requirements for daily work and whether they think the project can succeed. Potential personnel to question could include:

- audit personnel
- business unit managers
- database administrators
- end users
- legal counsel
- network administrators
- network technicians
- quality assurance personnel
- security administrators
- systems analysts
- technology department managers
- vendor personnel

After the project request makes it past the interview stage, the feasibility study can be used to flesh out the request by defining functional, system and organizational requirements included in the request-for-proposals and invitations-to-tender that management will distribute to third parties in the bid solicitation process.

When bids begin coming in based on the project request, the feasibility study should involve analyzing and comparing the bids with one another to see which is best. A solid bid will clearly address each requirement for the project as stated in the initial request. It will also cover issues such as:

- confidentiality standards
- compatible operating systems
- copyright standards
- delivery dates
- escrow criteria

- liability limitations
- licensing restrictions
- maintenance procedures
- next release date
- regulatory requirements
- software language
- subcontractor details
- testing standards
- training provided
- warranty specifications
- back up options for hardware
- memory capacities
- performance capabilities
- servicing options

Not all issues are necessary for each project request. For example you may need to check for "memory capacities" if you are acquiring hardware, but not if you're acquiring software. Defining procedures and issues to consider for different types of acquisitions will make the process simpler, and if possible you ought to do this.

Have you formulated an acquisition strategy?

Ah, strategies. Some of you may think that by avoiding sports or dropping out of law school that you avoided having to map out strategies forever. Well, think again. Strategizing is key in IT business management and it is equally as imperative to systems acquisition. For strategizing in the realm of IT systems acquisition, follow this control objective:

> *Once the organization determines whether a proposed acquisition is feasible, the next step will be to formulate an acquisition strategy. This strategy describes the criteria the organization will use to determine whether to develop or modify a system internally, acquire an IT system by external means, purchase software or service off-the-shelf, negotiate a contract with a third party vendor for systems or elect for a combination of strategies.*

Any acquisitions developed internally will follow the organization's own SDLC methodology, although as previously mentioned, many of the standards already consider systems acquisition to be part of the SDLC.

Guidance from the regulations and standards

Banking/Finance

FFIEC Development and Acquisitions divides development and acquisition into two separate projects, but does state that the feasibility study will help determine the acquisition strategy as a customization of pre-existing systems or off-the-shelf acquisition. In the case of customization, the standard points to SDLC practices, or through acquisition of contract system development.

FFIEC Development and Acquisitions Pg. 39 says organizations should develop acquisition strategies similar to the SDLC when acquiring significant hardware and software products. The difference is a bid solicitation process instead of design and development phases as in the SDLC. Establish vendor selection criteria, review vendors' financial strength, support levels, security controls, etc. before using them. Also, management should review contracts and licensing agreements to ensure the rights and responsibilities of each party are clear and equitable. Figure out risks as well – these can include poor definition of requirements, ineffective assessments of vendors and insufficient review of contracts and agreements.

Other concerns are contract and licensing issues. Ensure that legal counsel approves performance guarantees, source code accessibility, intellectual property considerations and software/data security issues before signing a contract.

If you work with foreign third-parties be sure to determine what country's laws apply to your interactions and how you will manage risks.

US Federal Security

The **Clinger-Cohen Act** provides an acquisition strategy that requires procurement of IT off-the-shelf or through contract and so the acquisition strategy, provided the government agency determines it is feasible, will always result in acquisition of IT from an outside source.

Records Management

DIRKS and **ISO 15489** both emphasize the need to consider whether to "buy, build, or both", included as a crucial element of recordkeeping system design strategy.

DIRKS § F.4.5.1 says you should determine whether you will buy services to build or build yourself. You can use in-house technology, additional technology brought from outside and tailored to suit needs or you can have someone else design additional technology. Cost, flexibility and integration speed are generally the biggest factors in choosing among these possibilities.

General Guidance

CobiT specifies the formulation of an acquisition strategy and at this stage calls for an acquisition plan, indicating that the strategy should be documented. The ISF Standard does not explicitly call for formulation of an acquisition strategy, as the acquisition section of the standard refers only to technology acquired through third parties; the **ISF Standard of Good Practices for Information Security**, like FFIEC, separates development and acquisition, so any other formulated strategy would most likely occur during initial planning for systems design.

Specifically, **CobiT** AI1.3 states that the SDLC should include provisions for acquisition strategy plans that define whether software will be acquired off-the-shelf, internally developed, through contract or by enhancing existing software, or a combination of all these.

Once you conduct a feasibility study and determine an acquisition makes sense, decided how the acquisition will take place. You can acquire the IT equipment you need off-the-shelf, develop it internally or contract with a third party vendor to have it created. Another possibility is a combination of all these strategies. Whatever you choose, keep in mind that internal development is the easiest way to ensure that the acquisition follows your organization's SDLC methodology closely, which is an important aspect of maintaining compliance with a number of standards.

Depending on what regulations you want to be compliant with, your acquisition strategy will fall under one of two categories. Either you'll need to include it as part of the SDLC, or develop it as a separate entity. In either case, there is a good deal of overlap. Acquisition needs many of the standards and details necessary for an SDLC.

Some special aspects of acquisition to include in your strategy are first and foremost, contract and licensing issues. If you're purchasing third party work or support, be sure you know what your criteria are for a hire, an acceptable contract, and the work to be delivered. If a third party vendor will be responsible for software or hardware support for something you purchase, find out details such as how stable the vendor is, how good their support is, what security controls they offer and how much experience they have before making a hire. If you are working with a foreign third party, determine which country's laws are applicable to your situation.

Before choosing a solution, the final step is to assess the risk of the acquisition. Using your organization's policies and procedures for risk assessment, determine if an acquisition offers an acceptable level of risk before purchasing or implementing anything.

What are third-party service requirements?

Working with a third party on a project can be highly beneficial to your organization. It can also look a lot like the sequel to #7 of the very popular and successful Nightmare on Elm Street series. To get the most out of a provider, you need to know what you want, what you don't want, and the opportunity to compare different third parties to one another. To ensure you achieve these things, keep in mind the following control objective:

> *Before signing a contract for a third-party service, the organization will develop and review service requirements. These requirements indicate what the organization expects to see from a third-party in terms of work, materials, quality of service, etc. The requirements will also indicate what you won't tolerate.*

All requirements should be written in clear, easy to understand terms so everyone knows what needs to be done, and so loopholes may be avoided.

Guidance from the regulations and standards

Banking/Finance

FFIEC Development and Acquisitions is the most detailed with regards to RFPs for third party vendor acquisitions, so much so that it defines a "bid solicitation process" for issuing third party service requirements for RFPs. FFIEC further details requirements for vendors when sending proposals, but since that is not applicable here we will not address it.

FFIEC Development and Acquisition Pgs. 40-43 specifically states that there are two key tools in managing acquisition projects: invitations-to-tender, and requests-for proposal. Invitations-to-tender involve soliciting bids from vendors when acquiring hardware or integrated systems of hardware and software. Requests-for-proposals involve soliciting bids when acquiring off the shelf or third-party developed software. FFIEC notes that these terms are sometimes used interchangeably.

Management should develop acquisition standards directly relating to these two procedures, and should make sure these acquisition standards are clearly detailed in the above documents.

US Federal Security

The **Clinger-Cohen Act** addresses third party service requirements only through its pilot programs (an alternate method of acquiring IT systems). It requires a "simple solicitation" that includes a functional work description, required qualifications, and terms and conditions.

NIST Special Publications

NIST 800-53 § SA-4 calls for the organization to include security requirements and or specifications in information system acquisition contracts based on an assessment of risk. The security requirements should describe:

- required security capabilities
- required design and development process
- required test and evaluation procedures
- required documentation

International Standards Organization

NIST 800-14 mentions contract solicitation documents but only in terms of ensuring security.

General Guidance

CobiT briefly addresses the need for an organization to evaluate requirements and specifications for a RFP.

CobiT AI1.4 states specifically that an organization's SDLC methodology should provide for the evaluation of the requirements and the specifications for an RFP when dealing with third-party service vendors.

From regulation to reality – sure signs you are complying

Acquiring information systems or applications from third-party service providers entails much more than going out and buying some software. Choosing the right system or the right application is a detailed process. You start by requesting proposals for the systems you want. Then you review each incoming proposal, compare it against others and weed out the bad ones. The final step is to pick one.

In greater detail, the first step of choosing a service provider begins with creating a request-for-proposal or invitation-to-tender. Due to the similarities between these two documents, and the tendency to use them interchangeably, we will refer to them as one – the request-for-proposal (RFP).

In order to issue the RFP, management must first define acquisition standards. These standards should address reliability and security issues, as well as functional and operational requirements. Then, these standards are integrated into the RFP. This will ensure that all third-party requirements are clearly identified and aid vendors in constructing proposals based on the needs of your organization.

Once you have received all the bids or proposals, the next step is to examine the bids and match them against each other and your requirements. Other applicable hardware and software issues such as confidentiality standards, compatibility, regulatory requirements, back-up options and so on should also be discussed during this process.

Narrow the proposals down to a short-list of the best proposals that can be given to management for review. Management will then take the short-list and investigate the vendors' financial stability, service commitment and other traits that will help them make a well-rounded decision based both on the organization's requirements and vendors' capabilities and reputation.

You may find it helpful to encapsulate this process in a documented procedure. Having a procedure for systems and software acquisition will ensure that steps are not overlooked and that your organization gets the best possible products from reliable vendors.

Have you prepared a risk analysis report?

Change is always scary. The question is-- how scary is change? If you don't have an answer to this question for each instance of change, especially when it involves acquiring and installing new systems or systems components, you need to start doing risk analysis reports.

> *The organization will prepare a risk analysis report as a key element of the systems acquisition process.*

Preparing a report also makes it easier to communicate issues and triumphs to the rest of your organization's management. If done well, a report is easily reference-able, and can be compared to other reports to determine new trends and patterns in the risks your organization faces.

Guidance from the regulations and standards

Public Companies

Though public standards do not directly address risk analysis reports for systems acquisition, they imply the need for risk management across all organizational functions.

Banking/Finance

FFIEC Development and Acquisitions does not specifically call for a risk analysis report with respect to systems acquisition, but does state that risk management must be a part of acquisition methodologies. It notes specific risks of IT procurement, including inadequate requirements definition, ineffective assessment of vendors, and insufficient review of contracts and agreements.

Healthcare and Life Sciences

HIPAA does not directly address risk analysis reports for systems acquisition, but does require a risk assessment that would relate to procurement of any IT systems or services pertaining to privacy information.

Credit Card

For systems acquired from third party vendors, **VISA CISP** requires a process to identify vulnerabilities associated with default settings and passwords.

US Federal Security

The **Clinger-Cohen Act** includes in its acquisition process requirements for quantifying risk but does not explicitly require a risk analysis report. **FISCAM, GAO Financial Audit Manual** and **FISMA** all provide guidance for assessing risk through all lifecycles of an organization, and other government standards imply this by mentioning risk management.

Records Management

Records management standards do not directly address risk analysis reports for systems acquisition, but **DIRKS** does require an assessment of business risk that could be applied to acquisition of recordkeeping resources.

General Guidance

CobiT is the only general standard that calls for a risk analysis report as part of the systems acquisition methodology. **COSO**, being a framework entirely focused on risk management, mentions that risk plays a role in systems acquisition, and the ISF Standard requires assessment of security deficiencies and security weaknesses in third party products.

Specifically, **CobiT** § AI1.8 calls for an organization's SDLC methodology to provide for an analysis and documentation of security threats, potential vulnerabilities and impacts, and the feasible security and internal control safeguards for reducing or eliminating risks. This is to be done in conjunction with each proposed information system development, implementation of modification project.

From regulation to reality – sure signs you are complying

Several regulations imply the procedure of risk measurement/analysis, and CobiT requires it. When undertaking a systems acquisition risk analysis, the following things need to be measured:

- Security threats
- Security weaknesses in third party products
- Potential vulnerabilities and impacts

- Feasibility security

- Internal control safeguards for reducing or eliminating risks

This kind of risk assessment should be done every time your organization decides to acquire systems or applications. After conducting the risk assessment, create a risk analysis report for management to review along with the RFPs.

Do you have procurement controls in place?

It's always fun to buy new stuff, and sometimes it's fun to fix up your existing stuff. What happens though, if several people in your organization decide to replace the same item? Or fix the same item? Instead of an improved system, you'll likely end up with a gigantic mess, and maybe even a few fights between staff members who prefer their ideas for changing something to everyone else's. To avoid this kind of problem, check out the following control objective:

> In addition to an acquisition methodology, the organization will create procurement controls for new systems, software and services. These controls enable you to organize and streamline the process used to purchase and implement new systems and system changes.

Leave out procurement controls and you'll have the same problem you get when too many cooks try to work on the same pot of soup – a finished product nobody wants to get near.

Guidance from the regulations and standards

Banking/Finance

The **FFIEC Development and Acquisitions handbook** defines procurement standards and procedures as "acquisition standards" and requires organizations to develop and document these standards for all procedures above.

US Federal Security

The **Clinger-Cohen Act** does not call for formal standards but refers to procurement procedures as a simplified process comprised of "management of risk, incremental acquisitions, and the need to incorporate information technology in a timely manner."

General Guidance

CobiT calls for a "central procurement approach" that describes a common set of standards and procedures for IT systems, software and services. The standard does not go into too much additional detail, other than to note that products should be reviewed and tested prior to their use and financial settlement. The **ISF Standard of Good Practice for Information Security** calls for standards and procedures that include software and hardware selection guidelines, risk management, licensing requirements, and review and approval mechanisms.

From regulation to reality – sure signs you are complying

The procurement of IT systems, software, and services can be a tedious task. Between requesting and reviewing proposals, conducting risk analyses and feasibility studies, and formulating acquisition strategies, there are a lot of little steps to remember. A good way to take the pressure off your brain is to create procurement controls. This includes developing, documenting and enforcing a set of policies and procedures to be adhered to any time your organization decides to procure systems, software or services.

These procurement controls are not the same thing as an acquisition plan; they only apply to the actual procurement of systems, rather than the acquisition methodology as a whole. Procurement controls (standards and procedures) should cover:

- RFP issuance and third-party vendor proposals
- Third-party contracts and software licensing
- Reviews of third-party vendors, contract, and licensing
- Security controls for product features and contract development
- Review and testing of the product before acquisition

What do you need to know about software product acquisition?

When it comes time in your organization's life to acquire software, there are several things to keep in mind. Consider this two part control objective before acquiring software products:

> *Software acquisition will be conducted in accordance with established organizational procurement controls. Additionally, the following five elements must be addressed: Escrowed documentation, Software licensing, Contract application programming, Pilot programs, and Third-party Software maintenance*

Once you have a handle on these aspects you'll be able to make good software product acquisition choices for your organization.

Guidance from the regulations and standards

Banking/Finance

FFIEC Development and Acquisitions calls for software development contracts and licensing agreements, and everything these contracts entail, from escrow agreements to third party regulatory and

US Federal Security

The **Clinger-Cohen Act** calls for a "modular contracting" and "incremental acquisition", basically meaning that agencies must employ contract developers to provide them with IT solutions, and incrementally, meaning each acquisition must be its own solution and not be reliant on subsequent increments to function properly. The one truly unique thing about this standard is that it calls for pilot programs, accomplished either through private sector organizations or contract software developers. The pilot programs solve acquisition needs by calling for contracted personnel to develop and test IT solutions independently.

NIST Special Publications

NIST 800-53 requires third party cooperation with security policies and procedures.

International Standards Organization

ISO 17799 requires that third party providers be held under contract to comply with an organization's security policies and controls. **ISO 17799** lists several security requirements for third party contracts. This list can be found on page 6- § 4.2.2- of the ISO 17799 document.

General Guidance

CobiT calls for software product acquisition to adhere to established procurement standards and procedures, but does not mention software licensing agreements or escrowed documentation. CobiT requires contract application programmers to be subject to the same SDLC methodology as the organization's own development team and also requires that third party providers of licensed software maintain the security and integrity of their products through maintenance agreements. For more information see CobiT Control Objectives AI 1.14-16.

The **ISF Standard of Good Practices for Information Security** requires selection from a list of approved vendors, software licensing contracts and contractual agreements with suppliers. The standard also calls for third party source code to be kept in escrow and updated regularly.

US State Laws

The **California Office of Privacy Protection** requires establishment of contracts with third party service providers to ensure that they follow privacy and security policies when handling an organization's information – this would apply directly to software development contracts.

From regulation to reality – sure signs you are complying

If you want to ensure you're acquiring appropriate software for your organization under terms you find acceptable, you'll need to address five elements: Escrow documentation, software licensing, contract application programming, pilot programs and third-party software maintenance.

Escrow documentation

According to the FFIEC Development and Acquisition Handbook, software can be written in three different ways: non-proprietary, open source code; proprietary, (licensed) open source code; or proprietary, closed source code. Non-proprietary, open source code is publicly available code and can be copied and modified without restriction. Proprietary, open source code software is also written in publicly available code but it is copyrighted and distributed through licensing agreements. Proprietary, closed source code software contains copyright trade secrets of the company that owns and/or wrote the software. Most vendors do not release the closed source code to the organizations that buy these products to protect software copyrights and integrity.

An alternative to receiving the source code is to install programs in object code and establish a source code escrow agreement. This agreement acts as a back-up, so that your organization can access the source code in the case that product support is discontinued or the vendor becomes insolvent. A third-party will hold the documentation in escrow, but it is your responsibility as the organization that bought or leased the program to periodically ensure that the third-party is holding the most recent version of the source information.

Remember, your rights will be most protected if you create a contract with the software vendor that requires them to inform you if they (the vendor) pledge the software as collateral. Be careful when forming escrow agreements and make sure all legal bases have been covered.

Software Licensing

Generally, software is licensed, not purchased. When licensing software, a detailed contract stipulating all the terms of the agreement should be drawn up and signed by both parties. These contracts must clearly define the rights and responsibilities of each of the parties to the contract.

The contract will lay out the scope of the licensing agreement, stating whether the software usage is exclusive or not exclusive, who can use the software, and whether there are any limitations on its use. The duration of the license should be stated with both parties understanding when it expires to plan for any renegotiation, if desired. Other issues to be included in the contract are source code accessibility, software and data security, and anything else either side deems important to the license. Finally, this may seem like a no-brainer, but make sure your legal counsel reviews the contract before you sign. You don't want to be stuck with contract terms that are unfavorable to your organization.

Contract Application Programming

When contracting for programming services, make sure that an IT manager justifies the need for this service with a written request. According to CobiT, the contract should include a provision indicating that software, documentation and other deliverables are subject to testing and review prior to acceptance. Completed contracted programming services should also be tested when finished, to ensure your organization gets what it contracted for. Only after these tests will payment be required. Testing includes: system testing, hardware and component testing, integration testing, procedure testing, load and stress testing, tuning and performance testing, user acceptance testing, and pilot testing. These tests are provided to protect against unexpected system failure.

Pilot Programs

According to the Clinger-Cohen Act, pilot programs are accomplished either through private sector organizations or contract software developers. Pilot programs solve acquisition needs by calling for contracted personnel to develop and test IT solutions independently. This can help you choose the appropriate IT solution to fit your organization's needs.

Third-Party Software Maintenance

For licensed software acquired from third-party providers, you should require that they have appropriate procedures to validate, protect and maintain the software product's integrity rights. In any maintenance agreement related to the delivered product, include terms relating to the support of the product.

Have you created acceptance procedures?

Acceptance procedures might sound a little bit like something you'd find in a 12-step program. And maybe they are a little bit similar. In a 12-step program you might hear 'if you don't accept yourself, then who will?' In your organization, the same thing applies – 'if you don't accept the stuff provided to you by third parties, then who will?' Hopefully, someone qualified to determine if incoming systems and equipment are appropriate. If you want to make sure you have the right goods and services coming into your organization, use this control objective:

> *The organization will develop acceptance procedures within to ensure that all software, systems and services provided to you by third parties are appropriate and compliant with agreed upon requirements.*

Good acceptance procedures let you easily separate the chaff from the wheat. Using them, you'll be able to chuck out useless systems, or poorly provided services, and keep the good ones.

Guidance from the regulations and standards

Banking/Finance

The **FFIEC Development and Acquisitions handbook** does not define specific acceptance procedures but does discuss development and licensing contracts at length, with the assumption being that fulfillment of contractual obligations and testing of development constitutes acceptance.

US Federal Security

The **Clinger-Cohen Act** does not specifically call for an acceptance mechanism, but includes review and approval as part of the overall acquisition process.

General Guidance

CobiT calls for the development of an acceptance plan as part of any contract with a third party vendor that details acceptance procedures for facilities and technology and appropriate testing for functionality. For more information see CobiT AI 1.17-18.

The **ISF Standard of Good Practice for Information Security** does not require an acceptance plan, but does note that appropriate personnel should be called upon to review the security features of any procured system and that management must formally approve the acquisition.

From regulation to reality – sure signs you are complying

The final step in systems acquisition is to develop and document acceptance procedures for testing and approval of the system, software or services provided. Make sure you include these procedures in any contract made with a third-party vendor. These procedures should provide for review by appropriate personnel of the security and other features of any procured system. Finally, have management formally approve the acquisition.

A last word about field editors

Ever wonder how we know so much? Field Editors! They keep us accurate, up-to-date, and honest. What do field editors get out of being able to contribute? *All* of the materials we work on together for *free*, an opportunity to collaborate with very smart people, and tons of deep discounts on everything we do.

Go ahead and read all about it at www.thecompliancebook.com/FE

We hope you sign up and here is some information about stuff that gets a 50% discount or more!

Systems Continuity Plan Pro

Disaster or auditor be ready for both! We worked with Palo Alto Softwware to bring you an application to conduct audits following our best practices , your audit guidelines, or with templates from well-known organization such as ISACA. Read all about it at http://www.paloalto.com/scpp

The Compliance Series

In addition to the main book, there are many parts to The Compliance Series. We have a slew of print and e-books available on topics ranging from Systems Continuity to How To Hire A Security Assessment Vendor. Just keep a look out at Amazon for our latest releases.

UCP Knowledgebase and Conferences

The Unified Compliance Project hosted by the IT Compliance Institute is based directly on The Compliance Series. Network Frontiers partners with ITCi on many conferences and the soon-to-be-released Control Objective Knowledgebase. Go ahead and take a look at:

http://www.itcinstitute.com/ucp